CW01464718

Full Stack Web Development For Beginners

Learn Ecommerce Web Development Using HTML5, CSS3, Bootstrap, JavaScript, MySQL, and PHP

Riaz Ahmed

Full Stack Web Development For Beginners

Copyright © 2021Riaz Ahmed

ISBN: 9798738951268

Dedicated To My Family

CONTENTS

Chapter 2 - Hypertext Markup Language (HTML) 15

Chapter 3 - Cascading Style Sheets (CSS) 59

About This Book

This book is written for absolute beginners who want to become full stack web application developer. To become a professional full stack web developer you have to put on many hats. HTML5, CSS3, Bootstrap, JavaScript, MySQL, and PHP are the core technologies that you must be acquainted with to develop moderate data-driven web applications. All these technologies are voluminous and you need ample time to learn each one of them.

In this fast changing technological world no one has time to go through bulky books of these core technologies. With so many web technologies out there in the market, novices are confused and do not have enough time to evaluate these technologies to decide what to pick for their career and where to start from. Keeping aside the least utilized features, I've written this book to focus on the more operational areas of these technologies that act as the first stepping stone and will provide you with a solid jump start into the exciting world of web development. This book is meant to help you learn web development quickly by yourself. It follows a tutorial approach in which hands-on exercises, augmented with illustrations, are provided to teach you web application development in a short period of time. Once you get grips on these core web development technologies through this book, you will be able to easily set the destination for your future.

With uncountable sites and freely available material, this book is written due to the following reasons:

- Assemble all scattered pieces in one place. This volume contains HTML5, CSS3, JavaScript, Bootstrap, PHP and MySQL. Sequential instructions are provided to download and install the required software and components to setup a complete development environment on your own pc.

- Focus on inspiring practical aspect of these web technologies.

- Last but not least, move novices gradually right from creating an HTML file with a text editor, through learning HTML, CSS, JavaScript, Bootstrap, MySQL and PHP all the way to creating and deploying a professional e-commerce website that comprises static and dynamic pages.

From web introduction to hands-on examples and from website designing to its deployment, this book surely is a complete resource for those who know little or nothing about professional web development.

Download Book Code: https://tinyurl.com/45sde94n

- Riaz Ahmed
oratech@cyber.net.pk

CHAPTER 1

THE WORLD WIDE WEB (WWW)
- AN INTRODUCTION

Web Development

Web development is the field in which you build, create, and maintain websites. It is a thrilling part of information technology which includes aspects such as web design, web publishing, web programming, and database management. Usually, website interfaces are designed using HTML and CSS, but a web developer may also write web scripts in languages such as PHP and Python. Basically there are two main types of website - static and dynamic. Static websites are ones that are fixed and display the same content for every user. Such websites are written exclusively in HTML. A dynamic website, on the other hand, is one that can display different content and provide user interaction, by making use of advanced programming and databases in addition to HTML. A dynamic site is powered by a server-side scripting language such as PHP. In such a site the content is called in by the scripting language from other files or from a database. In addition, a web developer may help maintain and update a database used by a dynamic website. In a broader sense, web development encompasses all the actions, updates, and operations required to build, maintain and manage a website to ensure its optimal performance, user experience, and speed. The professionals who maintain a website are called web developers or web devs.

Full Stack Web Development

Full stack development refers to the development of both front end and back end portions of a website or a web application. The front end is the visible part which is responsible for user experience. The user directly interacts with the front end portion of the web application or website using a browser. HTML, CSS, and JavaScript are used as front end tools. Back end refers to the server-side development of web application or website with a primary focus on how the website works. It is responsible for managing the database through queries. This type of website mainly consists of three parts front end, back end, and database. PHP server-side scripting language and MySQL database are being used for many years to serve as the main back end tools.

The Internet And The World Wide Web

The internet is playing a vital role in our lives and has become a mainstay in personal, work and education fields. It can be defined as a global system of interconnected computer networks that serve billions of users worldwide. It consists of millions of public, private, business, academic, and government networks that are linked by a wide range of electronic, wireless, and optical network technologies. It provides a huge information resource such as the inter-linked hypertext documents of the World Wide Web (WWW) and renders infrastructure support service for electronic mails (E-mails). It enables you to read the latest news, to do research, to shop, to communicate, to listen to music, to play games, and to access a wide variety of information. It has provided new means of human interactions through messaging, forums, and social networking and has boomed businesses through online shopping.

Are Web & Internet the same?
No they are not. The two are not synonymous. The Internet connects millions of computers together globally to form a massive network in which these computers can communicate with each other. The World Wide Web, on the other hand, is a system of interlinked hypertext documents accessed via the Internet. It is an information-sharing model that is built on top of the Internet. Additionally, there is one more term that is frequently used in the IT world and that is intranet. An intranet is a private network that can only be accessed by authorized users. The prefix *intra* means *internal* and therefore implies an intranet that is designed for internal communications. *Inter* (as in Internet) means *between* or *among*.

What is Internet Backbone?

A collection of fiber-optic cables and telephone lines spread all over the world form the Internet's backbone. Data travels at the speed of light along this backbone enabling you to access data within seconds from any part of the world.

Who is Internet Service Provider (ISP)?

The Internet cannot be accessed directly due to expensive communication equipments and communication lines. Instead, you have to rent a connection from an Internet Service Provider (ISP). An ISP is a company that has direct access to the Internet backbone. You're provided with a modem or wireless router that you use to connect to your ISP, which then transparently connects you to the Internet using their communication equipments.

Types of Internet Connections

Dial-up Connection: In the past, the most widely used connection to access the Internet was through dial-up modems. These connections provide a speed of 28.8 kilobits per second and do not exceed a speed of 56 kbit/s downstream (toward the end user) and 34 or 48 kbit/s upstream (toward the global Internet). Although inexpensive, it is the slowest connection and people have switched over to other high speed options.

Broadband Connection: This technology uses wires or fiber optic cables. Slightly more expensive than dial-up, broadband connections are extremely fast. They provide connection speed of 1 to several megabits per second. ISPs provide a high-speed modem to their subscribers to connect to the Internet. It commonly uses digital subscriber line (DSL) telephone service for the connection which uses existing 2-wire copper telephone line connected to the premise so service is delivered simultaneously with wired telephone service (it doesn't tie up your phone line as an analog dial-up connection does). The two main categories of DSL are called ADSL and SDSL. The data throughput of consumer DSL services typically ranges from 256 kbit/s to 20 Mbit/s in the direction to the customer (downstream), depending on DSL technology, line conditions, and service-level implementation. VDSL or VHDSL (very-high-bit-rate digital subscriber line) is a DSL standard that provides data rates up to 52 Mbit/s downstream and 16 Mbit/s upstream over copper wires and up to 85 Mbit/s down and upstream. VDSL2 is an enhanced second-generation version of VDSL. It is able to provide data rates exceeding 100 Mbit/s simultaneously in both the upstream and downstream directions. Cable broadband internet is another connection that is designed to operate over cable TV lines. Because the cable used by cable TV provides much greater bandwidth than telephone lines, a cable connection can be used to achieve extremely fast access. Wireless Internet or wireless broadband is also an Internet connection type that provide high-speed wireless Internet access or computer networking access. Instead of using telephone or cable networks for Internet connection, it uses radio frequency bands. Wireless Internet can be accessed from anywhere — as long as you're within a geographically network coverage area. It includes Wi-Fi, WiMAX, Satellite broadband, and Mobile broadband. Recently, fiber has emerged as the fastest, purest, and most reliable connection available. While DSL uses copper phone lines to transmit data, fiber uses ultra-thin glass strands that carry light instead of electricity. Since light can travel very quickly, fiber connection can see gigabit speeds 100x faster than DSL. With fiber, you can enjoy activities such as high-definition video streaming and online gaming without worrying about buffering or screen lags.

What is IP Address?

All data sent from one place to another across the Internet is addressed to a specific IP (Internet Protocol) address and from a specific IP address. These IP Addresses appear as four sets of numbers, separated by dots, like this: 999.999.999.999. To avoid conflicts, every Internet connection across the entire planet must possess a unique IP address. This uniqueness is necessary so that data could travel transparently between the two communicating devices. For example, when you request a page from a website, your computer needs to know the IP address of the destination website where to send the request. Conversely, the computer that is running the website needs to know the IP address that the request came from in order to serve the web page. IP addresses are broadly categorized in two forms – Dynamic and Static. In case of the Dynamic IP, when you connect to the Internet, your ISP allocates free IP address from its pool of IPs; when you disconnect from the Internet, the IP address that you were using goes back into the pool. The main drawback of Dynamic IP address is that the destination computer cannot keep track of requests sent by your computer. From security perspective, it is necessary for the recipient to know the performed activities, which can only be assessed through static IPs, that is, the requestor always uses the same (Static) IP address.

Web Address (URL) And Domains

Every site and page on the web is identified by its own unique address which is also called Uniform Resource Locator (URL). Visitors usually access a website by clicking a link found on another site. They can also access a site or a page within a site by typing its URL in the address bar of their web browsers. The URL of a website carries four pieces of information: A-the transfer protocol (http or https), B-the domain name, C-directory and D-filename:

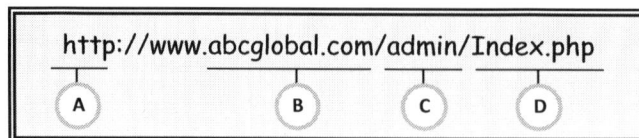

A domain name is a general Internet address, such as microsoft.com or bbc.co.uk. Domain names are formed by the rules and procedures of the Domain Name System (DNS). DNS is the most recognized system for assigning addresses to Internet web servers. Somewhat like international phone numbers, the domain name system helps to give every Internet server a memorable and easy-to-spell address. Simultaneously, the domain names keep the really technical IP address invisible from end users. IP Addresses are not particularly friendly for humans to deal with. A Domain Name, such as bbc.co.uk, is simply a human-friendly alias to an IP address. The BBC's website IP address is, for example, 212.58.251.195 but it would not be very helpful if the BBC announced "for further information, please visit our web site at http://212.58.251.195"!

Each domain name ends with a suffix that defines the type of organization. For example, any commercial enterprise or corporation that has a Web site will have a domain suffix of .com, which means it is a commercial entity. The domain suffix provides you with a clue about the purpose or audience of a website. The domain suffix might also give you a clue about the geographic origin of a website. Many sites from the United Kingdom will have a domain suffix of .uk. Here follows a list of the most common domain suffixes and the types of organizations that would use them.

Domain suffixes

.com Commercial site
.edu Educational institution
.gov Government
.org Non-profit organization
.mil Military
.net Network

Country domain suffixes

.au Australia
.ca Canada
.fr France
.it Italy
.mx Mexico
.uk United Kingdom

What IS Web Page?

The web provides information on almost every imaginable topic through billions of web pages. A webpage is a document, typically written in Hypertext Markup Language (HTML). Web pages are accessed and transported with the Hypertext Transfer Protocol (HTTP), which may optionally employ encryption (HTTPS - HTTP Secure) to provide security and privacy for the user of the web page content. The pages of a website can usually be accessed from a simple Uniform Resource Locator (URL) called the web address. When you seek some information, it is returned by a web server - that holds that information - to your computer using a web browser, such as Chrome, Firefox, or Edge. A web page can carry text, images, sounds, and videos on any subject.

Website vs. Web Application

A website is a set of related web pages associated with a particular person, business, government, school, or organization containing content such as text, images, video, audio, etc. A website is hosted on at least one web server, accessible via the Internet through an Internet address known as a Uniform Resource Locator (URL). Static and Dynamic are the two types of a website that we've already gone through at the beginning of this chapter. A web application or web app is a software that resides and runs inside a web server. Traditional desktop applications are installed on local PCs and run by your operating system. Web apps, on the other hand, are accessed from the web server through the Internet via a web browser. If you compare a web app with its counterpart, you will observe several advantages over desktop applications. First, web apps are accessed through web browsers and you do not need to develop web apps for multiple platforms. For example, a single application that runs in Chrome will work on both Windows and OS X. Another major advantage of a web app is that when you add new features to it, you are not required to distribute software updates to your users. Just update the application on the server and all users will have access to the updated version.

What Is Web Server?

Web server can either be the hardware (the powerful computer capable of handling thousands of site visitors at a time) or the software (the computer application, such as IIS and Apache) that delivers web content through the Internet. It is the primary function of web servers to deliver HTML documents and other content such as images, style sheets and scripts in shape of web pages to the requesting clients. Besides entertaining client requests, web servers also receive content from them through web forms and uploaded files. A large website is often run by hundreds of servers which is referred to as server farms or server cluster in web terminology. When someone requests a web page from a website on the Internet, the page is delivered by the web server hosting that website. A web server must be accessible 24 hours a day and should have a reliable high-speed connection to the Internet. Due to this reason, web servers are normally hosted by a web host. A web host, or web hosting service provider, is a business that provides the technologies and services needed for the website to be viewed via the Internet. Web hosting companies specialize in storing and serving websites.

What is Web Browser?

A web browser can be defined as an application software designed to enable users to access, retrieve and view documents and other resources on the Internet or a program designed to download and display web pages. The primary purpose of a web browser is to bring information resources to the users, allow them to view the information, and then access other information through navigational links. Although browsers are primarily intended to use the World Wide Web, they can also be used to access information provided by web servers in private networks or files in file systems. The major web browsers are Chrome, Firefox, Microsoft Edge, Opera, and Safari. All major web browsers allow the user to open multiple information resources at the same time, either in different browser windows or in different tabs of the same window. Major browsers also include pop-up blockers to prevent unwanted windows from popping up without the user's consent. Most web browsers can display a list of web pages that the user has bookmarked so that the user can quickly return to them.

What Are Cookies?

Cookies are small pieces of data that a website stores in the computer of the visitors. The main purpose of cookies is to identify returning visitor. When you revisit a site, the cookie stored on your computer helps in your identification. For example, if you log in to a website and check the remember me box, an identifier is stored in a cookie on your computer so that you do not need to log in again. This is the standard mechanism for identifying returning visitors to a site. This information also lets websites the user visits to keep track of a user's browsing patterns and preferences. You can set up your browsers to accept or not accept cookies.

What Is Responsive Page Design?

Responsive Web Design is about designing a website or web application in a way to automatically resize, hide, shrink, or enlarge to make it look good on all devices (desktops, tablets, and phones). A responsive web design will automatically adjust for different screen sizes and viewports. Most people nowadays access websites from mobile devices, rather than desktop computers or laptops. While most smartphones can display regular websites, the content is difficult to read and even harder to navigate.

Therefore, many web developers now use responsive web design to provide a better web browsing experience on small screens. There are some ways to make a website responsive. The simplest way is to add the following <meta> tag to all your web pages. This will set the viewport of your page, which will give the browser instructions on how to control the page's dimensions and scaling.

```
<meta name="viewport" content="width=device-width, initial-scale=1.0">
```

Another way to make web pages responsive is to use media queries. With media queries you can define completely different css rules for different browser sizes.

```
p {
    font-size: 12px /* The width is 12px by default */
}
```

This media query breakpoint would alter the font-size once the screen width dips below 414px.

```
@media screen and (max-width: 414px) {
  p {
    font-size: 16px;
  }
}
```

You can also use Bootstrap framework to make your web pages responsive. Bootstrap is a popular CSS framework, which uses HTML, CSS and jQuery to make responsive web pages. MaxCDN provides CDN support for Bootstrap's CSS and JavaScript. By adding the following CDNs to your web pages you can make them responsive:

```
<!-- Latest compiled and minified CSS -->
<link rel="stylesheet" href="https://maxcdn.bootstrapcdn.com/bootstrap/3.4.1/css/bootstrap.min.css">

<!-- jQuery library -->
<script src="https://ajax.googleapis.com/ajax/libs/jquery/3.5.1/jquery.min.js"></script>

<!-- Latest compiled JavaScript -->
<script src="https://maxcdn.bootstrapcdn.com/bootstrap/3.4.1/js/bootstrap.min.js"></script>
```

In this book, we are going to use a downloaded version of Bootstrap contained in a folder named css.

Finally, you can use W3.CSS, which is a free and easy to use framework. It is a modern CSS framework with support for desktop, tablet, and mobile design by default. W3.CSS is smaller, faster, easy to learn, and easy to use than similar CSS frameworks. It is rolled out as a high quality alternative to Bootstrap and its standard CSS only design makes it independent of jQuery or any other JavaScript library. To use W3.CSS in your web site, just add the following link to your web pages:

```
<link rel="stylesheet" href="https://www.w3schools.com/w3css/4/w3.css">
```

What Are Hyperlinks?

In computing, a hyperlink (or link) is a cross-reference to data that the reader can directly follow, or that is followed automatically. It takes visitors to another page on the same site or to a page on another website. A hyperlink points to a whole document or to a specific element within a document. A web browser usually displays a hyperlink in some distinguishing way, e.g. in a different color, font or style. The behavior and style of links can be specified using the Cascading Style Sheets (CSS) language. A link can also appear as an image. When you click a link the page loads in a new browser window or in a new tab in the existing window.

What Is File Transfer Protocol (FTP)?

The File Transfer Protocol (FTP) is a standard network protocol used for the transfer of computer files between a client and server on a computer network. You use FTP software (such as FileZilla) to receive (download) or send (upload) files from/to a web server. For example, once you complete a website or web application on your PC, you use FTP software to upload HTML, CSS, JS, and PHP files to your hosting company's web server.

What Is Search Engine?

You can use free search engines on the web to find information on a specific subject. A search engine is a web-based tool that helps you locate information on the World Wide Web. Google, Bing, and Yahoo! Search are the top ranking search engines. Search engines utilize automated software applications (referred to as robots, bots, or spiders) that travel along the web, following links from page to page, site to site. The information gathered by the spiders is used to create a searchable index of the web. You can either go to these search engine sites to find the required information or you can use search feature provided with your browser.

How Do Search Engines Work?

Every search engine uses different complex mathematical formulas to generate search results. The results for a specific query are then displayed on the search engine results page (SERP). Search engine algorithms take the key elements of a web page, including the page title, content and keyword density, and come up with a ranking for where to place the results on the pages. Each search engine's algorithm is unique, so a top ranking on Yahoo! does not guarantee a prominent ranking on Google, and vice versa. To make things more complicated, the algorithms used by search engines are not only closely guarded secrets, they are also constantly undergoing modification and revision. This means that the criteria to best optimize a site with must be surmised through observation, as well as trial and error — and not just once, but continuously.

Search engines only "see" the text on web pages, and use the underlying HTML structure to determine relevance. Large photos, or dynamic Flash animation mean nothing to search engines, but the actual text on your pages does. It is difficult to build a Flash site that is as friendly to search engines; as a result, Flash sites will tend not to rank as high as sites developed with well coded HTML and CSS (Cascading Style Sheets — a mechanism for adding styles to website pages above and beyond regular HTML). It will be very difficult for your website to yield high placement in the SERPs if the terms you want to be found do not appear in the text of your website.

What Is SEO?

Search Engine Optimization (SEO) is a procedure to make web pages rank as high as possible in search engines. By applying SEO techniques not only you can increase both the quality and quantity of your website traffic, you can also increase exposure to your brand through organic (non-paid) search engine results. It's the art of understanding what people are searching for on the Internet, the solutions they are seeking for their problems, the words they're using, and the type of content they wish to consume. Knowing the answers to these questions will allow you to connect to the people who are searching online for the solutions you offer.

What Are Web Logs or Blogs?

A Web log, or blog, is a discussion or informational site published on the World Wide Web consisting of frequently updated, reverse-chronological entries (the most recent post appears first) on a particular topic. Many blogs provide commentary on a particular subject; some function as more personal online diaries; others function more as online brand advertising of a particular individual or company. A typical blog combines text, images, and links to other blogs, Web pages, and other media related to its topic. The ability of readers to leave comments in an interactive format is an important contribution to the popularity of many blogs. Most blogs are primarily textual, although some focus on art (art blogs), photographs (photoblogs), videos (video blogs or "vlogs"), music (MP3 blogs), and audio (podcasts). Microblogging (such as twitter) is another type of blogging, featuring very short posts. In education, blogs can be used as instructional resources. These blogs are referred to as edublogs.

What Is Web Portal?

A Web Portal is like a management system where companies or organizations can build, share, interchange information, or data. It provides employees, customers and suppliers with a single access point to information. It is created to enhance the collaboration of information and improve the way employees, customers and suppliers interact with your business. Web portals help you to bring information from multiple sources together, allowing content to be shared amongst a variety of departments, customers and suppliers. Sales portal, CRM portal, Corporate portal, and Project Management portal are some examples of web portals that businesses usually deploy. There are two types of web portal - vertical or horizontal. Vertical web portals focus on a specific application or business function such as HR, accounting and finance, CRM, ERP, service management or warehouse management. They enable users from both inside and outside of your business to see, edit and contribute to processes within that given application(s). For example, an organization may wish to offer a customer web portal that enables suppliers to read, add to or amend order status details and other related information. Horizontal web portals provide users with the ability to see aggregated data from multiple applications. Some of the common examples of horizontal web portals are government portals, educational portals, corporate portals, cultural portals, etc. A common horizontal web portal could take the form of a managerial reporting system that presents Key Performance Indicator (KPIs) information from multiple business systems.

What Is E-Commerce?

Electronic Commerce, often referred to as simply ecommerce (or e-commerce), is a phrase used to describe business that is conducted over the Internet. Web sites such as Amazon.com, Buy.com, and eBay are examples of e-commerce sites. Electronic commerce can be between two businesses transmitting funds, goods, and services or between a business and a customer. These two forms of e-commerce are known as Business-to-Business (B2B) and Business-to-Consumer (B2C), respectively. While companies like Amazon.com cater mostly to consumers, other companies provide goods and services exclusively to other businesses. It is the buying and selling of product or service over electronic systems such as the Internet and other computer networks and draws on such technologies as mobile commerce, electronic funds transfer, supply chain management, Internet marketing, online transaction processing, electronic data interchange (EDI), inventory management systems, and automated data collection systems. You can use web-based stores to purchase books, theater tickets, and even cars. There are also many sites that enable you to sell or auction your products or household items. Sites like eBay (www.ebay.com) allow you to put your products online for auction. Thousands of websites are devoted to online shopping. Some focus on one product or service, while others, such as Amazon.com offer a wide range of goods. When you shop at an e-commerce site, you usually add the items that you want to purchase to a virtual shopping cart that keeps track of these items and the quantity. These sites have a View Cart link that enables you to view the contents of your shopping cart. The cart usually has a Proceed to Checkout link that leads you to a page where you provide your address and payment information. Payments on the web are usually made by credit cards. You are required to provide the credit card number, cvv number and expiry date. To ensure the security of this sensitive data, you must provide this information only on secured sites which are prefixed with https rather than http.

What Is Social Media?

Today we have many websites and applications that are created with the objective to support and facilitate online social networking. These websites are referred to as Social Media. The most popular examples of social media include Twitter, Facebook, Instagram, and Reddit. Social media is a collection of Internet-based communities that allow users to interact with each other online. This includes web forums, wikis, and user-generated content (UGC) websites. However, the term is most often used to describe popular social networking websites, which include Facebook, Twitter, LinkedIn, and Pinterest.

What Is Web Service?

A web service is an application or data source that is accessible via a standard web protocol (HTTP or HTTPS). Unlike web applications, web services are designed to communicate with other programs, rather than directly with users. Most web services provide an API, or a set of functions and commands, that can be used to access the data. For example, Twitter provides an API that allows developers to access tweets from the service and receive the data in JSON format. Yelp provides an API for programmers to access information about businesses, which can be displayed directly in an app or website. Google Maps provides an API for receiving geographical data and directions from the Google Maps database.

Launching a Website

The initial step in this process is to create web pages that constitute a website. To do so, you need a simple text editor such as Notepad or some special web page designing software such as Adobe Dreamweaver. After creating your site, the next step is to acquire a domain name (www.abcglobal.com) from a web-hosting company. Web hosting providers offer different packages (including free domain registration) to store your web pages on their servers from where the world can access your website.

Choosing The Right Hosting Company

There are thousands of Web Hosting Companies out there and counting. How do you choose the ideal plan for your website? The key here is to understand what your website needs are. Once you know what is required, you can eliminate many options. Listed below are the most important points that you need to focus on:

- How much storage space does your website require?

- How much Monthly Transfer (Bandwidth) do you need?

- How many e-mail accounts do you need?

- What type of database is required for your site?

- What Scripting Languages does your web site use?

- Does your site need Server-side scripting language?

- What Operating System should you go for?

- Should you use SHARED hosting or DEDICATED hosting?

Storage Space

Storage space refers to the amount of disk space allotted on the hosting web server to store your website files. If you have a 100MB limit, then you cannot store more than 100MB worth of files on the server. HTML files are not big, but if your website holds files such as images, videos, audio etc., you need to watch your limit.

Bandwidth

Bandwidth is a measure of how much of your data the server sends out. For example, if you have a page that is 10KB, including images, and 10 people access the page (either at the same time or over a period of time), the total bandwidth is 100KB. Most hosts give you a bandwidth limit (or cap), which is usually a specified number of megabytes or gigabytes per month.

Domain Name

The registration of domain names is usually administered by domain name registrars who sell their services to the public. A domain name registrar is an organization or commercial entity that manages the reservation of Internet domain names. Some hosting providers supply free domain name registration service with their packages.

What E-mail Is And How It Works?

Electronic mail, commonly referred to as email or e-mail, is a method of exchanging digital messages from an author to one or more recipients anywhere in the world. Modern email operates across the Internet or other computer networks. Today's email systems are based on a store-and-forward model. Email servers accept, forward, deliver and store messages. When you send an e-mail message, it travels along your Internet connection and then through your ISP's outgoing mail server. This server routes the messages to the recipient's incoming mail server, which then stores the message in his or her mailbox. The next time the recipient check for messages, your message is moved from the recipient's server to the recipient's computer.

To use e-mail, you have to have an e-mail account. There are three ways to get an e-mail account: through ISP, through your hosting plan, and through free services such as Gmail and Yahoo. An e-mail address is a set of characters that uniquely identifies the location of your Internet mailbox. A message sent to your address is delivered to you and no one else.

Example: admin@abcglobal.com

Each e-mail address, as shown above, carries three pieces of information:

Username: The username (admin in the above example) is the name of the person's account with the ISP or within an organization. This is often the person's first name, last name, or a combination of the two, but it could also be a nickname or some other text. No two people using the same ISP or within the same organization, can have the same username.

@ Symbol: The "@" sign separates the username from the domain name in an e-mail address.

Domain Name: The domain name (abcglobal.com) is the Internet name of the company that provides the person's e-mail account. This is usually the domain name of the ISP, an organization, or a free web e-mail service, such as gmail.com.

Scripting Languages

A scripting language or script language is a programming language that supports the writing of scripts, programs written for a software environment that automate the execution of tasks which could alternatively be executed one-by-one by a human operator.

Scripts are invisible to the visitor's eye but their availability within the code of a website defines how the website behaves in response to certain click requests sent by the user. Apart from the World Wide Web, scripts are also used for the automation of processes on a local computer. All in all, scripts have contributed a lot to making the web such a usable and flexibility driven environment as we are used to seeing it today.

Each script represents a text document containing a list of instructions that need to be executed by a certain program or scripting manager so that the desired automated action could be achieved. This will prevent users from having to go through many complicated steps in order to reach certain results while browsing a website or working on their personal computers. The text nature of the scripts allows them to be opened and edited with the help of a basic text editor.

Client-Side Scripting

Client-side scripting generally refers to the class of computer programs on the web that are executed client-side, by the user's web browser, instead of server-side (on the web server). Client-side scripts are often embedded within an HTML document, but they may also be contained in a separate file, which is referenced by the document (or documents) that use it. Upon request, the necessary files are sent to the user's computer by the web server where they reside. The user's web browser executes the script, and then displays the document, including any visible output from the script. Client-side scripts may also contain instructions for the browser to follow in response to certain user actions, (e.g., clicking a button).

Server-Side Scripting

Server-side scripting is normally used to provide an interface and to limit client access to proprietary databases or other data sources. These scripts may assemble client characteristics for use in customizing the response based on those characteristics, the user's requirements, access rights, etc. Server-side scripting also enables the website owner to reduce user access to the source code of server-side scripts which may be proprietary and valuable in itself.

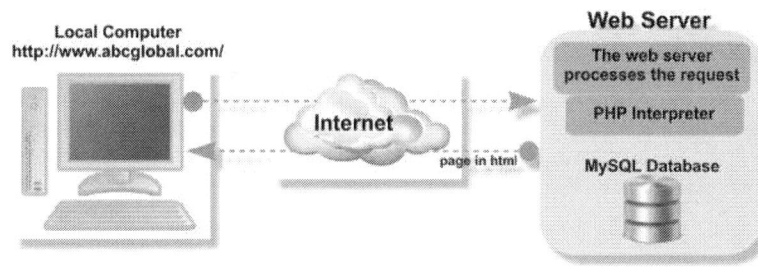

Figure 1-1 Server-side scripting (PHP and MySQL)

The server-side scripts are interpreted by the web server. Most server-side scripting languages usually embed their scripting components within a HTML file. So, when the web server reads them from the file system to serve a request from a browser, it interprets the script and generates the appropriate HTML to be returned to the browser. This contrasts with ordinary web pages where the server fetches an HTML-only static page directly from the file system and passes it onto the browser without any interpretation. The script interpretation might not actually be done by the web server but by a special software called CGI interpreter in the case of CGI scripts. For example, if the script language used is PHP, then it is PHP interpreter.

Server-side Scripting Languages
- PHP (*.php)
- Python via Django (*.py)
- Ruby (*.rb, *.rbw)
- SMX (*.smx)
- Lasso (*.lasso)
- WebDNA (*.dna,*.tpl)
- C via CGI (*.c, *.csp)
- ColdFusion (*.cfm)
- JavaServer Pages (*.jsp)
- Lua (*.lp *.op)
- Perl CGI (*.cgi, *.ipl, *.pl)

Some Interesting Facts
- The world # 1 video site YouTube is written in Python and Java.
- Amazon.com & Slashdot run on Perl.
- Flight simulator systems used to train commercial and military pilots are written in Perl.

Client-Side vs Server-side Scripting

Server side scripting, (ex. ASP.Net, ASP, JSP, PHP, Ruby, or others), is executed by the server (Web Server), and the page that is sent to the browser is produced by the serve-side scripting.

So when a server sends out a page, it executes server-side scripts, but does not execute client-side scripts. Once the browser receives the page, it executes the client-side scripts.

Server side scripting can connect to databases that reside on the web server or another server reachable from web server. Client side scripting cannot do that.

Server side scripting can access the file system that reside at the web server, client side cannot.

Server side scripting can access settings belonging to Web server while client side cannot.

The server may do things like database lookup, reading/writing files and user authentication that would be either impossible or very insecure to do in a browser.

Server-side scripts require that their language's interpreter be installed on the server, and produce the same output regardless of the client's browser, operating system, or other system details. Client-side scripts do not require additional software on the server (making them popular with authors who lack administrative access to their servers); however, they do require that the user's web browser understands the scripting language in which they are written. It is therefore impractical for an author to write scripts in a language that is not supported by popular web browsers.

Client side scripting is a script, (ex. JavaScript, VB script), that is executed by the browser (i.e. Firefox, Internet Explorer, Safari, Opera, etc.) that resides at the user computer.

Client side scripting consumes cycles from user's computer not web server one, while server side scripting consumes cycles form web server one.

Client side scripting can access files and settings that are local at the user computer.

Client-side scripts have greater access to the information and functions available on the user's browser, whereas server-side scripts have greater access to the information and functions available on the server.

Client side script such as JavaScript runs primarily in the browser, which server side languages like PHP, JSP, Ruby on Rails etc. cannot do.

There are also a couple of tasks that are commonly done both places, like form validation - on the client to give quick feedback. This validation can also be done on the server to ensure that what is submitted is actually safe and valid. Note that an attacker could easily skip any browser validation and submit illegal values.

CHAPTER 2

HYPERTEXT MARKUP LANGUAGE
<HTML>

About HTML

HTML stands for HyperText Markup Language. It is a markup language for structuring and presenting content in a web browser for the World Wide Web, and is a core technology of the Internet. HTML is written in the form of HTML elements consisting of tags enclosed in angle brackets (like <html>), within the web page content. HTML tags most commonly come in pairs like <h1> and </h1>, although some tags, known as empty elements, are unpaired, for example <img>. The first tag in a pair is the start tag, the second tag is the end tag (they are also called opening tags and closing tags). In between these tags web designers can add text, tags, comments and other types of text-based content.

HTML documents are read in a web browser (Chrome, Firefox, Microsoft Edge etc.) which is responsible to organize these documents into visible or audible web pages. The browser uses the HTML tags to interpret the content of the page. Web browsers can also refer to Cascading Style Sheets (CSS) to define the appearance and layout of text and other material.

HTML elements form the building blocks of all websites. HTML allows images and objects to be embedded and can be used to create interactive forms. It provides a resource to create structured documents by denoting structural semantics for text such as headings, paragraphs, lists, links, quotes and other items. It can embed scripts in languages such as JavaScript which affect the behavior of HTML web pages.

HTML5 is the fifth revision of the HTML standard and is focused in this book. Its core aims have been to improve the language with support for the latest multimedia while keeping it easily readable by humans and consistently understood by computers and devices. HTML5 is intended to subsume not only HTML 4, but XHTML 1 and DOM Level 2 HTML as well.

HTML5 is an attempt to define a single markup language. It includes detailed processing models to encourage more interoperable implementations and introduces markup and application programming interfaces (APIs) for complex web applications. For the same reasons, HTML5 is also a potential candidate for cross- platform mobile applications.

Many features of HTML5 have been built with the consideration of being able to run on low-powered devices such as smartphones and tablets. In particular, HTML5 adds many new syntactical features. These include <video>, <audio> and <canvas> elements, as well as the integration of scalable vector graphics (SVG) content that replaces the uses of generic <object> tags and MathML for mathematical formulas. These features are designed to make it easy to include and handle multimedia and graphical content on the web without having to resort to proprietary plugins and APIs. Other new elements, such as <section>, <article>, <header>, <footer> and <nav>, are designed to enrich the semantic content of documents.

New attributes have been introduced for the same purpose, while some elements and attributes have been removed. Some elements, such as <a>, <cite> and <menu> have been changed, redefined or standardized. The APIs and document object model (DOM) are no longer afterthoughts, but are fundamental parts of the HTML5 specification. HTML5 also defines in some detail the required processing for invalid documents so that syntax errors will be treated uniformly by all conforming browsers and other user agents.

DOCTYPE DECLARATION

NOTE

Each web page begins with a DOCTYPE declaration which informs the browser about the HTML version the page is using. Although this declaration is not mandatory, it helps browsers to correctly render a page. Due to various flavors of HTML, this declaration also varies as shown in the following table.

HTML Version	DOCTYPE Declaration
HTML 4	<!DOCTYPE html PUBLIC "-//W3C//DTD HTML 4.01 Transitional//EN" "http://www.w3.org/TR/html4/loose.dtd">
XML	<?xml version="1.0" ?>
Strict XHTML 1.0	<!DOCTYPE html PUBLIC "-//W3C//DTD XHTML 1.0 Strict//EN" "http://www.w3.org/TR/xhtml1/DTD/xhtml1-strict.dtd">
Transitional XHTML 1.0	<!DOCTYPE html PUBLIC "-//W3C//DTD HTML 4.01 Transitional//EN" "http://www.w3.org/TR/html4/loose.dtd">
HTML 5	<!DOCTYPE html>

Your First HTML Web Page

Open Notepad or any other text editor and type the following code:

```
CODE

<!DOCTYPE html>
<html>
  <head>
    <title>My First HTML Page</title>
  </head>
  <body>
    <h1>Grow your Business with us</h1>
    <p>This is a paragraph. Here you write your content.</p>
  </body>
</html>
```

Save the file as **MyWebPage.html** on your desktop or any other location you prefer. The icon of the saved file would change to the icon of your default browser. Double click the file to see your first web page in the browser as shown in the following figure.

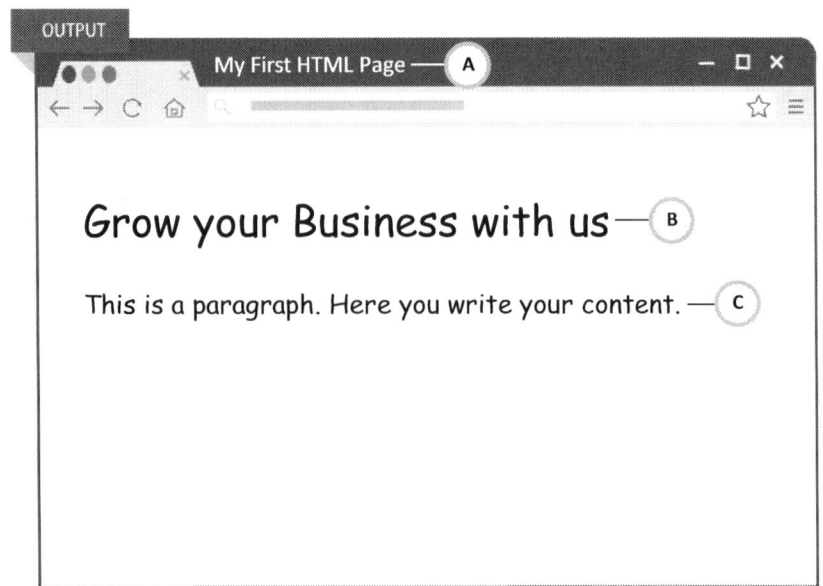

Figure 2-1

Let's go through the details of the above code.

Elements in HTML

Elements define an HTML document. Elements are usually made up of two tags: an opening tag (start tag) and a closing tag (end tag). Some HTML elements, such as <br>, are called empty elements. These elements are without a closing tag and are closed in the start tag. The first line in this example <!DOCTYPE html> defines the document type and is a declaration for the latest HTML5 generation. The text between <html> and </html> describes the web page. The <body></body> tags hold the visible page content. Only the content you provide in the <body> section is rendered in a browser, as illustrated in the previous output. Page heading is enclosed in the <h1></h1> tags whereas a paragraph is displayed within the <p></p> tags.

Opening Tag	Element Content	Closing Tag
<p>	This is a paragraph.	</p>
<h1>	This is the heading of my web page	</h1>
<body>	<h1>Grow your Business with us</h1> <p>This is a paragraph. Here you write your content. </p>	</body>
<html>	**<head>** <title>My First HTML Page</title> **</head>** **<body>** <h1> Grow your Business with us </h1> <p>This is a paragraph. Here you write your content.</p> **</body>**	</html>

The following elements can go inside an HTML file:

The <html> element: It defines the whole HTML document. It has a start tag <html> and an end tag </html>. Each HTML element contains some content that sits between its opening and closing tags and tells the browser something about the information. This one contains two other HTML elements - <head> and <body>.

The <head> element: The <head> element is a container for all the head elements. The <head> element must include a title for the document, and can include scripts, styles, meta information, and more.

<title> It defines a title (see A in Figure 2-1) for your HTML document and is a required element in the head section. When defined, the page title is shown in the browser's title bar and displayed in search engine results.

<style> It specifies how HTML elements will be rendered in a browser. The required type attribute defines the content of the <style> element. The only possible value is "text/css".

<link> Links to an external style sheet. See chapter 3 about external style sheets.

<script> It is used to define a client-side script, such as a JavaScript. The <script> element either contains scripting statements, or it points to an external script file through the src attribute. Common uses for JavaScript are image manipulation, form validation, and dynamic changes of content. See Chapter 4 to learn how scripts are added to a web page.

The <body> element: This element defines the body of the HTML document. It starts with the tag <body> and ends with </body>. In the current example, it is holding two other HTML elements – a heading <h1> element and a paragraph <p> element.

The <h1> element: You can use <h1> to <h6> tags to define HTML headings where <h1> is the most important heading and <h6> is the least one. Its content in the above example is: *Grow your Business with us* (B Figure 2-1).

The <p> element: Paragraphs in an HTML document are defined using the <p> element which has a start tag <p> and an end tag </p>. The element's content in the above example is: *This is a paragraph. Here you write your content* (C Figure 2-1).

Usage Recommendations

Keep the following recommendations in mind while using elements in HTML documents:

- Always put the end tags to avoid unexpected results and/or errors.
- Although HTML tags are not case sensitive, it is recommended to use lowercase.

Attributes in HTML

HTML elements can have attributes. Web page customization begins with HTML attributes. Attributes are responsible for customizing HTML elements and provide additional information about the contents of an element. While processing an HTML tag, the web browser looks to these attributes as guides for the construction of web elements. Without any attribute values specified, the browser will render the element using the default settings. Attributes are always specified in the start tag of the element and are made up of two parts - Name and Value - separated by an equals sign as shown in the following example for the <a> element.

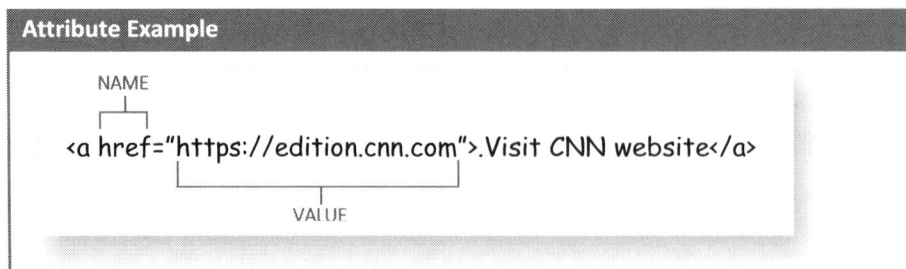

```
Attribute Example

        NAME
        ┌─┴─┐
   <a href="https://edition.cnn.com">.Visit CNN website</a>
              └──────────┬──────────┘
                       VALUE
```

Usage Recommendations

- Attribute values should always be enclosed in quotes. Double style quotes are the most common, but single style quotes are also allowed.
- Attribute names and attribute values are case-insensitive. However, recommended way is to use lowercase.

Headings in HTML

Headings and subheadings in a document are used to present information in a hierarchical format. For instance, a document usually starts with a big heading before the main introduction of a topic, followed by relevant subheadings.

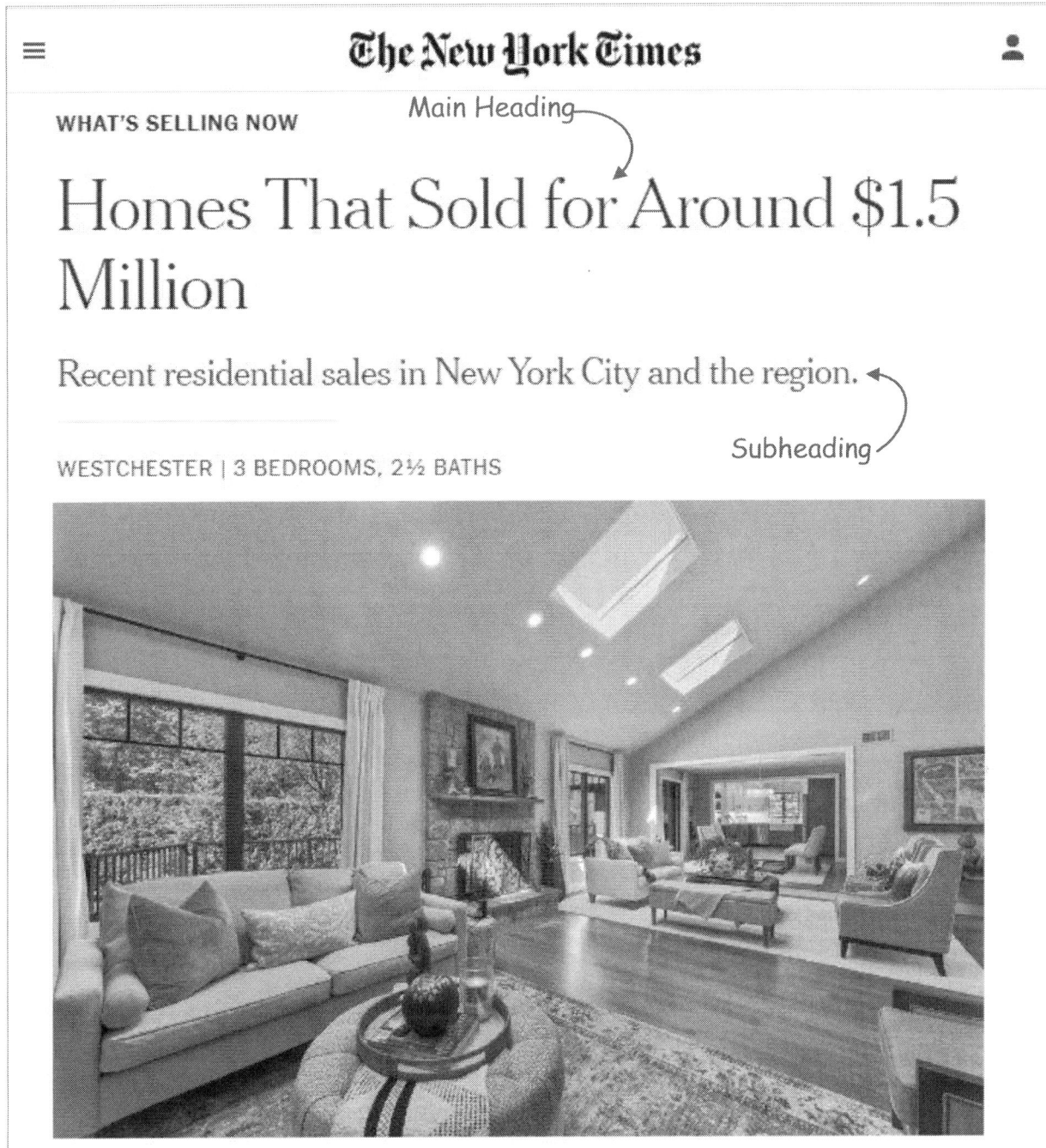

You can use <h1> to <h6> tags to define headings in your website where <h1> defines the most important heading while <h6> defines the least important one. Headings are displayed in different sizes by the browser. The content enclosed in <h1> is the largest, and that in <h6> is the smallest. You will learn how to set the size of content, its color, and font in the second part of this book where you'll be taught about Cascading Style Sheets (CSS).

CODE

```
<!DOCTYPE html>
<html>
  <body>
    <h1>This is heading 1</h1>
    <h2>This is heading 2</h2>
    <h3>This is heading 3</h3>
    <h4>This is heading 4</h4>
    <h5>This is heading 5</h5>
    <h6>This is heading 6</h6>
  </body>
</html>
```

OUTPUT

This is heading 1
This is heading 2
This is heading 3
This is heading 4
This is heading 5
This is heading 6

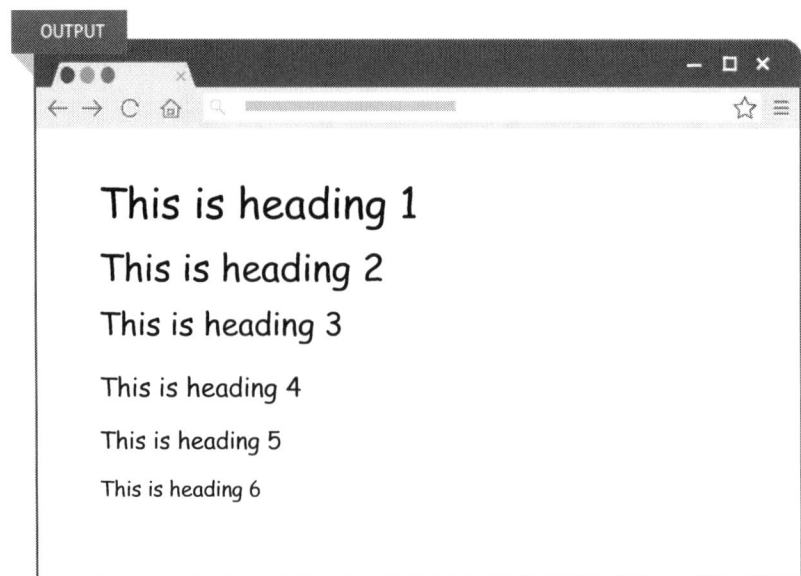

Usage Recommendations

Here are some tips on how to properly utilize these tags to improve your page structure for search engine ranking purposes.

- Don't use headings to make text bold.
- Header tag (h1, h2, h3 etc.) gives a specified amount of importance to the surrounding text on a page. So you can have as many h1 tags as necessary as long as you have the same amount of important sections on your page.
- Usually one h1 tag is enough for the search engine to see what the page is about.
- Multiple h1 tags on a website can trigger a penalty if you have other spamming techniques on your page.

Paragraphs in HTML

A paragraph is the composition of one or more sentences. Each paragraph is indicated by a new line. In HTML you use the paragraph tag <p> when you want to break up two streams of information into separate thoughts. Most browsers display paragraphs with one blank line between them. Here is an example of paragraph in HTML:

CODE

```html
<!DOCTYPE html>
<html>
<body>
    <p>
        Paragraph 1 - Lorem, ipsum dolor sit amet consectetur
        adipisicing elit. Harum labore sed, veniam nisi sunt
        laboriosam ducimus, odio aspernatur fugiat minima blanditiis
        dignissimos.
    </p>
    <p> Paragraph 1 - Lorem, ipsum dolor sit amet consectetur
        adipisicing elit. Harum labore sed, veniam nisi sunt
        laboriosam ducimus, odio aspernatur fugiat minima blanditiis
        dignissimos.</p>
</body>
</html>
```

OUTPUT

Paragraph 1 - Lorem, ipsum dolor sit amet consectetur adipisicing elit. Harum labore sed, veniam nisi sunt laboriosam ducimus, odio aspernatur fugiat minima blanditiis dignissimos.

Paragraph 2 - Lorem, ipsum dolor sit amet consectetur adipisicing elit. Harum labore sed, veniam nisi sunt laboriosam ducimus, odio aspernatur fugiat minima blanditiis dignissimos.

Lines and Breaks in HTML

In the previous example, you saw how browser automatically shows a new paragraph on a new line. Suppose you have a situation where you need to add a line break inside the middle of a paragraph. In such a case you can use the line break tag <br> as shown under. The <hr> (horizontal rule) tag is used to create a line between sections to separate content of your web page.

CODE

```
<!DOCTYPE html>
<html>
<body>
  <p>About Us: <br><br> Lorem, ipsum dolor sit amet consectetur adipisicing elit.
     Harum labore sed, veniam nisi sunt laboriosam ducimus, odio aspernatur
     fugiat minima blanditiis dignissimos.</p>
  <hr>
  <p> Lorem, ipsum dolor sit amet consectetur adipisicing elit. Harum labore sed,
     veniam nisi sunt laboriosam ducimus, odio aspernatur fugiat minima
     blanditiis dignissimos.</p>
  <hr>
</body>
</html>
```

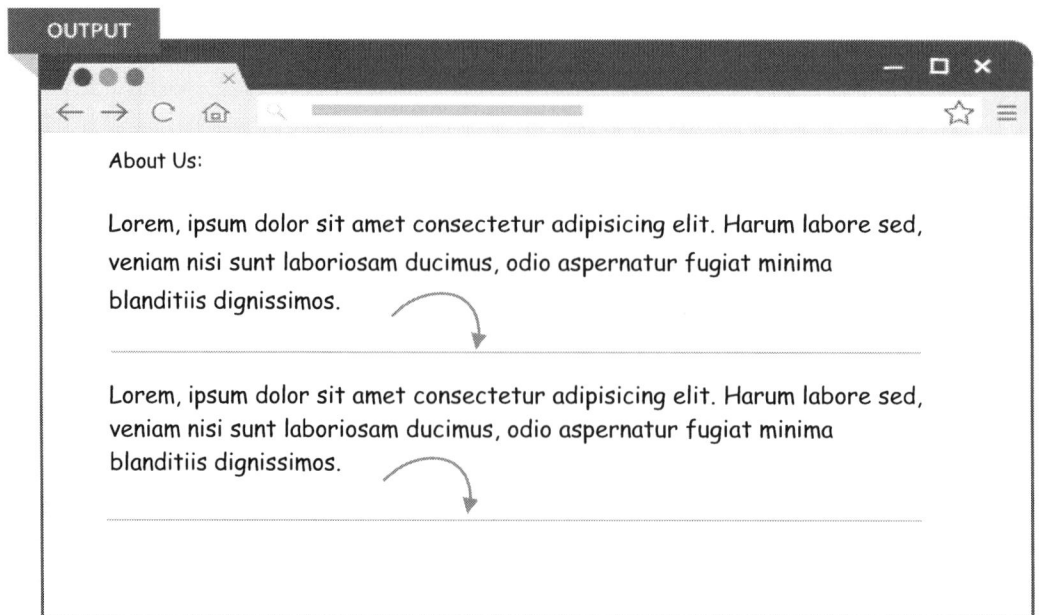

OUTPUT

About Us:

Lorem, ipsum dolor sit amet consectetur adipisicing elit. Harum labore sed, veniam nisi sunt laboriosam ducimus, odio aspernatur fugiat minima blanditiis dignissimos.

Lorem, ipsum dolor sit amet consectetur adipisicing elit. Harum labore sed, veniam nisi sunt laboriosam ducimus, odio aspernatur fugiat minima blanditiis dignissimos.

Comments In HTML

Web developers usually add comments to HTML to understand what the code is expected to do. The markup *<!-- Some comments -->* is used for this purpose as demonstrated in the example hereunder. Comments are ignored and are not displayed by the browser.

CODE

```
<!DOCTYPE html>
<html>
<body>
<!--Comments about the paragraph below – This line will be ignored-->
<p>Lorem, ipsum dolor sit amet consectetur adipisicing elit. Harum
    labore sed, veniam nisi sunt laboriosam ducimus, odio aspernatur
    fugiat minima blanditiis dignissimos.</p>
</body>
</html>
```

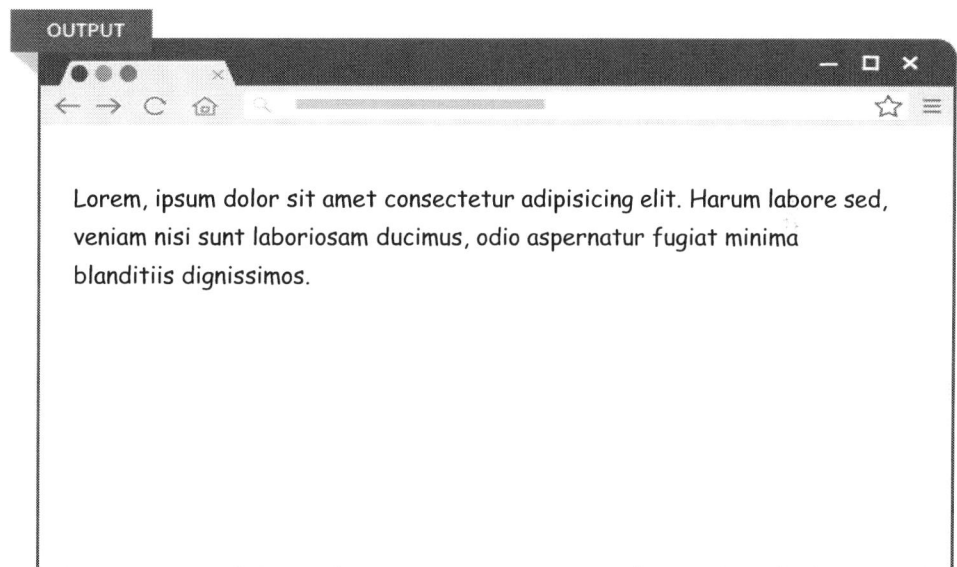

OUTPUT

Lorem, ipsum dolor sit amet consectetur adipisicing elit. Harum labore sed, veniam nisi sunt laboriosam ducimus, odio aspernatur fugiat minima blanditiis dignissimos.

Abbreviations / Acronyms In HTML

In HTML you can use <abbr> tag to present abbreviation or acronym. The optional title attribute of this tag can be used to provide the full form of the abbreviation, which is presented by browsers as a tooltip when the mouse cursor is hovered over the acronym. For example, when you rest your mouse over 4GL or API in the following example, you will see the full human readable description of these abbreviations.

CODE

```
<!DOCTYPE html>
<html>
<body>

<p>The <abbr title="Fourth-Generation Programming Language">4GL</abbr> is a
    programming language for commercial business software.</p>

<p>An <acronym title="Application Program Interface">API</acronym> is a
    description of the way one piece of software asks another program to perform
    a service.</p>

<p><b>Hold the mouse pointer over the acronym or abbreviation to see the
    spelled-out version that is displayed by the TITLE attribute.</b></p>

</body>
</html>
```

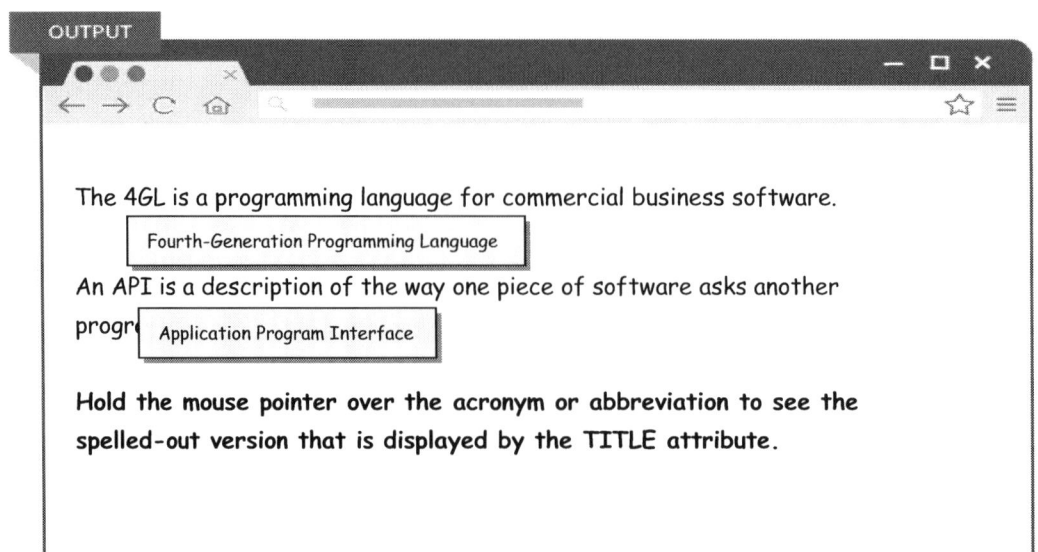

OUTPUT

The 4GL is a programming language for commercial business software.

Fourth-Generation Programming Language

An API is a description of the way one piece of software asks another

progr   Application Program Interface

Hold the mouse pointer over the acronym or abbreviation to see the spelled-out version that is displayed by the TITLE attribute.

Long and Short Quotations In HTML

Quotes are used to emphasize excerpts of text. According to HTML specifications, there are three elements which are supposed to semantically mark up quotations, namely <blockquote>, <q> and <cite>. Although all intended to markup quotes, they should be used in different contexts.

In HTML long quotation are defined by the tag <blockquote>. Blockquote are set off from the main text as a distinct paragraph or block. However, they refer to some external citation which isn't already mentioned in the article. This element can also have an optional attribute cite that specifies the location (in the form of a URL) where the quote has come from. The browser inserts white space before and after a blockquote element. It also inserts margins.

Short quotation is defined by the tag <q>. The browser inserts quotation marks around the short quotation. In practice, usually only blockquote and q are used.

CODE

```
<!DOCTYPE html>
<html>
<body>
  Example of long quotation:
  <blockquote>
    The Giant Eye is a telescope placed on Mount Palomar in Southern...
  </blockquote>
  Example of short quotation:
  <q>This is a short quotation</q>
</body>
</html>
```

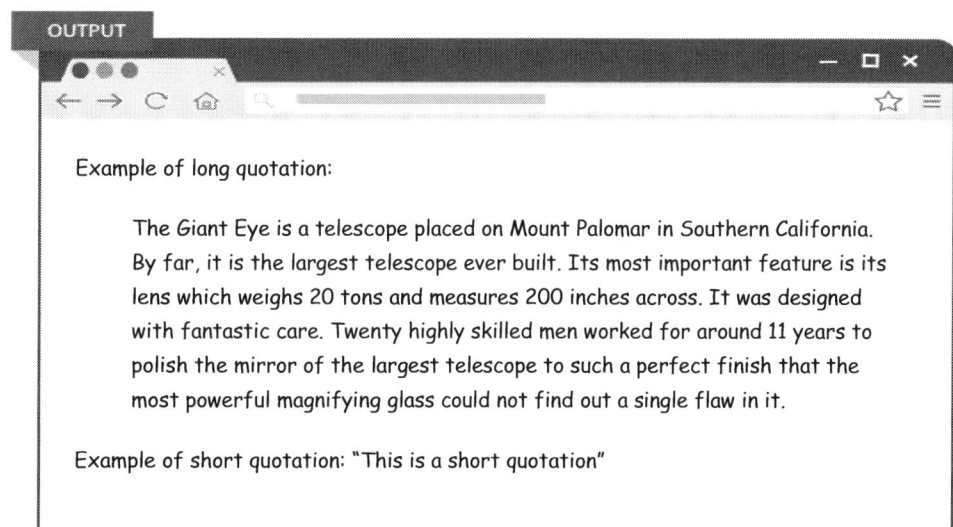

OUTPUT

Example of long quotation:

The Giant Eye is a telescope placed on Mount Palomar in Southern California. By far, it is the largest telescope ever built. Its most important feature is its lens which weighs 20 tons and measures 200 inches across. It was designed with fantastic care. Twenty highly skilled men worked for around 11 years to polish the mirror of the largest telescope to such a perfect finish that the most powerful magnifying glass could not find out a single flaw in it.

Example of short quotation: "This is a short quotation"

Web Links In HTML

The word Surfing is often used while discussing the internet which means moving from one web page to another. You can surf on the web using Links. Links are created using the HTML anchor tag **<a>**. An anchor is used in the following ways:

- Create links to access other pages on the same website
- Create a link to another website or page
- Create a link to send email
- Create a bookmark inside a web page

You define the link destination in the href attribute of the <a> element. The **target** attribute with the value **_blank** is used in the following example to open Amazon's website in a new window.

CODE

```
<!DOCTYPE html>
<html>
<body>
   <p>Link to other pages within a website:
      <a href="Index.php">Home</a>
      <a href="services.html">Services</a>
      <a href="about-us.html">About</a>
      <a href="contact.html">Contact</a>
   </p>
   <p>Link to another website:
      Buy from <a href="http://www.amazon.com/" target="_blank">Amazon!</a>.
   </p>
</body>
</html>
```

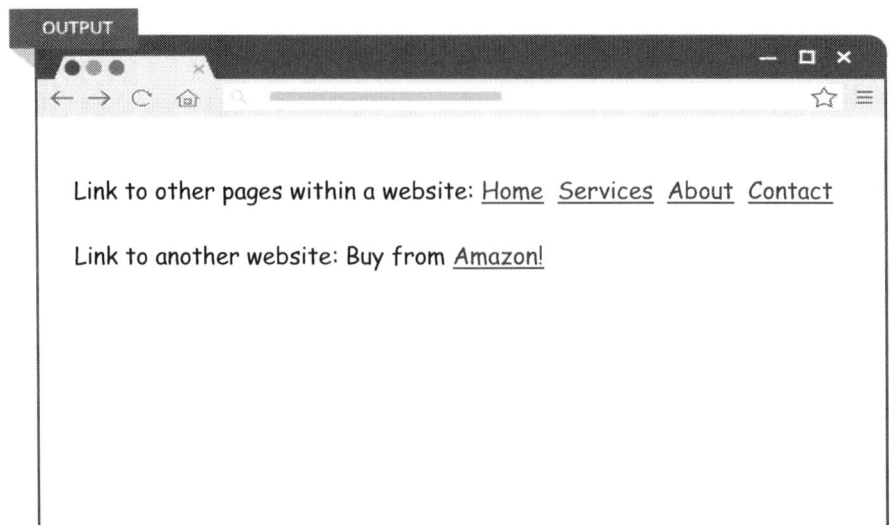

OUTPUT

Link to other pages within a website: Home Services About Contact

Link to another website: Buy from Amazon!

Using a shorthand known as relative URL, you can link to other pages within the same website and do not need to specify the domain name. The first four links in the previous example demonstrate relative URL.

When you link to a different website, the value of the href attribute will have the full web address for the site, which is known as an absolute URL as shown in the last link.

You can also create an image link in addition to text link.

Image Link Example

```
<!DOCTYPE html>
<html>
<body>
  <p>
    <a href="http://www.amazon.com/"><img src="amazon.jpg" alt="Amazon!" height="20"></a>
  </p>
</body>
</html>
```

Add to Shopping Cart

E-mail Links In HTML

The <a> element along with the href attribute can also be used to send email. You prefix mailto: to the email address of the recipient after the href attribute. When you click the email link, the default email program opens a new message displaying the recipient's address in the To: box. Optionally, you can also add a subject line as shown in the following example. Spaces between words should be replaced by %20 to ensure that the browser will display the text properly.

Email Link Example

```
<!DOCTYPE html>
<html>
<body>
  <p>
    Please <a href="mailto:someone@abc.com?Subject=Ticket%20Inquiry">Contact us</a> through email.
  </p>
</body>
</html>
```

Please Contact us through email.

Bookmarking In HTML

In your website, you have a long page with several sections. To make this page user-friendly, you use the bookmark feature in HTML by creating a list at the top of the page and link it to corresponding sections. Likewise, to save users from having to scroll back to the top, you also add a link at the bottom or at the end of each section which instantly takes the user to the top. You can achieve this task by using the **id** attribute which can be used with every HTML element. First you need to identify the points in the page the link will go to and mark them with the **id** attribute. Next, you link to these points using the # symbol followed by the value of the id attribute in the href attribute of the created list. You have to make your browser's window smaller to see the jumping effect.

CODE

```
<!DOCTYPE html>
<html>
<body>
    <!--The top link at the bottom will bring you here-->
    <h1 id="top">Education System Review</h1>
    <!--List of topics that points to corresponding section-->
    <a href="#topic1">First Topic</a><br>
    <a href="#topic2">Second Topic</a><br>
    <a href="#topic3">Third Topic</a><br><br>
    <!-- The first marked point with the id "topic1"-->
    <h2 id="topic1">First Topic</h2>
    <p> Lorem, ipsum dolor sit amet consectetur adipisicing elit... </p>
    <!--The second marked point with the id "topic2"-->
    <h2 id="topic2">Second Topic</h2>
    <p> Lorem, ipsum dolor sit amet consectetur adipisicing elit... </p>
    <!--The third marked point with the id "topic3"-->
    <h2 id="topic3">Third Topic</h2>
    <p> Lorem, ipsum dolor sit amet consectetur adipisicing elit... </p>
    <!--The top link which takes you to the main heading-->
    <p><a href="#top">Top</a></p>
</body>
</html>
```

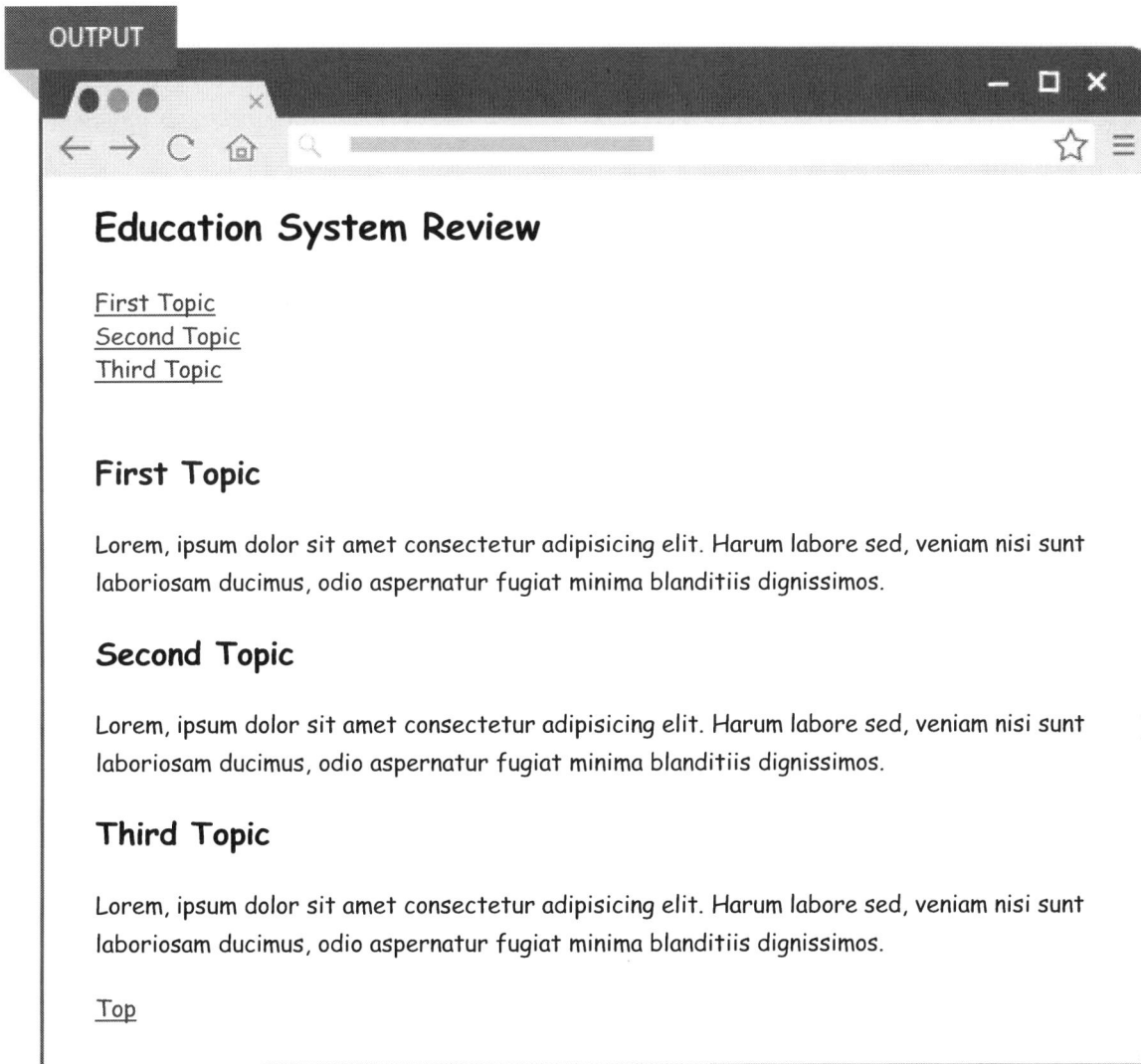

Images In HTML

The adage *"A picture is worth a thousand words"* refers to the notion that a complex idea can be conveyed with just a single still image. This fits more in the world of web than any other place. A web site having great images is more engaging than a dull text-based one.

You add images to your web page to display:

- Company logo
- Images
- Diagram, chart or illustration

Images are defined using the <img> tag in HTML which is an empty tag since it doesn't have an associated end tag. Some common attributes of <img> tag are src, alt, width, and height. The src attribute, which stands for source, is used to display images on a web page. Its value holds the location of the image. The alt attribute contains an alternate text that is displayed if the image cannot be displayed. The height and width attributes specify the image size (by default in pixels).

CODE

```
<!DOCTYPE html>
<html>
<body>
    <img border="0" src="airport.png" alt="Airport" width="1000" height="500">
</body>
</html>
```

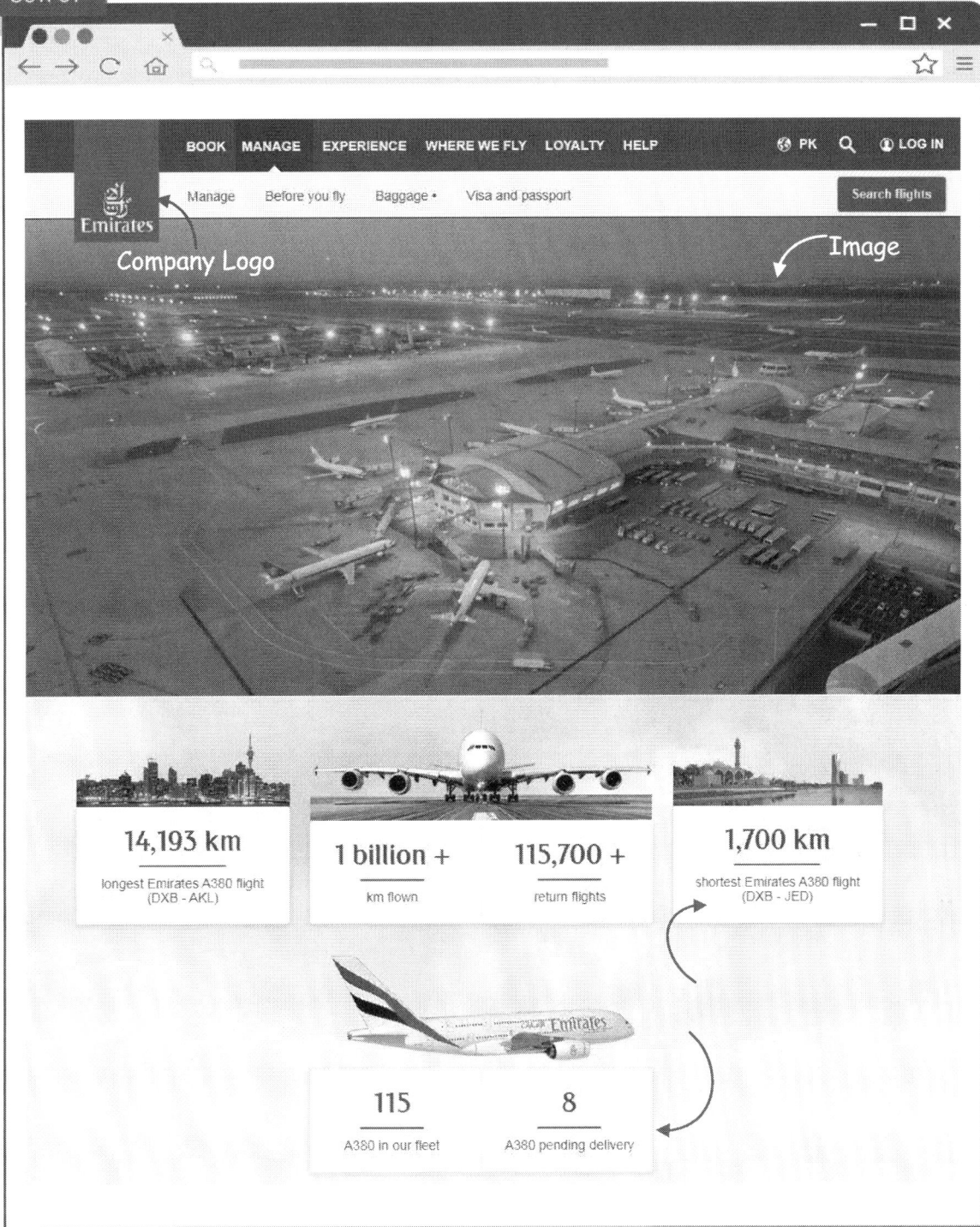

OUTPUT

BOOK **MANAGE** EXPERIENCE WHERE WE FLY LOYALTY HELP | 🌐 PK 🔍 ① LOG IN

Manage   Before you fly   Baggage •   Visa and passport | Search flights

Emirates

Company Logo

Image

14,193 km

longest Emirates A380 flight
(DXB - AKL)

1 billion +   115,700 +

km flown   return flights

1,700 km

shortest Emirates A380 flight
(DXB - JED)

115   8

A380 in our fleet   A380 pending delivery

Lists In HTML

HTML lists are great for calling your reader's attention to specific information. It has been a popular tool even when writing business and technical documents. Lists draw attention to important information. Readers like them because they are visually appealing and make it easy to quickly find pertinent information. In HTML you can use three types of lists:

Ordered List: This list has items marked with numbers. It is defined using the tag <ol> and each item starts with the tag <li>.

Unordered List: Items in this list are marked with bullets. It is defined with the tag <ul>. Each list item is enclosed in the <li> tag.

Definition List: This list contains description of each item and is defined with the <dl> tag in conjunction with <dt> and <dd> to define list items and corresponding descriptions respectively.

CODE

```
<!DOCTYPE html>
<html>
<body>
  <h4> Ordered List </h4>
  <ol>
    <li> Go to <b>Shared Components.</b> page </li>
    <li> Click <b>Lists</b> under Navigation section. </li>
    <li> Click the <b>Create</b> button. </li>
  </ol>
  <h4> Unordered List </h4>
  <ul>
   <li> HTML </li>
   <li> CSS </li>
   <li> JavaScript </li>
  </ul>
  <h4> Definition List </h4>
  <dl>
   <dt> - Coffee </dt>
     <dd> Black hot drink </dd>
   <dt> - Milk </dt>
     <dd> White cold drink </dd>
  </dl>
</body>
</html>
```

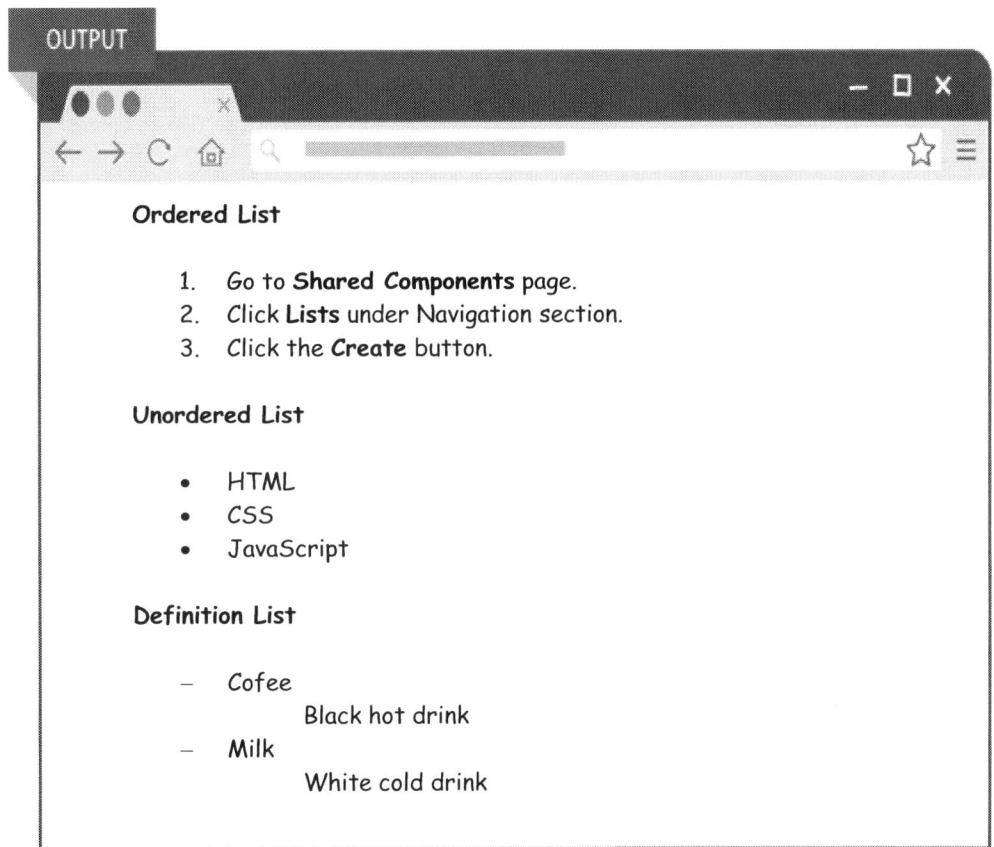

Ordered List

1. Go to **Shared Components** page.
2. Click **Lists** under Navigation section.
3. Click the **Create** button.

Unordered List

- HTML
- CSS
- JavaScript

Definition List

- Cofee
  Black hot drink
- Milk
  White cold drink

You can use different Ordered and Unordered list on your web page by applying the following TYPE attributes:

Ordered List		Unordered List	
List	Type	List	Type
Uppercase letters	<ol type="A">	Disc bullets	<ul type="disc">
Lowercase letters	<ol type="a">	Circle bullets	<ul type="circle">
Roman numbers	<ol type="I">	Square bullets	<ul type="square">
Lowercase Roman numbers	<ol type="i">		

You can also create nested listing as demonstrated below by putting a second list inside the existing one.

CODE

```
<!DOCTYPE html>
<html>
<body>
<h4>A Nested List</h4>
<ul>
  <li>Personal Computers</li>
  <li>Laptops
   <ul>
   <li>HP</li>
   <li>Dell
    <ul>
      <li>Inspiron 15R</li>
      <li>Inspiron 17R</li>
    </ul>
   </li>
   </ul>
  </li>
  <li>All-in-One</li>
</ul>
</body>
</html>
```

OUTPUT

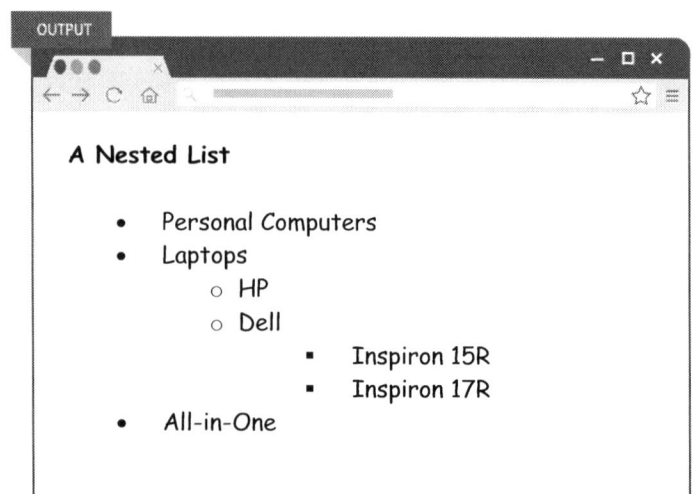

Tables In HTML

A table is a set of data elements (values) that is organized using a model of vertical columns and horizontal rows, the cell being the unit where a row and column intersect. In HTML you use the following elements while defining a table:

Element	Description
Table <table>	Defines the table itself
Table Rows <tr>	Rows in a table
Table Data <td>	Table cell that holds data
Header Cell <th>	Column heading
Table Heading <thead>	To group header content
Table Body <tbody>	To group body content
Table Footer <tfoot>	To group footer content

CODE

```
<!DOCTYPE html>
<html>
<body>
  <h4>Horizontal Table</h4>
  <table border="1">
    <thead><b>Product Information</b></thead>
    <tbody>
      <tr>
        <th>Product</th>
        <th>Quantity</th>
        <th>Price</th>
      </tr>
      <tr>
        <td>Ladies Shoes</td>
        <td>1</td>
        <td>$99.99</td>
      </tr>
    </tbody>
    <tfoot>
      <tr>
        <td><b>Total</b></td>
        <td><b>1</b></td>
        <td><b>$99.99</b></td>
      </tr>
    </tfoot>
  </table>
</body>
</html>
```

OUTPUT

Horizontal Table

Product Information

Product	Quantity	Price
Ladies Shoes	1	$99.99
Total	1	$99.99

CODE

```
<!DOCTYPE html>
<html>
<body>
<h4>Vertical Table</h4>
<table border="1">
  <tbody>
    <tr>
      <th>Product</th>
      <td>Jacket</td>
      <td><b>Total</b></td>
    </tr>
    <tr>
      <th>Quantity</th>
      <td>1</td>
      <td><b>1</b></td>
    </tr>
    <tr>
      <th>Price</th>
      <td>$70.00</td>
      <td><b>$70.00</b></td>
    </tr>
  </tbody>
</table>
</body>
</html>
```

OUTPUT

Vertical Table

Product	Jacket	Total
Quantity	1	1
Price	$70.00	$70.00

Divisions/Sections In HTML

The <div> tag defines a division or a section in an HTML document. It is used to group block-elements to format them with styles and is often used together with CSS to layout a web page. For example, you might create a <div> element to group header objects (such as logo and navigation links), a second one to group main content of the page, and the last one to group footer objects (links or copyright text). The code *&copy* displays the copyright symbol © while "id" attribute references css rules to style a single element. For further details, see CSS ID and Class in chapter 3.

CODE

```html
<!DOCTYPE html>
<html>
<body>
  <div id="header">
    <img src="logo.png" alt="ABC Global Consulting">
    <ul>
      <li><a href="company.html">Home</a></li>
      <li><a href="products.html">Products</a></li>
      <li><a href="services.html">Services</a></li>
      <li><a href="contact.html">Contact</a></li>
    </ul>
  </div>   <!-- end of header -->
  <div id="content">
    <h3>WELCOME</h3>
    <p>ABC Global Consulting, a provider of scalable business solutions.</p>
  </div>   <!-- end of content -->
  <div id="footer">
    <p>&copy; ABC Global Consulting</p>
  </div>   <!-- end of footer -->
</body>
</html>
```

OUTPUT

- Home
- Products
- Services
- Contact

DIV: **header**

WELCOME

ABC Global Consulting, a provider of scalable business solutions.

DIV: **content**

© ABC Global Consulting

DIV: **footer**

View HTML Source And Inspect Page Element

While surfing on the Internet you come across some very attractive websites and wonder how developers created those websites. All modern browsers allow you to see source code of websites. Just right-click an HTML page and select "View page source" (A) or similar option from the context menu. This will open a new tab or window showing the HTML source code of the page. In addition to this, you can also inspect an HTML element. Right-click on an element (B), and choose "Inspect" (C) or similar option from the context menu to see both the HTML and the CSS code of that element. Developers use Elements (D) and Styles panel (E) to modify both HTML and CSS on-the-fly.

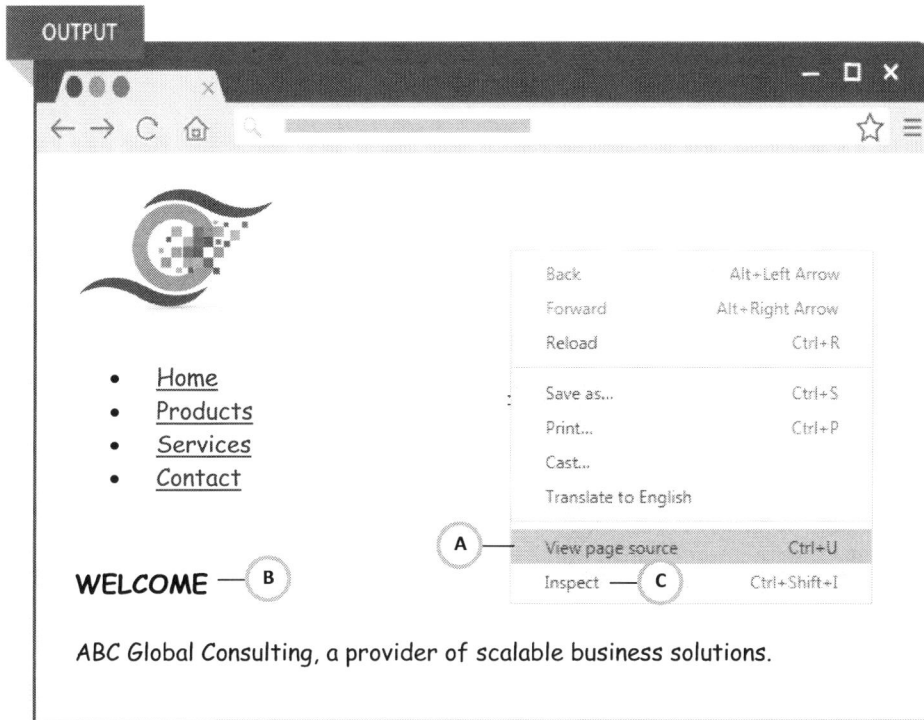

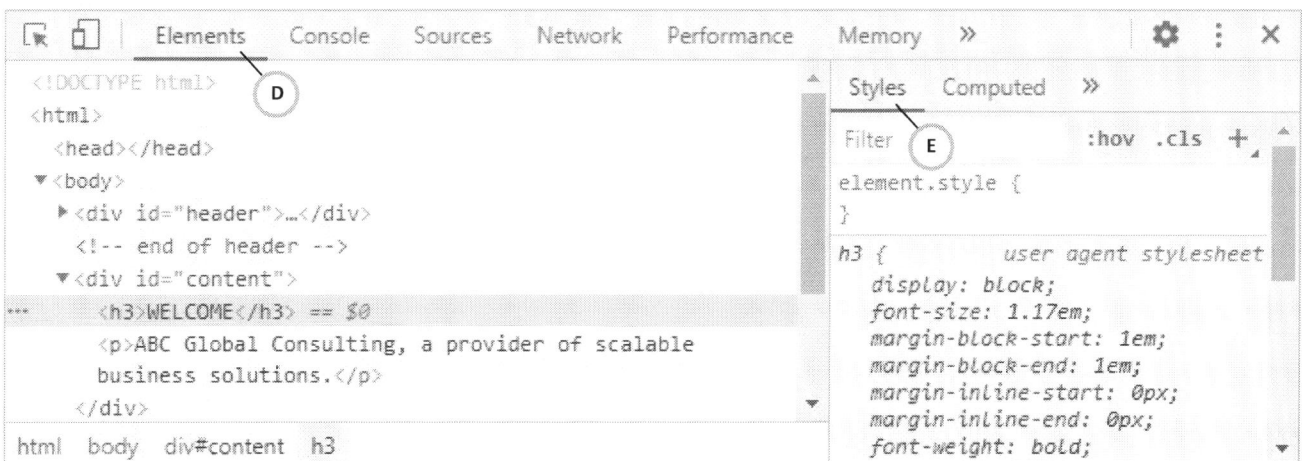

Forms In HTML

Forms are everywhere on the web. You might have interacted with HTML forms on web sites like Amazon, eBay, Yahoo!, and Google. The use of form on a page is a higher level phase of Web development to collect information from visitors. Whether it's through registration forms, mailing lists, site searches, or online ordering, forms facilitate interaction between organizations / individuals with their clients or end users.

Let's take Amazon as an example. You visit Amazon's website as a buyer and don't verbally tell Amazon to find an item. Instead, you interact with a form containing form controls in the shape of a search text box and a Search button. You enter your search criteria into the text box, click the Search button, and get the results in a clean list format that you can quickly browse through.

From a seller's perspective, the process is slightly more complex, but again, involves forms and form controls. When you want to sell an item on Amazon's Web site, the first step is to register as a seller. During the registration process, you'll see a form with numerous form controls that collect different types of information from you.

In HTML you use the <form> tag to create a form; all form controls reside inside this tag. Every <form> tag requires an action attribute which specifies where to send the form-data when a form is submitted. You also use form's *method* attribute to send or retrieve data to or from server. This attribute can have either a GET or a POST value. The GET method is the default and is used when you want to retrieve something from the server, while the POST method is used to manipulate information on the server.

As per functionality both GET and POST methods are same with the following differences:

- GET method shows the information to the users as it is sent appended to the URL. But in the case of POST method information will not be visible as it is sent encapsulated within the HTTP request body.

- GET method has limitation in the size of data transmitted, but POST method hasn't.

- Web browser can usually cache the response pages for GET requests, because they do not change. POST requests, however, cannot be cached, and the server is re-contacted each time the page is displayed.

- GET requests should be used for pure queries that don't affect anything on the server. POST requests are most suitable for queries where the response page will change over time – like a shopping cart.

The elements you can use in your web form include the following:

- Text and password fields
- Text area
- Radio buttons
- Checkbox
- Drop-down list box
- Button
- File input to upload a file
- Group box
- Label

Let's go through these form elements with some practical examples.

Text & Password Elements

These are the most commonly used input fields defined with the <input> tag. This <input> tag is an empty tag without a closing tag and contains a TYPE attribute which determines what kind of input is being created. The <input type="text"> defines a one-line input field that a user can enter text into whereas, <input type="password"> creates a password field. The characters in a password field are masked - shown as asterisks or circles. The following table shows a couple of most utilized attributes associated with the <input> tag:

Attribute	Description
name	Each form control should have a name to identify it on the server
maxlength	To limit the number of input characters

CODE

```
<!DOCTYPE html>
<html>
<body>
  <form action="http://www.abc.com/login.php">
   <p>Username:
      <input type="text" name="username" maxlength="30">
   </p>
   <p>Password:
      <input type="password" name="password"
maxlength="30">
   </p>
  </form>
</body>
</html>
```

OUTPUT

Username: Saad

Password: *************

Text Area Element

If you're acquainted with blogs, you must have seen a large text box under a blog post where users provide their comments. This box is a multi-line input control and is defined using its own tag called <textarea>. It can hold an unlimited number of characters and is specified by cols and rows attributes. The cols attribute, measured in numbers of characters, sets the width of the text area. The rows attribute indicates the height of the text area. The browser automatically adds a scroll bar when the text crosses the row attribute limit.

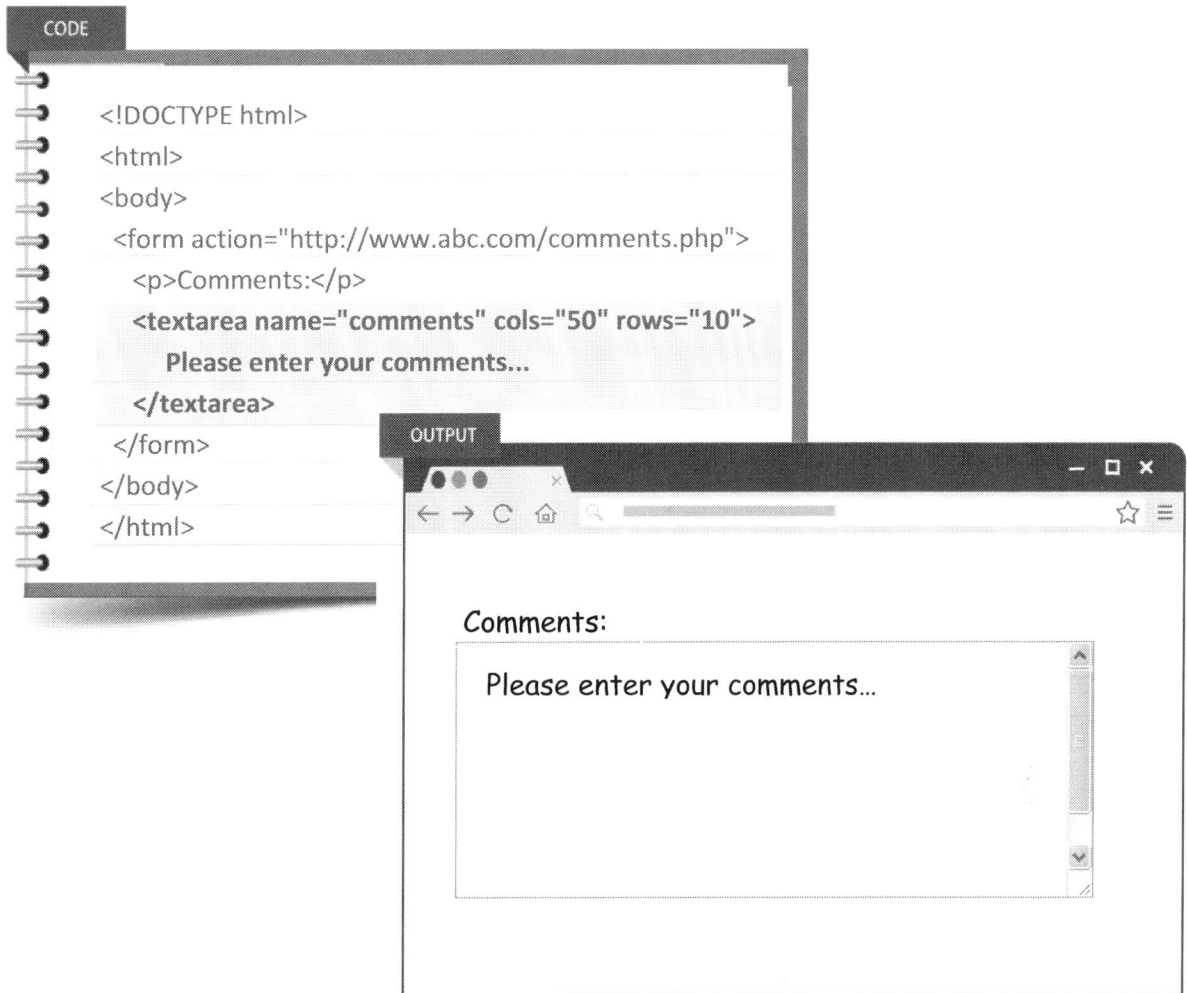

CODE

```
<!DOCTYPE html>
<html>
<body>
  <form action="http://www.abc.com/comments.php">
    <p>Comments:</p>
    <textarea name="comments" cols="50" rows="10">
       Please enter your comments...
    </textarea>
  </form>
</body>
</html>
```

OUTPUT

Comments:

Please enter your comments...

Radio Button Element

Radio buttons let a user select ONLY ONE of a limited number of choices. It is defined as <input type="radio"> and has three main attributes - name, value, and checked. The name is sent along with the selected value to the server. The value attribute is the value passed to a script or a CGI program to indicate which button is selected. Be sure you assign a different value to each button. The checked attribute sets a default value when the page loads into the browser and is used with only one radio button in a group.

The entire group of radio buttons shares a single name and a single object. To access the individual buttons, you treat the radio object as an array. The buttons are indexed, starting with 0. You use the checked property of a radio button to check its current state. The following statement checks the first radio button in the ctype group on the contact form:

document.contact.ctype[0].checked == true;

CODE

```
<!DOCTYPE html>
<html>
<body>
  <form action="http://www.abc.com/submit.php">
   <p><b>Customer Type:</b>
     <input type="radio" name="ctype" value="Corporate" checked="checked"> Corporate
     <input type="radio" name="ctype" value="Home User"> Home User
   </p>
  </form>
</body>
</html>
```

OUTPUT

Customer Type: ● Corporate ○ Home User

Checkbox Element

Defined using the tag <input type="checkbox">, checkboxes let a user select or de-select ONE or MORE options from the available choices. It has same attributes as radio buttons. It also has a single event, onClick, which occurs whenever the check box is clicked. This event examines the checked property to see whether the box was turned on or off.

CODE

```html
<!DOCTYPE html>
<html>
<body>
<form action="http://www.abc.com/submit.php">
 <p><b>Please select service(s) you're interested in:</b>
 <br>
 <input type="checkbox" name="service" value="accounts" checked="checked"> Accountancy
 <br>
 <input type="checkbox" name="service" value="it"> Information Technology
 <br>
 <input type="checkbox" name="service" value="hr"> Human Resource
 </p>
</form>
</body>
</html>
```

OUTPUT

Please select services(s) you're interested in:

☑ Accountancy
☑ Information Technology
☑ Human Resource

Dropdown List Box Element

Similar to radio buttons, a drop down list box also allows you to select a single option from the provided list. Usage depends on the scenario. For example, if the list has few options, use the radio buttons and to display a long list of products you must choose a drop down list box.

In HTML a dropdown list box is defined with the <select> tag in conjunction with two or more <option> elements. The <option> tags inside the <select> element define the available options in the list. An attribute called *selected* can be added to an option to mark it as the default selected option when the page loads.

Reading the value of a selected item is a two-step process. You first use the selectedIndex property, and then use the value property to find the value of the selected choice. Here's an example:

nIdx = document.contactform.category.selectedIndex;
sCat = document.contactform.category.options[nIdx].value;

This uses the nIdx variable to store the selected index, and then assigns the value of the selected choice to the sCat variable. Things are a bit more complicated with a multiple selection where you need to test each option's selected attribute separately.

CODE

```
<!DOCTYPE html>
<html>
<body>
  <form action="http://www.abc.com/submit.php">
    <p><b>Services - Subcategory</b></p>
    <select name="category">
      <option value="sw">Software</option>
      <option selected="selected" value="hw">Hardware</option>
      <option value="nw">Network</option>
    </select>
  </form>
</body>
</html>
```

OUTPUT

Services - Subcategory

| Hardware | ⌄ |

Software	⌄
Hardware	
Network	

Submit Button Element

After completing a web form you need something to inform the browser to send the information to the server. A submit button is used to accomplish this task and is the recommended way to submit HTML forms. It is defined using the tag <input type="submit"> and its value attribute acts as the button's label. After clicking this button, the data is sent to the page specified in the form's action attribute which performs some actions with the received input. In the following exercise, the information is sent to a page "xyz.php" on the server. The server processes the input and returns the answer as shown in the output pane. For this purpose, we used the GET method which retrieves the inputted information from the server. Server processing is an advanced topic and will be discussed in Chapter 5 and Chapter 6. At this stage, if you click the submit button after running the example code, you'll get an error indicating that the browser could not find the file 'submit.php'. Besides SUBMIT you can use two other types, RESET and BUTTON. The RESET button sets all the form fields back to their default value, or blank. The BUTTON performs an action associated with a JavaScript event handler. If the user presses a Submit or a Reset button, you can detect it with the onSubmit or onReset event handlers. For generic buttons, you can use an onClick event handler.

CODE

```
<!DOCTYPE html>
<html>
<body>
<form name="input" action="xyz.php" method="get">
  <input type="checkbox" name="service" value="accounts"> Accountancy <br>
  <input type="checkbox" name="service" value="it"> Information Technology <br>
  <input type="checkbox" name="service" value="hr"> Human Resource  <br><br>
  <input type="submit" value="Submit">
  <input type="reset" value="Reset">
</form>
<p>Click the Submit button to get the form-data from xyz.php page.</p>
</body>
</html>
```

OUTPUT

☑ Accountancy
☐ Information Technology
☑ Human Resource

Submit   Reset

Click the Submit button to get the form-data from xyz.php page.

OUTPUT

You selected the options(s):
accounts and hr

Button Element

Just like desktop application forms, you can create a push button on a web form as well using the markup <button type="button">text/image</button>. The main difference between this element and buttons created with the <input> element is that you can add text or image inside a button element which provides you more control over button's appearance.

CODE

```
<!DOCTYPE html>
<html>
<body>
  <form action="http://www.abc.com/add.php">
    <button><img src="add.gif" alt="add" width="10" height="10"> Add</button>
  </form>
</body>
</html>
```

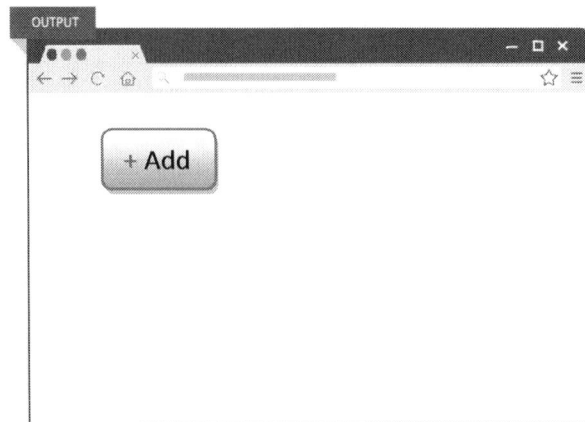

File Input Element

To allow users to upload their documents, images, videos or other files to your web server you again use the
<input> element with type="file" attribute. In such situations, you must set the method attribute value to POST.
The accept attribute specifies the types of files that the server accepts. To specify more than one value, separate
the values with a comma e.g. accept="audio/*,video/*,image/*".

CODE

```html
<!DOCTYPE html>
<html>
<body>
  <form action="http://www.abc.com/upload.php" method="post">
    <p>Upload your image in GIF format:</p>
    <input type="file" name="logo" accept="image/gif">
    <input type="submit" value="Upload">
  </form>
</body>
</html>
```

OUTPUT

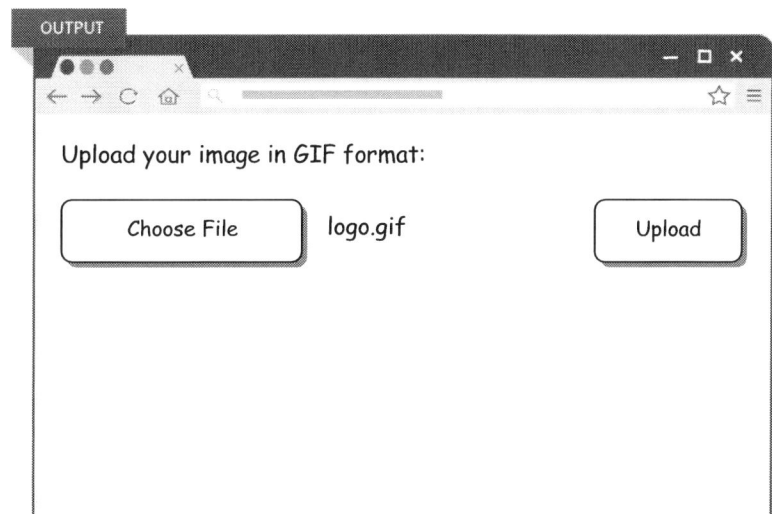

Grouping Form Elements

If your form has different sections, you can separate them using the <fieldset> element which draws a box around the related form controls to group them. You add the <legend> tag immediately after the opening <fieldset> tag to define a caption that informs the purpose of that section.

CODE

```
<!DOCTYPE html>
<html>
<body>
  <form>
    <fieldset>
      <legend>Contact Information</legend>
      <label>Name:<br>
      <input type="text" name="name"></label><br>
      <label>Email:<br>
      <input type="text" name="email"></label><br>
      <label>Cell No.:<br>
      <input type="text" name="mobile"></label>
    </fieldset>
  </form>
</body>
</html>
```

OUTPUT

Contact Information

Name:

Email:

Cell No.:

Some More HTML5 Elements

In previous sections you saw many examples of <input> HTML element. The following tables reveal some more elements of HTML5.

Structural Element	Description
<article>	Defines an article such as a blog post or main content on a web page
<aside>	Defines content aside from the page content like blog archives or events list
<figure>	Contains content like illustrations, diagrams, photos, code listings, etc.
<figcaption>	Defines a caption for a <figure> element
<footer>	Defines a footer for a document or section
<header>	Defines a header for a document or section
<hgroup>	Groups a set of <h1> to <h6> elements when a heading has multiple levels
<nav>	Defines navigation links
<section>	Defines a section in a document

Media Element	Description
<audio>	Defines sound content
<video>	Defines a video or movie
<source>	Defines multiple media resources for <video> and <audio>

HTML5 has several new input types for forms. These new features allow better input control and validation.

HTML5 New Input Types		
color	week	number
date	month	range
datetime	email	search
datetime-local	tel	url
time		

Calendar Element

In HTML5, a new date value is added to the type attribute which displays a calendar control on your web page from which users can select a desired date as demonstrated in the following example. As you can see this time we used a separate <label> tag to display a label for the calendar element. The for attribute of <label> element must be equal to the id attribute of the related element to bind them together.

CODE

```
<!DOCTYPE html>
<html>
<body>
  <form action="http://www.abc.com/info/" method="post">
    <label for="userDoB">Date of birth:</label>
    <input type="date" name="dob" id="userDoB">
    <input type="submit" value="Submit">
  </form>
</body>
</html>
```

OUTPUT

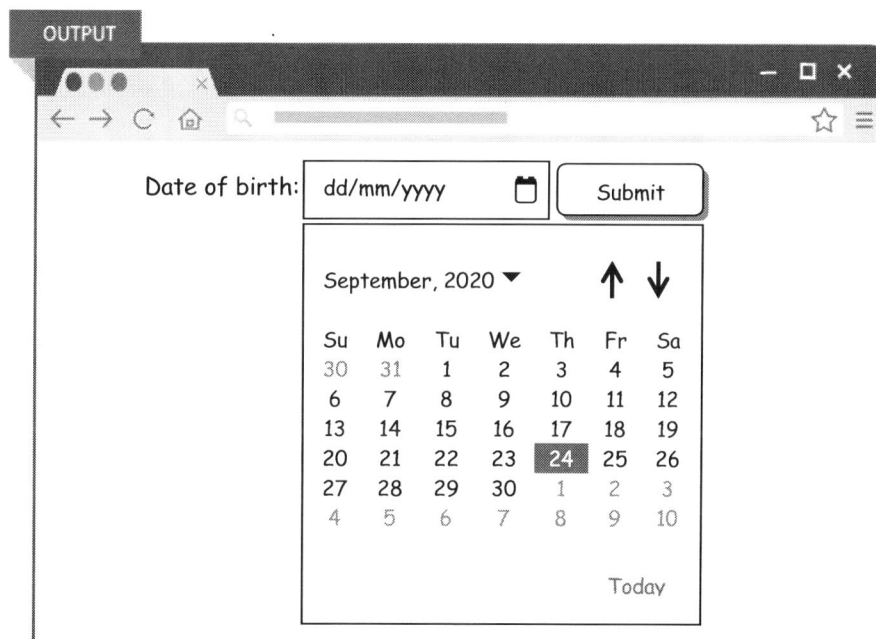

Form Validation

There are some mandatory fields in a form that must not be left blank e.g. User ID, Password etc. Users are alerted to provide such information if they omit them. This process is called form validation. Usually, a scripting language (such as JavaScript - discussed in Chapter 3) is used by developers to validate a form on client machines prior to posting data to the server. But now, HTML5 is introducing client side validation to quickly identify problems in a form. Some of these are listed below with examples.

Required & Placeholder Attributes

The required attribute applies to all input fields, and specifies that an input field must be filled out before submitting the form. It is defined as <input required>. The placeholder attribute specifies a short hint that describes the expected value of an input field (e.g. a sample e-mail address in the expected format). The hint is displayed unless you type something in the input field.

CODE

```
<!DOCTYPE html>
<html>
<body>
<form action="abc.php">
    User ID: <input type="text" name="userid" required
                     placeholder="me@example.com">
    Password: <input type="password" name="password" required>
    <input type="submit" value="Submit">
</form>
</body>
</html>
```

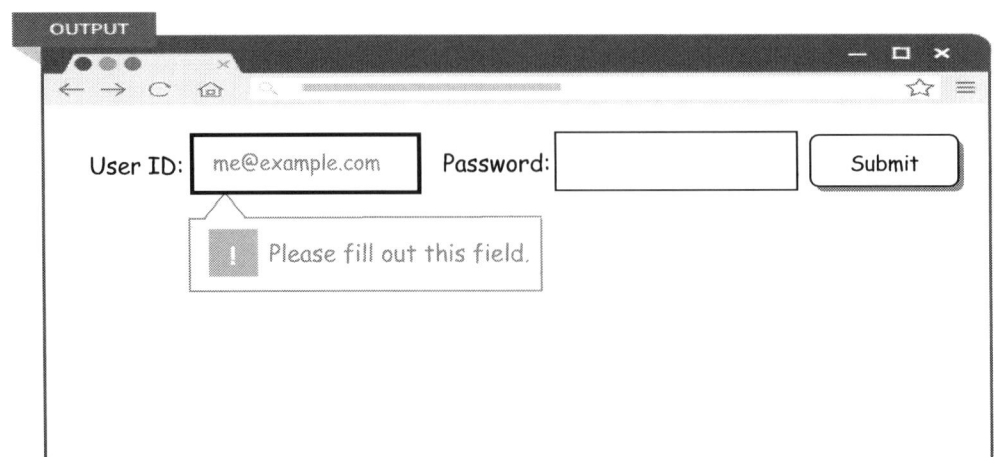

Validate E-mail and URL

If your form has mandatory email and url fields, you can validate them using the new input type values as shown in the following examples. Browsers supporting HTML5 will check and validate the correct format.

<input type="email" name="email">
<input type="url" name="website">

Add Search Box to a Web Page

Like every good website you can add search capabilities to your site. A search box allows users to search content that is not apparently visible to them. HTML5 has provided an input type called search to address search queries. Once again, the following code sends the search criteria to a page (abc.php) on the server to process the request.

CODE

```
<!DOCTYPE html>
<html>
<body>
  <form action="abc.php">
    Search Google: <input type="search" name="searchongoogle">
    <input type="submit">
  </form>
</body>
</html>
```

OUTPUT

Search Google: [   ] Submit

Play Videos on a Web Page

In HTML5 you can play movie clip and other video streams using the new <video> tag. The src attribute specifies the URL of the video file. The controls attribute displays video controls which include:

- Play
- Pause
- Seeking
- Volume
- Fullscreen toggle
- Captions/Subtitles (when available)
- Track (when available)

Internet Explorer 8 and earlier versions do not support the <video> tag. In order for users viewing your video through older or latest browsers you need to upload the video in at least two different formats as did in the example below. The <source> element inside the <video> element is used to run this video on all supported browsers. You specify alternative video/audio files which the browser may choose from, based on its media type or codec support. Use the <audio> tag to play audio files in HTML5.

CODE

```
<!DOCTYPE html>
<html>
<body>
  <video width="320" height="240" controls="controls">
    <source src="tennis.mp4" type="video/mp4">
    <source src="tennis.webm" type="video/webm">
    Your browser does not support the video tag.
  </video>
</body>
</html>
```

OUTPUT

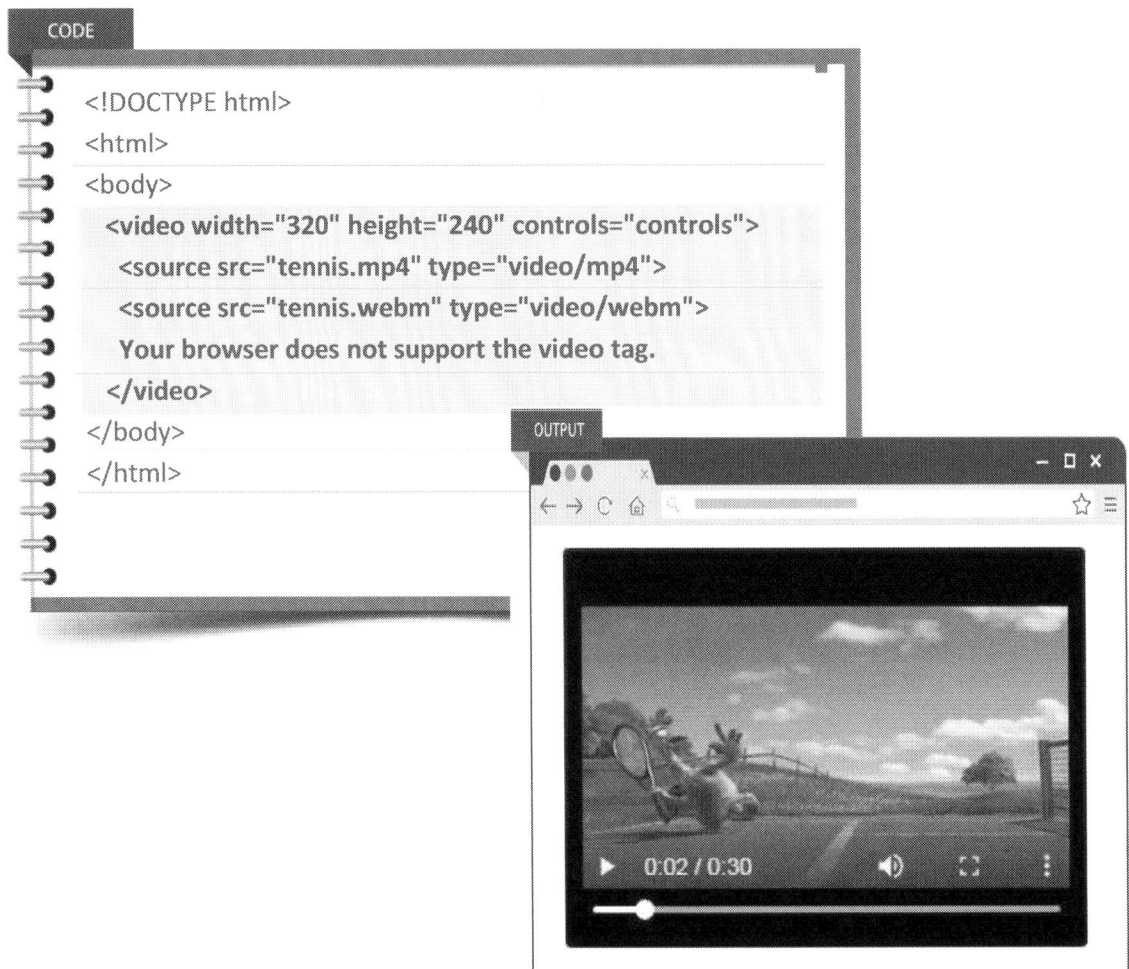

CHAPTER 3

CASCADING STYLE SHEETS
{CSS}

About Cascading Style Sheets

Having gone through the previous part, you might have observed that HTML is very restrictive with respect to web page formatting. This is because it was designed to format and send documents over sparse networks in a fastest possible way. Due to this limitation of HTML, the need for a styling language surfaced and caused the basis for the emergence of Cascading Style Sheet (CSS).

CSS is a style sheet language used for describing the presentation semantics of a document written in a markup language. Its most common application is to style web pages written in HTML. CSS is designed primarily to enable the separation of document content from document presentation, including elements such as the layout, colors, and fonts.

Prior to CSS, nearly all of the presentational attributes of HTML documents were contained within the HTML markup; all font colors, background styles, element alignments, borders and sizes had to be explicitly described, often repeatedly, within the HTML. This made documents more complex, larger, and more difficult to maintain. CSS allows developers to move much of that information to another file, the style sheet, resulting in considerably simpler HTML. CSS can define color, font, text alignment, size, borders, spacing, layout and many other typographic characteristics, and can do so independently for on-screen and printed views.

Style sheets are usually contained within an external CSS file (but they don't have to be) and are linked in to every web page that you are working with using the <link> tag. Therefore, any or all styles from that CSS file can be applied to the web pages that you are working with, ultimately providing you with the flexibility to quickly and easily modify one CSS file that propagates changes to all web pages that share the CSS file in your website. You can refer multiple style sheet files in your web page. For instance, use one file to control the presentation (such as fonts and colors) and use another to control the layout. Due to these capabilities of CSS, the use of all presentational HTML markups has been deprecated.

Style Sheet Rules
A style sheet is a collection of one or more styling instructions called rules that define how an element or a group of elements should appear on the web page. The initial step to learn CSS is to understand the parts of a rule.

Why CSS?

A consulting firm created a web site with more than a hundred pages. To provide a consistent look, they used the same font face, size, and color on all pages. After some time, they decided to change the font from Times to Arial, and the font color from gray to blue for their whole site. Just imagine how frustrating it would be to apply these changes to the whole bunch of pages individually. This is where CSS comes in to resolve the issue. It allows you to create just one file which holds all style rules that dictate how the text within your web site should look. Had the company used CSS, they would have made changes just to a single style sheet file to instantly change the style and layout of the entire web site all at once.

What is CSS3?

CSS3 is the latest standard for CSS. It is completely backward compatible, so you will not have to change existing designs. Browsers will always support CSS2. CSS3 is split up into "modules". The old specification has been split into smaller pieces, and new ones are also added.

Some of the most important CSS3 modules are:

- Selectors
- Box Model
- Backgrounds and Borders
- Text Effects
- 2D/3D Transformations
- Animations
- Multiple Column Layout
- User Interface

CSS Rules and Syntax

A CSS file consists of various rules that enhance the look of your web pages. These rules are associated with HTML elements and format the content of specified elements such as font properties, positioning properties, border properties, and much more. A CSS rule has two main parts: a selector, and one or more declarations (separated by a semi-colon):

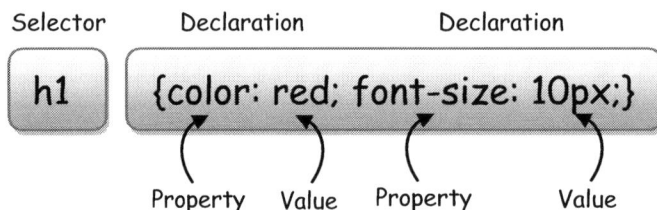

Figure 3-1

The selector is normally the HTML element you want to style. Selectors are case sensitive, so they must exactly match element names and attribute values. Declarations sit inside curly brackets. Each declaration consists of a property and a value. The property is the style attribute you want to change with an associated value. You can specify multiple selectors in a single rule as well as multiple alternative values for a single property like:

```
h1, h2 {
        font-family: Arial, Verdana, sans-serif;
    }
```

You create generic rules in a style sheet that apply to most elements and then override individual element properties that you need to display differently with inline styling.

> **NOTE**
>
> **CSS UNIVERSAL SELECTOR**
>
> In CSS the universal selector is represented by the symbol (*). It is used to select all HTML elements on the page. The CSS rule below will affect every HTML element on the page:
>
> ```
> * {
>     text-align: left;
>     color: gray;
> }
> ```

Creating Style Sheets

Usually, the following three methods are used to add style to your web pages:

External CSS: The most popular and time-efficient way to create style sheet is using an external CSS file. It is ideal when the style is applied to many pages. An external style sheet can be created in any text editor, should not contain any html tags, and must be saved with a .css extension. After creating an external style sheet file, you link each page to it using the <link> tag, which goes inside the <head> section. The href attribute holds name and path of the style sheet (.css file).

```
<head>
  <link rel="stylesheet" href="Style.css">
</head>
```

Where the referenced sytle.css file may contain the following rules to style body and h1 elements:

```
body {
  background-color: blue;
}

h1 {
  color: white;
  margin-left: 10px;
}
```

Later, when the time comes to make changes to the appearance or structure of your web site, you make modifications on the one CSS file, and all of the pages of your web site will instantly change to reflect the changes made within the CSS file.

Internal CSS: An internal style sheet, also known as document-wide style sheet, should be used when a single document (web page) is to be provided a unique style. It is defined in the <head> section of an HTML page using the <style> tag.

```
<head>
  <style>
    hr {color: gray;}
    p {margin-left: 10px;}
    body {background-image:url("images/bg.png");}
  </style>
</head>
```

Inline CSS: In this method a style attribute is directly added to the relevant element resulting in loss of advantages of a style sheet. It is not a recommended method and should be used sparingly. In the following example a text box is created and styled with a beveled border:

```
<input type="text" style="border-style:groove">
```

Understand the Cascade

As mentioned in a preceding section, you can reference multiple style sheets in a single web page. In a situation like this, if you've set some properties for the same selector in different style sheets, the values are taken and applied from the more specific style sheet. A question arises here: What is a specific style sheet? Looking at the scenario, you must first understand the cascading order prior to going through a practical example.

When you apply a style to an HTML element through multiple style sheets, all styles cascade into a new virtual style sheet using the following order of priority rules:

1. Inline style
2. Internal style sheet
3. External style sheet
4. Browser default

The above rule says that an inline style, specified within an HTML element, has the highest priority and will override a style defined in an internal style sheet, defined inside the <head> section, or in an external style sheet, or in a browser. Moreover, if an external style sheet link is placed after the internal style sheet in HTML <head> tag, the external style sheet will override the internal style sheet.

Let's try to understand the cascading concept through an example. You created an **external style sheet** that contains three declarations for the h3 selector:

```
h3
{
  color:blue;
  text-align:left;
  font-size:10pt;
}
```

You also set two properties in an **internal style sheet** for the same h3 selector:

```
h3
{
  text-align:right;
  font-size:20pt;
}
```

The properties for h3 selector will cascade into a new virtual style sheet as follows:

```
color:blue;
text-align:right;
font-size:20pt;
```

The color is taken from the external style sheet because this property is defined only in the external style sheet. Since the internal style sheet is more specific to the page and has higher priority, the text alignment and the font size are inherited from it.

One more concept relevant to the current scenario is the !important property. A rule that has the !important property will always be applied no matter where that rule appears in the CSS document. To make sure that a property always apply, you would add the !important property to the rule. So, to make the paragraph text always red, you would write:

```
p { color: #ff0000 !important; }
```

CSS ID and Class

Besides setting styles for HTML elements, CSS allows you to specify your own selectors called **"id"** and **"class"**.

The id selector is used to specify a style for a single, unique element. It uses the id attribute of the HTML element, and is defined with a "#" identifier. In the following example, the first paragraph in the HTML document is provided with an id "para1", which is referenced in the CSS file via "#para1" identifier to centralize this paragraph and to present it in red color. The second paragraph, on the other hand, neither have any id in the HTML code nor it has any corresponding rule in the CSS file. So, this element is presented normally by the browser.

CODE

```
HTML CODE (test.html)
<!DOCTYPE html>
<html>
<head>
    <link rel="stylesheet" href="styles.css" >
</head>
<body>
    <p id="para1">A paragraph styled with id selector</p>
    <p>This paragraph is not affected by the style rule.</p>
</body>
</html>
```

```
CSS CODE (styles.css)
#para1
    {
    text-align:center;
    color:red;
    }
```

OUTPUT

A paragraph styled with id selector

This paragraph is not affected by the style rule.

NOTE

In order to evaluate this example, create two separate files (for example, test.html and styles.css) in a text editor, such as Notepad, using the code provided in respective sections above. Place both files in the same folder so that the browser can access the style sheet.

The **class selector** is used to specify a style for a group of elements. This means you can set a particular style for many HTML elements with the same class. It uses the HTML class attribute, and is defined with a "." identifier. In this example, both <h1> and <p> elements are using a class selector. Since both elements are referencing the same "center" class selector in the CSS file, the texts in these elements are aligned centrally by the browser.

CODE

HTML CODE (test.html)
```
<!DOCTYPE html>
<html>
<head>
    <link rel="stylesheet" href="styles.css" >
</head>
<body>
   <h1 class="center">
      Heading aligned centrally using class selector
   </h1>
   <p class="center">
      Paragraph aligned centrally using the same class selector.
   </p>
</body>
</html>
```

CSS CODE (styles.css)
```
.center
   {
     text-align:center;
   }
```

OUTPUT

Heading aligned centrally using class selector

Paragraph aligned centrally using the same class selector.

Comments in CSS

Developers add comments to explain their code. Comments also help them assess the source code at a later date. In CSS comments are enclosed in **/*** and ***/** pair and are ignored by browsers. You'll see use of comments in the next example.

CSS Color Property

Powerful and important communication tool, colors are the life of modern websites. Without effective colors it is nearly impossible to design a winning site. In CSS, color and background-color properties are used to set foreground and background colors respectively and are specified by:

- **HEX value** - Hex values represent values for red, green, and blue in hexadecimal code like "#ff0000".

- **Color name** - Colors are represented by predefined names like red, blue, green etc. There are 147 color names defined in the HTML and CSS color specification.

- **RGB value** - Values for red, green, and blue are expressed as numbers between 0 and 255 like "rgb(255,0,0)".

- **RGBA colors** - Supported in latest browsers, these color values are an extension of RGB and are specified as: rgba(red,green,blue,alpha) where the alpha parameter is a number between 0.0 and 1.0. The lowest value is used for full transparency whereas the highest number is used for full opaque.

- **HSL colors** - An HSL color value is specified with: hsl(hue, saturation, lightness). Hue is a degree on the color wheel (from 0 to 360) - 0 (or 360) is red, 120 is green, 240 is blue. Saturation is a percentage value; 0% means a shade of gray and 100% is the full color. Lightness is also a percentage; 0% is black, 100% is white. Example: background-color:hsl(120,65%,75%);

- **HSLA colors** - An HSLA color value is specified with: hsla(hue, saturation, lightness, alpha), where the alpha parameter defines the opacity. The alpha parameter is a number between 0.0 (fully transparent) and 1.0 (fully opaque). Example: background-color:hsla(120,65%,75%,0.3);

In this example, we are using internal style sheet (A), which sets in HTML document's <head> tag.

CODE

```
HTML CODE
<!DOCTYPE html>
<html>          (A)
<head>
  <style>
      /* Body background color set using a HEX code */
      body {background-color: #f2f2f2;}

      /* Main heading font and background colors set using names */
      h1 {color:white;}
      h1 {background-color:deepskyblue;}

      /* Used RGB values for paragraph with a class */
      p.ex {color:rgb(255,255,255);}
      p.ex {background-color:rgb(0,112,192);}
  </style>
</head>
<body>          (A)
  <h1>Paragraph Heading</h1>
  <p class="ex">This is a paragraph with class="ex".</p>
  <p>This is an ordinary paragraph without any color applied.</p>
</body>
</html>
```

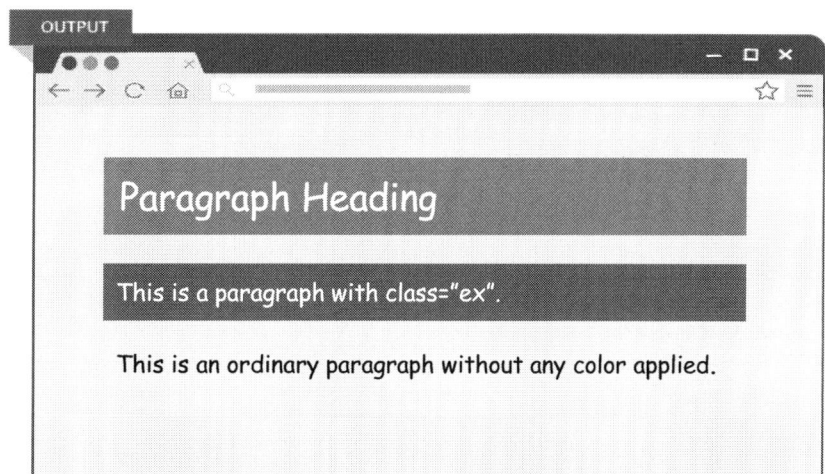

OUTPUT

Paragraph Heading

This is a paragraph with class="ex".

This is an ordinary paragraph without any color applied.

CSS Font

CSS font properties define the font family, boldness, size, and the style of a text.

Font Family

The font-family property allows you to specify the typeface that is applied to a text inside the element using a CSS rule. The font-family property should hold several font names as a "fallback" system. If the browser does not support the first font, it tries the next font. If the name of a font family is more than one word, it must be in quotation marks.

Examples:

body {font-family: Georgia, Times, serif;}
h1, h2 {font-family: Arial, Verdana, sans-serif;}
.fclass {font-family: "Courier New", Courier, monospace;}

In addition to standard HTML fonts, you can use the Google Fonts API to add hundreds of other fonts to your page by adding a stylesheet link and referencing a font family.

Example:

<link rel="stylesheet"
href="https://fonts.googleapis.com/css?family=Sofia">

Font Style

This property has three values:

normal - The text is shown normally

italic - The text is shown in italics

oblique - The text is leaning similar to italic, but less supported

Example:

.fontclass {font-style: italic;}

Font Size

To set the size of a text you use the font-size property. You can specify font size using Pixels (px), Percentages (%), em or vw.

Examples:

body {font-family: Arial, Verdana, sans-serif; font-size: 12px;}
h1 {font-size: 200%;}
h2 {font-size: 1.3em;}
<h1 style="font-size:10vw">Hello World</h1>

Font Weight

This property takes two values - normal and bold. The normal value displays text in normal weight, bold makes the text bold.

Example:

.fontclass {font-weight: bold;}

FONT SYNTAX

- *All font names, except generic font families, must be capitalized. For example, use "Arial" instead of "arial".*

- *Use commas to separate multiple font name.*

- *Font names that contain a character space (such as Courier New in the third example) must be placed within quotation marks.*

WHY USE MULTIPLE FONTS?

In CSS you can use a list of back-up fonts (font stack) if your first choice is not available. In the absence of the first specified font, the browser tries the next one, and down through the list until it finds one that works. For instance, in the first Font-Family example, if the browser does not find Georgia, it will use Times, and if Times is not available, it will substitute a generic serif font.

serif Examples: Times, Times New Roman, Georgia

sans-serif Examples: Arial, Arial Black, Verdana, Trebuchet MS, Helvetica, Geneva

monospaceExamples: Courier, Courier New, and Andale Mono

CSS Text

Described below are some common text properties that developers usually apply through CSS:

Text Transformation

Text-transform property is used to turn everything into uppercase or lowercase letters, or capitalize the first letter of each word.

Text Decoration

Text-decoration property is used to set or remove decorations from text. It is mostly used to remove underlines from links.

Text Alignment

Text-align property is used to set the horizontal alignment of a text. Text can be centered, or aligned to the left or right, or justified.

Text Indentation

Text-indent property is used to specify the indentation of the first line of a text.

Letter Spacing

The letter-spacing property increases or decreases the space between characters in a text.

Word Spacing

The word-spacing property increases or decreases the white space between words.

First Letter

The :first-letter selector is used to add a style to the first letter of the specified selector.

First Line

The :first-line selector is used to add a style to the first line of the specified selector.

A comprehensive example is presented on the next page to demonstrate CSS Fonts and CSS Text.

Style Links with Pseudo-Classes

CSS pseudo-classes are used to add special effects to some selectors. For example, you can set different styles to links that have or have not been visited.

:link - It is used to style links that have not been visited.

:visited - Sets styles for links that have been clicked.

:hover - Changes the appearance of an element when a pointing device such as a mouse is moved over it.

:active - It is applied when a button or a link is being clicked.

These classes should be used in the following order:

1. :link
2. :visited
3. :hover
4. :active

You'll see a complete example of these pseudo classes in Navigation section later in this chapter.

CODE

```
<!DOCTYPE html>
<html>
<head>
<style>
    h1{text-align: center; text-transform: uppercase; color: #0080ff;}
    p {text-indent: 50px; text-align:justify; letter-spacing:3px;}
    p.c1{font-weight: bold;}
    p.c2:first-letter{color:#ff0000; font-size: 40px;}
    p.c2:first-line{color:#ff0000; font-variant:small-caps;}
    .c3{font-style: italic; text-align: right;}
    a{text-decoration:none;}
    a:hover {text-decoration: underline;}
</style>
</head>
<body>
    <h1>heading transformed to upper case and aligned centrally</h1>
    <p class="c1">This paragraph is styled with p and p.c1 class selectors</p>
    <p class="c2">This paragraph is styled with some of the text formatting properties.
    The paragraph is indented, aligned, space between characters is specified, first
    character of the paragraph is capitalized with a larger font size. The first line is
    displayed in red color with all letters in small-caps – resize the browser window to
    see the first line effect. The underline is not visible in the   <a target="_blank"
    href=" https://edition.cnn.com">Visit our website</a> link but appears when
    mouse moves over it.</p>
    <p class="c3">by Riaz Ahmed</p>
</body>
</html>
```

OUTPUT

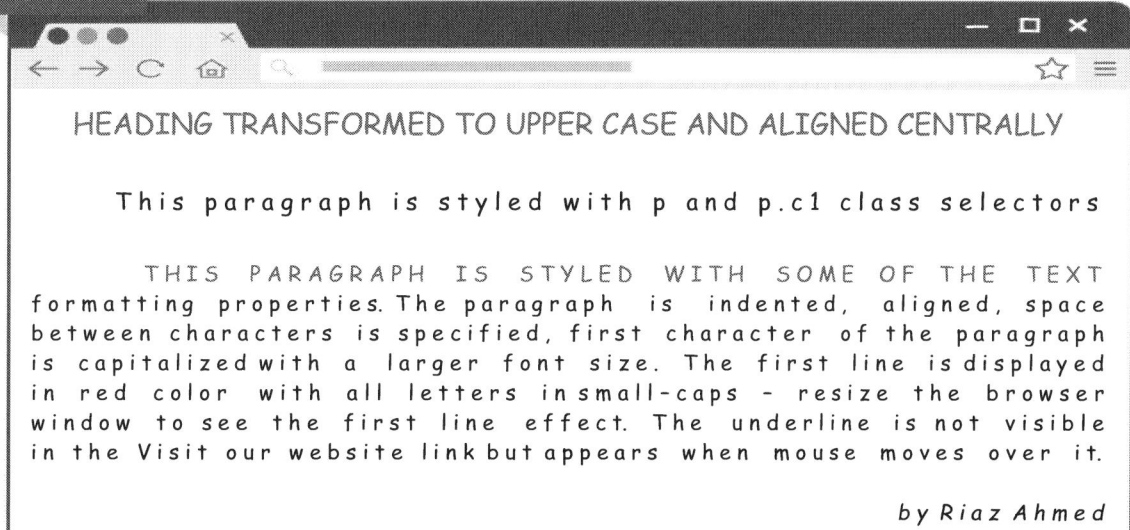

73

Styling Lists

In chapter 2 you saw three types of HTML lists: Ordered, Unordered, and Definition. Browsers automatically insert bullets before unordered list items and numbers before items in ordered lists. For the most part, the rendering of these markers is determined by the browser. In CSS, you can further style these lists and add images to act as list item marker instead of traditional bullet points.

CSS provides the following properties that allow you to choose the type and position of the marker, or turn them off entirely.

Property	Value
list-style-type	none
	disc
	circle
	square
	decimal
	decimal-leading-zero
	lower-alpha
	upper-alpha
	lower-latin
	upper-latin
	lower-roman
	upper-roman
	lower-greek
list-style-image	none
	url
list-style-position	Inside
	outside

list-style-type: With this property you can use various shapes and styles of markers. For example, you can use disc, circle, or square with unordered lists and decimal with leading-zero, lower/upper alpha, lower/upper roman etc. with ordered lists.

CODE

```
<!DOCTYPE html>
<html>
<head>
<style>
  ul.c1 {list-style-type:circle;}
  ul.c2 {list-style-type:square;}
  ol.c3 {list-style-type:upper-roman;}
  ol.c4 {list-style-type:lower-alpha;}
</style>
</head>
<body>
  <h3>Examples of list-style-type property</h3>
  <p><b>Unordered Lists:</b></p>
  <ul class="c1">
    <li>Accountancy</li>
    <li>Software</li>
    <li>Human Resource</li>
  </ul>
  <ul class="c2">
    <li>Accountancy</li>
    <li>Software</li>
    <li>Human Resource</li>
  </ul>
  <p><b>Ordered Lists:</b></p>
  <ol class="c3">
    <li>Accountancy</li>
    <li>Software</li>
    <li>Human Resource</li>
  </ol>
  <ol class="c4">
    <li>Accountancy</li>
    <li>Software</li>
    <li>Human Resource</li>
  </ol>
</body>
</html>
```

OUTPUT

Examples of list-style-type property

Unordered Lists:

- Accountancy
- Software
- Human Resource

- Accountancy
- Software
- Human Resource

Ordered Lists:

I. Accountancy
II. Software
III. Human Resource

a. Accountancy
b. Software
c. Human Resource

list-style-image: This property lets you specify an image as the list-item marker in a list. The example below uses an external style sheet. It also has margin property that is applied to set vertical space of 15 pixels among list items. The values specified for the margin property follow this order: top 15px, right 0px, bottom 0px, and left 0px.

CODE

HTML CODE (test.html)

```html
<!DOCTYPE html>
<html>
<head>
   <link rel="stylesheet" href="styles.css" >
</head>
<body>
  <ul>
    <li>Accountancy</li>
    <li>Software</li>
    <li>Human Resource</li>
  </ul>
</body>
</html>
```

CSS CODE (styles.css)

```css
ul {
    list-style-image:url('marker.png');
  }
li {
    margin: 15px 0px 0px 0px;
  }
```

OUTPUT

- Accountancy
- Software
- Human Resource

list-style-position: Use this property to place markers outside (A) or inside (B) the content flow.

CODE

HTML CODE (test.html)

```html
<!DOCTYPE html>
<html>
<head>
  <link rel="stylesheet" href="styles.css" >
</head>
<body>
  <ul class="c1">
    <li>Accountancy: ABC Global Consulting provides accountancy services...</li>
    <li>Software: We design tailor-cut desktop and web-based solutions to...</li>
  </ul>
  <ul class="c2">
    <li>Accountancy: ABC Global Consulting provides accountancy services...</li>
    <li>Software: We design tailor-cut desktop and web-based solutions to...</li>
  </ul>
</body>
</html>
```

CSS CODE (styles.css)

```css
ul {
    width: 250px;
    list-style-image:url('marker.png');
}
ul.c1 {
        list-style-position: outside;
}
ul.c2 {
        list-style-position: inside;
}
```

OUTPUT

— □ ×

(A) ▥ Accountancy: ABC Global Consulting provides accountancy services...

▥ Software: We design tailor-cut desktop and web-based solutions to...

(B) ▥ Accountancy: ABC Global Consulting provides accountancy services...

▥ Software: We design tailor-cut desktop and web-based solutions to...

Styling Tables

You can also improve the look of a table through CSS as done in the following example.

CODE

```
<!DOCTYPE html>
<html>
<head>
<style type="text/css">
  /*Rule 1*/
  table, td, th {border-spacing: 0px;}
  /*Rule 2*/
  th {background-color:#0066cc; color:white;}
  /*Rule 3*/
  table {width:100%;}
  /*Rule 4*/
  tr.head th:first-child {
       -webkit-border-top-left-radius: 5px;
        -moz-border-radius-topleft: 5px;
        border-top-left-radius: 5px;
  }
  /*Rule 5*/
  tr.head th:last-child {
        -webkit-border-top-right-radius: 5px;
        -moz-border-radius-topright: 5px;
        border-top-right-radius: 5px;
  }
  /*Rule 6*/
  tr.even {background-color: #e0e9f0;}
  /*Rule 7*/
  td {
      border-top: 1px solid #f1f8fe;
      border-bottom: 1px solid #cbd2d8;
      border-right: 1px solid #cbd2d8;
  }
  /*Rule 8*/
  th {height:30px;}
  /*Rule 9*/
  .c1 {text-align:right;}
</style>
</head>
```

CSS RULES EXPLAINED

Rule 1: Zero pixel border-spacing is set at once for table, table data, and table heading. This is called selector grouping.

Rule 2: Table header background color is set to #006cc and font color to white.

Rule 3: Table's width is set to 100% to use the whole browser's width.

Rule 4: Adds a rounded border to the top-left corner of the table. Firefox requires the prefix -moz- while Chrome and Safari requires the prefix -webkit-.

Rule 5: Adds a rounded border to the top-right corner of the table.

Rule 6: Sets a different color for even rows; odd rows will have the default white.

Rule 7: Added top, bottom, and right borders to data cells.

Rule 8: Set heading height to 30 pixels.

Rule 9: Right-aligned salary data.

Code Continued...➔

CODE

```
<body>
<table>
  <tr class="head">
     <th>Firstname</th>
     <th>Lastname</th>
     <th>Salary</th>
  </tr>
  <tr>
     <td>Peter</td>
     <td>Griffin</td>
     <td class="c1">$100</td>
  </tr>
  <tr class="even">
     <td>Lois</td>
     <td>Griffin</td>
     <td class="c1">$150</td>
  </tr>
  <tr>
     <td>Joe</td>
     <td>Swanson</td>
     <td class="c1">$300</td>
  </tr>
  <tr class="even">
     <td>Cleveland</td>
     <td>Brown</td>
     <td class="c1">$250</td>
  </tr>
</table>
</body>
</html>
```

OUTPUT

Firstname	Lastname	Salary
Peter	Griffin	$100
Lois	Griffin	$150
Joe	Swanson	$300
Cleveland	Brown	$250

Understanding the Box Model

In order to set the width and height of an element correctly in all browsers, CSS presents a box model. In this model each HTML element is wrapped in a box that has multiple layers as indicated in the following illustration:

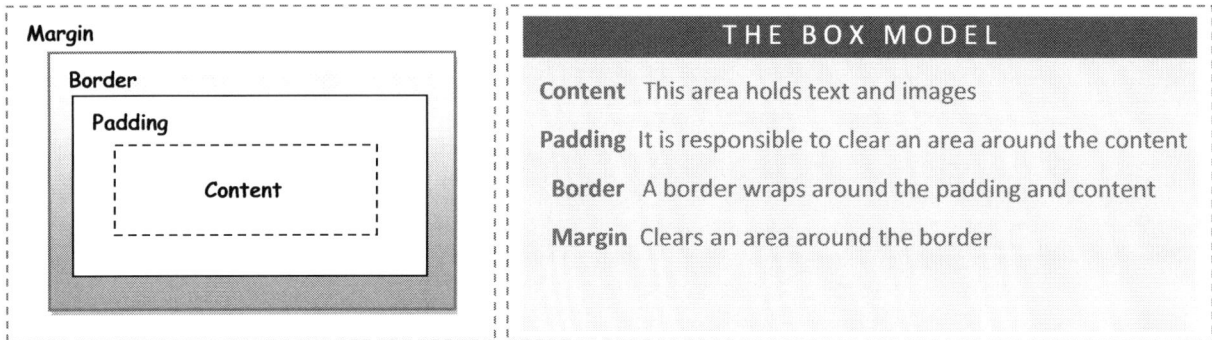

Margin		THE BOX MODEL
Border		**Content** This area holds text and images
Padding		**Padding** It is responsible to clear an area around the content
Content		**Border** A border wraps around the padding and content
		Margin Clears an area around the border

Figure 3-2

Let's do some practical exercise to understand this model. In the following example, you're shown how a 250px space is used.

CODE

```
<!DOCTYPE html>
<html>
<head>
<style>
  div.c1 {width:240px; border:5px solid gray; border-color:#ff0000 #0000ff;}
  div.c2 {width:240px; padding:0px; border:5px solid gray; margin:0px;}
</style>
</head>
<body>
  <div class="c1"></div>
  <br>
  <div class="c2">The line above is 250px wide (width+left and right borders).<br>
    The total width of this element is also 250px (width+borders).</div>
</body>
</html>
```

*The first CSS rule **div.c1{}** applies to **<div class="c1"></div>** which draws a red line to act as a guage.*

OUTPUT

The line above is 250px wide (width+left and right borders).
The total width of this element is also 250px (width+borders).

The total width of an element is calculated like this:

Total element width = width + left padding + right padding + left border + right border + left margin + right margin

The total height of an element is calculated like this:

Total element height = height + top padding + bottom padding + top border + bottom border + top margin + bottom margin

So, as per the first equation, the width of the above element is calculated as under:

240px (width) + 0px (left and right padding) + 10px (left and right border) + 0px (left and right margin) = 250px

This is how you control content within the specified limits. Now, change the value of padding to 10px. This change adds a space of 10px (between content and surrounding border) on all four sides of the content resulting in expansion of width from the allowed 250px space, as shown in the illustration below.

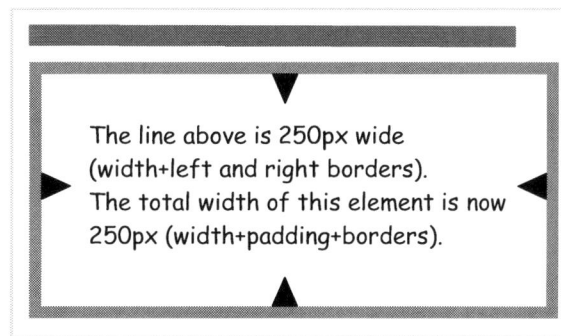

The line above is 250px wide (width+left and right borders). The total width of this element is now 250px (width+padding+borders).

Figure 3-2

Considering the equation mentioned above, the browser calculated the width of the element like this:

240px (width) + 20px (left and right padding) + 10px (left and right border) = 270px

The above example demonstrated that you must also consider the padding, borders and margins to calculate the full size of an element.

Control Element Positioning

CSS has the following positioning schemes that allow you to control the layout of a page:

- Static
- Fixed
- Relative
- Absolute
- Sticky

These positioning properties allow you to position an element. Besides placing an element behind another, you can also handle large content with them. You position elements using the top, bottom, left, and right properties. However, these properties require that you set the position scheme first. You specify the positioning scheme using the position property in CSS. Let's go through these positioning methods using some examples.

Static Positioning: By default, all HTML elements have static positions, which mean that such elements are always positioned according to the normal flow of the page. Every element appears on a new line, causing each new item to appear under the previous one. No two elements sit side-by-side even if there is space. These elements do not take effect of top, bottom, left, and right properties. The following example shows that <h1> and all <p> elements appear on a new line.

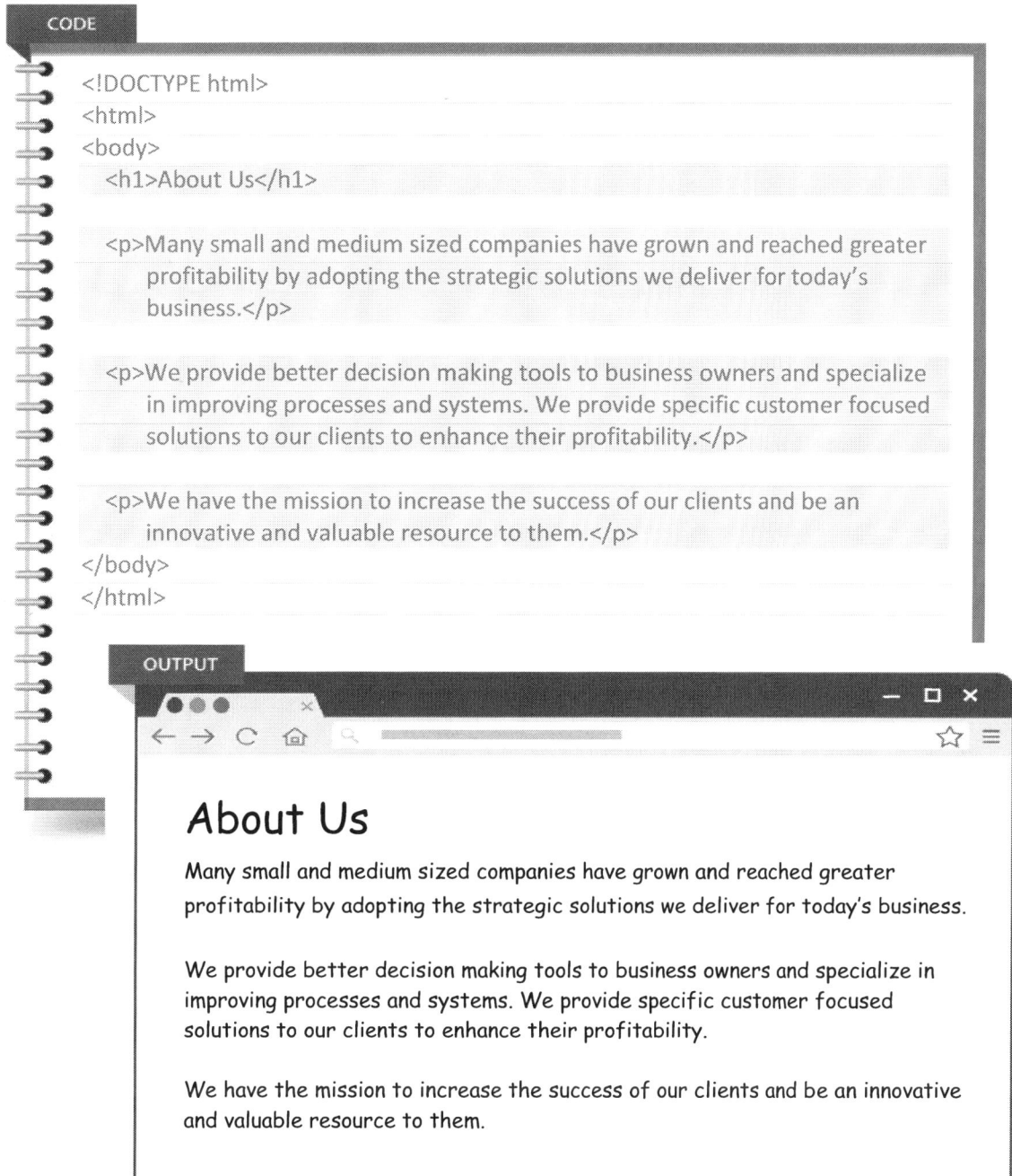

CODE

```
<!DOCTYPE html>
<html>
<body>
  <h1>About Us</h1>

  <p>Many small and medium sized companies have grown and reached greater
     profitability by adopting the strategic solutions we deliver for today's
     business.</p>

  <p>We provide better decision making tools to business owners and specialize
     in improving processes and systems. We provide specific customer focused
     solutions to our clients to enhance their profitability.</p>

  <p>We have the mission to increase the success of our clients and be an
     innovative and valuable resource to them.</p>
</body>
</html>
```

OUTPUT

About Us

Many small and medium sized companies have grown and reached greater profitability by adopting the strategic solutions we deliver for today's business.

We provide better decision making tools to business owners and specialize in improving processes and systems. We provide specific customer focused solutions to our clients to enhance their profitability.

We have the mission to increase the success of our clients and be an innovative and valuable resource to them.

Fixed Positioning: In this scheme, an element is positioned relative to the browser window and doesn't move when the user scrolls up or down the page. In the following example, <h1> element is marked with fixed position. After adding few more paragraphs, the About Us heading remains fixed and doesn't move when you scroll through the page.

CODE

```
<!DOCTYPE html>
<html>
<head>
<style>
    h1.fixed {position:fixed; background-color: #efefef;}
</style>
</head>
<body>
    <h1 class="fixed">About Us</h1>
    <p>Many small and medium sized companies have grown and
        reached greater profitability....</p>
    <p>We provide better decision making tools to business owners
        and specialize in improving ...</p>
    <p>We have the mission to increase the success of our clients
        and be an innovative and ...</p>
    <p>New paragraph</p>
    ...
</body>
</html>
```

OUTPUT

business.

About Us   on making tools to business owners and specialize in systems. We provide specific customer focused solutions to our clients to enhance their profitability.

We have the mission to increase the success of our clients and be an innovative and valuable resource to them.

New paragraph

New paragraph

New paragraph

Relative Positioning: Set the value of position property to relative to move an element relative to its normal position. This scheme moves an element in relation to where it would have been in normal flow. You use top, bottom, left, or right properties to indicate how far to move the element from where it would have been in normal flow. In the following example, you moved the second paragraph 10 pixels from the top and 50 pixels from the left. If you increase the top value to 40 pixels, the second paragraph will overlap the third one.

CODE

```html
<!DOCTYPE html>
<html>
<head>
<style>
    p.relative {position:relative; top: 10px; left: 50px;}
</style>
</head>
<body>
   <h1>About Us</h1>

   <p>Many small and medium sized companies have grown and reached greater
profitability...</p>
   <p class="relative">We provide better decision making tools to business
owners and specialize in improving processes and systems. We provide specific
customer focused solutions to our clients to enhance their profitability.</p>

   <p>We have the mission to increase the success of our clients and be an
innovative...</p>
</body>
</html>
```

OUTPUT

About Us

Many small and medium sized companies have grown and reached greater profitability by adopting the strategic solutions we deliver for today's business.

We provide better decision making tools to business owners and specialize in improving processes and systems. We provide specific customer focused solutions to our clients to enhance their profitability.

We have the mission to increase the success of our clients and be an innovative and valuable resource to them.

Absolute Positioning: With absolute positioning, an element can be placed anywhere on a page. The heading below is placed 170px from the left of the page and 0px from the top of the page. If you change the value of the top property to 90px, the heading is pushed below the paragraph.

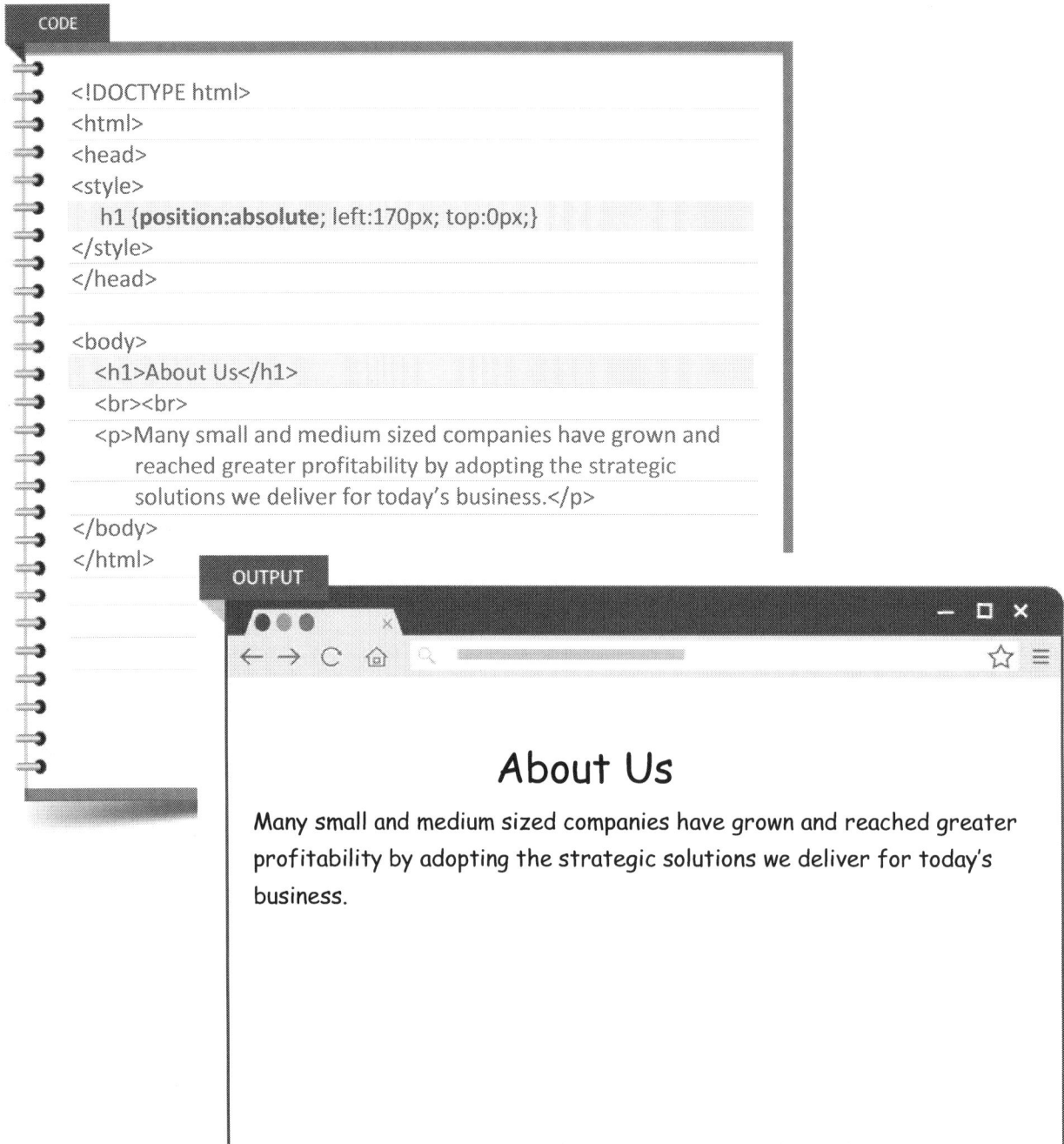

CODE

```
<!DOCTYPE html>
<html>
<head>
<style>
    h1 {position:absolute; left:170px; top:0px;}
</style>
</head>

<body>
  <h1>About Us</h1>
  <br><br>
   <p>Many small and medium sized companies have grown and
       reached greater profitability by adopting the strategic
       solutions we deliver for today's business.</p>
</body>
</html>
```

OUTPUT

About Us

Many small and medium sized companies have grown and reached greater profitability by adopting the strategic solutions we deliver for today's business.

Sticky Positioning: In the Sticky positioning scheme an element is positioned based on the user's scroll position. The Sticky positioning is a mix of relative and fixed positioning. The element is treated as relative positioned until it crosses a specified threshold, at which point it is treated as fixed positioned. In the following example, the <dt> sticky element (capital alphabet headings (A) used in the list) sticks to the top of the page (top: -1px), when you reach the threshold.

CODE

HTML CODE (test.html)

```
<!DOCTYPE html>
<html>
<head>
 <link rel="stylesheet" href="styles.css" >
</head>
<body>
<div>
 <dl>
  <dt>A</dt>
  <dd>This is some text</dd>
 </dl>
 <dl>
  <dt>B</dt>
  <dd>This is some text</dd>
 </dl>
 <dl>
  <dt>C</dt>
  <dd>This is some text</dd>
 </dl>
 <dl>
  <dt>D</dt>
  <dd>This is some text</dd>
 </dl>
</div>
</body>
</head>
```

CSS CODE (styles.css)

```
dl {
 margin: 0;
 padding: 24px 0 0 0;
}

dt {
 font: bold 20px/30px Helvetica,
       Arial, sans-serif;
 color: white;
 background: #0066cc;
 padding: 2px 0 0 12px;
 position: sticky;
 top: -1px;
}

dd {
 font: bold 20px/45px Helvetica,
       Arial, sans-serif;
 margin: 0;
 padding: 0 0 0 15px;
 border-top: 1px solid lightgray
}
```

OUTPUT

A

A

This is some text

This is some text

A

B

This is some text

This is some text

Overlapping Elements: When you use relative, fixed, or absolute positioning, boxes can overlap. In such case, the element that appears later in the HTML code sits on top of those that are earlier in the page. If you want to control which element sits on top, you can use the z-index property. Its value is a number, and the higher the number the closer that element is to the front. For example, an element with a z-index of 10 will appear over the top of one with a z-index of 5.

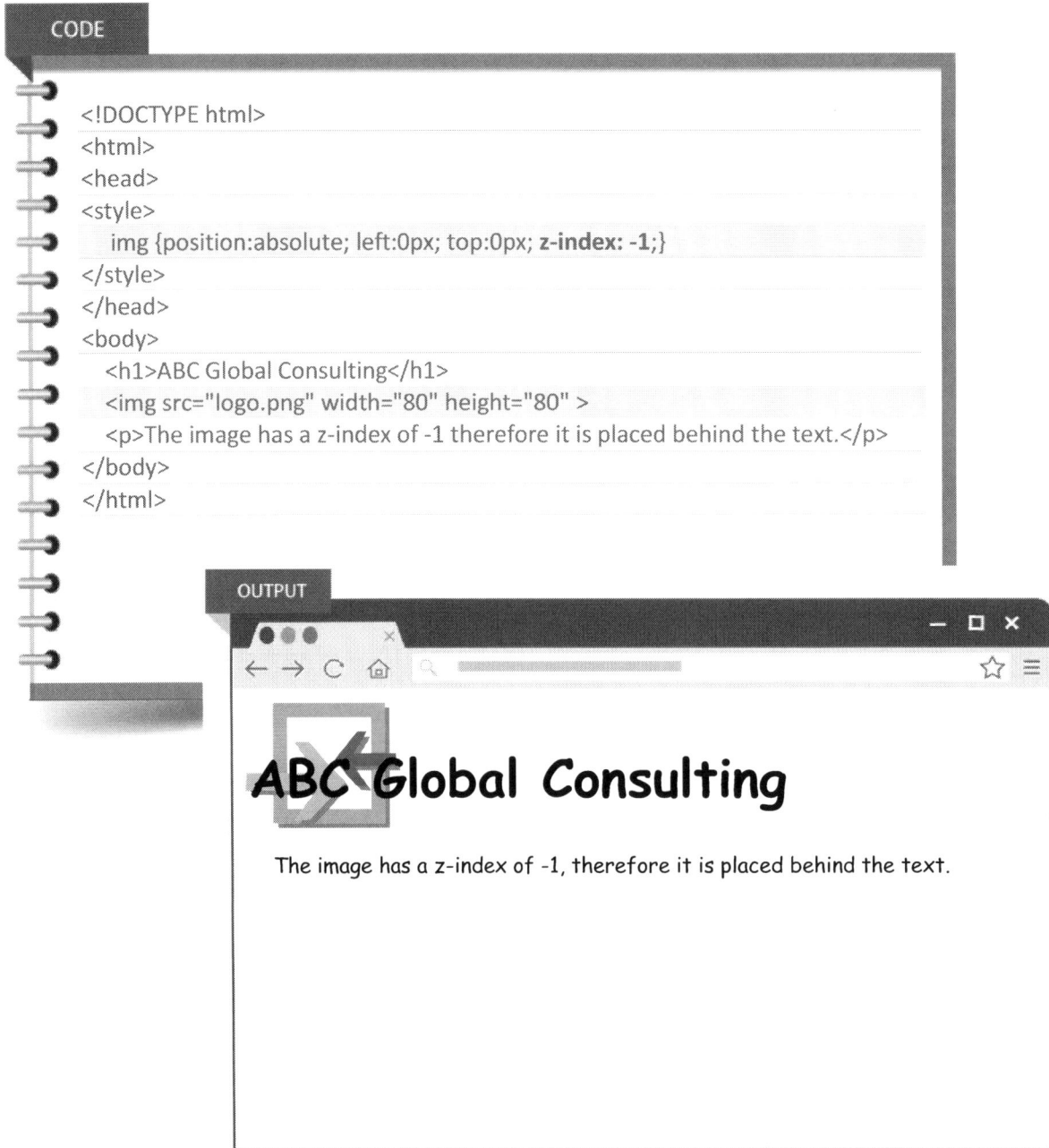

CODE

```
<!DOCTYPE html>
<html>
<head>
<style>
    img {position:absolute; left:0px; top:0px; z-index: -1;}
</style>
</head>
<body>
    <h1>ABC Global Consulting</h1>
    <img src="logo.png" width="80" height="80" >
    <p>The image has a z-index of -1 therefore it is placed behind the text.</p>
</body>
</html>
```

OUTPUT

ABC Global Consulting

The image has a z-index of -1, therefore it is placed behind the text.

Floating Elements

In situations where elements are to be placed side-by-side, CSS provides a property called float. Elements are floated horizontally, which means that an element can either be pushed to the left or right. Elements before the floating elements are not affected, but those that follow will flow around it. The float property takes one of the five values: left, right, none, or inherit. The inherit value specifies that the value of the float property should be inherited from the parent element. In the first example below, an image is added with a style *float:left*. The result is that the image will float to the left in the paragraph.

CODE

```
<!DOCTYPE html>
<html>
<head>
<style>
   img {float:left;}
   p {width:500px; font-family: Verdana, Arial, sans-serif; font-size: 12px;}
</style>
</head>
<body>
  <p>
  <img src="freight.png" width="200" height="100" >
  Successful importers utilize technology to better manage the movement
  of cargo, create accurate documentation, and execute financial
  transactions. We have designed an imports software...
  </p>
</body>
</html>
```

OUTPUT

Successful importers utilize technology to better manage the movement of cargo, create accurate documentation, and execute financial transactions. We have designed an imports software, The Import Manager, to provide the innovative technology you need to operate your import entries more efficiently, profitably and competitively. It is designed to address importers' unique requirements, accelerate the entire import process from end-to- end. Automates critical import activities such as duty management, compliance, landed cost calculations, customs clearance etc. Close management of these functions results in reduced shipment delays, taxes, fees and fines.

Multiple floating elements float next to each other if there is room as demonstrated in the following example. Make your browser's window small and see that the images scroll down when there in not enough room.

CODE

```
<!DOCTYPE html>
<html>
<head>
<style>
    img {float:left; width:250px; height:250px; margin:5px;
    border-style: ridge;}
</style>
</head>
<body>
  <h3>Illustrations</h3>
  <img src="img1.png">
  <img src="img2.png">
  <img src="img3.png">
  <img src="img4.png">
</body>
</html>
```

OUTPUT

Navigation

Every website has an important section on each page that allows visitors to surf. This is called a navigation bar and it is created using a list of links with <ul> and <li> elements. CSS allows you to create fancy navigation bars like the one presented below. The *list-style-type* CSS property specifies appearance of a list item element and sets the type of bullet or numbering to a list. Here, we set it to none which mean no item marker are shown. See Styling Lists earlier in this chapter.

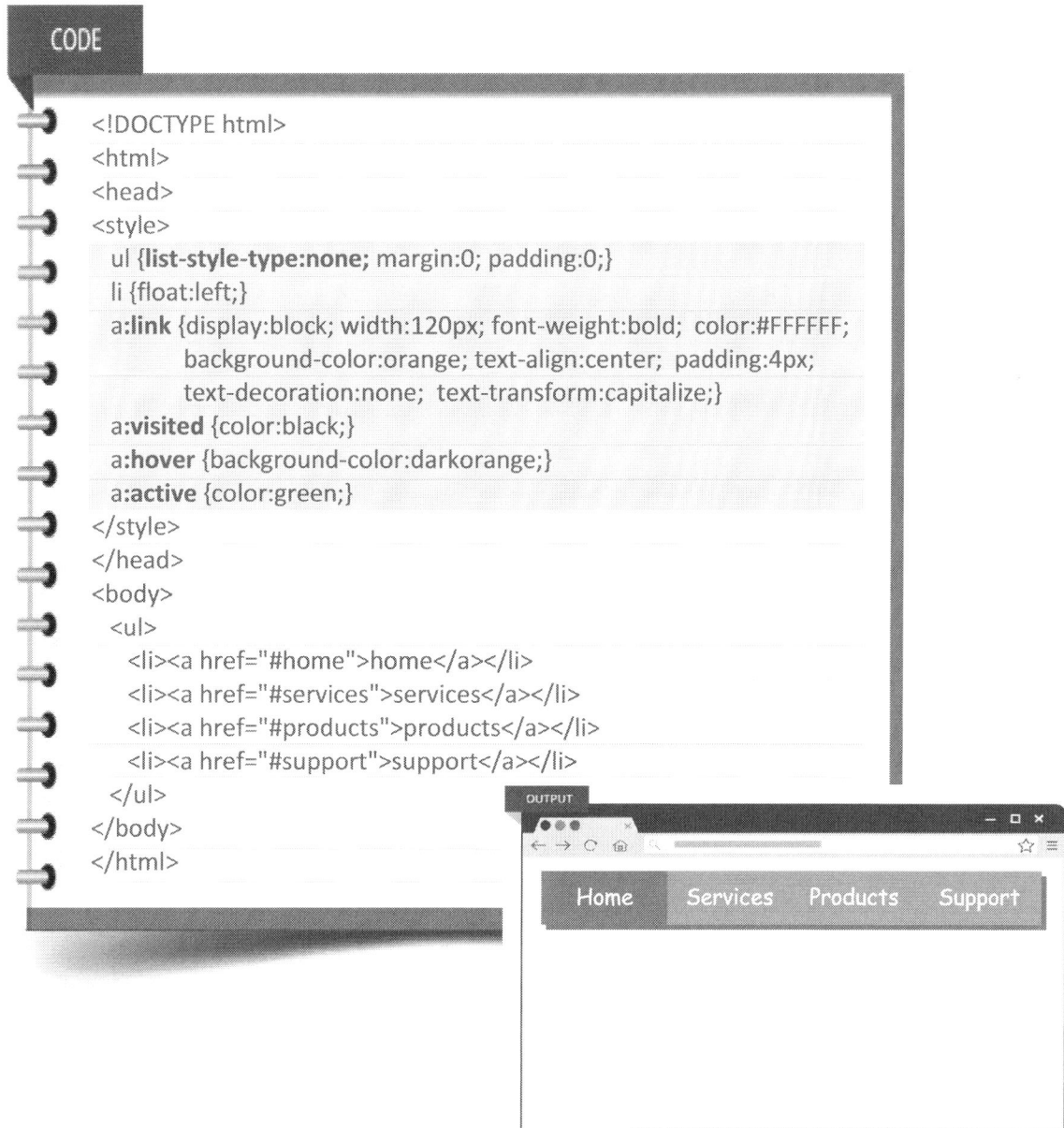

CODE

```html
<!DOCTYPE html>
<html>
<head>
<style>
  ul {list-style-type:none; margin:0; padding:0;}
  li {float:left;}
  a:link {display:block; width:120px; font-weight:bold;  color:#FFFFFF;
          background-color:orange; text-align:center;  padding:4px;
          text-decoration:none;  text-transform:capitalize;}
  a:visited {color:black;}
  a:hover {background-color:darkorange;}
  a:active {color:green;}
</style>
</head>
<body>
  <ul>
    <li><a href="#home">home</a></li>
    <li><a href="#services">services</a></li>
    <li><a href="#products">products</a></li>
    <li><a href="#support">support</a></li>
  </ul>
</body>
</html>
```

OUTPUT

| Home | Services | Products | Support |

We also added special effects to these links using the four pseudo classes that we went through in Style Links with Pseudo-Classes section earlier in this chapter. When you press and hold the left mouse button, the *:active* pseudo class activates and displays the link in green. Clicking any of the four navigation options would turn the link color to black through the *:visited* class. By default, the *:link* class presents the links in white color whereas, the *:hover* changes the background color to dark orange when you just move the mouse over these links.

Opacity and Transparency

To make pictures or other elements transparent, CSS provides a property called opacity. It takes a value from 0.0 - 1.0. The lower value makes the element more transparent. In the following example, we are using the hover pseudo class to show actual picture by setting the opacity to 1.0 when the user hovers over it. When the mouse pointer moves away from the image, the image will be transparent again.

CODE

```
<!DOCTYPE html>
<html>
<head>
<style>
   .images { float:left; width:200px; height:200px; margin:5px;
             border-style:groove;}
   img {opacity:0.5;filter:alpha(opacity=40);}
   img:hover {opacity:1.0;filter:alpha(opacity=100);}
</style>
</head>

<body>
   <img class="images" src="img1.png">
   <img class="images" src="img2.png">
</body>
</html>
```

OUTPUT

CSS3 Borders

The border property in CSS allows you to specify the width, color, and style of an element's border. The border-style property can have from one to four values (for the top border, right border, bottom border, and the left border). The following list shows the different border styles:

- border-style: none;
- border-style: hidden;
- border-style: solid;
- border-style: dotted;
- border-style: dashed;
- border-style: double;
- border-style: groove;
- border-style: ridge;
- border-style: inset;
- border-style: outset;
- border-style: dotted dashed solid double;

For specific browser support, use the following prefix:

-moz- for Firefox

-webkit- for Chrome and Safari

-o- for Opera

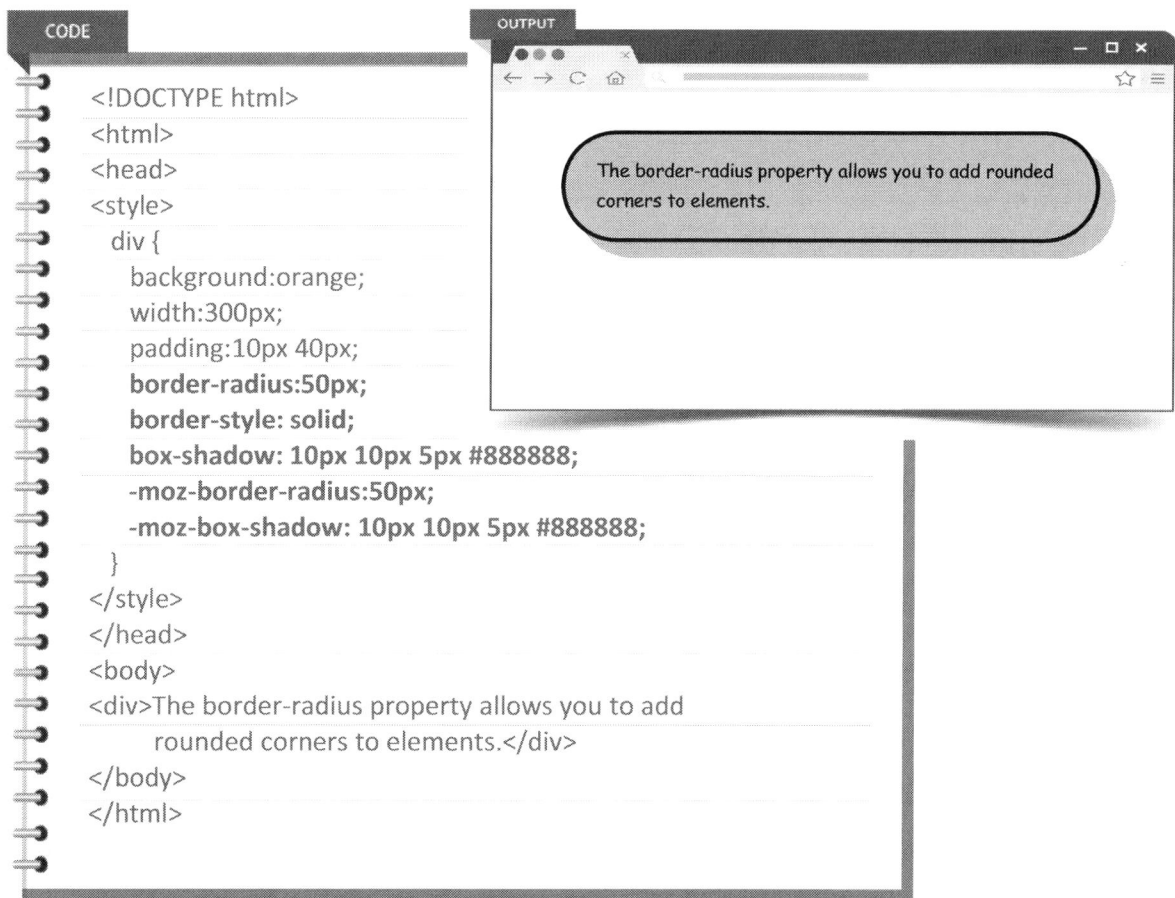

```
CODE

<!DOCTYPE html>
<html>
<head>
<style>
  div {
    background:orange;
    width:300px;
    padding:10px 40px;
    border-radius:50px;
    border-style: solid;
    box-shadow: 10px 10px 5px #888888;
    -moz-border-radius:50px;
    -moz-box-shadow: 10px 10px 5px #888888;
  }
</style>
</head>
<body>
<div>The border-radius property allows you to add
     rounded corners to elements.</div>
</body>
</html>
```

OUTPUT

The border-radius property allows you to add rounded corners to elements.

CSS3 Fonts

Before CSS3, you had to use fonts that were already installed on the user's computer. But now, with CSS3, you can use any font you want. You've to get the desired font and upload the font file to your web server so that it is downloaded with your web page. To use your own font you must add *@font-face* rule to your style sheet. Within this rule you have to define a name for the font (e.g. myFont), and then specify the path to the font. In the rule that you set for HTML element, refer this name (myFont) through the font-family property. In the following example we're using a custom font named Redressed, which is available in the book code. Just double-click the ttf file (Redressed.ttf) and then click the install button to use this font in the following exercise.

CODE

```
<!DOCTYPE html>
<html>
<head>
<style type="text/css">
  @font-face {font-family: myFont; src: url('Redressed.ttf'); }
  h2 {font-family:myFont; font-size:48px;}
</style>
</head>
<body>
  <h2>This is a Custom Font</h2>
</body>
</html>
```

OUTPUT

This is a Custom Font

Google Fonts

In addition to using standard and custom fonts in your web pages, you can also use hundreds of Google Fonts. For this, you have to use Google Fonts API by adding a stylesheet link and refer to a font family of your choice. The major advantage of this approach is that you are neither required to download any fonts, nor you need to upload them to your server - just add the stylesheet link to your web pages. In this exercise, we are using a font named Tangerine. For a list of all available Google Fonts, visit https://fonts.google.com.

CODE

```
<!DOCTYPE html>
<html>
<head>
<link rel="stylesheet" href="https://fonts.googleapis.com/css?family=Tangerine">
<style>
  body {
    font-family: 'Tangerine', serif;
    font-size: 48px;
    text-shadow: 4px 4px 4px #aaa;
  }
</style>
</head>
<body>
  <h2>Google Font Tangerine</h2>
</body>
</html>
```

OUTPUT

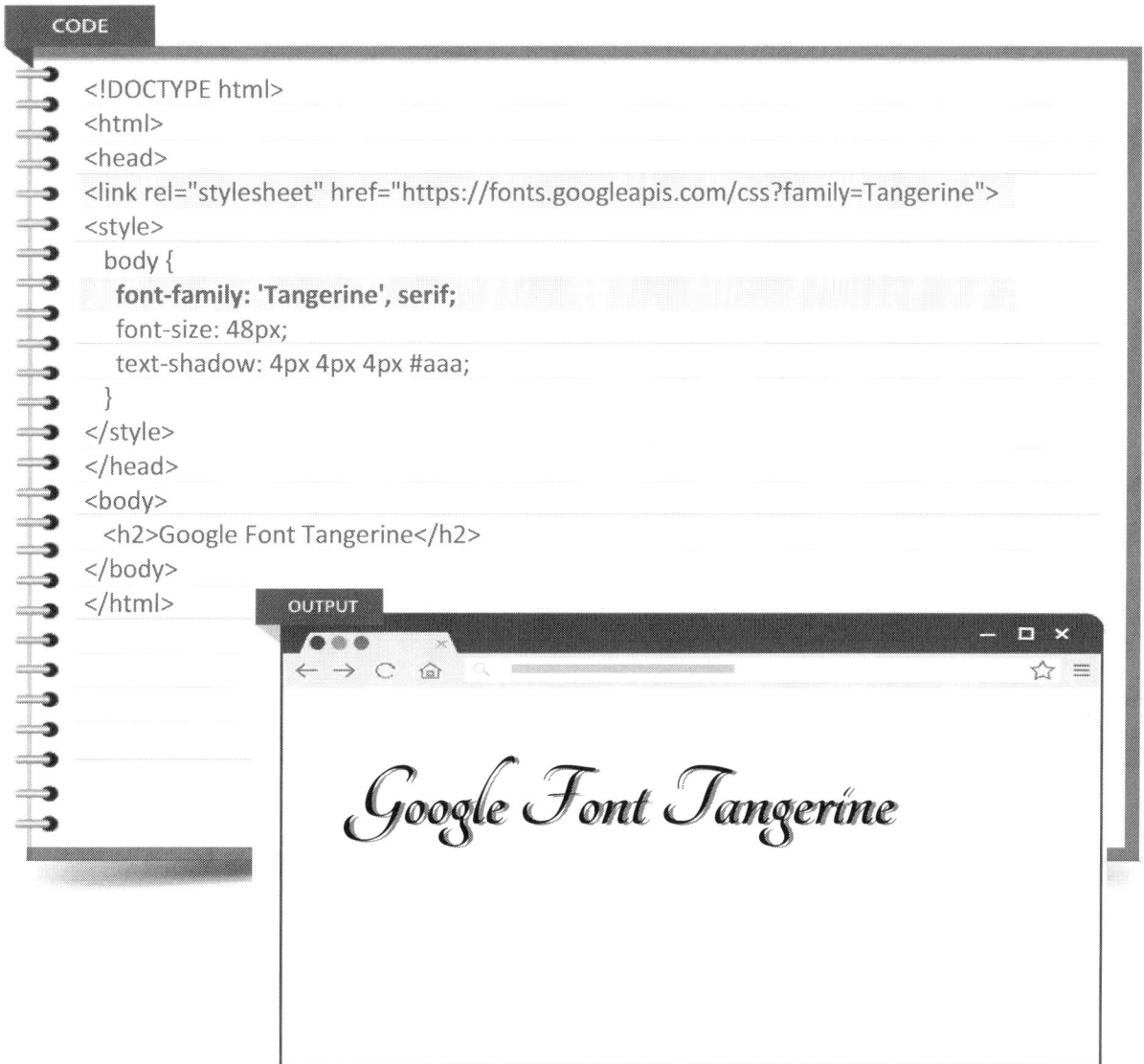

CSS3 Animation

Animation is another great feature included in CSS3; it is an effect that lets an element gradually change from one style to another. You can use CSS3 animations in place of animated images, Flash animations, and JavaScript. The rule @keyframes is added to the style sheet to achieve this objective. You have to set appropriate prefix (-moz-, -webkit-, or -o-) according to your browser. This example assumes that you are running it under Google Chrome.

CODE

```html
<!DOCTYPE html>
<html>
<head>
<style>
/* Point # 1*/
@-webkit-keyframes myAnimation {
    0% {opacity:1;}
    50% {opacity:0;}
    100% {opacity:1;}
  }
/* Point # 2*/
  #f1 img {position:absolute;}
/* Point # 3*/
  #f1 img {
    -webkit-animation-name: myAnimation;
    -webkit-animation-timing-function: ease-in-out;
    -webkit-animation-iteration-count: infinite;
    -webkit-animation-duration: 10s;
  }
/* Point # 4*/
  #f1 img:nth-of-type(1) {-webkit-animation-delay: 5s;}
  #f1 img:nth-of-type(2) {-webkit-animation-delay: 0s;}
</style>
</head>
<body>
<!-- Point # 5 -->
  <div id="f1">
    <img src="img1.png" width=100% height=100% >
    <img src="img2.png" width=100% height=100% >
  </div>
</body>
</html>
```

OUTPUT

In this example, we're using two images that will cross fade infinitely one after the other.

Point # 1:
Created a keyframe rule for Chrome and named it myAnimation. Specified when the change will happen in percent, which ranges from 0% to 100%. Initially, we will display actual picture by setting the opacity to 1. When the animation is at 50%, it will become transparent (opacity:0), and again to actual when the animation is 100% complete. This rule will be applied to all images defined in Point 5.

Point # 2:
In this rule we provided absolute position to images. If you omit this rule, both pictures will appear relatively (side-by-side).

Point # 3:
The animation-name property specifies the name of the keyframe you want to bind to the selector. Here, you have provided the name myAnimation to the keyframe and bound it to #f1 selector that has <img> elements.

The animation-timing-function property describes how the animation will progress over one cycle of its duration. We set it to ease-in-out which means that the animation has both a slow start and a slow end.

The animation-iteration-count property specifies the number of times an animation is played. The infinite value is set to play the animation forever.

The animation-duration property specifies how many seconds or milliseconds an animation takes to complete one cycle. We set the value to ten seconds (5 seconds for each picture).

Point # 4:
The :nth-of-type pseudo-class matches elements based on their position within the parent element's list of child elements of the same type. This pseudo-class accepts an argument (N) which can be a number, keyword, or expression. In our example we're referencing the two images defined in Point#5.

The animation-delay property defines when the animation will start.
The total duration of this animation is 10s (Point#3). The animation will start with the second image (img2.png) and will last for 5 seconds. Then the first image (img1.png) will appear and it too will last for 5 seconds.

Point # 5:
We defined two images in a <div> element. These images will act as the source for the animation and will appear and fade in a cycle.

Calculate Keyframe Points:

For proper animation, you need to set appropriate points (in percentage) while defining the keyframe rule. This section explains how to calculate these points. There are two factors that help in evaluating the proper range: number of images and display time of each image. In our example, there are two images and each one will be displayed for 5 seconds. We also know that an animation cycle starts with 0% and finishes at 100%. The first calculation that you will perform is to divide the value of 100 with the number of images to get the change point. In our scenario the answer is 50 (100/2). Based on this calculation, we added a new point as 50% and set the opacity to 0. We set total animation duration to 10s in Point 3 and, in Point 4, equally divided this duration between the two images.

Let's do some more experiments to further evaluate this theory:

1. Add another picture (img3.png) to Point 5
2. Set animation-duration property in Point 3 to 15s (5 seconds x 3 images)
3. Add another rule to Point 4 with nth-of-type(3), and set animation delay as under:
   - nth-of-type(1) delay 10s
   - nth-of-type(2) delay 5s
   - nth-of-type(3) delay 0s
4. Add another point to keyframes in Point 1 using the 100/3 formula. The keyframe should now hold four points:
   - 0% {opacity:1;}
   - 33% {opacity:0;}
   - 66% {opacity:0;}
   - 100% {opacity:1;}
5. Run the animation and see smooth transition of images

The following table contains parameters (for six pictures) that you can use and follow if you want to add more images to your animation.

Property	2 Images	3 Images	4 Images	5 Images	6 Images
Duration (seconds)	10	15	20	25	30
Delay (seconds)	0/5	0/5/10	0/5/10/15	0/5/10/15/20	0/5/10/15/20/25
Keyframes (%)	0/50/100	0/33/66/100	0/25/50/75/100	0/20/40/60/80/100	0/17/34/51/68/85/100
Opacity	1/0/1	1/0/0/1	1/0/0/0/1	1/0/0/0/0/1	1/0/0/0/0/0/1

CHAPTER 4

JAVASCRIPT
<SCRIPT>

About JavaScript

HTML is a simple text markup language, it can't respond to the user, make decisions, or automate repetitive tasks. Interactive tasks such as these require a more sophisticated language: a programming language, or a scripting language.

Although many programming languages are complex, scripting languages are generally simple. They have a simple syntax, can perform tasks with a minimum of commands, and are easy to learn. Web scripting languages enable you to combine scripting with HTML to create interactive web pages.

JavaScript is one of the most popular and widely used scripting language of the web and is used in billions of web pages to add functionality, validate forms, communicate with the server, and much more. It is primarily a client-side scripting language for use in web browsers. Its main focus is to help developers interact with Web pages and the Web browser window itself. Because it is embedded in all modern browsers, it has an extraordinary wide distribution.

One of the most powerful features of the language is its flexibility. As a JavaScript programmer, you can make your programs as simple or as complex as you wish them to be. The language also allows several different programming styles. You can write your code in the functional style or in the slightly more complex object-oriented style. It also lets you write relatively complex programs without knowing anything at all about functional or object-oriented programming; you can be productive in this language just by writing simple functions. It allows programmers to accomplish useful tasks with a very small, easy-to-learn subset of the language.

JavaScript is almost as easy to learn as HTML, and it can be included directly in HTML documents. Here are the few things you can do with JavaScript:

' Display messages to the user as part of a web page, in the browser's status line, or in alert boxes.

' Validate the contents of a form and make calculations (for example, an order form can automatically display a running total as you enter item quantities).

' Animate images or create images that change when you move the mouse over them.

' Create ad banners that interact with the user, rather than simply displaying a graphic

' Detect the browser in use or its features and perform advanced functions only on browsers that support them.

' Detect installed plug-ins and notify the user if a plug-in is required.

' Modify all or part of a web page without requiring the user to reload it.

' Display or interact with data retrieved from a remote server.

You can do all this and more with JavaScript, including creating entire applications. A JavaScript is added to an HTML document using the <script> tag. It is typically used to manipulate existing HTML elements using the *id* attribute of those elements. To access these elements JavaScript provides a method called document.getElementById(). Within the parenthesis of this method you specify the id of the element you're trying to access.

Let's go through a simple example to embed JavaScript in an HTML document. In this example a JavaScript is used to manipulate text of a paragraph using the paragraph's id p1. The innerHTML property returns the inner HTML of an element. In this example, the innerHTML property is used to change p1's text. If you remove the equal to sign and the text defined for the innerHTML property, you will get p1's actual text.

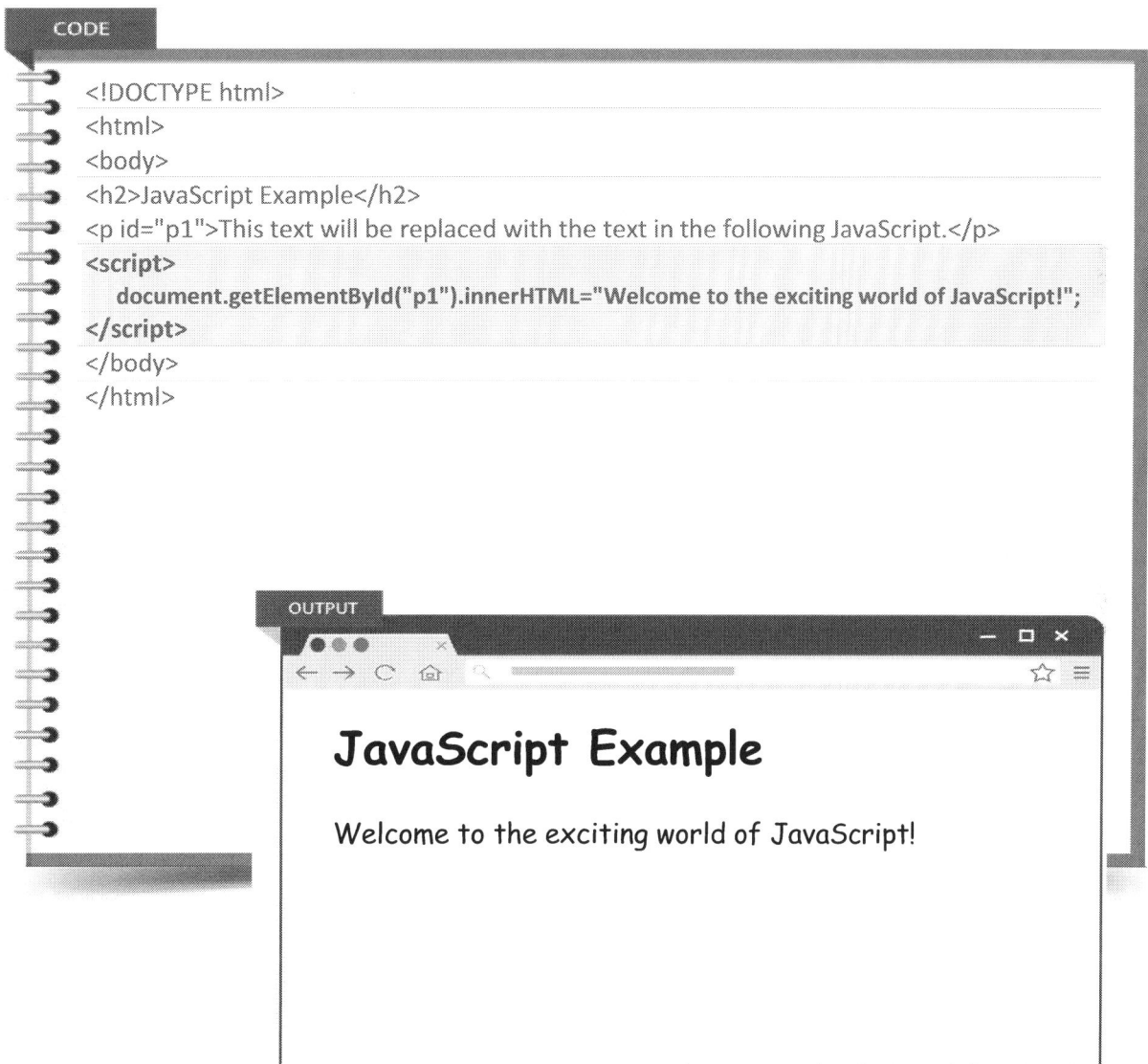

CODE

```html
<!DOCTYPE html>
<html>
<body>
<h2>JavaScript Example</h2>
<p id="p1">This text will be replaced with the text in the following JavaScript.</p>
<script>
    document.getElementById("p1").innerHTML="Welcome to the exciting world of JavaScript!";
</script>
</body>
</html>
```

OUTPUT

JavaScript Example

Welcome to the exciting world of JavaScript!

Comments in JavaScript

Like HTML and CSS, JavaScript too allows you to add comments to your code. You do this for two purposes:

- To explain your code
- To prevent its execution

Here as well, browsers ignore JS comments. Comments in JavaScript are added using the following two methods:

Single Line Comments: In this method you add two forward slashes before your comment or before a JS statement, for example:

```
// Added elements to JS
//document.write("<h1>Added h1 element to JS</h1><p>Added p HTML element to JS</p>");
```

The first line above is used to provide an explanation whereas the second one is a JS statement that is prevented from being executed.

Multi Line Comments: Use the symbols /* and */ pair to add comments that span multiple lines.

```
/*
The write() method does not add a new line
The writeln() method adds a new line
*/
```

> **NOTE**
>
> *PHP also uses the same set of characters for single and multi line comments.*

```
/*
document.writeln("The Writeln() method");
document.writeln("Added a new line");
*/
```

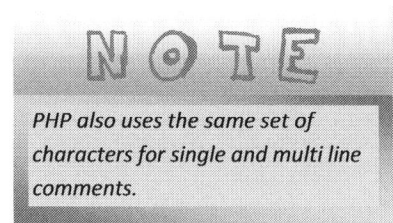

You can also add comments at the end of each statement to describe its functionality:

```
document.writeln("The Writeln() method");   //writeln() method adds a new line
document.writeln("Added a new line");
```

Few Points To Remember

- JavaScript code is a sequence of JavaScript statements. Each statement is executed by the browser in the sequence they are written. For example:
  document.write("JavaScript Example");
  document.getElementById("p1").innerHTML="Welcome to the exciting world of JavaScript!";

- Statements that execute together in a block are enclosed in curly brackets {} and are known as JavaScript functions.
  function jsFunction()
  {
  document.write("<h1>Added h1 element to JS</h1><p>Added p HTML element to JS</p>");
  document.write("The write() method does not add a new line");
  }

- JavaScripts are placed in the <head> and in the <body> sections.

- JavaScripts can be added both to the body and the head sections at the same time. Usually, all scripts are placed in one place either in the head section, or at the bottom of the page. If you're referencing elements in the script, place the script at the bottom to make sure it is not executed before the element. Placing scripts at the bottom of the <body> element improves the display speed, because script interpretation slows down the display.

- There is no limit to the number of scripts in a document; we added two scripts in the next example.

- To use the same JavaScript code in multiple web pages, you have to create an external file with a .js extension. Such external scripts are referenced through the src attribute of the <script> tag such as: <script src="External.js"></script>. External scripts are useful when the same code is used in many different web pages.

- Unlike HTML, JavaScript is case sensitive - therefore pay close attention to alphabets' case when you write JavaScript statements, create or call variables, objects and functions.

- Add a semicolon at the end of each executable JS statement. Although it is optional, the use of semicolon allows you to write multiple statements on one line.

Using HTML Elements in JavaScript

You can also add HTML elements to JS code using write() and writeln() methods. Methods define functions performed by an object. Making a reference to an object method is similar to referencing its property. Thus, document.write(); calls the write() method of the document object. Methods are always followed by a pair of parenthesis. There is a little difference between the write() and the writeln() methods. The write() method does not add a new line while writeln() adds a new line after each statement. The HTML <pre> tag used in this example defines preformatted text. Text in a <pre> element is displayed in a fixed-width font, and the text preserves both spaces and line breaks. The text will be displayed exactly as written in the HTML source code.

CODE

```
<!DOCTYPE html>
<html>
<body>
<pre>
  <script>
    document.write("<h1>Added h1 element to JS</h1>
                    <p>Added p HTML element to JS</p>");
    document.write("The write() method ");
    document.write("does not add a new line");
  </script>
</pre>
<pre>
  <script>
    document.writeln("The Writeln() method");
    document.writeln("Added a new line");
  </script>
</pre>
</body>
</html>
```

OUTPUT

Added h1 element to JS

Added p HTML element to JS

The write() method does not add a new line

The Writeln() method
Added a new line

Variables in JavaScript

A variable is a storage location and an associated symbolic name which contains some known or unknown quantity or information. Every variable has a name, called the variable name, and a value. For example, in the expression x=10, x is the variable name and it holds the value 10. A variable can have a short name, like x, or a more descriptive name, like ntotalAmount. Variables can represent numeric values, character strings, or memory addresses. They can hold values or expressions, such as n = x + y. To be able to operate on variables, it is important to know something about the data type. JavaScript variables can hold many data types, such as numbers, strings, boolean, objects, arrays and more.

Data Type	Variable Declaration
Number	var ntotalAmount = 25.56;
String	var sService="Accountancy";
Boolean	(x == y) If both values are equal, true is returned, else false is returned.

Types of Variables

In JavaScript variables are of two types:

Local Variables: These variables are declared within a JavaScript function and are specific to that function. You can access these variables in the function you created them. Since these variables have a local scope, you can use same variable name in different functions. Local variables are destroyed upon completion of the function.

Global Variables: Contrary to local variables, these variables are declared outside a function and can be accessed by all scripts and functions within a web page. If you declare a new variable that does not already exist, and assign a value to it, such variable automatically becomes a global variable. These variables are wiped out when the page is closed.

You must consider the following rules while declaring a variable in JavaScript:

- JavaScript is case-sensitive therefore variable names are also case sensitive - *a* and *A* are two different variable names.
- Start variable names with a letter, underscore, or $ character.
- Use the var keyword to declare JavaScript variables (e.g. var ntotalAmount;).
- Use the (=) operator to assign a value to a variable (e.g. var ntotalAmount = 1000; or var sService="Accountancy";). For visual recognition, you can optionally add a prefix to variables. For example prefix numeric variables with n and string variables with an s.
- Enclose text values in quotes and do not put quotes around numeric values. Numeric values enclosed in quotes are treated as text.

CODE

```
<!DOCTYPE html>
<html>
<body>
   <p>Click the button to create and display two variables.</p>
   <button onclick="myVariables()">Click Me</button>
   <p id="number"></p>
   <p id="string"></p>
   <p id="boolean"></p>
   <script>
      function myVariables()
      {
        var ntotalAmount=1000;
        var sService="Accountancy";
        document.getElementById("number").innerHTML="Amount: "+ntotalAmount;
        document.getElementById("string").innerHTML="Service: "+sService;
        document.getElementById("boolean").innerHTML=(ntotalAmount == 1000);
      }
   </script>
</body>
</html>
```

OUTPUT

Click the button to create and display two variables.

Click Me

Amount: 1000

Service: Accountancy

true

The example above contains a JavaScript function named myVariables (you will learn more about functions soon). This function is triggered by the onclick event of the button element. The function holds two variables: a numeric variable ntotalAmount with a value of 1000 and a string variable sService having the value Accountancy. The first two document.getElementById statements in the script concatenate variable values with appropriate labels. The last one evaluates whether the value held in the variable ntotalAmount equals 1000. Since both are equal, a boolean true value is returned.

Assignment & Arithmetic Operators in JavaScript

The Assignment Operators are used to assign values to JavaScript variables and Arithmetic operators are used to perform mathematical calculations between variables and/or values. We used couple of these operators in the preceding example in the myVariables function.

Examples of Arithmetic Operators

The following table explains the use of arithmetic operators in JavaScript assuming that z=5.

Operator	Symbol	Formula	Description	Value of a	Value of z
Addition	+	a=z+2	Add 2 to the value of z	7	5
Subtraction	-	a=z-2	Subtract 2 from the value of z	3	5
Multiplication	*	a=z*2	Multiply z and 2	10	5
Division	/	a=z/2	Divide z by 2	2.5	5
Increment	++	a=++z	Increment z by 1 and assign new value to a	6	6
		a=z++	Assign old value to a and then increment z by 1	5	6
Decrement	--	a=--z	Decrease z by 1 and assign new value to a	4	4
		a=z--	Assign old value to a and then decrease z by 1	5	4

Examples of Assignment Operators

Assuming that the value of a=10 and z=5, the following table demonstrates the use of assignment operators in JavaScript:

Operator	Formula	Description	Output	Equivalent
=	a=z	a is equal to z	a=5	
-=	a-=z	subtract z from a	a=5	a=a-z
+=	a+=z	add a to z	a=15	a=a+z
/=	a/=z	divide a by z	a=2	a=a/z
*=	a*=z	multiply a by z	a=50	a=a*z

You can also join multiple string variables with the help of + operator and can also add spaces between variables.

```
fname="Saad";
lname="Muavia";
fullname=fname+" "+lname;
```

Comparison Operators in JavaScript

In computer programming, comparison of two data items is affected by the comparison operators mentioned in the table below. These operators produce the logical value true or false, depending on the result of the comparison. For example, in the pseudo-code

if a > 1 then ...

the statements following *then* are executed only if the value of the variable "a" is greater than 1 (i.e. when the logical value of a > 1 is true).

Assuming that the value of a=5, the following table demonstrates the comparison operators:

Operator	Symbol	Compare	Return & Reason
Is greater than	>	a>8	False – The value of a is 5 and is less than 8
Is less than	<	a<8	True – 5 is less than 8
Greater than or equal to	>=	a>=8	False – 5 is not greater than or equal to 8
Less than or equal to	<=	a<=8	True – One condition is true i.e. 5 is less than 8
Is equal to	==	a==8	False – 5 is not equal to 8
		a==5	True – 5 is equal to 5
Is exactly equal to (both value and type)	===	a==="5"	False – Cannot compare number to string
		a===5	True – Both value and type are same
Is not equal	!=	a!=8	True – 5 is not equal to 8
Is not equal (neither value nor type)	!==	a!=="5"	True – types are not same
		a!==5	False – values are equal

Logical Operators in JavaScript

The logical operators compare expressions and return a Boolean result (true or false).

The NOT operator: It performs logical negation on an expression. It yields the opposite of the expression it evaluates. If the expression evaluates to True, Not yields False; if the expression evaluates to False, Not yields True.

The And operator: It performs logical conjunction on two expressions. That is, if both expressions evaluate to True, then the And operator returns True. If both expressions evaluate to False, And returns False.

The Or operator: It performs logical disjunction on two expressions. If either expression evaluates to True, it returns True. If neither expression evaluates to True, it returns False.

The following table describes logical operators through examples. Here the value of a=6 and z=3.

Operator	Symbol	Expression	Return & Reason
not	!	!(a==z)	True – a and z are not equal
and	&&	(a < 10 && z > 1)	True – Both expressions are true
		(a > 10 && z > 1)	False – First expression a>10 is false
or	||	(a==5 || z==5)	False – Both expressions evaluate to false
		(a==6 || z== 6)	True – First expression meets the criteria

Conditional Operators

JavaScript provides a special conditional operator that assigns a value to a variable based on some condition.

Syntax

variablename=(condition) ?value1:value2

Example

sReorder=(nStock<10)?"Low":"High";

In the above example, if the value of variable nStock is less than 10, move *Low* to the reorder level variable (sReorder), otherwise set the value of reorder to *High*.

The IF Conditional Statement

In computer science, conditional statements are features of a programming language which perform different computations or actions depending on whether a programmer-specified condition evaluates to true or false. In other words, conditional statements are used to perform different actions based on different conditions.

For example, x > 0 means "the variable x contains a number that is greater than zero". The computer evaluates this condition. If the condition is true, the statements within the braces are executed. Otherwise, the execution continues in the following branch – either in the else block (which is usually optional), or if there is no else branch, then after the closing brace. After either branch has been executed, control returns to the point after the ending brace.

You can also combine several conditions using "else if". Only the statements following the first condition that is found to be true will be executed. All other statements will be skipped.

CODE

```
<!DOCTYPE html>
<html>
<body>
  <h3>Check Stock Level</h3>
  <button onclick="StockLevel()">Click Me</button>
  <p id="stockStatus"></p>
  <script>
    function StockLevel()
    {
      var stock=5;
      var reorder=10;
      if (stock<reorder) {
        Alert="Low";
      }
      else if (stock < 100)
      {
        Alert="Good";
      }
      else
      {
        Alert="High";
      }
      document.getElementById("stockStatus").innerHTML=Alert;
    }
  </script>
</body>
</html>
```

OUTPUT

Check Stock Level

Click Me

Low

Example Explained:

The onclick event of the button calls the StockLevel function. Two variables (stock and reorder) are declared with respective values on the first two lines of this function. Initially, with stock value equal to 5, the first condition stock<reorder will evaluate to true and the alert Low will be displayed. If you change the stock value to 99, the else if condition will be triggered to show the Good alert. Finally, if you set the stock to 100 or more, the else condition will come into action and will throw the High alert. Using this technique you can check different conditions and perform some actions based on the evaluation.

The Switch Statement

Typically, nested if-else statements are used in the program's logic where there isn't only one condition to evaluate. A switch statement, on the other hand, evaluates only one variable and starts to work there. You can think of a switch statement as a simplified (and stripped-down) version of an if-else block.

```
switch(x) {
  case 1: // do this
  case 2: // do this
  case 3: // do this
  // etc
}
```

The nested if-else statement's power comes from the fact that it is able to evaluate more than one condition at once, and/or use lots of different conditions in one logical structure.

```
if(x == 0) {
  // do this
} else if(y == 1) {
  // do this
} else if(x == 1 && y == 0) {
  // do this
}
```

If you're going to evaluate only one variable in the condition statement, you're better off going with a switch statement, since it looks a lot neater than nested ifs. The following example evaluates a product's price based on a single variable (sjacketColor). Change color in the variable declaration from Black to Brown or Green and see display of relevant price. We used break to prevent the code from running into the next case and added the default keyword to specify what to do if there is no match.

```
<!DOCTYPE html>
<html>
<body>
  <h3>Price Checker</h3>
  <button onclick="checkPrice()">Click Me</button>
  <p id="price"></p>
  <script>
  function checkPrice() {
    var sjacketColor = "Black";
    var result;
    switch (sjacketColor) {
     case "Black":
       result = "Price $300";
       break;
     case "Brown":
       result = "Price $200";
       break;
     case "Green":
       result = "Price $100";
       break;
     default:
       result = "No color selected";
    }
    document.getElementById("price").innerHTML=sjacketColor+" Jacket: "+result;
  }
  </script>
</body>
</html>
```

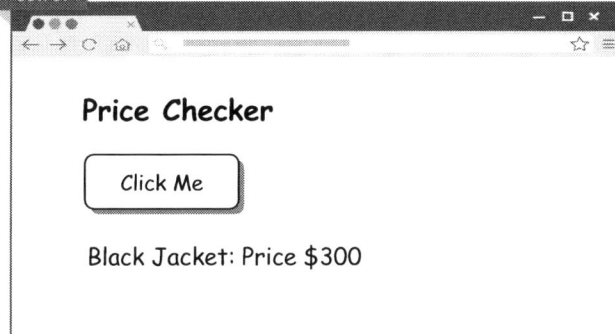

OUTPUT

Price Checker

Click Me

Black Jacket: Price $300

Alert Box

It is a small box that appears on the display screen to give you some information. For example, it might alert you to provide the mandatory email address that you left blank in the subscription form. Unlike dialog boxes, alert boxes do not require any user input. However, you need to acknowledge the alert box by pressing the Enter key or clicking the OK button to make it go away. Alert boxes are also called message boxes.

CODE

```
<!DOCTYPE html>
<html>
<head>
    <script>
    function testAlert()
    {
        alert("Please enter a valid email address");
    }
    </script>
</head>
<body>
    <input type="button" onclick="testAlert()" value="Click Me" >
</body>
</html>
```

OUTPUT

Click Me

This page says

Please enter a valid email address

OK

Confirm Box

You use a confirm box to verify some information or ask the user to accept something. This box has two buttons: OK and Cancel. The box returns true if the user clicks OK, and returns false if Cancel is selected.

CODE

```
<!DOCTYPE html>
<html>
<body>
  <button onclick="cbox()">Click me to display a confirm box</button>
  <p id="p1"></p>
  <script>
  function cbox() {
    var x;
    var r=confirm("Click on a button!");
    if (r==true)
    {
      x="You clicked OK!";
    }
    else
    {
      x="You clicked Cancel!";
    }
    document.getElementById("p1").innerHTML=x;
  }
  </script>
</body>
</html>
```

OUTPUT

Click me to display a confirm box

You clicked OK!

This page says

Click on a button!

OK   Cancel

Prompt Box

A prompt box is used to accept a value from the user before proceeding to the desired page. This box also presents two buttons to move ahead or stay on the same page. The OK button returns the input value while clicking the Cancel button gives null.

CODE

```html
<!DOCTYPE html>
<html>
<body>
    <button onclick="pBox()">Click me to bring up a Prompt Box</button>
    <p id="p1"></p>
    <script>
    function pBox()
    {
      var msg;
      var name=prompt("What is your name? ","Enter Your Name");
      if (name!=null)
      {
        msg="Hello " + name + "! Welcome to the world of JS";
        document.getElementById("p1").innerHTML=msg;
      }
    }
    </script>
</body>
</html>
```

OUTPUT

Click me to bring up a Prompt Box

Hello Saad! Welcome to the world of JS

This page says

What is your name?

Enter Your Name

OK   Cancel

Using Functions in JavaScript

A function is a collection of statements that executes when:

- An event occurs (such as a button is clicked)
- Called from a script
- Called from another function

Functions are declared with the keyword *function*, followed by a set of arguments, and finally by the code to execute enclosed in braces. The basic syntax is:

```
function functionName(var1, var2,..., varN) {
  statements
}
```

Remember the following points associated with functions:

- Functions can be placed both in the <head> and in the <body> section of a document.

- The keyword *function* must be written in lowercase letters.

- You must call a function with the exact same capitals as in the function name.

- You can pass some values, called parameters, when you call a function.

- You can specify any number of parameters, separated by commas.

- Functions receive parameters as variables in the expected order i.e. the first variable receive the value of the first passed parameter and so on.

- A function can return a value (which is optional) back to where the call was made using the *return* statement.

- When the *return* statement in encountered, the function stops executing and returns the value, if any.

- Any code that comes after a *return* statement is not executed.

- The *return* statement stops only the function, not the whole JavaScript.

- The *return* statement can also be used to exit a function.

- All variables declared within a function are destroyed when you exit the function.

Example 1:
```
function Greeting(sName, sMessage){
  alert("Hello " + name + ", " + sMessage);
}
```

The above function will be called like this:

Greeting ('Saad', 'welcome to the world of JS');

In the above calling statement, we are passing two parameters enclosed in parentheses to the function named Greeting. The function will receive these parameters in the two variables, sName and sMessage, respectively and will show the alert illustrated in the output section below.

Example 2 – Code after a return statement is not executed:
```
function sum(iNum1, iNum2) {
  return iNum1 + iNum2;
  alert(iNum1 + iNum2);  // this line will not execute
}
```

Example 3 – Function with multiple return statements based on some condition:
```
function diff(iNum1, iNum2) {
  if (iNum1 > iNum2)
  {
    return iNum1 – iNum2;
  }
  else
  {
    return iNum2 – iNum1;
  }
}
```

Example 4 – Exit a function without a return value:
```
function Greeting(sMessage) {
  if (sMessage == " ")
  {
    return;
  }
  alert(sMessage);
}
```

```html
<!DOCTYPE html>
<html>
<body>
  <button onclick="Greeting('Saad', 'welcome to the world of JS')">Click Me</button>
  <script>
  function Greeting(sName, sMessage){
    alert("Hello " + sName + ", " + sMessage);
  }
  </script>
</body>
</html>
```

This page says

Hello Saad, welcome to the world of JS

OK

```html
<!DOCTYPE html>
<html>
<body>
  <p>Call a function to perform mathematical operation</p>
  <p id="p1"></p>
  <script>
  function Add(x,y)
  {
    return x+y;
  }
  document.getElementById("p1").innerHTML="Sum of 10 and 3 is: "+Add(10,3);
  </script>
</body>
</html>
```

Call a function to perform mathematical operation

Sum of 15 and 5 is: 20

Iterative Statements

Iterative statements, also called loop statements, specify certain commands to be executed repeatedly until some condition is met.

The FOR loop

This loop iterates through a block of code a specified number of times and is used when the number of iteration is known. Its syntax is:

for (initialization; expression; post-loop-expression) {block of code}

The following example creates a loop to generate a sequence of number from 1-9. The variable i is initialized with 1 (i=1) and is incremented by 1 on each iteration (i++). The loop terminates when the value of i reaches 10.

CODE

```html
<!DOCTYPE html>
<html>
<body>
   <button onclick="fLoop()">Click Me</button>
   <p id="p1"></p>
   <script>
   function fLoop()
   {
     var a="",i;
     for (i=1;i<10;i++)
     {
       a=a + "The number is " + i + "<br>";
     }
     document.getElementById("p1").innerHTML=a;
   }
   </script>
</body>
</html>
```

OUTPUT

Click Me

The number is 1
The number is 2
The number is 3
The number is 4
The number is 5
The number is 6
The number is 7
The number is 8
The number is 9

The WHILE Loop

This loop executes a block of code while a specified condition is true. It has two variants while and do...while. While loops are conditional loops where a condition is checked at the starting of the loop and if the condition is true then the statements inside the loop are executed.

CODE

```
<!DOCTYPE html>
<html>
<body>
    <button onclick="wLoop()">Click Me</button>
    <p id="p1"></p>
    <script>
    function wLoop()
    {
      var a="",i=1,c=true;
      while (c==true)
      {
        a=a + "This is loop number " + i + "<br>";
        i++;
        if(i == 10){
          c=false;
        }
      }
      document.getElementById("p1").innerHTML=a;
    }
    </script>
</body>
</html>
```

OUTPUT

Click Me

This is loop number 1
This is loop number 2
This is loop number 3
This is loop number 4
This is loop number 5
This is loop number 6
This is loop number 7
This is loop number 8
This is loop number 9

The DO...WHILE Loop

Do...While loop is little different than while loop. Here the condition is checked at the end of the loop. Statements inside the loop will be executed at least once even if the expression is FALSE. This is the basic difference between do while loop and while loop.

CODE

```
<!DOCTYPE html>
<html>
<body>
   <button onclick="dwLoop()">Click Me</button>
   <p id="p1"></p>
   <script type="text/javascript">
   function dwLoop()
   {
     var a="",i=1,c=false;
     do
     {
       a=a + "This is loop number " + i + "<br>";
       i++;
       if(i == 10){
         c=false;
       }
     }
     while (c==true)
     document.getElementById("p1").innerHTML=a;
   }
   </script>
</body>
</html>
```

OUTPUT

Click Me

This is loop number 1

Break & Continue Statements

Break leaves a loop, continue skips the current iteration and jumps to the next iteration. Break is used in *switch, for, while, and do-while* statements continue is used in *for, while, and do-while* loop. Continue means, whatever code that follows the continue statement WITHIN the loop code block will not be executed and the program will go to the next iteration, in the following example, when the program reaches i=5 it checks the condition in the if statement and executes *continue*, everything after continue will not be executed and the control will be transferred to the beginning of the loop.

Break statement will just stop execution of the loop and go to the next statement after the loop if any. In this case when i=8 the program will jump out of the loop. Meaning, it will not continue to show 8 and 9. The following example demonstrates the use of these two statements. The code will print 1 to 7 except 5.

CODE

```
<!DOCTYPE html>
<html>
<body>
  <button onclick="BreakContinue()">Click Me</button>
  <p id="p1"></p>
  <script>
  function BreakContinue()
  {
    var a="",i=0;
    for (i=1;i<10;i++)
    {
      if (i==5)
      {
        continue;
      }
      if (i==8)
      {
        break;
      }
      a=a + "This is loop number " + i + "<br>";
    }
    document.getElementById("p1").innerHTML=a;
  }
</script>
</body>
</html>
```

OUTPUT

Click Me

This is loop number 1
This is loop number 2
This is loop number 3
This is loop number 4
This is loop number 6
This is loop number 7

Objects in JavaScript

An object can be defined as a special kind of data that comprises properties and methods.

Properties are the values associated with the object. For example, a car is an object. Its properties include model, color, doors, speed, etc. All cars have these properties, but the values vary from car to car. Property values can be a number, a string or a Boolean. When you call them, like object.property, you get (or set) this value. For example, to get and set the innerWidth property of the window object you use window.innerWidth and window.innerWidth=pixels respectively.

Methods are the actions that can be performed on objects. Some of the car methods are start(), gearshift(), stop, etc. When you call them, like object.method(), something happens. For example, if you write document.write('Hello World!') you execute the pre-defined write() method of the document object.

As properties basically hold values associated with the object, the methods provide the definitions of how the object can be acted on which can include changing the values of the properties. For example, the gearshift() method of a car would update the speed property to indicate which speed the car is now running at.

In JavaScript, you have two types of Objects: built-in and user defined. We will start by looking at the user defined objects that you create yourself, and will explain the built-in objects later.

Declaring an Object

Objects are created by using the new keyword followed by the name of the class you wish to instantiate:

```
var oCar = new Object();
var oStringObject = new String();
```

The first line creates a new instance of Object and stores it in the variable oCar; the second line creates a new instance of String and stores it in the variable oStringObject. The parentheses aren't required when the constructor doesn't require arguments, so these two lines could be rewritten as follows:

```
var oCar = new Object;
var oStringObject = new String;
```

NOTE

Avoid String, Number, and Boolean objects. They complicate your code and slow down execution speed.

Add Properties to Objects

Properties are added to an object by simply giving them values like this:

```
oCar=new Object();
oCar.model="VTI";
oCar.color="Red";
oCar.door=4;
oCar.speed=250;
```

To get the color property of this object, the following code will be used:

```
document.write(oCar.color);
```

This code will render "Red" as the output.

Why Use Objects?

In JavaScript you use variables and arrays to store data, but there are situations that are more complicated and where you need another mechanism to act differently. For instance, you want to access and display a list of software along with title, price, and description on your web page from a database table.

To deal with a situation like this, you create objects. In the following section, we will try to understand objects and their utilization through the scenario mentioned above. First, you need to define an object named oSWList, add properties (title, price, description), and finally create methods to work with the information.

Creating Objects and Defining Properties

You create a function to make the new oSWList objects. This function is called the constructor for an object. The constructor is a simple function that accepts parameters to initialize a new object and assigns them to the corresponding properties. The function below accepts several parameters from the statement that calls the function, and then treats them as objects' properties. Because the function is called oSWList, the object is the oSWList object. The "this" keyword is referring to the current object that is being created by the function. The last line is referencing a method mSoftware(), which is created in the next section to make the method part of the function definition for oSWList objects.

```
function oSWList(title,price,description) {
  this.title = title;
  this.price = price;
  this.description = description;
  this.mSoftware = mSoftware;
}
```

Creating a Method

After defining the object oSWList, you create a method named mSoftware() to work with it. Note that all oSWList objects will have the same properties. The mSoftware() function is created to act as a method for oSWList objects, so you do not have to ask for the parameters. Again, you will use the "this" keyword to refer to the current object's properties.

```
function mSoftware() {
  sTitle = "Title: "+ this.title + "<br>\n";
  nPrice = "Price: "+ this.price + "<br>\n";
  sDescription = "Description: "+ this.description + "<br>\n";
  document.write(sTitle, nPrice, sDescription);
}
```

This function simply reads the properties from the current object (this), displays each one with a label, and skips to a new line. To officially make mSoftware() part of the oSWList object, you already added a line while defining the object above.

Creating an Object Instance

To use an object definition, you create an instance of that object with the new keyword. The following statement creates a new oSWList object instance called accounts:

accounts = new oSWList("The Millennium Accountant", 100, "A handy software to manage finance of an organization");

The above statement creates an instance (accounts - to hold accounting software information), and calls the oSWList function (the object definition) and passes it the required attributes in the defined order. This is called an instance of the oSWList object. In JavaScript, you can define several instances of an object.

After creating an instance of an object, you can use the mSoftware() method to show the information. For example, this statement displays the properties of the accounts software:

accounts.mSoftware();

Testing Objects

After scratching the basics, let's see a complete example of the subject scenario. This section demonstrates how to use objects in a web page to display software information. The first step is to create a test.js file having mSoftware(), oSWList, and three software records as shown below. Finally, create an HTML file (test.html) that calls the JavaScript file and displays the result in a browser. Save both .js and .html files in the same folder and run test.html.

CODE

HTML CODE (test.html)

```html
<html>
<head>
<title>Software Products</title>
</head>
<body>
  <h1>Software Products</h1>
  <p></p><hr>
  <script src="test.js">
  </script>
</body>
</html>
```

JAVASCRIPT CODE (test.js)

```javascript
// This is the method
function mSoftware() {
  sTitle = "<b>Title: </b>" + this.title + "<br>\n";
  nPrice = "<b>Price: </b>" + this.price + "<br>\n";
  sDescription = "<b>Description: </b>" + this.description + "<br>\n<hr>";
  document.write(sTitle, nPrice, sDescription);
}
// The object function
function oSWList(title,price,description) {
  this.title = title;
  this.price = "$"+price;
  this.description = description;
  this.mSoftware = mSoftware;
}
// Create instance of the objects
accounts = new oSWList("The Millennium Accountant", 100, "A handy software to manage finance of an organization");

imports = new oSWList("The Import Manager", 200, "A software to manage your import processes");

demo = new oSWList("Demo Creator", 300, "Create professional videos of your products");

// And print them
accounts.mSoftware();
imports.mSoftware();
demo.mSoftware();
```

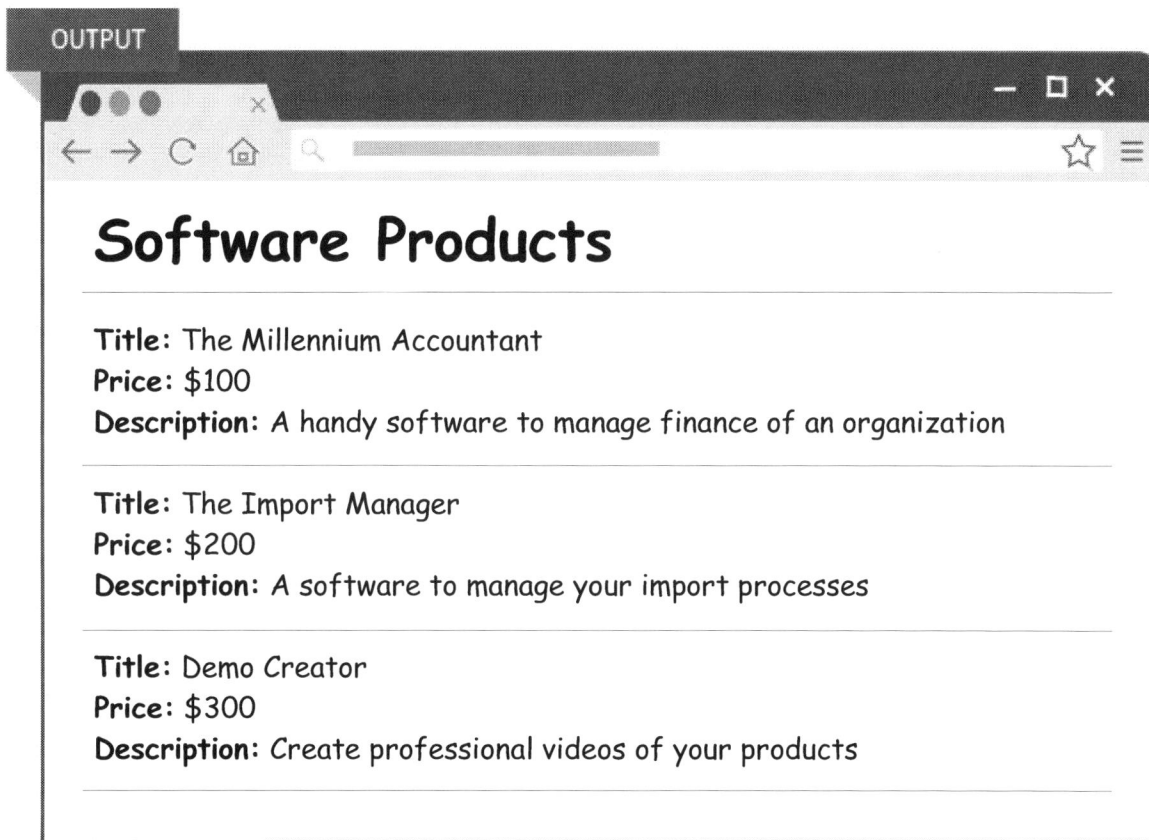

JavaScript Events

Events are actions that happen when a button is clicked on a web page, the mouse pointer is moved, key is pressed on a keyboard, or a web page or image loads from the server. JavaScript programs detect events and react to them. This reaction makes web documents interactive. The script that you use to detect and respond to an event is called an event handler.

Each event has a name. For instance, the onMouseOver event occurs when the mouse pointer moves over an object on the page. An event handler attribute can be added to an individual HTML tag as:

```
<a href="https://edition.cnn.com" onMouseOver="window.alert('You are over the link');">Click Me</a>
```

The above statement shows an alert when the mouse moves over the link. It is recommended to use a function in case of multiple statements. Function is defined in the header of the document, and is called as the event handler like this:

```
<a href="#tlink" onMouseOver="GoTop();">Hover over this link</a>
```

This example calls a function called GoTop() when the mouse is moved over the link.

Common Events

Here are some most common JavaScript events you use in your web pages.

onMouseOver: This handler is called when the mouse pointer moves over an object on a web page. For example, change an image when the mouse moves over the image.

onMouseOut: Opposite to onMouseOver, this handler is called when the pointer leaves the object's border. It is used to reverse the action taken with onMouseOver handler such as, changing an image back to its previous status.

onClick: This event handler comes into action when the mouse button is clicked on an object. For example, the following statement displays an alert when the link is clicked:

```
<a href="https://edition.cnn.com" onClick="alert('You will be taken to CNN site');">Go to CNN.com</a>
```

The statement below displays a confirmation box and returns a value. If the user clicks Cancel, false is returned and prevents the link from being followed.

```
<a href="https://edition.cnn.com" onClick="return(window.confirm('Are you sure?"));">Click Here</a>
```

onMouseDown: It is used when the user presses the mouse button.

onMouseUp: This handler is used when the user releases the mouse button.

onLoad: This event is triggered when the current page finishes loading from the server.

```
<body onLoad="alert('Loading complete.');">
```

onUnload: It happens when another page is loaded or when the browser window is closed.

Using JavaScript with HTML Forms

We went through HTML forms in chapter 2 (Forms in HTML) and exercised various aspect of it using different form controls. In this section, you will learn how to make a form interactive with JavaScript. In JavaScript, each form is represented as an object with the same name as the NAME attribute mentioned in the <form> tag.

Form Attributes

name: Using this attribute, you provide a name to your form in the <form> tag. You assign a name to a form to recognize it in JavaScript.

method: It has two values, GET and POST. You send data to the server using these methods. For further details on these two method, see Chapter 2.

action: Using this attribute you send form's data to the desired destination.

Form Methods

The form object has two methods, submit() and reset(). The former one lets you submit the form's data whereas the later one clears the form.

Form Events

You can use two event handlers for a form object in JavaScript, onSubmit and onReset. The onSubmit event is called before the data is submitted. If the statement or function returns true, the data is submitted. This submission can be prevented by returning a value of false for the event handler. Similarly, the functionality of a Reset button can be prevented with the onReset event handler.

Referring Form Elements

You can refer to a form element either by its name or by its index. For example, the two expressions below correspond to the first element (the fname text field) in the contact form.

```
document.contactform.elements[0]
document.contactform.fname
```

CODE

```
<!DOCTYPE html>
<html>
<head>
<title>Using JavaScript with HTML Form</title>
<script>
  function showData() {
    oPopWin=window.open('','Window1','toolbar=no,status=no,width=300,height=100')
    message = "<ul><li><b>Name: </b>" + document.contactform.name.value;
    message += "<li><b>E-mail: </b>" + document.contactform.email.value;
    message += "<li><b>Cell No.: </b>" + document.contactform.mobile.value + "</ul>";
    oPopWin.document.write(message);
  }
</script>
</head>
<body>
<form name="contactform">
  <fieldset>
    <legend>Contact Information</legend>
    <label>Name:<br>
    <input type="text" name="name" ></label><br>
    <label>Email:<br>
    <input type="text" name="email" ></label><br>
    <label>Cell No.:<br>
    <input type="text" name="mobile" ></label>
  </fieldset>
  <p><input type="BUTTON" value="Show Data" onClick="showData();"></p>
</form>
</body>
</html>
```

This example is an extension to the one we went through in chapter 2 (Grouping Form Elements). Here, we added JavaScript to display data from the form in a pop-up window through a function named showData().

OUTPUT

Contact Information

Name:

Saad Muavia

Email:

fsdy2k@gmail.com

Cell No.:

0123-1234567

Show Data

- **Name:** Saad Muavia
- **Email:** fsdy2k@gmail.com
- **Cell No.:** 0123-1234567

Validating Form's Data

You saw how JavaScript is used in HTML forms, but its most significant use is to validate data entered in these forms. For example, you can check that the form's mandatory fields are not left blank or, if entered, they are in the correct format. Data in the previous form could be validated as shown in the following example. The checkData() JavaScript function is used to check data in the name field through the field's length. If you leave the field blank and hit the submit button, the submission is stopped and an alert message comes up with relevant information.

We used document.contactform.name.focus() statement to place the cursor on the field where the error occurred. The function checkData() is called using the onSubmit event handler in the <form> tag. The value returned by the checkData() function is determined by the return keyword to assess whether to submit the form. You can use the onChange event handler in each form field to validate data individually prior to submission.

```
<!DOCTYPE html>
<html>
<head>
<title>JavaScript in HTML Form</title>
<script>
  function checkData() {
      if (document.contactform.name.value.length < 1) {
        alert ("Please enter your name");
        document.contactform.name.focus();
        return false;
      }
    return true;
  }
</script>
</head>
<body>
  <form name="contactform" onSubmit="return checkData();">
    <fieldset>
      <legend>Contact Information</legend>
      <label>Name:<br>
      <input type="text" name="name" ></label><br>
      <label>Email:<br>
      <input type="text" name="email" ></label><br>
      <label>Cell No.:<br>
      <input type="text" name="mobile" ></label>
    </fieldset>
    <p><input type="SUBMIT" value="Submit"></p>
  </form>
</body>
</html>
```

Contact Information

Name:

Email:

fsdy2k@gmail.com

Cell No.:

0123-1234567

Submit

This page says

Please enter your name

OK

At this point, we have seen how to handle different aspects of HTML Forms using client side scripting to avoid server round trips. Forms are designed to receive input from users and then to store this input into a database. This functionality lacks in client side scripting languages, and this is where server-side scripting comes into action. In the next part, you will learn how to validate and store HTML Form data on the server using PHP and MySQL.

JavaScript & PHP

Although PHP offers plenty of power for creating dynamically generated Web pages, it is strictly a server-side language. There's a common category of Web site tasks that perhaps don't require all the

processing power of a server and would best be done quickly—for instance, changing the look of a button on mouseover. JavaScript, a purely client-side language, can be easily integrated into our projects to fill in many of these gaps.

Client-side JavaScript itself has many limitations. For example, because it can't communicate directly with a database, JavaScript cannot update itself with fresh data depending on the page. Even worse, it's impossible to depend on client-side technologies, because they may not be present in a visitor's browser or may be disabled. PHP can help to mitigate the effects of client-side indeterminacy.

Where to use JavaScript

Some places you should definitely consider replacing or enhancing PHP with JavaScript include:
- Simple arithmetic in forms and calculators (such as shopping cart running total, mortgage calculator etc.)
- Simple form validation (such as making sure e-mail addresses have @ symbols)
- Site navigation (such as pull-down navigation menus)
- Pop-ups (alerts, search boxes)
- Browser events (mouseover, onClick)
- With the introduction of Electron.js (https://www.electronjs.org/), it is even possible to make desktop applications using JavaScript. Visual Studio Code, Slack, Figma, Twitch, WhatsApp(desktop), WordPress(desktop), etc. are made with electron.js.
- Python and R languages are mainly used in Machine Learning and Artificial Intelligence projects, but now ML/AI is possible with JavaScript using Google's TensorFlow.js library (https://www.tensorflow.org/js).

Where to use PHP

Server-side scripting languages such as PHP perfectly serve most of the truly useful aspects of the Web, as such as the items in this list:
- Content sites (both production and display)
- Community features (forums, bulletin boards, Groupware, and so on)
- E-mail (Web mail, mail forwarding, and sending mail from a Web application)
- Customer-support and technical-support systems
- Web-based business applications
- Surveys, polls, and tests
- Filling out and submitting forms online
- Catalog, brochure, and informational sites
- Games (for example, chess) with lots of logic but simple/static graphics
- Any other application that needs to connect a backend server

CHAPTER 5

PHP & MYSQL

Introduction to PHP and MySQL Database

In this part, you will be introduced to PHP, MySQL, and the interaction of the two.

What is PHP?

PHP stands for *PHP: Hypertext Preprocessor*. It is a server-side scripting language, which can be embedded in HTML or used as a standalone binary (although the former use is much more common). PHP is a powerful tool for making dynamic and interactive Web pages and is the widely-used, free, and efficient alternative to competitors such as Microsoft's ASP.

Below are some basic general facts about PHP:

- PHP is a server-side scripting language and its scripts are executed on the server.
- PHP is an open source software and is free to download and use.
- PHP files have ".php" extension. These files can hold text, HTML tags and scripts.
- PHP files are returned to the browser as plain HTML.
- PHP supports many databases (MySQL, Oracle, PostgreSQL, Sybase, Informix, Solid, Generic ODBC, etc.)
- PHP is easy to learn.

What is MySQL?

MySQL (pronounced My Ess Q El) is a Relational Database Management System (RDBMS). It is used to store data. Data in MySQL is stored in objects called tables. For example, a database of a company can have the following tables:

- Customers
- Vendors
- Products
- Orders
- Contact

A table consists of rows and columns and holds related records. For instance, the Contact table holds feedback data from customers as shown below:

ID	Name	Email	Age	Message
1	Saad Muavia	saad@abc.com	30	This is feedback message # 1
2	Daniel Clarke	daniel@gmail.com	25	This is feedback message # 2
3	Michael Peter	mpeter@yahoo.com	40	This is feedback message # 3
4	Michael Jackson	mjackson@hotmail.com	55	This is feedback message # 4

This table (Contact) consists of five columns (ID, Name, Email, Age, and Message) and contains four records (rows 1 through 4). Each row holds same type of record with unique IDs and different values.

Set Up Environment for Server-Side Scripting

To make things simple, you will create a development environment on your own PC using AMPPS, which is a solution stack of Apache, MySQL, MongoDB, PHP, Perl and Python for Windows NT, Linux and macOS. This desktop software stack includes everything you need for website development.

Download & Install AMPPS

To make your website visible to the world, it has to be placed on a web server. During the development phase your own PC can act as a web server if you install AMPPS, which is free, easy to install and ideal for developing and testing websites and web applications.

Here are the steps to download and install this free software on your PC:

1. Go to **http://www.ampps.com/downloads** and download the version available for your operating system. I downloaded Windows 64 bit version 3.9 for my Windows 10 PC.

2. After downloading, double click **Ampps-3.9-x86_64-setup** file to start the installation process.

Figure 5-1

3. Accept the license agreement and click **Next** twice.

4. Accept the default installation folder and click **Next**.

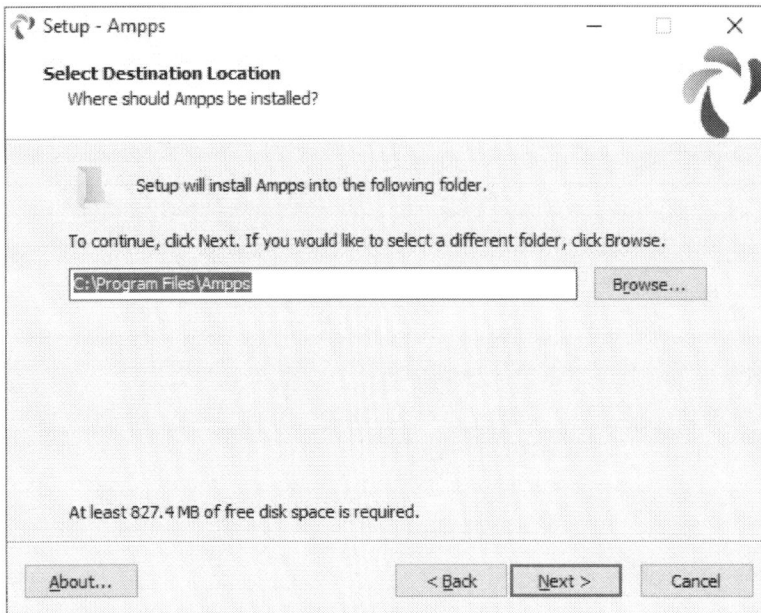

Figure 5-2

5. Accept the Start Menu Folder and click **Next**.

6. Click **Next** on the additional tasks screen and then click on **Install** on the final wizard screen. At this stage you will be asked to install Microsoft Visual C++ Redistributable software. Accept the installation of this software.

7. Click **Finish** to launch the application. Click **OK** if you see an update notification. The AMPPS application will start as shown in the following figure. It will start Apache, PHP, and MySQL services. An icon of this application will be placed on your desktop that you can use subsequently to start the application before starting any development task.

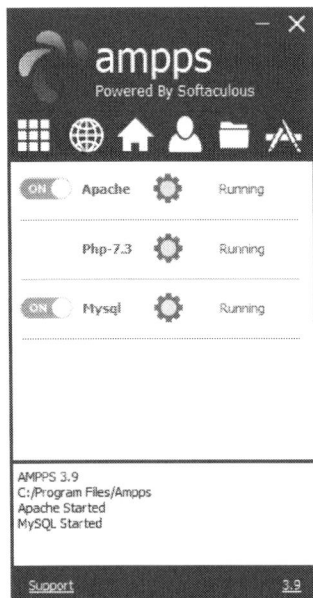

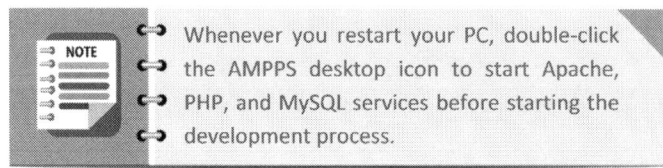

Whenever you restart your PC, double-click the AMPPS desktop icon to start Apache, PHP, and MySQL services before starting the development process.

Figure 5-3

Download & Install Visual Studio Code

Visual Studio Code is a lightweight but powerful source code editor which runs on your desktop and is available for Windows, macOS and Linux. It comes with built-in support for JavaScript, TypeScript and Node.js and has a rich ecosystem of extensions for other languages, such as C++, C#, Java, Python, PHP, and Go. Here are the easy steps to download and install this software.

1. Go to **https://code.visualstudio.com/download** and choose the version for your OS. I downloaded 64 bit User Installer for my Windows 10 PC.

2. Double-click the downloaded .exe file to start the installation.

3. Accept the license agreement on the first wizard screen and click **Next**.

4. Select the default destination location and click **Next**.

5. Accept the default Start Menu Folder and click **Next**.

6. On the Select Additional Tasks wizard screen, accept all the options as illustrated in the following figure and click **Next**.

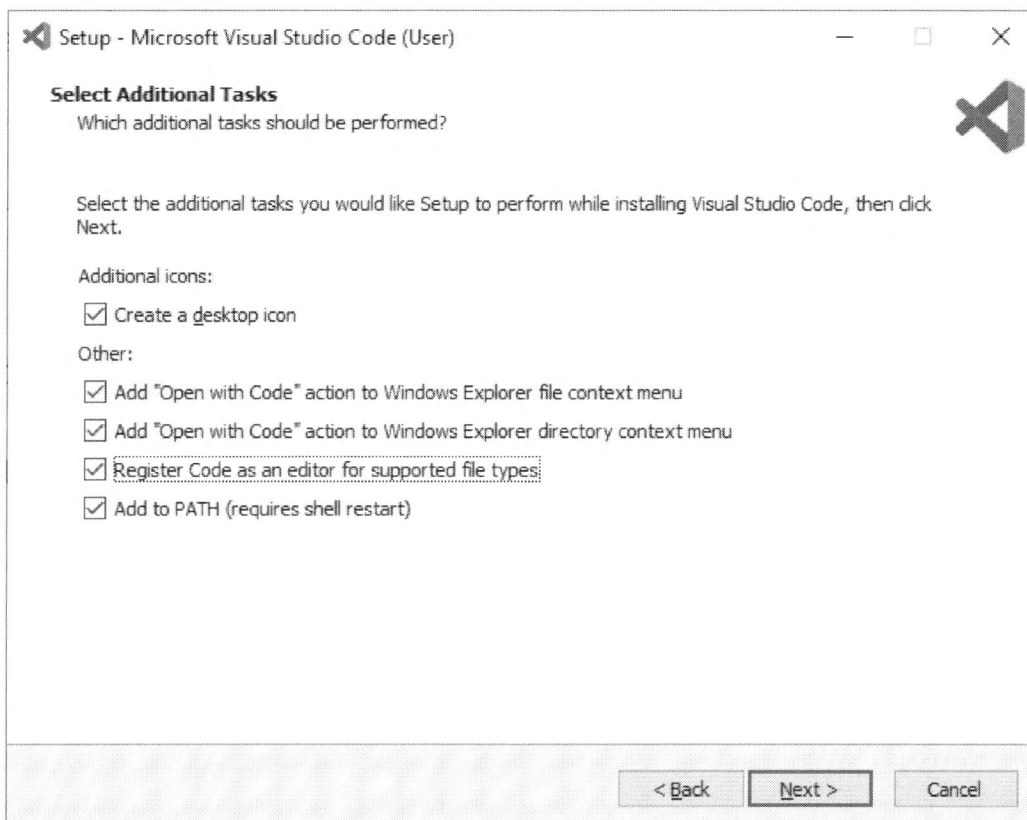

Figure 5-4

7. Click **Install** on the final wizard screen.

8. Click **Finish** to complete the installation process. Make sure that **Launch Visual Code** checkbox is checked to immediately start the application.

Test PHP

The development environment is set on your computer. Let's give it a try by creating and running a small .php file.

1. In Visual Studio Code, select **New File** from the **File** menu (A) and type the following code (B).

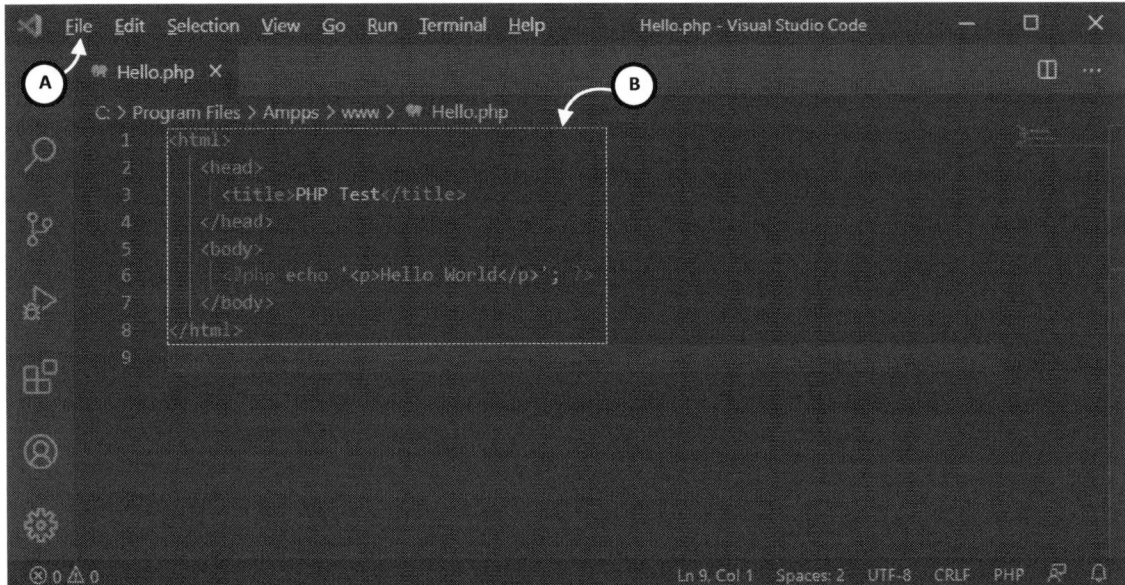

Figure 5-5

2. Select **Save** from the **File** menu (A). Enter **Hello** for File name (C), select **PHP** (D) as its type and save this file in **C:\Program Files\Ampps\www** folder (E). From now on, you will place all your project files under AMPPS www folder. Whenever you create a project under AMPPS, the pages and folders for the project must go into this folder.

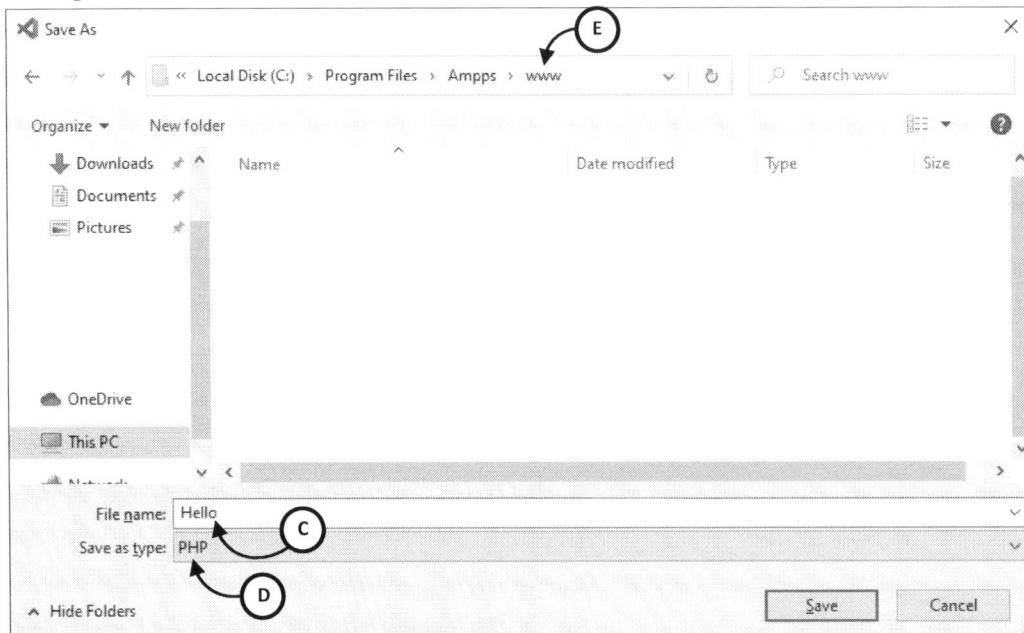

Figure 5-6

3. Open a browser session and type **http://localhost/hello.php** to see the text "Hello World" in the browser.

We will dig further PHP details in an upcoming sections, but first you must explore some basics of MySQL database.

Structured Query Language (SQL)

A discussion about database is meaningless without mentioning SQL. SQL is the language of relational databases. It is the common vocabulary and syntax that enables you to interact with numerous databases including Oracle, SQL Server, MySQL etc. Instructions that you pass to these databases through SQL are called statements. SQL statements are broadly categorized as: DML, DCL, and DDL.

Data Definition Language (DDL) is the part of SQL that you use to CREATE, ALTER, and DROP database objects (database, tables, users and so on).

Data Control Language (DCL) statements are used to control database access such as GRANT and REVOKE statements which you use to grant and revoke privileges on database objects to users.

Data Manipulation Language (DML) statements let users move data into and out of a database. The four basic data-manipulation statements supported by essentially all SQL databases are: SELECT, INSERT, UPDATE, and DELETE. SELECT gets data out of the database, INSERT puts in a new entry, UPDATE edits pieces of the entry in place, and DELETE gets rid of an entry.

Handling A Database

A new database is created using the CREATE DATABASE DDL syntax. Follow the procedure outlined below to create a database named TESTDB:

1. Enter **http://localhost/phpmyadmin** in your browser's address bar. phpMyAdmin is a free software tool written in PHP, intended to handle the administration of MySQL over the Web. phpMyAdmin supports a wide range of operations on MySQL and MariaDB. Frequently used database operations (managing databases, tables, columns, relations, indexes, users, permissions, etc) can be performed via the user interface, while you still have the ability to directly execute any SQL statement. The phpMyAdmin interface, as illustrated in the following figure, should be displayed when you use the URL specified above.

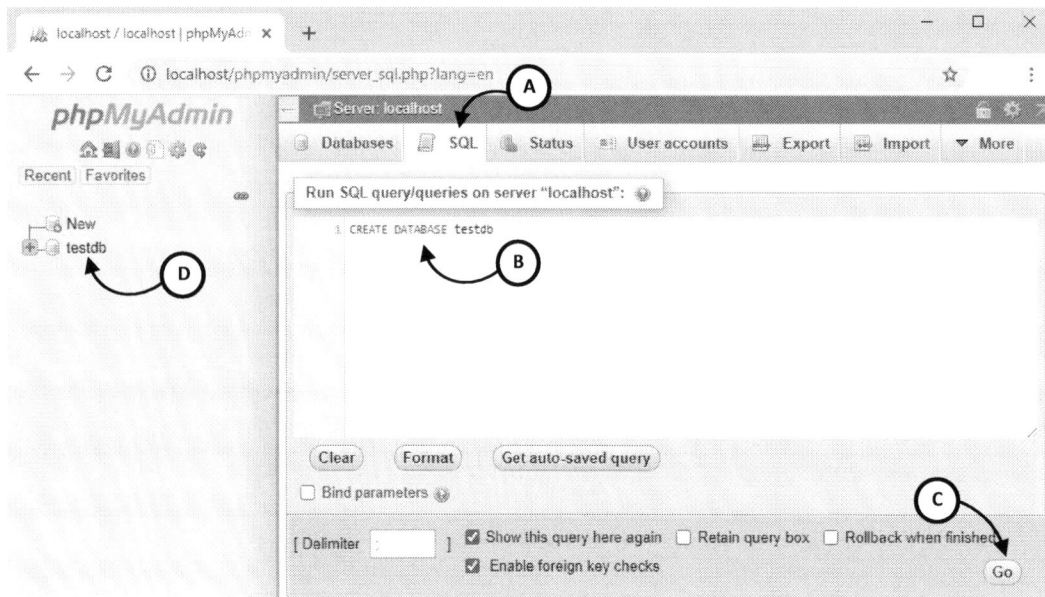

Figure 5-7

2. Click the **SQL** tab (A).
3. In the SQL pane, type **CREATE DATABASE testdb** (B) and click the **Go** button (C). The new database will be created (D).

MySQL Data Types

All RDBMS require the user to specify the data type of each column in a table. The available data types vary from one programming language to another, and from one database application to another, but the following usually exist in one form or another:

- Character (text): Readable text
- Integer : An integer is a whole number; a number that has no fractional part.
- Floating-point : A number with a decimal point. For example, 3 is an integer, but 3.5 is a floating-point number.

In MySQL data types are divided into three main categories: text, number, and Date/Time.

Text Types:

Type	Description
CHAR(size)	Stores string (letters, numbers, and special characters) of fixed length up to 255 characters
VARCHAR(size)	Values in VARCHAR columns are variable-length strings. The length can be specified as a value from 0 to 255 before MySQL 5.0.3, and 0 to 65,535 in 5.0.3 and later versions.
BLOB	A BLOB is a binary large object that can hold a variable amount of data such as images. The four BLOB types are TINYBLOB, BLOB, MEDIUMBLOB, and LONGBLOB.
TEXT	TEXT values are treated as nonbinary strings (character strings). The four TEXT types are TINYTEXT, TEXT, MEDIUMTEXT, and LONGTEXT.

Number Types:

Type	Description
INT(size)	An integer is what is more commonly known as a whole number. It may be positive, negative, or the number zero. MySQL supports the SQL standard integer types including INTEGER or (INT), SMALLINT, TINYINT, MEDIUMINT, and BIGINT.
Fixed-Point Types	The DECIMAL and NUMERIC types store exact numeric data values. These types are used when it is important to preserve exact precision, for example with monetary data. In MySQL, NUMERIC is implemented as DECIMAL. In a DECIMAL column declaration, the precision and scale can be (and usually is) specified; for example: *salary DECIMAL(5,2)* In this example, 5 is the precision and 2 is the scale. The precision represents the number of significant digits that are stored for values, and the scale represents the number of digits that can be stored following the decimal point.

Date Type:

Type	Description
DATE()	The DATE type is used for values with a date part but no time part. MySQL retrieves and displays DATE values in 'YYYY-MM-DD' format. The supported range is '1000-01-01' to '9999-12-31'.
DATETIME()	The DATETIME type is used for values that contain both date and time parts. MySQL retrieves and displays DATETIME values in 'YYYY-MM-DD HH:MM:SS' format. The supported range is '1000-01-01 00:00:00' to '9999-12-31 23:59:59'.
TIMESTAMP()	The TIMESTAMP data type is used for values that contain both date and time parts. TIMESTAMP has a range of '1970-01-01 00:00:01' UTC to '2038-01-19 03:14:07' UTC.
YEAR()	The YEAR type is a type used to represent year values. It can be declared as YEAR(4) or YEAR(2) to specify a display width of four or two characters. The default is four characters if no width is given.
TIME()	MySQL retrieves and displays TIME values in 'HH:MM:SS' format (or 'HHH:MM:SS' format for large hours values). TIME values may range from '-838:59:59' to '838:59:59'. The hours part may be so large because the TIME type can be used not only to represent a time of day (which must be less than 24 hours), but also elapsed time or a time interval between two events (which may be much greater than 24 hours, or even negative).

Creating Table

After creating an empty database and understanding different data types, you can now add tables to your database to hold data. Tables are created using the CREATE TABLE DDL syntax.

CREATE TABLE table_name
(
column_name1 data_type,
column_name2 data_type,
column_name3 data_type,
....
)

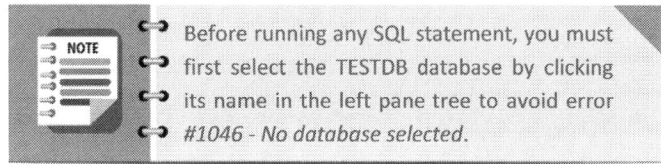

> **NOTE** Before running any SQL statement, you must first select the TESTDB database by clicking its name in the left pane tree to avoid error *#1046 - No database selected.*

Let's add a table named Contact to the new TESTDB database.

1. Click the **SQL** tab again, and type the following CREATE TABLE statement (A) in the SQL pane and hit **Go**.

   CREATE TABLE contact (id int, name varchar(50), email varchar(100), age int(3), message varchar(2000))

   The new table will be created under the TESTDB database. Expand the tree to see the table's definitions (B) in the left pane.

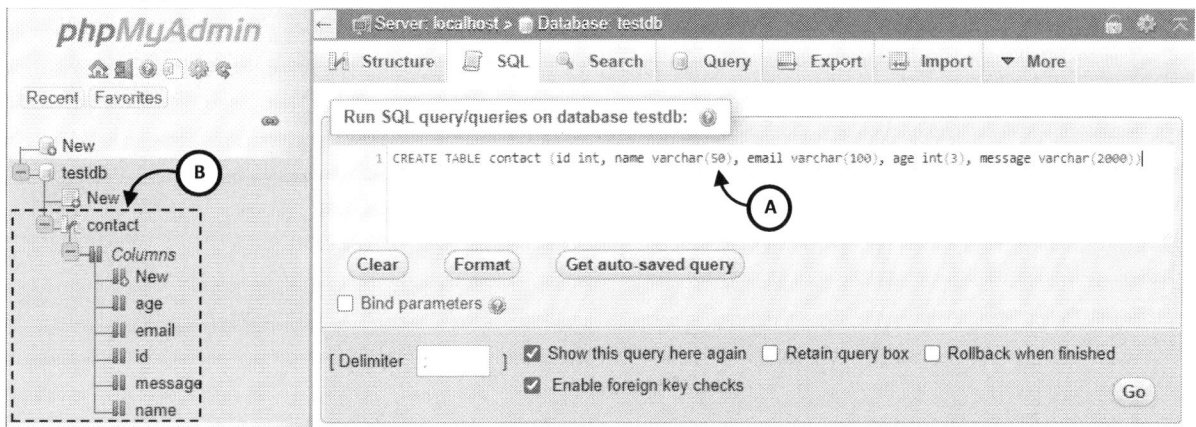

Figure 5-8

2. In the tree view, click on the **Columns** node (C) in the left pane to see the structure of this table (D) – as illustrated in the following screenshot.

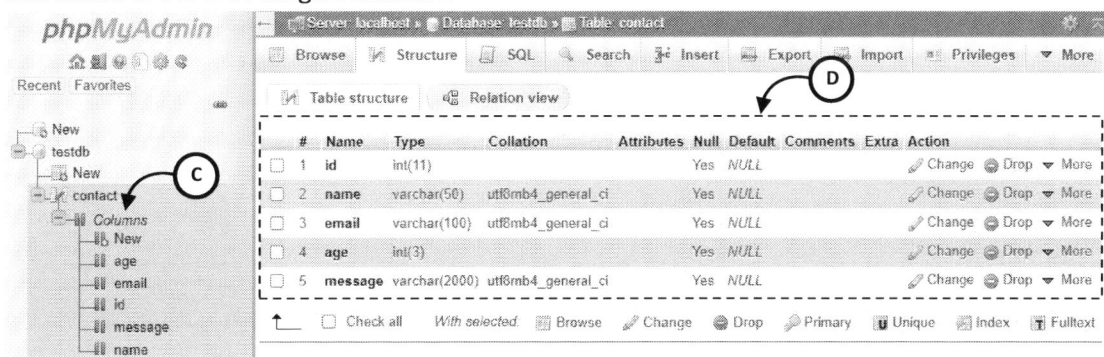

Figure 5-9

Adding Data

The INSERT INTO statement is used to insert new records in a table. This statement has the following two forms:

INSERT INTO table_name VALUES (value1, value2, value3,...)

Use the above syntax (without mentioning column names) if you want to populate all columns in a table with some data. If you wish to add values to specific columns in a table, then use the following syntax specifying column names. In this example, you skipped column2 and column4 and inserted values in column 1, 3, and 5.

INSERT INTO table_name (column1, column3, column5,...) VALUES (value1, value2, value3,...)

1. Type the following two INSERT statements in the SQL pane and hit Go to add two records to the Contact table. These statements will populate all table columns with relevant information.

> **Examples**
> Insert into contact values (1, 'Saad', ' saad@abc.com', 30, 'Feedback message');
> Insert into contact values (2, 'Daniel Clarke', 'daniel@gmail.com', 25, 'This is a comment');
> Insert into contact (id, email, message) values (99, 'abc@abc.com', 'This is a message');

2. Add another record by using the second syntax:

> **Example**
> Insert into contact (id, email, message) values (99, 'abc@abc.com', 'This is a message');

The above statement will insert values only in id, email, and message columns, leaving name and age columns blank.

Querying Data

You now have three records in your Contact table. To query this data you will use the SELECT statement. Its syntax is:

SELECT column_name(s) FROM table_name

1. Type the following statement in the SQL pane and hit Go to retrieve all rows from the Contact table:

> **Example**
> SELECT id, name, email, age, message FROM Contact

The result should resemble the following figure.

> ✔ Showing rows 0 - 2 (3 total, Query took 0.0005 seconds.)
>
> SELECT id, name, email, age, message FROM Contact
>
> ☐ Show all | Number of rows: 25 ▾   Filter rows: Search this table
>
> + Options

id	name	email	age	message
1	Saad	saad@abc.com	30	Feedback message
2	Daniel Clarke	daniel@gmail.com	25	This is a comment
99	NULL	abc@abc.com	NULL	This is a message

Figure 5-10

2. To select all columns at once, you can use the asterisk (*) character instead of individual column names like this:

> **Example**
> SELECT * FROM Contact

This statement will provide the same output as shown in the above figure.

3. Use the WHERE clause to get only those records that satisfy a specified criterion. The syntax is:

SELECT column_name(s) FROM table_name WHERE column_name operator value

> **Example**
> SELECT * FROM Contact where Name = 'Saad'

This statement fetches only one record, the one having value Saad in the Name column. You can use the following operators in the WHERE clause:

Operator	Description	Example
=	Equal	SELECT * FROM Contact where Name = 'Saad' *Returns record # 1* | id	name	email	age	message | |---|---|---|---|---| | 1 | Saad | saad@abc.com | 30 | Feedback message |
<> or !=	Not Equal	SELECT * FROM Contact where Name <> 'Saad' *Returns* | id	name	email	age	message | |---|---|---|---|---| | 2 | Daniel Clarke | daniel@gmail.com | 25 | This is a comment | | 3 | Michael Peter | mpeter@yahoo.com | 35 | This is a feedback message |
>	Greater than	SELECT * FROM Contact where Age > 30 *Returns* | id	name	email	age	message | |---|---|---|---|---| | 3 | Michael Peter | mpeter@yahoo.com | 35 | This is a feedback message |
>=	Greater than or equal	SELECT * FROM Contact where Age >= 25 *Returns* | id	name	email	age	message | |---|---|---|---|---| | 1 | Saad | saad@abc.com | 30 | Feedback message | | 2 | Daniel Clarke | daniel@gmail.com | 25 | This is a comment |
<	Less than	SELECT * FROM Contact where Id < 2 *Returns* | id	name	email	age	message | |---|---|---|---|---| | 1 | Saad | saad@abc.com | 30 | Feedback message |
<=	Less than or equal	SELECT * FROM Contact where Id <= 2 *Returns* | id	name	email	age	message | |---|---|---|---|---| | 1 | Saad | saad@abc.com | 30 | Feedback message | | 2 | Daniel Clarke | daniel@gmail.com | 25 | This is a comment |
BETWEEN	Data range between two values	SELECT * FROM Contact where Id BETWEEN 2 AND 100 *Returns* | id	name	email	age	message | |---|---|---|---|---| | 2 | Daniel Clarke | daniel@gmail.com | 25 | This is a comment | | 99 | NULL | abc@abc.com | NULL | This is a message |
LIKE	Matches a pattern	SELECT * FROM Contact where message like '%feed%' *Returns* | id	name	email	age	message | |---|---|---|---|---| | 1 | Saad | saad@abc.com | 30 | Feedback message |
IN	Search multiple values	SELECT * FROM Contact where name IN ('Saad', 'Daniel Clarke') *Returns* | id	name	email	age	message | |---|---|---|---|---| | 1 | Saad | saad@abc.com | 30 | Feedback message | | 2 | Daniel Clarke | daniel@gmail.com | 25 | This is a comment |

AND	Filter records	SELECT * FROM Contact where name='Saad' AND age=30
		Returns
&		
			id	name	email	age	message	
OR			1	Saad	saad@abc.com	30	Feedback message	
		SELECT * FROM Contact where name='Saad' OR age=25
		Returns
			id	name	email	age	message	
			1	Saad	saad@abc.com	30	Feedback message	
			2	Daniel Clarke	daniel@gmail.com	25	This is a comment	
		SELECT * FROM Contact where name='Saad' AND (age=25 or age=30 or age=99)
		Returns
			id	name	email	age	message	
			1	Saad	saad@abc.com	30	Feedback message	

Updating Data

We inserted record number 99 with some missing values that we wish to populate now. The process of updating existing records in a table is accomplished through the UPDATE statement whose syntax is:

UPDATE table_name SET column1=value, column2=value2,...
WHERE some_column=some_value

1. Type the following statement in the SQL pane and click Go to update record number 99:

> **Example**
>
> UPDATE Contact SET name='ABC', age=99 WHERE id=99
>
> Type the following statements to check the updated row:
>
> SELECT * FROM Contact

Here is the output.

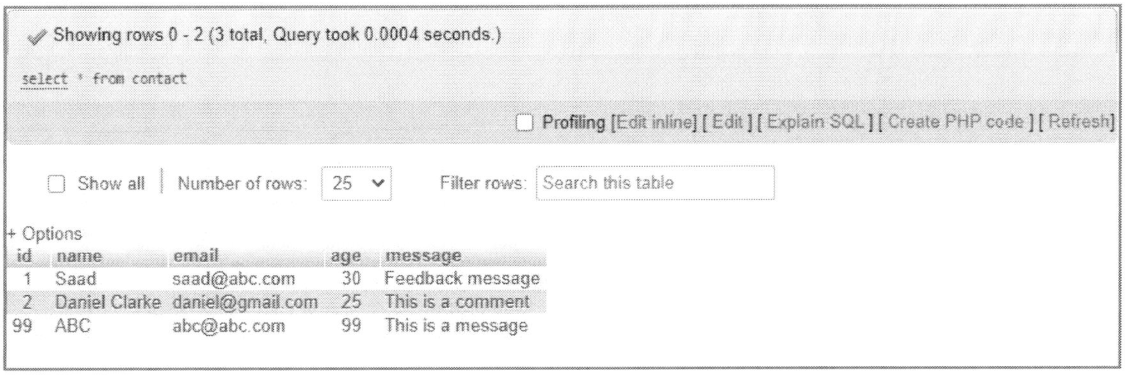

Figure 5-11

> **WARNING**
>
> *It is important to use the WHERE clause, which is used to set conditions while updating table records. The WHERE clause states which record(s) are to be updated. If you omit the WHERE clause, all records will be updated!*

Removing Data

In this exercise you will remove record number 99 from the table using the DELETE statement. Syntax for the DELETE statement is:

DELETE FROM table_name WHERE some_column=some_value

1. Click the **TESTDB** database in the tree pane to your left to select this database.
2. Type any of the following statement in the SQL tab's command interface and hit **Go** to remove record number 99. When prompted, click **OK** in the confirmation box.

> **Example**
>
> DELETE FROM Contact WHERE id=99
>
> Alternatively, you can use a string condition in the WHERE clause like this:
>
> DELETE FROM Contact WHERE name='ABC'

Both the above statements will delete record number 99. Again, you must use the WHERE clause, if you omit, all records will be deleted!

Database and SQL are huge topics that require dedicated books. In this section, I merely scratched the surface to give you some basic knowledge about database and how to interact with it using SQL. You'll need this information in the last part of this book where you will create a database to store data received from your website visitors. The next section, which discusses PHP, will tell you how to connect to your database and insert users' feedback in a table.

PHP: Hypertext Preprocessor

We discussed the significance of PHP earlier in this chapter. Now, we're going to dig deeper to evaluate this robust server-side technology to fulfill the purpose of our project – taking users' feedback, newsletter subscription, and e-commerce modules. Following is the basic syntax of PHP script that starts with *<?php* and ends with *?>*:

```
<?php
   ...
   ...
   ...
?>
```

Basic Information:

- A PHP script can be placed anywhere in the document.
- It is executed on the server, and the result is sent back to the browser in plain HTML.
- It usually has a .php extension and carries HTML tags besides PHP scripting code as we saw in while testing PHP installation.
- Each PHP code line terminates with a semicolon to separate a set of instructions from another.

Variables in PHP

Variables are temporary containers for storing information. Consider the following points while declaring variables in PHP.

- In PHP, variables start with a $ sign, followed by a name e.g. $s_Phone1.
- Variable name should not contain spaces.
- Variable name must start with a letter or the underscore character and can contain alphabets (A-z), numbers (0-9) and the underscore (_).
- Variable names are case sensitive e.g. $s_Phone1 is different from $s_phone1.
- Variables in PHP are created when you assign value to them like:
  $s_Phone1="800-235-4365";
  $n_Age=30;
  $d_Today = date("d/m/Y");
  $b_Married = false;
- To concatenate two string variables together, use the concatenation operator (.):
  $s_Address1 = "301 S. Prospect Rd.";
  $s_Address2 = "Bloomington, IL 61704";
  echo "Address: " . $s_Address1 . " " . $s_Address2;
- Local variables can only be accessed within the function they are declared in.
- Global variables, declared using the *global* keyword, can be accessed from any part of the script.

PHP Code – Variables.php

```php
<html>
 <head>
  <title>PHP Variable Examples</title>
 </head>
 <body>
  <?php
   // String Variable  – The "echo" language construct is used to output one or more strings
   $s_Address1 = "301 S. Prospect Rd.";
   $s_Address2 = "Bloomington, IL 61704";
   echo "Address: ".$s_Address1 . " " . $s_Address2;
   echo ("<br>");
   // Numeric Variable
   $n_Age = 30;
   echo "Your age is ".$n_Age;
   echo ("<br>");
   // Store and display system date
   $d_today = date("d/m/Y");
   echo "The date today is ".$d_today;
   echo ("<br>");
   // Boolean Example
   $b_Married = false;
   if($b_Married == true)
   {
     echo "You're married";
   }
   else
   {
     echo "You're unmarried";
   }
  ?>
 </body>
</html>
```

> **NOTE**
>
> *Just like JavaScript, PHP too uses // for single line and /* */ combination for multi line comments.*

> Address: 301 S. Prospect Rd. Bloomington, IL 61704
> Your age is 30
> The date today is 01/01/2021
> You're unmarried

Arrays in PHP

In PHP arrays are used to store data. It can be defined as a super-variable containing a collection of variables called elements. Each element has three components: index, datatype, and value. An element's value can be accessed through its corresponding index. By default, PHP uses integer indices starting with 0. Indices can be either strings or numbers, and are presented in square brackets. For example, the expression $categories[0] refers to the first value stored in $categories array.

Syntax:

Create an array: *$array_name = array(value1,value2,...)*

Access value in an element: *$array_name[index];*

Example:

$categories = array('Software','Hardware','Network');

Alternate method:

$categories = array();
$categories[0] = 'Software';
$categories[1] = 'Hardware';
$categories[2] = 'Network';

Besides the default numeric indices, you can also define strings index values. This type of array is called associative array. The indices in an associative array are called keys. Instead of element values separated by commas, you supply key-value pairs separated by commas, where the key and value are separated by the special symbol =>.

Syntax:

array('key' => value ...)

Example:

$product = array('PRODUCT' => 'The Import Manager', 'PRICE' => 99.99);

Many PHP built-in environment variables are in the form of arrays. For instance $_SESSION, which carries all the variable names, types, and values and propagates this data from one page to the other via PHP's session mechanism.

PHP Session

Sessions and cookies are closely allied concepts in PHP and in web programming more generally, largely because the best way to actually implement sessions is by using cookies. PHP uses cookies to work with sessions and only works when cookies are enabled in client browsers. For clients who have cookies disabled, PHP presents an alternative which called URL encoding.

What's a Session?

In Web terminology, a session is a period of time during which a person visits a number of different Web sites using his or her browser. A session ends when the visitor quits the browser. From the perspective of a single website, the session runs from that person's first download of a page from the site through the last. Session tracking is a term that refers to keeping track of users as they move around a website.

Why Track Session?

Web applications use HTTP by which browsers talk to Web servers. Since HTTP doesn't maintain state, it is known as a stateless protocol. Here, your Web server reacts independently to each individual request it receives and has no way to link requests together even if it is logging requests. For example, a client browser requests a page from a web server. After rendering the page, the server closes the connection. When a subsequent request is forwarded from the same client, the web server doesn't know how to associate the current request with the previous one.

> **NOTE**
>
> *After starting a session, you can store data in session variables with the help of a global array called $_SESSION. To remove an element from this array, you use the UNSET() function. Similarly, by setting it to an empty array you can remove its contents. A session ends when the browser is closed, or specified amount of time elapses without a request, or when a function such as session_destroy() is called. You'll be using this array extensively throughout the e-commerce module.*

Session Tracking in PHP

PHP provides a strong session tracking mechanism to cope with a situation like the one mentioned above. When a client sends a request, PHP evaluates whether the request has a PHP session ID. If not, it creates a new session on the server and assigns it a unique ID. This ID is sent back to the client browser as a cookie. The client includes this session ID with all subsequent requests. PHP uses this ID to access the session data stored on the web server and thus links requests sent against individual sessions.

Starting a Session

In PHP, you can start a new session or resume a previously defined session by calling the *SESSION_START()* built-in function. It prompts PHP to check for session ID in the sent request and to create a new session ID and cookie if one doesn't already exist. It returns true on success and false otherwise. Since it sets a cookie, it must be called before the page sends any HTML output to an application. PHP stores session ID in the client browser using the default per-session cookie mechanism. This type of session ends when the users closes the browser. You can use *session_set_cookie_params()* function to create a session cookie that persists longer.

Creating a PHP Function

Just like JavaScript, you can create your functions in PHP. A function created in PHP is executed by a call to it from anywhere within a page. Functions in PHP are created using the following syntax:

```
function functionName($para1,$para2,...)
{
  function code;
}
```

Guidelines:

- Start the function name with a letter or underscore
- Give function a meaningful name to reflect its purpose
- You can add parameters (arguments) to your functions
- Use the return statement to get back a value from a function

The first example on the next page demonstrates a simple function named Greeting which doesn't pass or receive any values. In this code the text *Hello* is displayed and just after that, the function Greeting() is called which in turn displays the text *Saad* next to the word *Hello*.

The second example passes two numeric values to the function named sum - *sum(5,10)*. On line 4 the function receives these values in two variables *($a,$z)*, adds them up on the next line, and returns the result through the variable *$n_Sum* using the keyword *return*.

PHP Code Function.php

```
<html>
<body>

<?php
  function Greeting()
  {
    echo "Saad";
  }
  echo "Hello ";
  Greeting();
?>

</body>
</html>
```

Output

Hello Saad

PHP Code Pfunction.php (Parameterized Function)

```
<html>
<body>

<?php
  function sum($a,$z)
  {
    $n_Sum=$a+$z;
    return $n_Sum;
  }
  echo "The sum of 5 + 10 is: " . sum(5,10);
?>

</body>
</html>
```

Output

The sum of 5 + 10 is: 15

Dealing With Forms

In chapter 2, you saw how to create a form in HTML and made that form interactive with JavaScript in chapter 4. In this part of the book, you are going to use PHP and SQL's DML statements to insert information in MySQL database that is provided by users. But initially, you will learn how to connect to the MySQL database and fetch records from the Contact table that you manually entered in the previous section.

Connect to MySQL Database and Query Records

Before you can access data in a database, you must create a connection to the database. In PHP, this is done through:

- MySQL extension
- MySQLi extension
- PHP Data Objects (PDO)

The MySQLi Extension (MySQL Improved) is a relational database driver used in the PHP programming language to provide an interface with MySQL databases. MySQLi is an improved version of the older PHP MySQL driver, offering various benefits. The developers of the PHP programming language recommend using MySQLi when dealing with MySQL server versions 4.1.3 and newer. If the MySQL database you are connecting to is less than or equal to 4.1.3, use mysql_connect.

In MySQLi extension, you access the database with the *mysqli_connect()* function. Its syntax is:

mysqli_connect(servername,username,password);

servername: This parameter specifies the server running your database. Since we have the database on the same machine, we'll set this parameter to *localhost*. In computer networking, localhost (meaning this computer) is the standard hostname given to the address of the loopback network interface. This mechanism is useful for programmers to test their software during development.

username: A default user, *root*, was created during MySQL database installation. Right now, we are going to connect the database through that user's credentials.

password: The default password for the user root is *mysql*. So we'll pass it over to the function: *mysqli_connect()*.

To close the database connection, you'll use *mysqli_close()* function.

The initial example presented on the next page is named SELECT.PHP to demonstrate the use of SELECT statement after connecting to the database.

Line	Select.php - SELECT Statement Example
1	`<html>`
2	`<head>`
3	`<title>PHP Test</title>`
4	`</head>`
5	`<body>`
6	`<?php`
7	`Print "Connecting...";` // Like echo Print is also used to output string
8	`echo " ";`
9	`$con = mysqli_connect("localhost","root","mysql");`
10	`if (!$con)`
11	`{`
12	`die('Could not connect: ' . mysqli_error());`
13	`}`
14	`mysqli_select_db($con, "testdb");`
15	`$result = mysqli_query($con, "SELECT * FROM Contact");`
16	`while($row = mysqli_fetch_array($result))`
17	`{`
18	`echo $row['name'] . " - " . $row['email'] . " - " . $row['age'];`
19	`echo " ";`
20	`}`
21	`mysqli_close($con);`
22	`?>`
23	`</body>`
24	`</html>`

Output

Connecting…
Saad - saad@abc.com - 30
Daniel Clarke - daniel@gmail.com - 25

- Code on line # 9 stores the connection string in a variable *$con*.
- The statement *if(!$con)* (line 10) evaluates whether the connection failed. The symbol (!) represents the NOT operator. In case of failure, the PHP die() function is called (line 12) that prints a message and exits the current script. The PHP function, *mysqli_error()*, returns the error description of the last MySQL operation.
- On line # 14, another PHP function named *mysqli_select_db()* is called to set the active MySQL database i.e. testdb. We also specified to use $con for connection. The function *mysqli_select_db()* returns TRUE on success, or FALSE on failure.
- The *mysqli_query()* function (line 15) executes a query on the database. In this scenario, we asked to fetch all rows from the Contact table and then store the result set in the *$result* variable.
- Next, we used the *mysqli_fetch_array()* function to return the first row from the record set as an array. Each call to *mysqli_fetch_array()* returns the next row in the record set. The *while* loop iterates through all the records in the record set. To print the values from each row, we used the PHP *$row* variable (*$row['column name']*). The code, echo "<br>", displays each record on a new line.
- Finally, we closed the connection through mysqli_close($con) function.
- Save this file as *select.php* in the www folder.
- Open a browser and type *http://localhost/select.php* in the address bar and hit Enter to see the output.

Insert Form's Data in MySQL Database

As you already know, HTML and JavaScript are unable to process form data on the server. A scripting language such as PHP must be used with HTML forms to process data captured by HTML form elements. HTML form elements rely on action and method attributes to identify where to send the form data for processing (action) and how to process the data (method).

An HTML form has one required attribute, ACTION, specifying the URL of a CGI script which processes the form and sends back feedback. The URL to a document may be on the same server (for example, a shared CGI folder that has various form-processing scripts), or even a page or script on an entirely separate server.

There are two methods to send form data to a server. GET, the default, will send the form input in a URL, whereas POST sends it in the body of the submission. The latter method means you can send larger amounts of data, and that the URL of the form results doesn't show the encoded form.

Upon receipt, PHP stores form values in $_GET array that it receives through the form GET method. For example, the following portion of the URL requests a page named Member.php and passes two values to it using the default GET method:

member.php?fName=Riaz&lName=Ahmed

Here, the question mark indicates that there is some data following the symbol. Each data item carries the name of the form element, an equals sign, and a corresponding value. The ampersand symbol (&) is used to separate the items. In the above example, the URL carries data from two form text boxes named *fName* and *lName* along with respective values *Riaz* and *Ahmed*. After receiving these values, PHP creates the $_GET array as shown in the following illustration.

Later on, to retrieve the values from the $_GET array and store it in a PHP variable; you use the following code:

$first_name = $_GET['fName'];
$last_name = $_GET['lName'];

The above code will create two PHP variable $first_name and $last_name to get values from fName and lName array elements.

The HTTP POST method works just like the GET method without appending the parameters to the URL. Values passed to PHP using the POST method are held under another built-in array called $_POST that you'll see shortly.
In the previous example you fetched existing records from the database using the SELECT statement and used PHP code in conjunction with HTML in a .php file. In this exercise, you will use an html file with form action

attribute to call a server-side script (.php) to INSERT form's data into the database. To accomplish this task follow the steps listed below:

1. In VS Code, press Ctrl+N to open a new file. Add the code listed in the HTML Code section on the next page, and save the file as **insert.html** in the www folder.
2. Create another file named **insert.php**, as shown in the PHP Code section on the subsequent page, and save it in the same folder.
3. Open a browser session and type **http://localhost/insert.html** to see the form as illustrated on the next page.
4. Fill in the form using the credentials as shown in the figure, and click the **Submit** button. If everything goes well, you will see a message *"1 record added"*.
5. Type **select * from contact** in SQL tab to check the new record.

HTML Code (insert.html) - Insert Form Data

```
<html>
<body>
<form action="insert.php" method="post">
  <fieldset>
    <legend>Contact Us</legend>
    <label>Name:<br>
    <input type="text" name="s_Name" >
    </label><br>
    <label>Email:<br>
    <input type="text" name="s_Email" >
    </label><br>
    <label>Age:<br>
    <input type="text" name="n_Age" >
    </label><br><br>
    <textarea name="s_Message" cols="50" rows="10">Please enter your comments...</textarea>
    <br>
    <input type="submit" >
  </fieldset>
</form>
</body>
</html>
```

```
┌─ Contact Us ────────────────────────────────┐
│ Name:                                        │
│ ┌──────────────────────┐                     │
│ └──────────────────────┘                     │
│ Email:                                       │
│ ┌──────────────────────┐                     │
│ └──────────────────────┘                     │
│ Age:                                         │
│ ┌──────────────────────┐                     │
│ └──────────────────────┘                     │
│ ┌──────────────────────────────────────────┐ │
│ │ Please enter your comments...            │ │
│ │                                          │ │
│ │                                          │ │
│ │                                          │ │
│ │                                          │ │
│ │                                          │ │
│ │                                          │ │
│ └──────────────────────────────────────────┘ │
│ ┌─────────┐                                  │
│ │ Submit  │                                  │
│ └─────────┘                                  │
└──────────────────────────────────────────────┘
```

Line	PHP Code (insert.php)
1	`<?php`
2	`$con = mysqli_connect("localhost","root","mysql");`
3	`if (!$con)`
4	`{`
5	`die('Could not connect: ' . mysqli_error($con));`
6	`}`
7	`mysqli_select_db($con, "testdb");`
8	`//Move form values to local PHP variables`
9	`$s_Name = $_POST['s_Name'];`
10	`$s_Email = $_POST['s_Email'];`
11	`// Assess $_POST['n_Age'] as a valid integer, or move 0 to $n_Age`
12	`$n_Age = (is_numeric($_POST['n_Age']) ? (int)$_POST['n_Age'] : 0);`
13	`$s_Message = $_POST['s_Message'];`
14	`//Insert record using PHP variable values`
15	`$sql="INSERT INTO Contact VALUES (3,'$s_Name','$s_Email',$n_Age,'$s_Message')";`
16	`if (!mysqli_query($con,$sql))`
17	`{`
18	`die('Error: ' . mysqli_error($con));`
19	`}`
20	`echo "1 record added";`
21	`mysqli_close($con);`
22	`?>`

Example Explained:

- The html code (insert.html) uses <fieldset> to group form control.
- The form's ACTION attribute in the html code calls insert.php file using the POST method. This file is called when the *Submit* button is clicked.
- In the php file, the database connection method is similar to the one you saw in the previous example.
- In PHP, the predefined $_POST array is used to collect values - *$_POST['s_Name']* - from a form sent with *method="post"*. These values are then stored in corresponding local variables: *$s_Name, $s_Email* etc.
- The code *$n_Age = (is_numeric($_POST['n_Age']) ? (int)$_POST['n_Age'] : 0)* evaluates the $_POST['n_Age'] to be a number, if not, 0 is inserted in the Age column. The is_numeric() function is used to check whether a variable is numeric or not.
- All the values are written to the database table using INSERT INTO statement (line 15). Note that we used a static value 3 for the ID column. In our final project, we will use the AUTO_INCREMENT attribute of MySQL to automatically generate a unique number when a new record is inserted in a table.

Update Form's Data in MySQL Database

Create a new file named update.php using the following code in VS code. Run this example in the browser by typing **http://localhost/update.php** in the address bar.

PHP Code (Update.php)

```
<html>
 <head>
  <title>PHP Test</title>
 </head>
<body>

<?php
 $con = mysqli_connect("localhost","root","mysql","testdb") or die("Error connecting to MYSQL server.");

 $sql="UPDATE contact SET Age=35 WHERE name like 'Michael%' and id=3";

 mysqli_query($con,$sql) or die('Error: ' . mysqli_error($con));

 echo "<br>";

 printf ("Updated records: %d\n", mysqli_affected_rows($con));

 mysqli_close($con);
?>

 </body>
</html>
```

Example Explained:

- The mysqli_connect() function adds a fourth parameter allowing you to select a database, testdb, in the same function you used to connect. A function with the name mysqli_select_db() also exists to select a database, but you'll need it only if you want to use multiple databases on the same connection. The die() function is also used on this line.
- The UPDATE statement is used to modify the record of Michael Peter having id=3 to change his age from 40 to 35.
- The printf() function outputs a formatted string to display number of rows affected.
- The mysqli_affected_rows() gets number of affected rows in the last MySQL Insert, Update or Delete operation.

Deleting Form's Data from MySQL Database

Create a new feedback record in the Contact table. I created one with id=9 and mentioned it in the WHERE clause in the DELETE statement. The IF condition is used in conjunction with mysqli_affected_rows() function to evaluate number of deleted rows. If the number returned by this function is greater than zero, the message *Deleted records:* is printed with the number.

PHP Code (Delete.php)

```php
<html>
 <head>
  <title>PHP Test</title>
 </head>
 <body>

<?php
 $con = mysqli_connect("localhost","root","mysql","testdb") or die("Error connecting to MYSQL server.");

 $sql="DELETE FROM Contact WHERE id = 9";

 mysqli_query($con,$sql) or die('Error: ' . mysqli_error($con));

 echo "<br>";

 if (mysqli_affected_rows($con) > 0)
 {
   printf ("Deleted records: %d\n", mysqli_affected_rows($con));
 }
 else
 {
   printf ("No records deleted");
 }

 mysqli_close($con);
?>

 </body>
</html>
```

PHP Data Objects (PDO)

The previous section demonstrated older techniques to interact with MySQL database (using MySQLi extension). This topic shows you how to use PDO (PHP Data Objects) to work with a database. PDO is relatively new to PHP, and it supports most popular databases. It defines a consistent interface for accessing databases and uses the same PHP code with more than one type of database. PDO doesn't work with earlier versions of PHP. To maintain legacy code, you have to use techniques mentioned in the previous section. For new development, though, PDO is recommended.

Connect to MySQL Database through PDO

```
$con = 'mysql:host=localhost; dbname=testdb';
$username = 'root';
$password = 'mysql';
$db = new PDO($con, $username, $password);
```

The first line assigns a DSN (Data Source Name) to the variable *$con*. This code specifies a MySQL database named *testdb* that is running on the same computer (localhost) as the PHP. Then, the *$username* and *$password* variables are assigned values, as we did in former sections. Finally, these variables are used as the arguments for creating a new PDO object that is assigned to the variable named *$db*. Alternatively, you can write it as under:

```
$con = new PDO('mysql:host=localhost; dbname=testdb', 'root', 'mysql');
```

Execute the SELECT Statement

```
$query = 'SELECT * FROM contact';
$rs = $con->query($query);        // $rs contains the result set
```

Here, *$con* is an object and query is a method. To call a method from any object, you define the name of the object (*$con*), followed by a special symbol (->) and then by the name of the method (*query*). Within the method parentheses, you provide the argument (*$query*).

In the next example, you are using "query" method of the PDO object to execute a SELECT statement. It requires just one argument, which is the SELECT statement. This argument can be a variable (*$query*) that contains the SELECT statement, as we used above, or the statement itself.

Execute a SELECT Statement

PHP Code (SelectPDO.php)

```php
<html>
  <head>
    <title>Test PDO</title>
  </head>
  <body>
   <?php
    $con = new PDO('mysql:host=localhost; dbname=testdb', 'root', 'mysql');
    $rs = $con->query('SELECT * FROM contact');
    echo '<br><br>';
    $count = 0;
    // Fetch() is for getting current row from result set
    while ($row = $rs->fetch())
    {
      print "ID:{$row[0]} Name:{$row[1]} Email:{$row[2]} Age:{$row[3]} Message:{$row[4]}";
      $count++;
      echo '<br>';
    }
    echo '<br>';
    print "Number of rows in result set: ". $count;
   ?>
  </body>
</html>
```

Output

ID:1 Name:Saad Email:saad@abc.com Age:30 Message: Feedback message
ID:2 Name:Daniel Clarke Email:daniel@gmail.com Age:25 Message: This is a comment
ID:3 Name:Michael Peter Email:mpeter@yahoo.com Age:35 Message: This is a feedback

Number of rows in result set: 3

Example Explained:

- Fetch() is used to get current row from the result set.
- By default, PDO returns each row as an array indexed by column name and 0-indexed column position in the row. For example, $row[0] returns data from column number 1, $row[1] gives column 2 and so on.
- We used $count++ as a record counter to evaluate number of records in the result set.

Execute an INSERT Statement

For INSERT, UPDATE, and DELETE statements the *exec* method of the PDO object is used with the SQL statement as the argument. The variables $rec_insert, $rec_update, and $rec_delete store the number of rows affected by each statement.

HTML Code (InsertPDO.html)

```html
<html>
<body>
<form action="insertPDO.php" method="post">
  <fieldset>
    <legend>Contact Us</legend>
    <label>Name:*<br>
    <input type="text" name="s_Name">
    </label><br>
    <label>Email:*<br>
    <input type="text" name="s_Email">
    </label><br>
    <label>Age:<br>
    <input type="text" name="n_Age">
    </label><br><br>
    <textarea name="s_Message" cols="50" rows="10">Please enter your  comments...</textarea>
    <br>
    <input type="submit">
  </fieldset>
</form>
</body>
</html>
```

PHP Code (InsertPDO.php)

```php
<?php
  $con = new PDO('mysql:host=localhost; dbname=testdb', 'root', 'mysql');
  $s_Name = $_POST['s_Name'];
  $s_Email = $_POST['s_Email'];
  // Assess $_POST['n_Age'] as a valid integer, or move 0 to $n_Age
  $n_Age = (is_numeric($_POST['n_Age']) ? (int)$_POST['n_Age'] : 0);
  $s_Message = $_POST['s_Message'];

  // Validate inputs
  if (empty ($s_Name) || empty ($s_Email))
  {
    Print "Invalid data. Click the back button and enter all fields.";
  }
  else
  {
    $query = "INSERT INTO Contact VALUES (4,'$s_Name','$s_Email',$n_Age,'$s_Message')";
    $rec_insert = $con->exec($query);
  }
  echo '<br>';
  print "Number of records added: ".$rec_insert;
?>
```

Execute an UPDATE Statement

```php
$n_Id = 4;
$n_Age = 29;
$query = "UPDATE Contact SET age = $n_Age WHERE id = $n_Id";
$rec_update = $db->exec($query);
```

Execute a DELETE Statement

```php
$n_Id = 4;
$query = "DELETE FROM Contact WHERE id = $n_Id";
$rec_delete = $db->exec($query);
```

Using FOREACH Loop

In a previous section we saw how to loop through database records using the WHILE statement. In this exercise, we're going to use FOREACH for the same purpose. Please note that FOREACH works only on arrays and objects, and will issue an error when you try to use it on a variable with a different data type or an uninitialized variable. It has two syntaxes:

foreach (array_expression as $value)
   statement

foreach (array_expression as $key => $value)
   statement

The first form loops over the array given by *array_expression*. On each iteration, the value of the current element is assigned to *$value* and the internal array pointer is advanced by one and the next iteration gives the next element.

The second form will additionally assign the current element's key to the *$key* variable on each iteration. The symbol => is the separator for associative arrays. In the following example, the keys (Saad/Daniel) of the array ($users) is assigned to *$user* and the values (mypassword123/Dc5649) to *$password*.

Example:

```
$users = array(
   'Saad' => 'mypassword123',
   'Daniel' => 'Dc5649'
);

foreach ($users as $user => $password) {
   echo "{$user}'s password is: {$password}\n";
}
```

Prints:
 Saad's password is: mypassword123
 Daniel's password is: Dc5649

You can also use this symbol for numerically indexed arrays.

Example:

```
$vehicles = array('airplane', 'bus', 'train', 'car', 'bike');
foreach ($vehicles as $idx => $vtype) {
   echo "{$idx}: {$vtype}\n";
}
```

Prints:
0: airplane
1: bus
2: train
3: car
4: bike

PHP Code (foreach.php)

```
<html>
<head>
  <title>Test FOREACH Loop</title>
</head>
<body>

  <?php
  $con = new PDO('mysql:host=localhost; dbname=testdb', 'root', 'mysql');
  $rs = $con->query('SELECT * FROM contact');

  foreach ($rs as $currentrow)
  {
   echo $currentrow['id'];
   echo ' - ';
   echo $currentrow['name'];
   echo '<br>';
  }

?>
</body>
</html>
```

1 - Saad
2 - Daniel Clarke
3 - Michael Peter

Include and Require Statements

One of the great benefits of dynamic web page generation over static HTML is the opportunity to fight redundancy. It's very common to use the same set of functions across a set of web site pages. PHP makes it very easy to drop anything into your scripts, from one character to a whole separate program, by using the *include* or *require* statements.

These statements import the contents of some other file into the file being executed. Using either one of these forms is vastly preferable and saves a lot of work. You can create a standard header, footer, or menu file for all your web pages. When you want to modify your website functions or appearance, you will have to do it only once. For example, when the header needs to be updated on all web pages, you only need to update the included header file.

Both *require* and *include* are identical except upon failure require produces a fatal E_COMPILE_ERROR. In other words, it will halt the script; whereas, include only emits a warning (E_WARNING) which allows the script to continue. So, if you want the execution to go on and show users the output, even if the included file is missing, use "include". Otherwise, always use require to add in a key file to the flow of execution. This will help avoid compromising your application's security and integrity. You can use the "include" and "require" functions to pass control to another web page. When that page finishes, control returns to the statement after the "include" or "require" function.

To better understand the functionality, let's see a simple example. This example has two file: Testinclude.html and bio.php. The first four PHP statements in the html file do not show name and age values. After adding bio.php (*include 'bio.php'*), the values are fetched from the file and included in the text.

TestInclude.php

```
<html>
 <head>
  <title>Test PHP Include Statement</title>
 </head>
 <body>

  <?php
    echo "My name is $s_Name"; // Displays My name is
    echo "<br>";
    echo "My age is $n_Age";   // Displays My age is
    echo "<br>";
    include 'bio.php';
    echo "My name is $s_Name, I'm aged $n_Age"; // Displays My name is Saad Muavia, I'm aged 20
  ?>


</body>
</html>
```

```
My name is
My age is
My name is Saad Muavia, I'm aged 20
```

Bio.php

```
<?php
 $s_Name = 'Saad Muavia';
 $n_Age = 30;
?>
```

Send E-Mail From PHP

You can use PHP's built-in MAIL() function to send emails from PHP scripts. It is a cost effective way of notifying users on important events. It has the following basic syntax:

```php
<?php
  mail($to,$subject,$message,[$headers],[$parameters]);
?>
```

$to is the email address of the recipient.

$subject is the email subject.

$message is the message to be sent.

[$headers] is optional, it can be used to include information such as CC and BCC. CC stands for carbon copy. It is used when you want to send a copy to an interested person. BCC is the acronym for blind carbon copy. It is similar to CC. The email addresses included in the BCC section are not visible to the other recipients. Multiple extra headers should be separated with a CRLF (\r\n).

[$parameters] is also optional, and it can be used to pass additional flags as command line options to the program configured to be used when sending mail, as defined by the *sendmail_path* configuration setting. For example, this can be used to set the envelope sender address when using sendmail with the -f sendmail option.

PHP must be configured correctly via the php.ini file with the details of how your system sends email. Windows users should ensure that two directives are supplied. The first is called SMTP that defines your email server address. The second is called *sendmail_from* which defines your own email address. PHP MAIL() function uses Simple Mail Transmission Protocol (SMTP) to send emails. On a hosted server, the SMTP settings would have already been set. However, to send emails from your PC, you need to modify php.ini configuration file. Execute the following steps to configure SMTP email settings on your local PC.

1. Go to **C:\Program Files\Ampps\php-7.3** folder. Right-click the file named **php.ini** and select **Open with Code** to open this file in VS Code.

2. In VS Code, press **ctrl+f** and type **mail function** in the find box (A) to locate this entry in the php.ini file. In the *mail function* section set SMTP address (B), which is provided by your ISP (Internet Service Provider). Type your email address next to the *sendmail_from* parameter (C). If there are semi colons before these parameters, remove them.

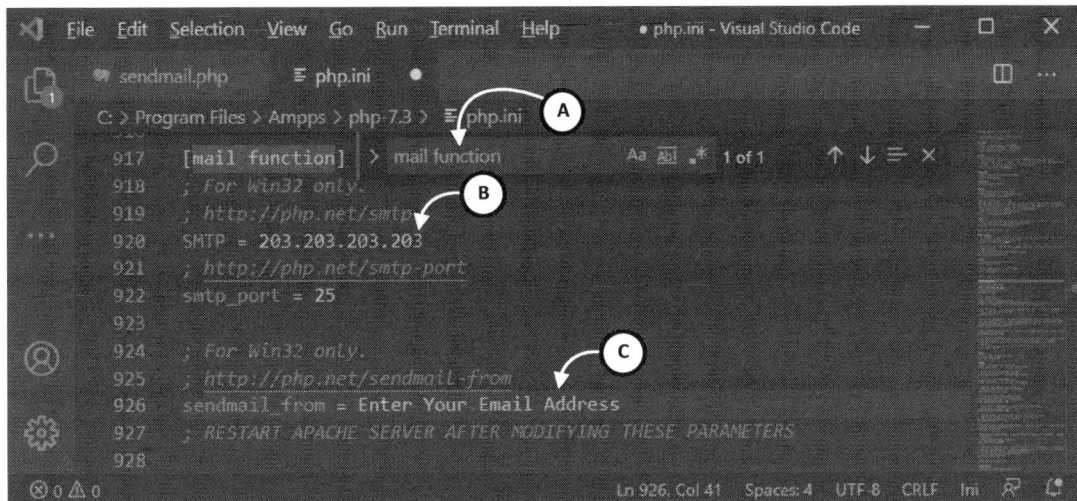

Figure 5-12

3. Press **ctrl + s** to save the configurations.

4. Restart Apache server (C) – turn the switch off and then back on.

Figure 5-13

5. In VS Code, press **ctrl + n**, and type the following code to send a test email. I saved this file as **sendmail.php** in C:*Program Files\Ampps\www* folder.

SendMail.php

```html
<html>
  <head>
    <title>Sending Test Email</title>
  </head>
  <body>
    <?php
      function sanitize_email($recipient_email) {
        $recipient_email = filter_var($recipient_email, FILTER_SANITIZE_EMAIL);
        if (filter_var($recipient_email, FILTER_VALIDATE_EMAIL)) {
          return true;
        } else {
          return false;
        }
      }
      $to = "Recipient email address";
      $subject = "This is a test email sent using PHP script";

      $message = "<b>Hello! This is HTML message.</b>";
      $message .= "<h1>This is headline.</h1>";

      $header = "From:Your email address \r\n";
```

```
      $header .= "Cc:techies@gmail.com \r\n";
      $header .= "MIME-Version: 1.0\r\n";
      $header .= "Content-type: text/html\r\n";

      $valid_email = sanitize_email($to);
      if ($valid_email == false) {
        echo "Invalid input - message not sent";
      } else { //send email
        mail($to, $subject, $message, $header);
        echo "Message sent successfully!";
      }
    ?>
  </body>
</html>
```

6. Open a browser session and type **http://localhost/sendmail.php**. If followed all the steps in order, you'll see *Message sent successfully*. You can check the "to" email account which should receive a message as shown in the following illustration.

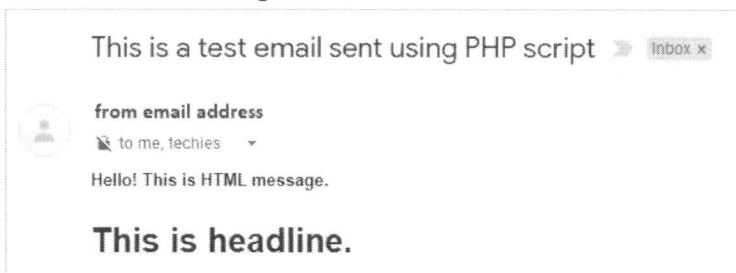

Figure 5-14

Users can accidently or intentionally inject code in the headers which can result in sending spam mails. To prevent such mishaps, we added a custom function (sanitize_email) that sanitizes and validates the values before sending the email using the *filter_var* built in function.

filter_var() is the validation and sanitization function.

$recipient_email is the value to be sanitized.

FILTER_SANITIZE_EMAIL removes illegal characters from email addresses. admin/@abc.{com) returns *admin@abc.com*.

FILTER_VALIDATE_EMAIL returns true for valid email addresses and false for invalid email addresses.

FILTER_SANITIZE_URL removes illegal characters from URLs. https://www.abc@.comé returns *https://www.abc.com*

FILTER_SANITIZE_STRING removes tags from string values. bold faced text becomes *bold faced text*.

All the examples till now warmed you up for the next and final part of the book where you will undergo a web site project for ABC Global Consulting company and will apply most of the techniques you learned throughout the previous chapters. In that project you will create a Contact Form, a Newsletter subscription module and an E-Commerce module.

CHAPTER 6

E-COMMERCE WEBSITE PROJECT

Project's Introduction

You've landed to the most interesting part of this book. Here, you'll create a professional website for ABC Global Consulting and will apply the techniques you've learned so far. The project is divided into two categories:

Dynamic
Dynamic web pages are generated at the time of access by a user or change as a result of interaction with the user. These pages can give the website owner the ability to simply update and add new content to the site. For example, news and events could be posted to the site through a simple browser interface. Dynamic features of a site are only limited by imagination. Some examples of dynamic website features could be: content management system, e-commerce system, bulletin / discussion boards, intranet or extranet facilities, ability for clients or users to upload documents, ability for administrators or users to create content or add information to a site. In this part of the book, you'll create an e-commerce system and couple of more interfaces with the help of PHP and MySQL database:

Contact Form - This page is meant to interact with the site visitors. A form will be provided to the visitors of the website to add their comments and feedback. This form will use PHP and MySQL to store the comments in a database table. Besides, it will receive contact details such as e-mail address and other relevant information.

Newsletter Subscription - Using a form site visitors would enter their e-mail address to subscribe to company's newsletters. This form will appear in the footer of every website page. A process will be created with the help of PHP and MySQL to interact with site visitors.

Admin Interface – As just mentioned, you'll create an e-commerce prototype application that will comprise admin and members sections. The admin section will be accessible only to the site administrators who will use this interface to manage tasks such as products and orders management.

Members Interface - This module will allow end users to become site members and will allow them to view and purchase products from the website.

Static
A static web page is a page that is delivered to the user exactly as stored. An obvious example of a static page is an old style HTML document which can only be changed by uploading a new or updated version. Every time a static file is viewed, the file contents that are sent to the browser are the same for everyone who access that file. In this project the you'll be taught to create the following static pages:

Index.php - This is the Home page of our website. Everyone who visits the website will be greeted by this page.

Header_Admin.php - This page will contain static HTML and PHP code to display company name, logo, sign-in link, and main navigation menu for site administrators.

Header_Member.php – Just like header_admin.php file, this file will show similar content with a specific navigation menu for site members, which is different from the admin navigation menu.

Footer.php – The content in this file will display company and contact information on every website page. Additionally, it will display a newsletter subscription form that will allow visitors to subscribe to company's newsletters.

STATIC VS DYNAMIC

When you create a normal web page with HTML and CSS, all the content is fixed by the webmaster. Everyone who visits the page sees the same content—it's static.

By contrast, the content of a dynamic web page frequently changes. For example, the Products page in our project would displays three most recent products (marked as featured products) from the database. When a new item is added to the database, the PHP code in the page automatically displays it. Whenever this page is called, the content changes to display a list of newly added featured products. The code in the page controls the content depending on the request it receives from the browser.

Website Security

A web site designed, built, and deployed with security as a prime feature is more robust than one deployed with security features added as an afterthought. However, as web sites become more complex, it also becomes more difficult to make them secure. Security cannot be achieved by setting a few particular properties, or using a specific tool; instead you must take a holistic approach and address security in all stages of site planning, development, and deployment. People just consider the job is done once the website is up. It definitely is not. There are no point and click software available to secure a website. Protecting a website or web server is possible only by continued efforts. Unlike a poorly protected desktop in your place of business, a hacked website will reflect poorly on you, your business or brand. There may not be *fit it and forget* solutions for protecting a website in a world where threats emit constantly. But there are always some time tested fundamental ground work that should be done to get the first line of defense up while figuring out a detailed security plan. This section is aimed at detailing some basic proactive security considerations that can help you lay the foundation for your site security.

Use a Secure Connection

If you web application receives sensitive data such as credit card number or passwords from visitors, you must use a secure connection to transmit data. Failing to do so may allow hackers or other malicious minds to intercept and view this data. Regular HTTP connections send data in plain text and are not suitable for sites like online stores or e-commerce websites. For such sites, you should consider HTTPS (HyperText Transfer Protocol with Secure Sockets Layer). HTTPS is a protocol to transfer encrypted data over the Web. Although hackers can still intercept this data, they cannot read it unless they break the encryption code. Most web customers know that they should look for the https in the URL and the lock icon in their browser when they are making a transaction. So if your storefront is not using HTTPS, you will lose customers.

NOTE

It is possible to run your entire web site on https, but it slows down the connection. You should only secure those pages that request and collect data.

🔒 https://kdp.amazon.com/

What is SSL Certificate?

An SSL Certificate (Secure Sockets Layer), also called a Digital Certificate, creates a secure link between a website and a visitor's browser. With SSL, the browser encrypts all data that's sent to the server and decrypts all data that's received from the server. Similarly, the server encrypts all data that's sent to the browser and decrypts all data that's received from the browser. By ensuring that all data passed between the two remains private and secure, SSL encryption prevents hackers from stealing private information. SSL can also determine if data has been tampered with during transit and can also verify both client and server. Another new protocol that is used by the Internet for secured connection is Transport Layer Security (TLS). A successor to SSL, TLS is supported only by latest browsers.

Before establishing a secure connection, the server uses SSL server authentication to authenticate itself by providing a digital secure certificate to the browser. The browser accepts the certificate and a secure connection is established.

A digital secure certificate can be purchased from certification authorities (CA) like VeriSign, Thawte, Instantssl, Entrust etc. These authorities verify with a registration authority the validity of the company or person requesting the certificate. To obtain the certificate, you provide the name of a registration authority (RA) with your company information. After approval from RA, the CA issues a certificate. Once you get the certificate, provide it to your hosting provider who will set up the certificate in your web server so that every time a page is accessed via the https protocol, it hits the secure server. Once that is set up, you can start building your web pages that need to be secure.

Use Authentication

Authentication is the process of identifying an individual, usually based on a user id and password. In a web application, you can implement authentication to some or all of the web pages to allow access only to authorized users. Form-based authentication in the most common type of authentication where a web form is presented to the user to get his/her id and password. To prevent hackers from intercepting this sensitive information, a secure connection is used along with an encryption algorithm to send the information to the server. You'll follow this approach in the final chapter where you will create a website project.

Encrypting Password

In this project you'll store userid and password in a database table. Following the best practice method, you'll encrypt the data before storing it in the database. That way, if a hacker gains access to the database, he will not be able to easily read the password.

THE BOTTOM LINE TO SECURE YOUR WEBSITE

You should consider the following points in order to host your website in a secured environment:

- *A web server such as Apache with mod_ssl that supports SSL encryption*
- *A Unique IP address - this is what the certificate providers use to validate the secure certificate*
- *An SSL Certificate from an SSL certificate provider*

Build Website's Static Pages

Taking the simple route first, you'll build the static page of your project in this section. While creating this web page, you'll apply the skills learned in earlier parts of this book with the addition of some more useful stuff.

General Steps:

1. If not yet done, download the book's code from the url provided in the About This Book section at the beginning of this book.
2. Extract this file in a folder using WinRAR or WinZIP utilities. I extracted it in c:\bookcode and will refer to this folder as 'source' in subsequent sections.
3. Create a folder named ABCGLOBAL under C:\Program Files\Ampps\www\. This folder will be referred to as 'site folder'.
4. Copy css, images, model, utility, and view folders from source\project to C:\Program Files\Ampps\www\abcglobal.

The Home Page

Usually a site is visited by typing its URL without specifying a file name like: *www.abcglobal.com*. Every web server needs a file in order to serve a website. This file is called the default file. On most Web servers, this default file is named "Index.php". What this means is that when you go to a URL without a file named at the end, the server looks for a default file and displays that automatically. Just as if you had typed in that file name in the URL:

http://www.abcglobal.com/Index.php.

When you start building your website, you should create your main page and name it Index.php. That way, when people come to your website, they automatically get your main page.

In this project our home page (shown in the figure below) is named Index.php. This will be the initial page that will come up when a visitor enters website's url (www.abcglobal.com) in a browser. Let's begin the project by creating the home page of the website.

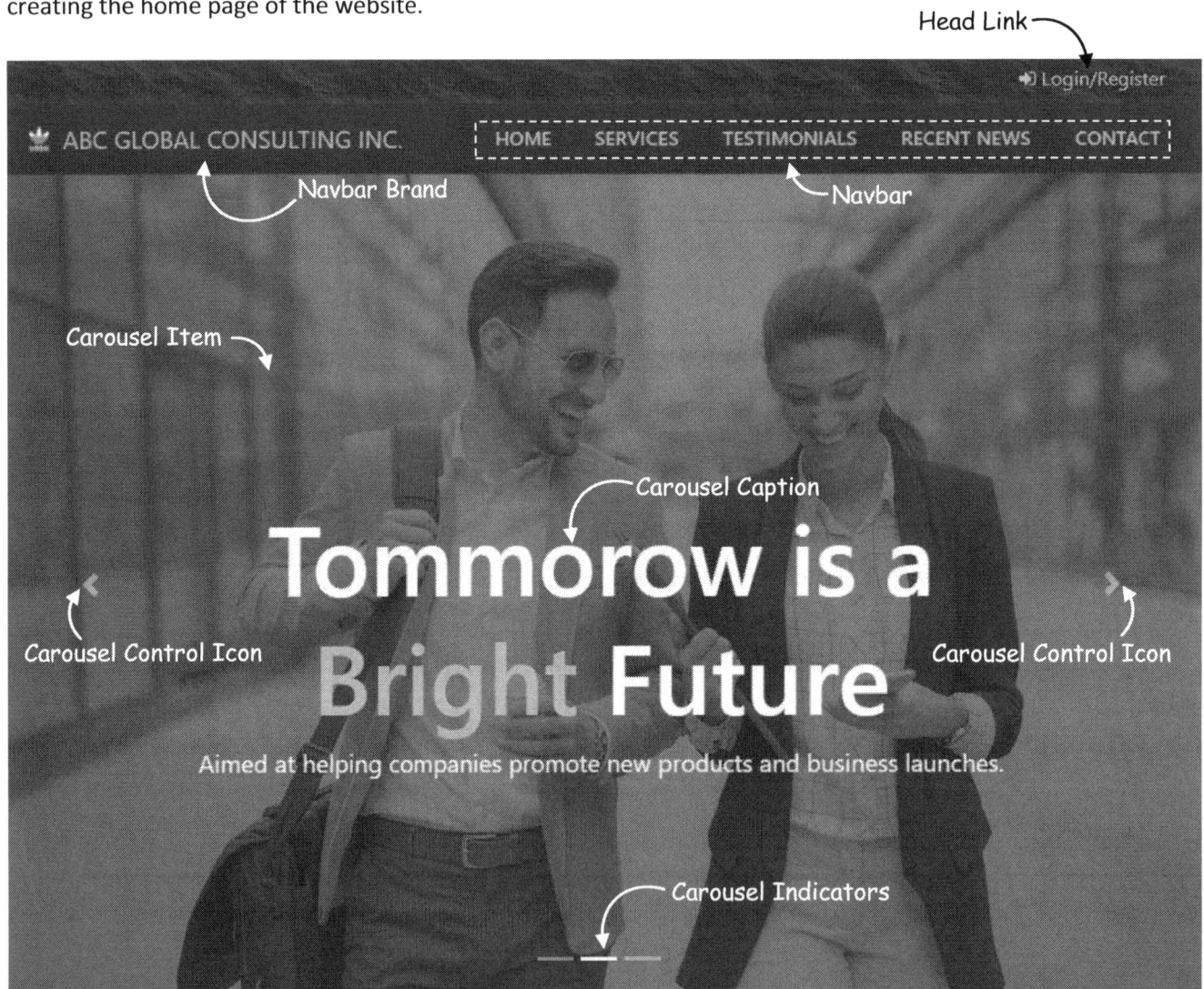

Figure 6-1 - The Home Page

Since you are building and testing this website on your own PC, you'll type *http://localhost/abcglobal/Index.php*, or simply, *http://localhost/abcglobal* in your preferred browser.

1. From source\project folder, copy **Index.php** to the site folder. Make sure the site folder contains the css, images, model, utility, and view folders that we copied in the previous section.
2. Open up your browser and type *http://localhost/abcglobal/Index.php* in the address bar and hit Enter. You'll see an un-organized website whose content will be scattered from top to bottom. Why is it so? It's just because we didn't specify any style to this page and that's what we're going to do next.
3. Copy Style.css file from source\project to the site folder (abcglobal) and run Index.php again. Now you'll see the page similar to figure 6-1.

Let's dig deeper and see how this page was built and how did the CSS file give it a professional look. To understand the whole process, first you'll see HTML and PHP code from Index.php, Header_Member.php, and Navbar.php files and then we'll move on to Style.css to check how the rules specified in this file work. You can open all these files by right-clicking on them and selecting *Open with Code (i.e. Visual Studio Code)* from the context menu.

Index.php

```php
<?php
    require_once('utility/Main.php');
    include 'view/Header_Member.php';
?>
```

The initial PHP code in Index.php file makes a call to Main.php file (stored in the Utility folder) and Header_Member.php file (stored in View folder). The Main.php file is discussed in a later section. The rest of the code in Index.php file is also discussed ahead according to the program flow.

Header_Member.php

```
<!DOCTYPE html>
```

Each web page begins with a DOCTYPE declaration which informs the browser about the HTML version the page is using. This line defines the document type and is a declaration for the latest HTML5 generation. This is not an HTML tag. It is an "information" to the browser about what document type to expect.

```html
<html lang="en">       <!-- The tag terminates in Footer.php file -->
```

This is the starting html tag. The HTML *lang* attribute is used to identify the language of text content on the web. This information helps search engines return language specific results, and it is also used by screen readers that switch language profiles to provide the correct accent and pronunciation. The following css rule is defined for this element in Style.css file, which allows a smooth animated scroll effect. The *scroll-behavior* property specifies whether to smoothly animate the scroll position, instead of a straight jump, when the user clicks on a link – for example, a link in the main navigation menu.

CSS Rule

```css
html { scroll-behavior: smooth; }
```

\<head\>
The starting head tag.

\<title\>ABC Global Consulting Inc.\</title\>
Title tag displays page title in the browser.

\<link rel="stylesheet" href="\<?php echo $app_path ?\>Style.css"\>
Referencing the external style sheet file (Style.css) used for this page. All the rules specified in Style.css file will be explained individually during the development process of each web page. The $app_path variable holds the root folder name – ABCGLOBAL. This variable is initialized in Main.php file and is discussed later.

\<link rel="stylesheet" href="\<?php echo $app_path ?\>css/Bootstrap.css"\>
Reference to the Bootstrap.css file placed under the css folder. Bootstrap is a popular CSS framework of prewritten stylesheets. In this book you will use this framework to design layouts over a 12-column grid system.

\<link rel="stylesheet" href="https://stackpath.bootstrapcdn.com/font-awesome/4.7.0/css/font-awesome.min.css"\>
Font Awesome is a font and icon toolkit based on CSS. Font Awesome has a PRO edition, and a FREE edition with more than 1500 icons. In this book we will use the FREE edition using this single line Font Awesome CDN code, which is the easiest way to get Font Awesome icons in our project. CDN is a public content delivery network. It enables users to load CSS, JavaScript and images remotely from its servers. StackPath's global content delivery network makes websites using its service resilient to unexpected surges in web traffic.

\<meta charset="utf-8"\>
\<meta name="viewport" content="width=device-width, initial-scale=1, shrink-to-fit=no"\>
The \<meta\> tag defines metadata about an HTML document. These tags always go inside the \<head\> element, and are typically used to specify character set, page description, keywords, author of the document, and viewport settings. To display an HTML page correctly, a web browser must know which character set to use. The *charset* attribute is used to serve this purpose. It specifies the character encoding for the HTML document. The default character set for HTML5 is UTF-8, which covers almost all of the characters and symbols in the world. The *viewport* meta information sets the viewport of your page, which will give the browser instructions on how to control the page's dimensions and scaling.

\</head\>
The ending head tag.

\<body\>   *\<!-- The tag terminates in Footer.php file --\>*
The starting body tag. The \<body\> element is styled using the following css rules. We set a background image, background-color (if the background image fails to load), font properties, and link hover effects that will be applied to every page in the website.

CSS Rules

```css
body {
    background-image: url(images/bg-pattern.jpg);
    margin: 0;
    font-family: Objective, sans-serif;
    font-size: .9375rem;
    font-weight: 400;
    line-height: 1.75;
    color: white !important;
    text-align: left;
    background-color: #252525 !important;
}
```

```css
body a {
    color: #c3c3c3 !important;
    text-decoration: none;
}


body a:hover {
    color: #ffc107 !important;
    text-decoration: none;
}
```

```php
<?php
    $member_url = $app_path . 'member';
    $logout_url = $member_url . '?action=logout';
    if (isset($_SESSION['user'])) :
?>
```

This embedded PHP code checks whether site member is logged in. The first line of this code stores *abcglobal/member* in the $member_url variable to point to the member folder that we will create in a subsequent section to handle the Member module. The next line stores *abcglobal/member?action=logout* in the $logout_url variable. This value will enable users to logout. The next line checks whether the user is logged in. If the condition is true, then the following <div> displays the name of the logged in user with a logout link. The isset() PHP function determines whether a certain variable has already been set. It returns a boolean value true if the variable has already been set, or false otherwise. Here, the IF condition checks whether the built-in $_SESSION array carries the value 'user' (this value is set in $_SESSION when a user successfully logs into the website). Note that in the previous chapter we used curly-brace-style IF conditions, and here we use the colon-style IF that terminates with ENDIF and is more visible than an ending curly brace.

```
<div class="row mr-0 mt-n2 mb-n2">
  <div class="col-md-12">
    <div id="headlinks">
      <p>
        <span class="fa fa-user"></span><b><?php echo ' Hi, ' . $_SESSION['user'][1] . ' ' .
                                        $_SESSION['user'][2].'!'; ?></b>
          <a href="<?php echo $logout_url; ?>"><span class="fa fa-sign-out">Logout</a>
      </p>
    </div>
  </div>
</div>
```

This <div> displays first and last names of the logged in user using 2nd and 3rd elements in the $_SESSION global variable along with the Logout link. The main <div> utilizes bootstrap row class to set right (mr), top (mt), and bottom (mb) margins. We added a font awesome icon (fa fa-user) just before the greeting message. When the Logout link is clicked, the program flow is switched to abcglobal/member/Index.php file with the *logout* POST action to unset *user* information from the $_SESSION global variable.

```
<?php else: ?>
  <div class="row mr-0 mt-n2 mb-n2">
    <div class="col-md-12">
      <div id="headlinks">
        <p>
          <a href="<?php echo $member_url; ?>"><span class="fa fa-sign-in"></span> Login/Register</a>
        </p>
      </div>
    </div>
  </div>
<?php endif; ?>
```

This <div> is enclosed in PHP ELSE block. It displays Login/Register link with a sign-in icon if the user is not logged in. Note that at this stage clicking this link will throw *Not Found – 404* message due to absence of the required module. The two *headlinks* divs are styled using the following css rule.

CSS Rule
#headlinks {
color: rgb(197, 197, 197); /*The link in displayed in light gray color*/
float: right; /*Floats the element from the right side*/
margin-top: 15px;
margin-right: 10px;
}

```
<?php require_once('view/navbar.php'); ?>
```
This PHP code makes a call to the following Navbar.php file in the View folder to display main navigation menu for site members just under the Login/Register link specified above.

Navbar.php

```
<div id="nav-bar" (1) >
   <nav class="navbar (2) navbar-expand-lg (3) navbar-dark (4)">
     <a class="navbar-brand" (5) href="#">
        <!-- /abcglobal/images/logo.png -->
        <img src="<?php echo $app_path . 'images/' ?>logo.png" width="30" height="30"
          class="d-inline-block align-top" alt=""> ABC Global Consulting Inc.
     </a>
     <!-- Links -->
     <button class="navbar-toggler" (6) type="button" data-toggle="collapse" (7)
        data-target="#navbarNav" (8) aria-controls="navbarNav" aria-expanded="false"
        aria-label="Toggle navigation">
        <span class="navbar-toggler-icon"></span>
     </button>
     <div class="collapse (10) navbar-collapse" id="navbarNav" (9)>
        <ul class="navbar-nav ml-auto">
           <li class="nav-item active">
              <!-- calls abcglobal/Index.php -->
              <a class="nav-link" href="<?php echo $app_path ?>Index.php">Home</a>
           </li>
           <li class="nav-item">
              <!-- Scrolls down to the Services section -->
              <a class="nav-link" href="#services">Services</a>
           </li>
           <li class="nav-item">
              <!-- Scrolls down to the Testimonials section -->
              <a class="nav-link" href="#testimonials">Testimonials</a>
           </li>
           <li class="nav-item">
              <!-- Scrolls down to the Recent News section -->
              <a class="nav-link" href="#news">Recent News</a>
           </li>
           <li class="nav-item">
              <!-- Scrolls down to the Contact section -->
              <a class="nav-link" href="#crsl">Contact</a>
           </li>
        </ul>
     </div>
   </nav>
</div>
```

CSS Rules

```
#nav-bar {
    position: sticky;
    background-image: url(images/bg-info.jpg);
    z-index: 100;
    top: 0;
    filter: drop-shadow(10px 10px 10px grey);
    left: 0;
    width: 100%;
    text-transform: uppercase;
}
```

```
/* Rules for Navigation Menu Unordered List items */
.navbar-nav li {
    padding: 0 10px;
}

.navbar-nav li a {
    font-weight: 500;
    float: right;
    text-align: left;
}

.navbar-toggler {
    outline: none;
}
```

The Navbar.php file uses HTML <nav> tag and bootstrap navbar classes to create and style the member's navigation menu. The main <div> is provided with an id named *nav-bar* (1). A single CSS rule for this <div> element is created to set custom attributes. For example, the sticky position will make the menu visible all the time, while the z-index property will place it on top of all other page elements. The background-image property sets a background for the menu. We also applied a shadow around the menu. The menu utilizes 100% screen width. The Bootstrap's *navbar* class (2) controls the display of this navigation menu. The *navbar-expand-lg* class (3) displays the menu only on large (lg) screens. To add a white text color to all links in the navbar, we used the *navbar-dark* class (4). Using the *navbar-brand* class (5) we added a logo from the Images folder to the main navigation menu. Next, we added a <button> with *navbar-toggler* class (6) that presents the button as hamburger icon on small screens. The *data-toggle="collapse"* (7) and *data-target* (8) attributes are added to the button class to automatically assign control of the <div> element *navbarNav* (9) that contains the navigation menu. The *data-target* attribute accepts a CSS selector (in this case navbarNav) to apply the collapse to. Be sure to also add the *collapse* (10) class to the collapsible element, which in this case is the navbarNav <div>. Accessible Rich Internet Applications (ARIA) defines ways to make Web content and Web applications more accessible to people with disabilities. Dynamic content on a web page can be particularly problematic for users who, for whatever reason, are unable to view the screen. Stock tickers, live twitter feed updates, progress indicators, and similar content modify the DOM in ways that an assistive technology (AT) may not be aware of. That's where ARIA comes in. After delivering the menu on your screen, the program flow is returned to Header_Member.php file that switches the flow back to the following code in Index.php file.

The Home Section – Index.php

```
<div id="home">
  <div id="carouselIndicators" class="carousel slide" data-ride="carousel" data-pause="hover">
    <!-- Slide Indicators -->
    <ol class="carousel-indicators">
      <li data-target="#carouselIndicators" data-slide-to="0" class="active"></li>
      <li data-target="#carouselIndicators" data-slide-to="1"></li>
      <li data-target="#carouselIndicators" data-slide-to="2"></li>
    </ol>
    <!-- Slide Show -->
    <div class="carousel-inner">
      <div class="carousel-item active">
        <img src="images/3.jpg" class="d-block w-100" alt="...">
        <div class="bg-overlay"></div>
        <div class="carousel-caption">
          <h1>Tommorow is a<br><span>Bright</span> Future</h1>
          <p>Aimed at helping companies promote new products and business launches.</p>
        </div>
      </div>
      <div class="carousel-item">
        <img src="images/2.jpg" class="d-block w-100" alt="...">
        <div class="bg-overlay"></div>
        <div class="carousel-caption">
          <h1>Tommorow is a<br><span>Bright</span> Future</h1>
          <p>Aimed at helping companies promote new products and business launches.</p>
        </div>
      </div>
      <div class="carousel-item">
        <img src="images/1.jpg" class="d-block w-100" alt="...">
        <div class="bg-overlay"></div>
        <div class="carousel-caption">
          <h1>Tommorow is a<br><span>Bright</span> Future</h1>
          <p>Incline is set of landing and support pages aimed at helping companies.</p>
        </div>
      </div>
    </div>
    <a class="carousel-control-prev" href="#carouselIndicators"
       role="button" data-slide="prev">
      <span class="carousel-control-prev-icon" aria-hidden="true"></span>
      <span class="sr-only">Previous</span>
    </a>
    <a class="carousel-control-next" href="#carouselIndicators"
       role="button" data-slide="next">
      <span class="carousel-control-next-icon" aria-hidden="true"></span>
      <span class="sr-only">Next</span>
    </a>
  </div>
</div>
```

CSS Rules

```
.carousel-caption {
    position: absolute;
    top: 240px;
}


.carousel-caption h1 span {
    color: #ffc107;  (Presents the word "Bright" in yellow)
}


.carousel-caption p {
    font-size: 20px;
}


.carousel-item img {
    max-height: 100vh;
}


.bg-overlay {
    position: absolute;
    top: 0;
    bottom: 0;
    left: 0;
    right: 0;
}
```

```
.bg-overlay::before {
    content: ";
    position: absolute;
    top: 0;
    bottom: 0;
    left: 0;
    right: 0;
    background-color: #212529;
    opacity: .55;
}

/* Rules for small screens */
@media (max-width: 992px) {
    .carousel-indicators li {
        visibility: hidden;   /*Hide Carousel indicators*/
    }
    .carousel-caption {
        top: 30%;          /*Bring caption down*/
    }
    .carousel-caption h1 {
        font-size: 20px;   /*Reduce caption h1 element size*/
    }
    .carousel-caption p {
        font-size: 15px;
    }
}
}
```

After receiving the control back, the first <div> element identified as "home" in Index.php file displays a bootstrap carousel, which creates a slider comprising three images. Carousels require the use of an id (in this case id="carouselIndicators") for carousel controls to function properly. The class="carousel" specifies that this <div> contains a carousel. The data-ride="carousel" attribute tells Bootstrap to begin animating the carousel immediately when the page loads. The data-pause="hover" attribute set in the main carousel <div> pauses the slide show when you rest your mouse on any slide image.

We created three slide indicators using the <ol> and <li> tags and added three <div> elements to show three different images with captions. The slides are specified in a <div> with carousel-inner class. Finally, two <a> tags are added to display previous and next icons that appear on the images for navigation purpose. The carousel-caption and carousel-item classes have their respective rules in Style.css file. The max-height: 100vh rule set for carousel images utilizes 100% of viewport height to display complete image on the screen. If you see the website on your smartphone, the images will also shrink to fit the screen size. Using an image with a dark overlay is the quickest way to make a beautiful hero header. An overlay on an image makes text much more readable. For this purpose, we added a <div> with a class bg-overlay to all three carousel images along with a couple of rules that create a grayish overlay with .55% opacity. We also set top, bottom, left, and right properties that are normally used in conjunction with the Position property to tweak an element. The @media rule is used in css files to apply different styles for different media types/devices. For example, it is used to check width and height of the viewport, orientation (landscape or portrait mode), and resolution. For the Home page, we used it to hide carousel indicators, caption placement, and set size of caption heading and paragraph elements when the screen size dips below 992px, which is the size of smartphones and tabs.

The Services Section – Index.php

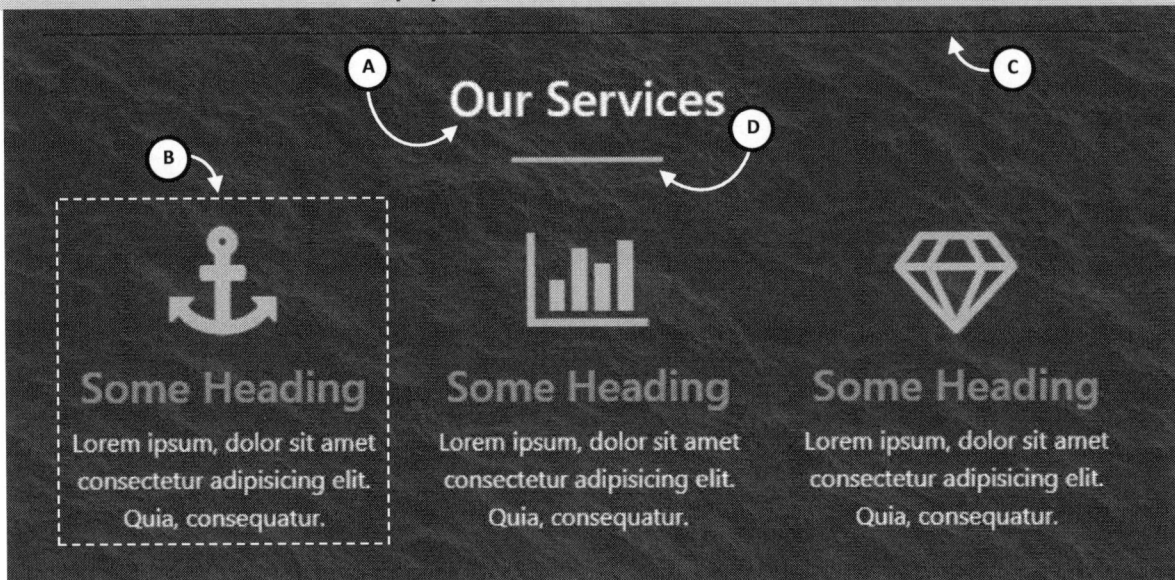

Figure 6-2

```
<div id="services">
    <div class="container section">
        <div class="row">
            <div class="col-md-12">
                <h2 class="section-head">Our Services</h2>          (A)
            </div>
            <div class="col-md-4">
                <div class="service-box">          (B)
                    <i class="fa fa-anchor"></i>
                    <h3>Some Heading</h3>
                    <p>Lorem ipsum, dolor sit amet consectetur adipisicing elit. Quia, consequatur.</p>
                </div>
            </div>
            <div class="col-md-4">
                <div class="service-box">          (B)
                    <i class="fa fa-bar-chart"></i>
                    <h3>Some Heading</h3>
                    <p>Lorem ipsum, dolor sit amet consectetur adipisicing elit. Quia, consequatur.</p>
                </div>
            </div>
            <div class="col-md-4">
                <div class="service-box">          (B)
                    <i class="fa fa-diamond"></i>
                    <h3>Some Heading</h3>
                    <p>Lorem ipsum, dolor sit amet consectetur adipisicing elit. Quia, consequatur.</p>
                </div>
            </div>
        </div>
    </div>
</div>
```

CSS Rules

```css
.service-box {
   color: #fff;
   text-align: center;
   margin-bottom: 30px;
}

/* Rule for font awesome icon*/
.service-box i.fa {
   color: #ffc107;
   font-size: 70px;
   margin-bottom: 15px;
}
```

```css
.section {
   padding-top: 60px;
   padding-bottom: 10px;
   border-top: solid 1px #333;
   box-shadow: #000 0 -1px 0;
   margin: 0 10% 0 10%;
}

.section h2.section-head,
h4.section-head {
   color: rgb(255, 255, 255);
   text-align: center;
   margin-bottom: 40px;
}

.section h2.section-head::after,
h4.section-head::after {
   background: #ffc107;
   content: '';
   display: block;
   width: 100px;
   height: 3px;
   margin: 20px auto;
}
```

After rendering the Home section, the Services section is presented. It utilizes Bootstrap's Container class along with a custom class named Section to style elements in this part of the page. Bootstrap provides a powerful mobile-first twelve column flexbox grid to build layouts. Bootstrap's grid system uses a series of containers, rows, and columns to layout and align content. It's build with flexbox and is fully responsive.

After defining the Bootstrap's container class, we defined the row class. Next, we specified the column class (col-md-12) that will utilize all twelve columns on medium screen. These settings will allow the "Our Services" heading to span 12 columns. The next three child <div> elements utilize 4 columns each (col-md-4) to avail the width of 12 columns grid. The objective of this section is to teach how to display information in three different columns in a 12 columns grid. On small screens these divs will be stacked on top of each other. Try this out by shrinking your browser screen.

The .section css rules are general rules that will apply to other sections on the Home page as well as to elements on other pages in the website. The border-top and box-shadow rules draw a shadowed horizontal line (C) that acts as a section separator. The *::after* selector is used to insert something after the content of an element. Here, we used it to underline section headings (D).

The Testimonials Section – Index.php

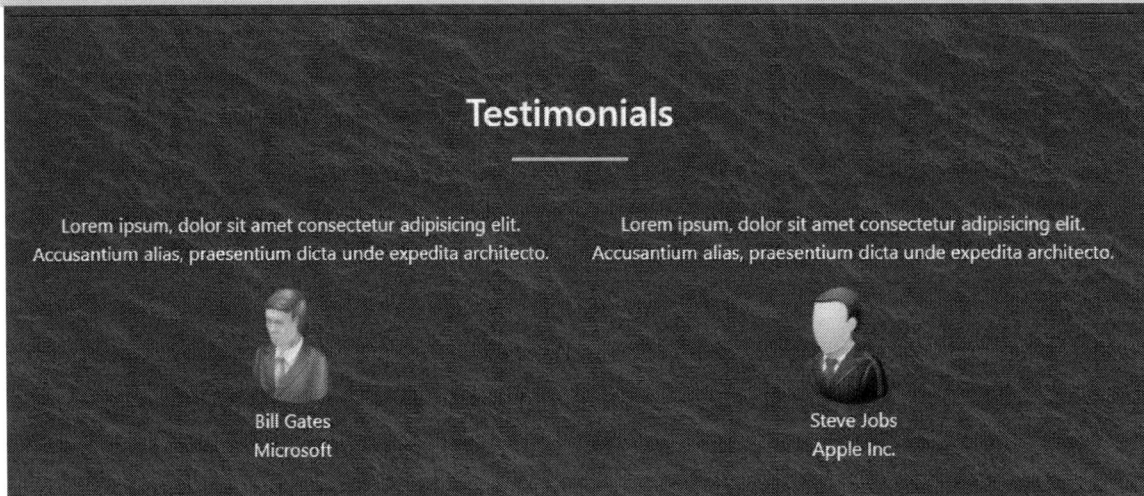

Figure 6-3

```
<div id="testimonials">
    <div class="container section">
        <div class="row">
            <div class="col-md-12">
                <h2 class="section-head">Testimonials</h2>
            </div>
            <div class="col-md-6">
                <div class="testimonial">
                    <p>Lorem ipsum, dolor sit amet consectetur adipisicing elit. Accusantium alias,
                        praesentium dicta unde expedita architecto.</p>
                    <img src="images/bill gates.png" width="100" height="100" alt="">
                    <div>Bill Gates</div>
                    <div>Microsoft</div>
                </div>
            </div>
            <div class="col-md-6">
                <div class="testimonial">
                    <p>Lorem ipsum, dolor sit amet consectetur adipisicing elit. Accusantium alias,
                        praesentium dicta unde expedita architecto.</p>
                    <img src="images/steve jobs.png" width="100" height="100" alt="">
                    <div>Steve Jobs</div>
                    <div>Apple Inc.</div>
                </div>
            </div>
        </div>
    </div>
</div>
```

```
CSS Rule
.testimonial {
    text-align: center;
    margin-bottom: 30px;
}
```

This code is similar to the code defined for the Services section. The objective of this section is to show how to split information in two columns using col-md-6 Bootstrap class, which divides the 12 column grid into half. The two divs under the column class use the same custom *testimonial* class. The only rule defined for this class is used to centrally align the elements in these divs, and to add a bottom margin of 30px.

The Recent News Section – Index.php

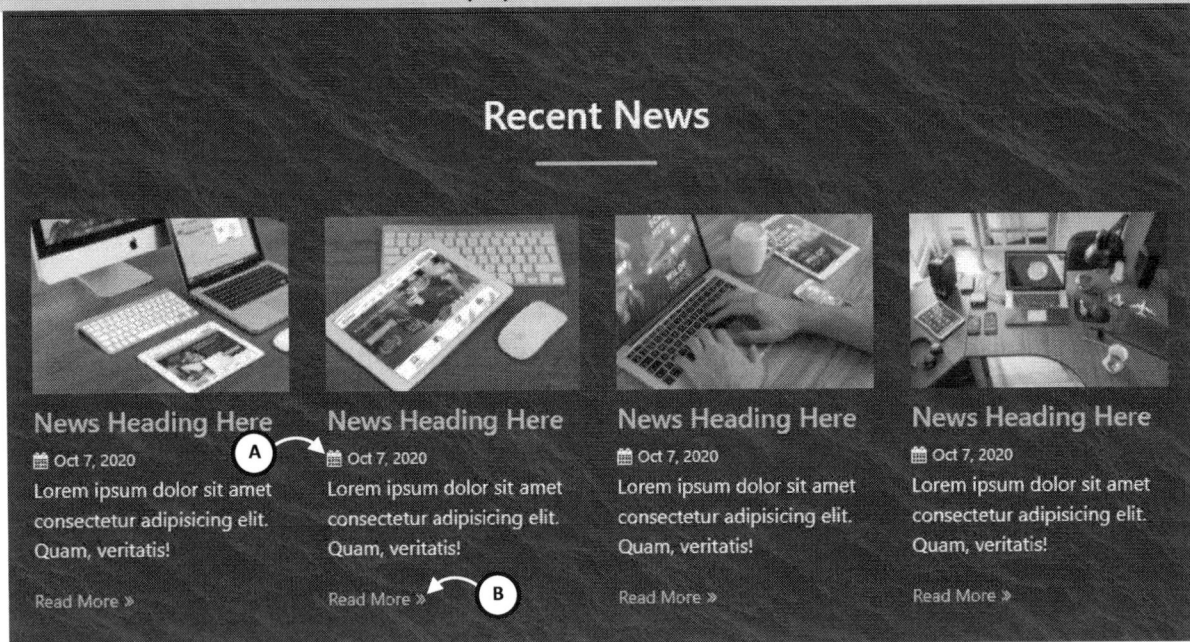

Figure 6-4

```
<div id="news">
    <div class="container section">
      <div class="row">
        <div class="col-12">
          <h2 class="section-head">Recent News</h2>
        </div>
        <div class="col-md-3">
          <div class="news-post">
            <img src="images/pexels-2.jpg" alt="image missing">
            <h3><a href="">News Heading Here</a></h3>
            <div class="post-date">Oct 7, 2020</div>
            <p>Lorem ipsum dolor sit amet consectetur adipisicing elit. Quam, veritatis!</p>
            <a href="" class="readmore">Read More</a>
          </div>
        </div>
        <div class="col-md-3">
          <div class="news-post">
            <img src="images/pexels-3.jpg" alt="image missing">
            <h3><a href="">News Heading Here</a></h3>
            <div class="post-date">Oct 7, 2020</div>
            <p>Lorem ipsum dolor sit amet consectetur adipisicing elit. Quam, veritatis!</p>
            <a href="" class="readmore">Read More</a>
          </div>
        </div>
        <div class="col-md-3">
          <div class="news-post">
            <img src="images/pexels-5.jpg" alt="image missing">
            <h3><a href="">News Heading Here</a></h3>
            <div class="post-date">Oct 7, 2020</div>
```

```
                <p>Lorem ipsum dolor sit amet consectetur adipisicing elit. Quam, veritatis!</p>
                <a href="" class="readmore">Read More</a>
            </div>
        </div>
        <div class="col-md-3">
            <div class="news-post">
                <img src="images/pexels-6.jpg" alt="image missing">
                <h3><a href="">News Heading Here</a></h3>
                <div class="post-date">Oct 7, 2020</div>
                <p>Lorem ipsum dolor sit amet consectetur adipisicing elit. Quam, veritatis!</p>
                <a href="" class="readmore">Read More</a>
            </div>
        </div>
      </div>
    </div>
  </div>
  <!----Display Page Footer---->
  <?php include 'view/Footer.php'; ?>
```

CSS Rules

```css
.news-post {
  color: rgb(255, 255, 255);
  margin-bottom: 30px;
}


.news-post img {
  width: 100%;
  margin-bottom: 10px;
}


.news-post h3 {
  font-size: 1.35rem;
}


.news-post h3 a {
  color: #ffc107;
}
```

```css
.post-date {
  font-size: 13px;
  margin-bottom: 2px;
}


.post-date::before {
  content: "\f073";
  font-family: FontAwesome;
  padding-right: 5px;
}


a.readmore {
  font-size: 14px;
  color: #ffc107;
}


a.readmore::after {
  content: "\f101";
  font-family: FontAwesome;
  padding-left: 5px;
}
```

Just like the previous two sections, the Recent News section also utilizes Bootstrap's container, row, and column structure to display information. This time, it splits the 12 columns grid row into 4 sub-sections using col-md-3 class. In order to provide a consistent look, all the four divs are assigned to the *news-post* custom class. The *::before* selector inserts something before the content of each selected element(s). The *content* property is used to specify the content to insert. The *::before* selector specified in the *post-date* class adds a font awesome calendar icon (f073 - A) via the *content* property. The *::after* selector is used to insert something after the content. We used this selector in the *readmore* class to insert a double arrow font awesome icon (f101 - B) after the Readmore text. The last line in Index.php file calls Footer.php file in the View folder to display page footer that is discussed next.

The Footer Section – Footer.php

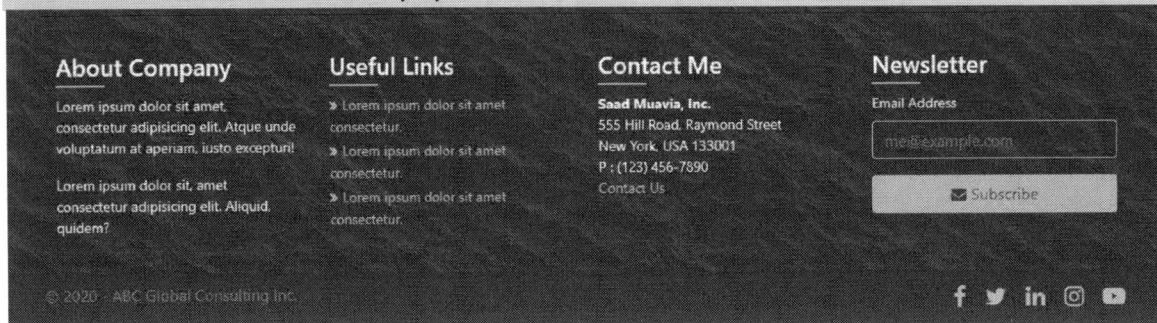

Figure 6-5

```
<!----Company/Contact Info---->
    <div class="info">
      <div class="container">
        <div class="row">
          <div class="col-md-3">
            <div class="info-widget">
              <h4>About Company</h4>
              <p>Lorem ipsum dolor sit amet, consectetur adipisicing elit. Atque unde voluptatum at aperiam,
                 iusto excepturi!</p>
              <p>Lorem ipsum dolor sit, amet consectetur adipisicing elit. Aliquid, quidem?</p>
            </div>
          </div>

          <div class="col-md-3">
            <div class="info-widget">
              <h4>Useful Links</h4>
              <ul class="latest-news">
                <li><a href="">Lorem ipsum dolor sit amet consectetur.</a></li>
                <li><a href="">Lorem ipsum dolor sit amet consectetur.</a></li>
                <li><a href="">Lorem ipsum dolor sit amet consectetur.</a></li>
              </ul>
            </div>
          </div>

          <div class="col-md-3">
            <div class="info-widget">
              <h4>Contact Me</h4>
              <address>
                <b>Saad Muavia, Inc.</b><br>
                555 Hill Road, Raymond Street<br>
                New York, USA 133001<br>
                P : (123) 456-7890
                <p> <a href="contact_form.php">Contact Us</a> </p>
              </address>
            </div>
          </div>
```

```html
        <div class="col-md-3">
          <div class="info-widget">
            <h4>Newsletter</h4>
            <form action="<?php echo $app_path; ?>subscribe.php" method="post">
              <div class="form-group">          <!-- A Bootstrap class to wrap labels and form controls -->
                <label>Email Address</label>
                <input type="email" maxlength="35" size="35" name="subemail" required="vital"
                        placeholder="me@example.com" class="form-control">
              </div>
              <button class="btn btn-warning btn-block"><span class="fa fa-envelope"></span>
                Subscribe</button>
            </form>
          </div>
        </div>
      </div>
    </div>
  </div>
</div>
```

> Bootstrap includes the following predefined button styles. In this section of the page we used btn and btn-warning classes to show the button in yellow. We also added btn-block class to create block level button. A block level button spans the entire width of the parent element.
>
> Primary   Secondary   Success   Danger   Warning   Info   Light   Dark   Link

```html
<!----Copyright & Social Links---->
<div id="crsl">
  <div class="container">
    <div class="row">
      <div class="col-md-6">
        &copy; <?php echo date("Y"); ?> - ABC Global Consulting Inc.
      </div>
      <div class="col-md-6">
        <ul id="social-icons" class="float-md-right">
          <li>
            <a href="Facebook social link goes here" class="fa fa-facebook"></a>
          </li>
          <li>
            <a href="Twitter social link goes here" class="fa fa-twitter"></a>
          </li>
          <li>
            <a href="Linkedin social link goes here" class="fa fa-linkedin"></a>
          </li>
          <li>
            <a href="Instagram social link goes here" class="fa fa-instagram"></a>
          </li>
          <li>
            <a href="Youtube social link goes here " class="fa fa-youtube-play"></a>
          </li>
        </ul>
      </div>
    </div>
  </div>
</div>
```

```html
    <script src="https://code.jquery.com/jquery-3.5.1.slim.min.js"
        integrity="sha384-DfXdz2htPH0lsSSs5nCTpuj/zy4C+OGpamoFVy38MVBnE+IbbVYUew+OrCXaRkfj"
        crossorigin="anonymous">
    </script>
    <script src="https://cdn.jsdelivr.net/npm/bootstrap@4.5.3/dist/js/bootstrap.bundle.min.js"
        integrity="sha384-ho+j7jyWK8fNQe+A12Hb8AhRq26LrZ/JpcUGGOn+Y7RsweNrtN/tE3MoK7ZeZDyx"
        crossorigin="anonymous">
    </script>
  </body>      <!-- The tag commenced in Header_Member.php file -->
</html>      <!-- The tag commenced in Header_Member.php file -->
```

CSS Rules

```css
.info-widget {
   font-size: 14px;
}

.info-widget h4::after {
   content: '';
   background: #ffc107;
   display: block;
   width: 50px;
   height: 2px;
   margin: 5px 0;
}

.info-widget a {
   color: #fff;
}

.latest-news {
   list-style: none;
   padding: 0;
   margin: 0;
}

.latest-news li {
   margin-bottom: 3px;
}

.latest-news li::before {
   content: "\f101";
   font-family: FontAwesome;
   padding-right: 5px;
}
```

```css
/*----- Copyright & Social Links -----*/
#crsl {
   color: rgb(126, 126, 126);
   padding: 10px 0;
   background-image: url(images/bg-info.jpg);
}

#social-icons {
   list-style: none;
   margin: 0;
   padding: 0;
}

#social-icons li {
   display: inline-block;
   padding-left: 5px;
   margin: 5px;
}

#social-icons li a {
   color: rgb(126, 126, 126);
   font-size: 23px;
}

@media (max-width: 992px) {
   #crsl {
      text-align: center;
   }
}
```

The Footer section is displayed on every page in this project via Footer.php file. To avoid redundancy, the footer code is placed in this separate file and is called from every website page using the code specified in the last section. This section is divided into two divs - *info* and *crsl*. The initial code of this file displays company and contact info. This information is split into four bootstrap columns using col-md-3 class. The fourth column in this section contains a newsletter subscription form. All these four sections are styled using info-widget class in the css file. The second div (crsl) displays copyright and social links. The two JavaScripts cdns control the functionality of carousel slides that we specified in the Home section earlier. Finally, the Body and HTML elements that started in Header_Member.php file are terminated here to complete the document. Right-click anywhere in the Home page in your browser, and select *View page source* from the context menu to see the complete HTML document.

Make the Website Dynamic

In previous sections you completed the static parts of the website. Now it's time to create the dynamic segments using PHP and MySQL. In this part you will enable your website to interact with its visitors by adding the following modules.

Contact Form

All modern websites provide some means of communication with their visitors; a contact form is one of them. You'll be guided to add a contact form to the website so that visitors could input their comments. This data will then be stored in a table named Contact in the MySQL database.

Newsletter Subscription

E-mail newsletters are a very popular way to open a channel of communication with your site visitors. Newsletters provide great benefit of keeping a site's user base up-to-date on the latest news and offerings from an organization. Moreover, they have the potential for turning site visitors into customers. For newsletters to be successful, they have to be easy to subscribe to and—just as importantly—unsubscribe from. Recall that while creating the Home page we added the interface of this module.

E-Commerce Module

Besides consulting services, ABC Global Consulting Inc. also deals in IT related products and intends to sell them through their website. To achieve this task you have to add interactive functionalities to the website. You have to build a products page that will show relevant information (image, description, price etc.) from a database and will allow users to buy those products. But before that, you have to create some modules that will manage administrative tasks such as uploading categories and products information. These modules will be accessible only to the site administrators.

Tasks List

The following table lists the tasks you will be performing in this chapter:

Task	Module	Description
General Tasks		
Task 1	Contact Form	Add contact form to receive visitor's comments and store them in the database.
Task 2	Newsletter Subscription	Allow visitors to subscribe to company's newsletter.
Admin Interface Tasks		
Task 3	Admin Login Module	Create login interface for site administrators.
Task 4	Manage Categories	View, add, update and delete product categories.
Task 5	Manage Products	View, add, update and delete individual products.
Task 6	Manage Orders	View, ship, and delete orders placed by customers.
Task 7	Manage Accounts	Add, update, and delete admin users.
Member Interface Tasks		
Task 8	Member Login Module	Interface for site members.
Task 9	Register New Member	Allow new users to become members.
Task 10	Reset Password	Provides new passwords to site members.
Task 11	Manage Your Account	This page lets users edit their information and review their orders.
Task 12	Featured Products Catalog	This page will be added to the website and will be accessible to all through the *Products* main navigation link. This page will show featured products along with images, short description, and prices.
Task 13	Product Details	This page will provide complete details about a particular product and will have an Add to Cart button.
Task 14	Shopping Cart	Once the member clicks the Add to Cart button, he will be brought to this page to check the cart.
Task 15	Checkout (Confirm Order)	The cart page will contain a checkout link. The module will ask the member to login before placing an order. Once logged in successfully, he or she will proceed to the payment page, which will accept credit card information from the member.
Task 16	Website Deployment	After completion, the website will be deployed on a host server so that the world could access it.

Directory Structure

The table on the next page presents the directory structure for the tasks mentioned above. Each module is stored in a separate directory. For example, Checkout module files are stored in the checkout directory. Member, Catalog, Cart, and Checkout directories hold files for the end users of the web site.

In contrast, administrative modules are stored under the Admin directory. This directory has four sub-directories (Users, Category, Product, and Orders) to manage admin users, categories, products, and orders placed by customers, respectively.

Each directory contains a controller file (Index.php) which is the default file that runs for each directory. This file in turn calls relevant functions and presentation files stored in respective directories. The web site's root directory has a Product.php file that is executed when the user clicks the Products link on the main navigation bar. This file calls Show_Product.php file to display featured products from the database.

The Errors directory contains PHP scripts for displaying application errors, while the Images directory holds all the image files used in the web site. Files in the Model directory provide database functions, whereas the Utility directory carries files that provide parsing, global and session functions. The View directory contains files (header, footer, sidebar etc.) that are used by all modules to provide a consistent look.

This directory structure is ideal to maintain and enhance a web site. For instance, if you decide to use two different headers, one for the end user and one for the administrators, you just add a new header file to the View directory and modify the files that use it. You will create separate headers for admin and end users to display separate navigation bar. Similarly, if you wish to change something in the cart module, you can go to the Cart directory that contains all relevant files to this module. The following illustration presents a general PHP process pattern called MVC (Model, View, and Controller).

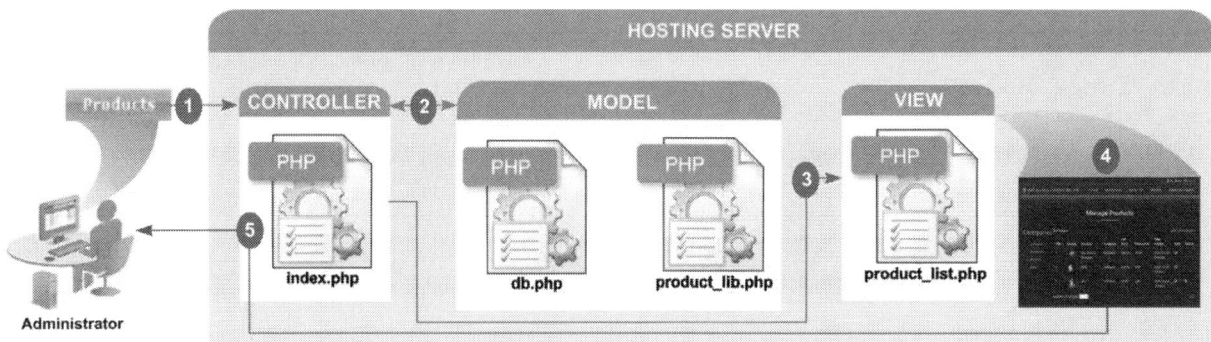

Figure 6-6

In this example, the process initiates when an administrator clicks the Products link on the main navigation bar. The flow is received by the controller - Index.php file (1). Then, the controller gets appropriate data from the model (2). The model connects to the database and fetches data through various functions. For instance, here the administrator requested for products data. So, a file named Product_Lib.php is called to fetch products information. After receiving the information, the controller calls a file (Product_List.php) from the view layer (3). This file contains HTML and PHP code to render the list of products (4). The products list is then presented to the administrator through the controller (5).

Directory	Sub-Directory	PHP Files
ABCGLOBAL (root)	-	Index.php contact.php, contact_form.php, success.php, subscribe.php, confirm_subscribe.php, products.php, show_product.php,
Admin		Index.php
	Category	Index.php, category_list.php
	Orders	Index.php, order.php, order_delete.php, order_status.php
	Product	Index.php, product_add_edit.php, product_list.php, product_view.php
	Users	Index.php, admin_delete.php, admin_edit.php, admin_login.php, admin_view.php
CSS	-	Bootstrap framework files
Cart	-	Index.php, cart_view.php
Catalog	-	Index.php, category_view.php, product_view.php
Checkout	-	Index.php, checkout_confirm.php, checkout_payment.php
Errors	-	db_error_connect.php, error.php, member_db_connect_error.php, member_error.php
Images	-	All images used in the website
Member	-	Index.php, member_address.php, member_edit.php, member_login.php, member_orders.php, member_password.php, member_pw_sent.php, member_register.php, member_view.php
Model	-	address_lib.php, admin_lib.php, cart.php, category_lib.php, db.php, member_lib.php, order_lib.php, product_lib.php
Utility	-	check_admin.php, images.php, main.php, secure.php, tags.php, validation.php
View	-	footer.php, header_admin.php, header_member.php, navbar.php, navbar_admin.php, product.php, sidebar_admin.php, sidebar_member.php

The Controller File (Index.php)

Before commencing the project, it is important to get some know how about the function of controller files. As pointed out in the previous section, Index.php exist under all module directories. The main purpose of this file is to control the process of a module it represents. The directory structure you saw in the previous section contains several directories that basically fall under the following two categories:

Main Module Folders

These are the directories that hold php files to process a specific segment of the project. For example, the Cart directory carries couple of files to control the process of shopping cart module. Other main folders in this category are: Admin, Member, Catalog, and Checkout. The Admin folder has four child folders and each one of them takes care of individual admin task.

Subordinate Folders

This category has Errors, Images, Model, Utility, and View directories. All these five directories assist the files in the main directories, mentioned above, in several different ways. For instance, files in the Errors directory handle errors and display appropriate message whenever an error is encountered while executing a task through the main module.

Each main module folder has a controller file that calls files listed under the subordinate folders to achieve some tasks, and all the controller files have more or less the same structure as illustrated in the figure presented on the next page.

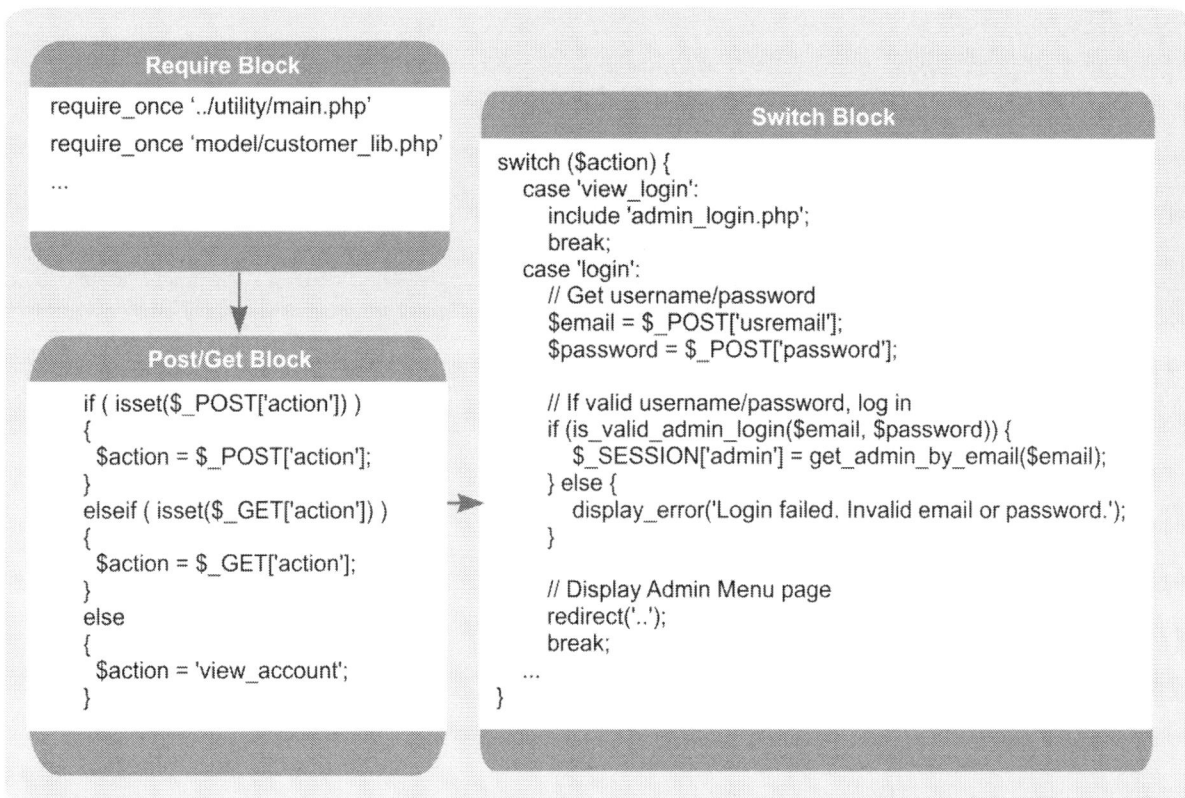

Require Block
```
require_once '../utility/main.php'
require_once 'model/customer_lib.php'
...
```

Post/Get Block
```
if ( isset($_POST['action']) )
{
  $action = $_POST['action'];
}
elseif ( isset($_GET['action']) )
{
  $action = $_GET['action'];
}
else
{
  $action = 'view_account';
}
```

Switch Block
```
switch ($action) {
    case 'view_login':
        include 'admin_login.php';
        break;
    case 'login':
        // Get username/password
        $email = $_POST['usremail'];
        $password = $_POST['password'];

        // If valid username/password, log in
        if (is_valid_admin_login($email, $password)) {
            $_SESSION['admin'] = get_admin_by_email($email);
        } else {
            display_error('Login failed. Invalid email or password.');
        }

        // Display Admin Menu page
        redirect('..');
        break;
    ...
}
```

Figure 6-7

As the illustration depicts, every controller file has three blocks: Require, Post/Get, and Switch.

The Require block includes several files from the subordinate directories to perform a job. For example, every controller file includes Main.php file. This file is responsible to prepare the environment by setting some global variables and database connection.

The second block is a conditional block which evaluates whether the received request is either POST or GET. A request is sent to the controller through a parameter defined as 'action' and holds a value which indicates which action to perform. The block also has a default ELSE statement which executes if the request is neither POST nor GET.

The final block evaluates the received request using several Case statements sorted under the main Switch statement. Each case is assessed based on the received request stored in a variable $action. The Switch statement in php is similar to the one you saw in JavaScript chapter. When a case match is found, statements under that case are executed. Just like the second block, this one also has a default case that executes when no case is satisfied. You'll go through almost all the controller files in this project individually while performing a particular task.

Database Structure

To accomplish the above tasks, you need to create the following tables in the MySQL database to store information. You'll be guided on how to create these tables in the MySQL database.

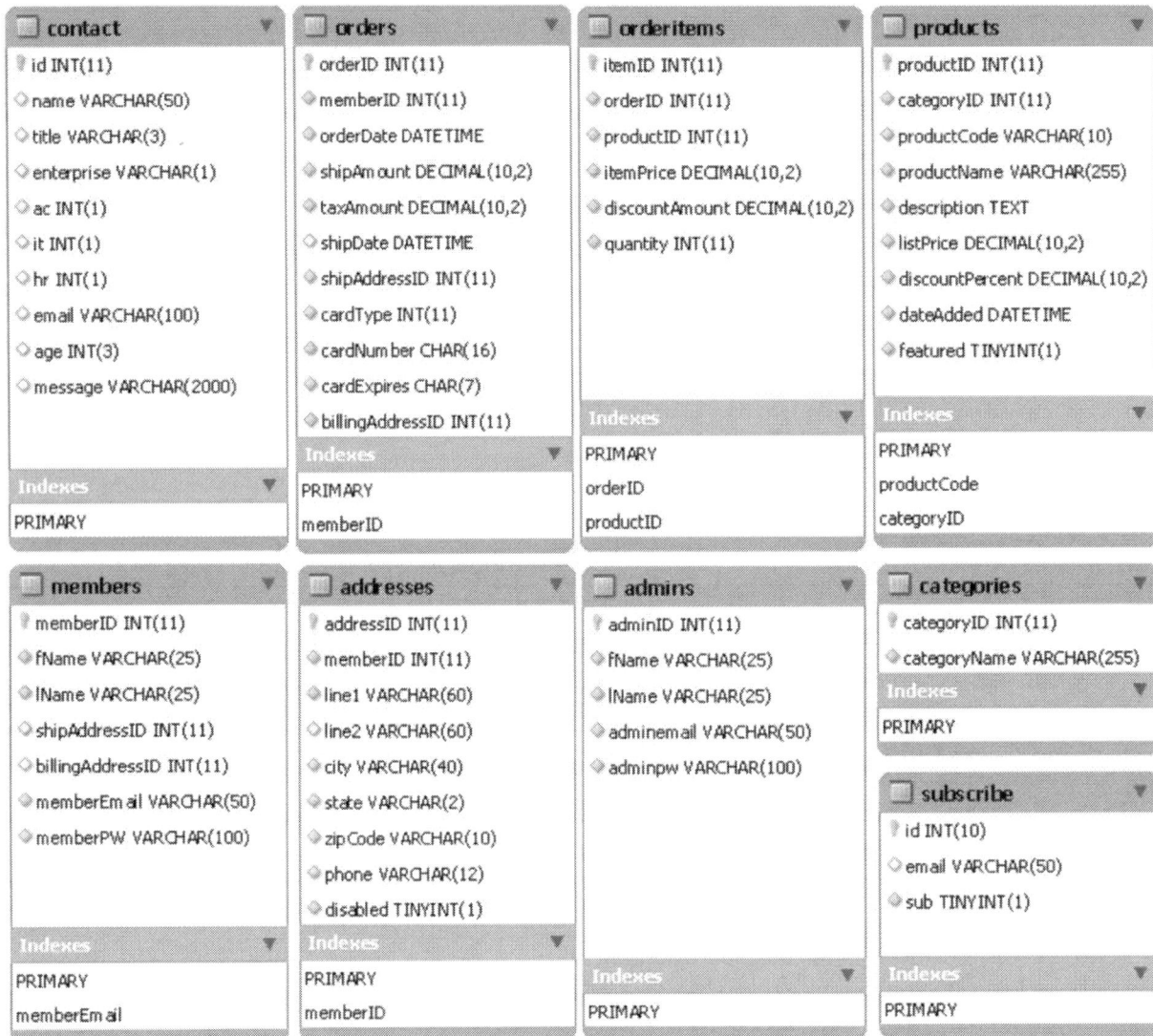

contact
- id INT(11)
- name VARCHAR(50)
- title VARCHAR(3)
- enterprise VARCHAR(1)
- ac INT(1)
- it INT(1)
- hr INT(1)
- email VARCHAR(100)
- age INT(3)
- message VARCHAR(2000)

Indexes
- PRIMARY

orders
- orderID INT(11)
- memberID INT(11)
- orderDate DATETIME
- shipAmount DECIMAL(10,2)
- taxAmount DECIMAL(10,2)
- shipDate DATETIME
- shipAddressID INT(11)
- cardType INT(11)
- cardNumber CHAR(16)
- cardExpires CHAR(7)
- billingAddressID INT(11)

Indexes
- PRIMARY
- memberID

orderitems
- itemID INT(11)
- orderID INT(11)
- productID INT(11)
- itemPrice DECIMAL(10,2)
- discountAmount DECIMAL(10,2)
- quantity INT(11)

Indexes
- PRIMARY
- orderID
- productID

products
- productID INT(11)
- categoryID INT(11)
- productCode VARCHAR(10)
- productName VARCHAR(255)
- description TEXT
- listPrice DECIMAL(10,2)
- discountPercent DECIMAL(10,2)
- dateAdded DATETIME
- featured TINYINT(1)

Indexes
- PRIMARY
- productCode
- categoryID

members
- memberID INT(11)
- fName VARCHAR(25)
- lName VARCHAR(25)
- shipAddressID INT(11)
- billingAddressID INT(11)
- memberEmail VARCHAR(50)
- memberPW VARCHAR(100)

Indexes
- PRIMARY
- memberEmail

addresses
- addressID INT(11)
- memberID INT(11)
- line1 VARCHAR(60)
- line2 VARCHAR(60)
- city VARCHAR(40)
- state VARCHAR(2)
- zipCode VARCHAR(10)
- phone VARCHAR(12)
- disabled TINYINT(1)

Indexes
- PRIMARY
- memberID

admins
- adminID INT(11)
- fName VARCHAR(25)
- lName VARCHAR(25)
- adminemail VARCHAR(50)
- adminpw VARCHAR(100)

Indexes
- PRIMARY

categories
- categoryID INT(11)
- categoryName VARCHAR(255)

Indexes
- PRIMARY

subscribe
- id INT(10)
- email VARCHAR(50)
- sub TINYINT(1)

Indexes
- PRIMARY

Figure 6-8

Task 1 - Contact Form

You did some work in the contact page in chapter 5 where you took users' comments and stored them in the MySQL database through a PHP script. Let's take a step forward and enhance that form by adding some more input elements (select list, radio, checkbox etc.) and incorporate website theme to give it a consistent look as shown below.

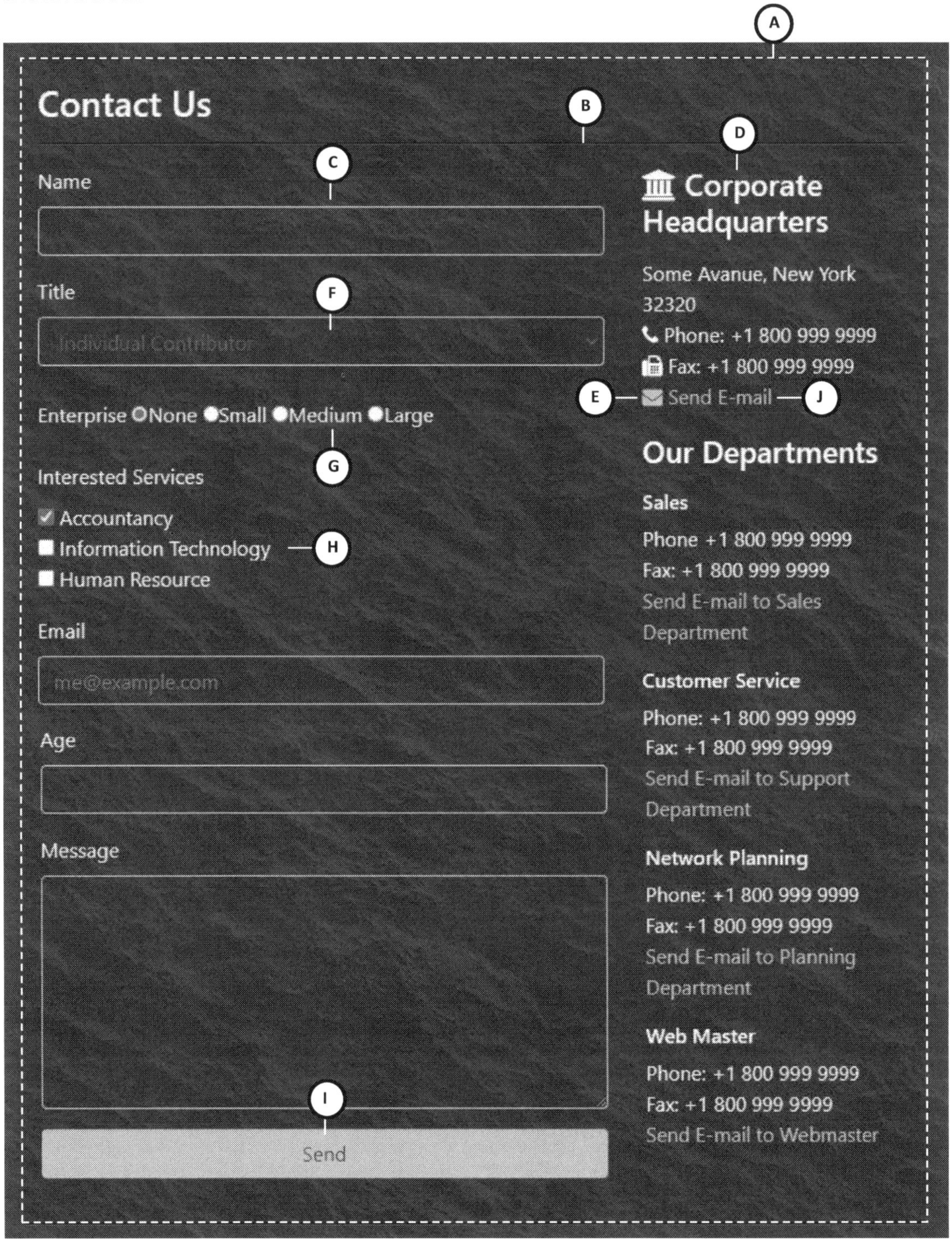

Figure 6-9

Create Database Tables

Execute the following steps to create a new database named ABCGLOBAL in MySQL and populate it with tables and some seed records using a script file.

1. If not open, access phpMyAdmin interface by typing **http://localhost/phpmyadmin/** in your browser address bar and hit **Enter**.

2. Click the **New** link (A) to create the new database. Type **abcglobal** (B) for the database name and click the **Create** button (C). The new database name will be added to the tree pane.

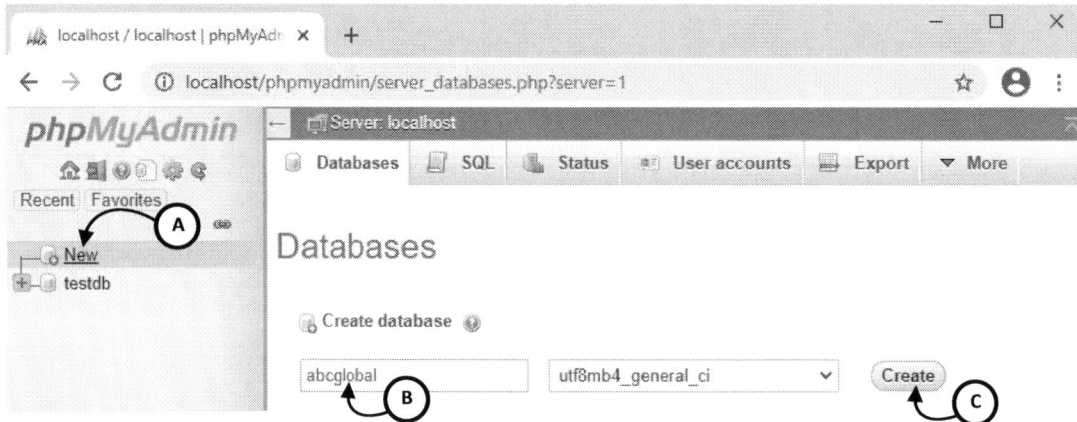

Figure 6-10

3. Select the **abcglobal** database by clicking its name in the left pane. On the **Import** tab (D), click the **Choose File** button (E), and select **abcglobal.txt** script file (F), which is provided in the source folder. After selecting the file, click the **Go** button provided at the bottom of this tab. The file will be imported with a message "*Import has been successfully finished, 16 queries executed. (abcglobal.txt)*" and some warnings. Ignore these warnings and go through the imports stats provided on this screen to get some know how, especially the INSERT statements that created some seed records for the project. Expand the abcglobal database tree node and view the nine tables discussed earlier in the Database Structure section.

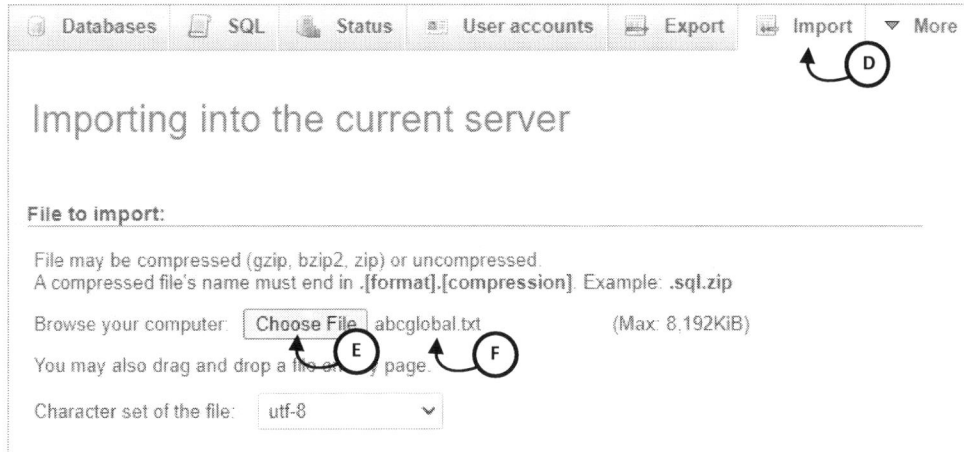

Figure 6-11

4. Copy **Contact.php**, **Contact_Form.php**, and **Success.php** files from the source folder to the project folder (C:\Program Files\Ampps\www\ABCglobal).

Let's go through the code from these files.

Contact_Form.php

```
<!DOCTYPE html>
<html lang="en">
<head>
    <title>Contact Form</title>
    <meta charset="utf-8">
    <meta name="viewport" content="width=device-width, initial-scale=1, shrink-to-fit=no">
    <link rel="stylesheet" href="https://stackpath.bootstrapcdn.com/font-awesome/4.7.0/css/font-awesome.min.css">
    <link rel="stylesheet" href="style.css">
    <link rel="stylesheet" href="css/bootstrap.css">
    <style>
        input[type="radio"] { margin-top: 15px; }
    </style>
</head>
<body>
<?php require_once('view/navbar.php'); ?>
```

The html code generates the contact form while the css code styles it in a desired format. We have already gone through most of the above code while creating the Home page. We applied inline style to radio group input element by providing a top margin of 15px. This element will be used to receive input from users to specify the type of enterprise they represent. The last line in this code calls Navbar.php file to display the navigation bar.

```
<!---- Contact Form ---->
<form action="contact.php" method="POST">
   <div class="container page-overlay">
       <h3>Contact Us</h3>
```

CSS Rule
```
.page-overlay {
    background: rgb(0 0 0 / 18%);
    color: white;
    margin-top: 50px !important;
    padding: 20px;
}
```

The input form is created with the POST method. When submitted, it calls Contact.php file (explained in the next section) to store information in the Contact database table. The form elements are styled using Bootstrap's *container* and *form-group* classes. A custom class named *page-overlay* is also applied to the main div to put a transparent background (see point A in Figure 6-9).

```
<hr class="hr">
```

CSS Rule
```
. hr {
    border-top: solid 1px #333;
    box-shadow: #000 0 -1px 0;
}
```

The <hr> element is most often displayed as a horizontal rule that is used to separate content (or define a change) in a web page. We used it in the Contact form under the main form heading (B) and styled it using a separate css rule, which displays it as a grooved line. The .hr class will be used throughout this project to style the <hr> tag used in other pages.

```html
<div class="row">
  <div class="col-md-8">
    <div class="form-group">
      <label>Name</label>
      <input type="text" size=40 name="s_Name" required="vital" class="form-control">
    </div>
    <div class="form-group">
      <label>Title</label>
      <select name="s_Title" class="form-control">
        <option selected="selected" value="ind">Individual Contributor</option>
        <option value="ceo">CEO/Managing Director</option>
        <option value="cfo">CFO/Finance Director</option>
        <option value="cio">IT Director</option>
        <option value="vp">Vice President</option>
        <option value="dir">Director</option>
        <option value="mgr">Manager</option>
      </select>
    </div>
    <div class="form-group">
      <label>Enterprise</label>
      <input type="radio" name="s_Enterprise" value="N" checked="checked">None
      <input type="radio" name="s_Enterprise" value="S">Small
      <input type="radio" name="s_Enterprise" value="M">Medium
      <input type="radio" name="s_Enterprise" value="L">Large
    </div>
    <div class="form-group">
      <label>Interested Services</label><br>
      <input type="checkbox" name="ac" checked=checked> Accountancy<br>
      <input type="checkbox" name="it"> Information Technology<br>
      <input type="checkbox" name="hr"> Human Resource
    </div>
    <div class="form-group">
      <label>Email</label>
      <input type="email" size=40 name="s_Email" required="vital" placeholder="me@example.com"
          class="form-control">
    </div>
    <div class="form-group">
      <label>Age</label>
      <input type="text" maxlength="2" size=2 name="n_Age" class="form-control">
    </div>
    <div class="form-group">
      <label>Message</label>
      <textarea name="s_Message" class="form-control" rows="7"></textarea>
    </div>
    <div class="form-group">
      <button class="btn btn-warning btn-block">Send</button>
    </div>
  </div>
```

CSS Rule

```
. form-control {
    background: transparent !important;
    color: rgb(165, 165, 165);
}
```

The main row is divided into two Bootstrap columns. The first one (col-md-8) utilizes eight columns to hold form input elements (C), while the second one utilizes the remaining four columns to display a sidebar (D). Some form input elements are styled using the *form-control* class that makes the background of these elements transparent.

The "Title" field (F) is a select list named "s_Title" with some pre-defined values. It is defined using the <select> html element and holds six designations. A visitor can optionally select one of these values to represent him/her. The next field is labeled "Enterprise" (G). It is named "s_Enterprise" and demonstrates how a radio input element could be used to receive a single value in a web page. It presents four options (None, Small, Medium, and Large) to the visitor to select a single value from. The next field "Interested Service" (H) allows visitor to select one or more options from the provided values. We used three checkbox input elements with different names. Each checkbox corresponds to a column in the Contact database table. The checked attribute of the first checkbox is turned on and that's why it contains a small checked icon when the form initially appears on the screen. At the bottom of the input form, we added a Bootstrap <button> element (I) that will be used to send the message. When clicked, this button calls contact.php file (discussed next) to process the form.

```html
      <div class="col-md-4">
        <address>
          <h4><i class="fa fa-university"></i> Corporate Headquarters</h4>
        </address>
        <p>
          Some Avenue, New York 32320<br>
          <i class="fa fa-phone"></i> Phone: +1 800 999 9999<br>
          <i class="fa fa-fax"></i> Fax: +1 800 999 9999<br>
          <a href="mailto:hq@abcglobal.com?Subject=Inquiry%20Ticket">
          <i class="fa fa-envelope"></i> Send E-mail</a>
        </p>
        <p>
          <h4>Our Departments</h4>
        </p>
        <h6>Sales</h6>
        <p>Phone +1 800 999 9999<br> Fax: +1 800 999 9999<br>
          <a href="mailto:sales@abcglobal.com?Subject=Inquiry%20Ticket">Send E-mail to Sales Department</a>
        </p>
        <h6>Customer Service</h6>
        <p>Phone: +1 800 999 9999<br> Fax: +1 800 999 9999<br>
          <a href="mailto:customer@abcglobal.com?Subject=Support%20Ticket">
            Send E-mail to Support Department</a>
        </p>
        <h6>Network Planning</h6>
        <p>Phone: +1 800 999 9999<br> Fax: +1 800 999 9999<br>
          <a href="mailto:customer@abcglobal.com?Subject=Inquiry%20Ticket">
            Send E-mail to Planning Department</a>
        </p>
        <h6>Web Master</h6>
        <p>Phone: +1 800 999 9999<br> Fax: +1 800 999 9999<br>
          <a href="mailto:customer@abcglobal.com?Subject=Website%20Ticket">
            Send E-mail to Webmaster</a>
        </p>
      </div>
    </div>
  </div>
</form>
<!----Main Footer---->
<?php require_once('view/footer.php'); ?>
```

This is the second column on the page that displays company contact information in the remaining four columns of the grid. We used font awesome icons with the <i> tag to display relevant icons (E). We also added some e-mail links (J) that, when clicked, invoke email client with a new message window and a default subject line. The final line of this code displays page footer using Footer.php file in the View folder. Recall that the same Navbar.php and Footer.php files were utilized in the Home page to display the main navigation menu and page footer. This approach will be adopted for all project pages to eliminate duplication.

Contact.php

```php
<?php

$con = mysqli_connect("localhost","root","mysql");
if (!$con) {
  die('Could not connect: ' . mysqli_error($con));
}

mysqli_select_db($con, "abcglobal");

$s_Name = $_POST['s_Name'];
$s_Title = $_POST['s_Title'];
$s_Enterprise = $_POST['s_Enterprise'];
```

When you press the Send button in the contact form, the information entered in the form elements is passed to this file via the form action attribute and the POST method, discussed earlier. This file initiates connection with the database, inserts data in the Contact table and displays a message through Success.php page. You have already gone through this process in previous sections. Here, we will discuss the untouched areas.

```php
if (isset($_POST['ac'])) {    <!-- Accountancy -->
  $n_Ac = 1;
} else {
  $n_Ac = 0;
}

if (isset($_POST['it'])) {         <!-- Information Technology -->
  $n_It = 1;
} else {
  $n_It = 0;
}

if (isset($_POST['hr'])) {         <!-- Human Resource -->
  $n_Hr = 1;
} else {
  $n_Hr = 0;
}

$s_Email = $_POST['s_Email'];
$n_Age = (is_numeric($_POST['n_Age']) ? (int)$_POST['n_Age'] : 0);
$s_Message = $_POST['s_Message'];
```

We used checkbox input element to present multiple options to the visitor. Now it's up to the visitor to select any number of options from none to all or a mix of them. To evaluate the selections, we used isset() function. The isset() PHP function determines whether a certain variable has already been declared. It returns a Boolean value true if the variable has already been set, or false otherwise. In the first IF condition below we checked whether the built-in $_POST array carries the value 'ac' (this value is passed to this script by the contact form when the send button is pressed). If so, the variable $n_Ac is assigned the value 1 indicating the visitor has selected the Accountancy option. If the 'ac' value is not set in $_POST, a value of 0 is moved to the $n_Ac variable via the ELSE block, which signifies that the option was not selected. The same process is repeated for the other two options.

```
$sql="INSERT INTO contact (name,title,enterprise,ac,it,hr,email,age,message) VALUES
('$s_Name','$s_Title','$s_Enterprise','$n_Ac','$n_It','$n_Hr','$s_Email',$n_Age,'$s_Message')";

if (!mysqli_query($con,$sql)) {
  die('Error: ' . mysqli_error($con));
}
```

The above INSERT SQL statement stores the input values in the Contact database table. Note that this time the INSERT SQL statement doesn't have the ID column because we set this column's attribute to generate automatically while creating the table through the script file.

```
header('Location: ' . 'success.php');
mysqli_close($con);
?>
```

Finally, a message is displayed through the header() PHP function by calling Success.php file, which displays a successful submission message and contains the stuff we have already discussed. To redirect a request, you use the header() function. This function returns an HTTP response to the browser that contains a Location header. The header() function sends a raw HTTP header to a client. The values within the parentheses specify the header string to send. The header causes the browser to request the specified URL resulting in a second round trip to the server.

The page is ready to launch.

1. Type **http://localhost/abcglobal** in your browser address bar and hit Enter to access the Home page.
2. In the main navigation bar, click **Contact**. This action will take you to the bottom of the page.
3. Click the **Contact Us** link to see the contact form.
4. Enter and select values from the provided options and click the **Send** button. If everything goes well, you'll see Success.php page with the message "**Thank you for contacting us - We have received your message**".
5. In phpMyAdmin select the abcglobal database and use the statement **select * from contact** in the SQL tab to check this record.

Task 2 – Newsletter Subscription

In this section, you'll learn how subscription application works in a website. In this module, a visitor will sign up for a subscription on the site (to receive newsletters from the company) and will receive a confirmation e-mail. The newsletter subscription form is displayed on every page of this project through Footer.php file that we have already discussed while creating the Home page.

You'll use a database table named *Subscribe* to hold data of users who request subscription. The Subscribe table has three data columns: ID, Email, and Sub. The ID column is the primary key and uses an integer format that is automatically incremented. The Email column has a text format and is intended to hold the subscribers e-mail addresses. The final column Sub stores 0 or 1 to denote whether a user is currently subscribed or not – 1 indicates subscribed and 0 stands for unsubscribed. Unsubscribed records are usually deleted but you may keep users' e-mail addresses on file. You can use these addresses other than just the newsletter in case your site offers more opportunities through emails.

	Browse	Structure	SQL	Search	Insert	Export	Import	Privileges	▼ More

	Table structure		Relation view				

#	Name	Type	Collation	Attributes	Null	Default	Comments	Extra	Action		
1	id	int(10)			No	None		AUTO_INCREMENT	Change	Drop	▼ More
2	email	varchar(50)	utf8mb4_general_ci		Yes	NULL			Change	Drop	▼ More
3	sub	tinyint(1)			No	None			Change	Drop	▼ More

Figure 6-12

Execute the following steps to initiate the process:

1. From project source folder copy **Subscribe.php** and **Confirm_Subscribe.php** files and paste them into the site folder (C:\Program Files\Ampps\www\ABCglobal).

Footer.php

```
<div class="info-widget">
  <h4>Newsletter</h4>
  <form action="<?php echo $app_path; ?>subscribe.php" method="post">
    <div class="form-group">
      <label>Email Address</label>
      <input type="email" maxlength="35" size="35" name="subemail" required="vital"
          placeholder="me@example.com" class="form-control">
    </div>
    <button class="btn btn-warning btn-block"><span class="fa fa-envelope"></span> Subscribe</button>
  </form>
</div>
```

The code presented above already exist in relevant files, therefore nothing is to be done on your part. Here's the newsletter code from Footer.php file, which comprises an email input element and a Subscribe button styled with Bootstrap classes. When visitors provide their email addresses and hit the Subscribe button, the form action attribute calls Subscribe.php file (discussed next) with the POST method, which forwards the email addresses.

Subscribe.php

```php
<?php
 $con = mysqli_connect("localhost","root","mysql");
 if (!$con)
 {
   die('Could not connect: ' . mysqli_error($con));
 }
 mysqli_select_db($con, "abcglobal");
 $s_Email = $_POST['subemail'];
 $sql="INSERT INTO subscribe (email,sub) VALUES ('$s_Email', 1)";

 if (!mysqli_query($con,$sql))
  {
   die('Error: ' . mysqli_error($con));
  }

 mysqli_close($con);

 function sanitize_email($recipient_email) {
  $recipient_email = filter_var($recipient_email, FILTER_SANITIZE_EMAIL);
  if (filter_var($recipient_email, FILTER_VALIDATE_EMAIL)) {
   return true;
  } else {
   return false;
  }
 }

 $to = $_POST['subemail'];
 $subject = "Newsletter Subscription Confirmation";
 $message = "Hi,\n\nThis message is sent to you from ABC Global Consulting Inc. as a confirmation to
            your newsletter subscription request.";
 $header = "From:Administrator <admin@abc.com> \r\n";
 $header .= "MIME-Version: 1.0\r\n";
 $header .= "Content-type: text/html\r\n";

 $valid_email = sanitize_email($to);
 if ($valid_email == false) {
  echo "Invalid input - message not sent";
 } else {    //send email
  mail($to, $subject, $message, $header);
  include 'confirm_subscribe.php';
 }
?>
```

The initial code in this file establishes connection with the ABCGLOBAL database and inserts email address of the subscriber in the Subscribe table along with a constant value of 1 (which stands for subscribed). The rest of the code sends a confirmation e-mail to the subscriber. Recall that we configured email settings and discussed all email parameters used here in the previous chapter . The final line in this code includes Confirm_Subscribe.php file if the e-mail is sent successfully.

Confirm_Subscribe.php

```php
<?php include 'view/header_member.php'; ?>
<div class="container page-overlay">
  <h2>Thank you for subscribing to our newsletter</h2>
  <hr class="hr">
  <p>A confirmation of your subscription has been sent to your email address <?php echo $to ; ?>,
      with instructions for unsubscribing.</p>
</div>
<?php include 'view/footer.php'; ?>
```

This file presents a confirmation message to the subscribers, as illustrated in the screenshot below. It is enclosed in the same header and footer files discussed earlier to display the navigation and footer content on this page as well.

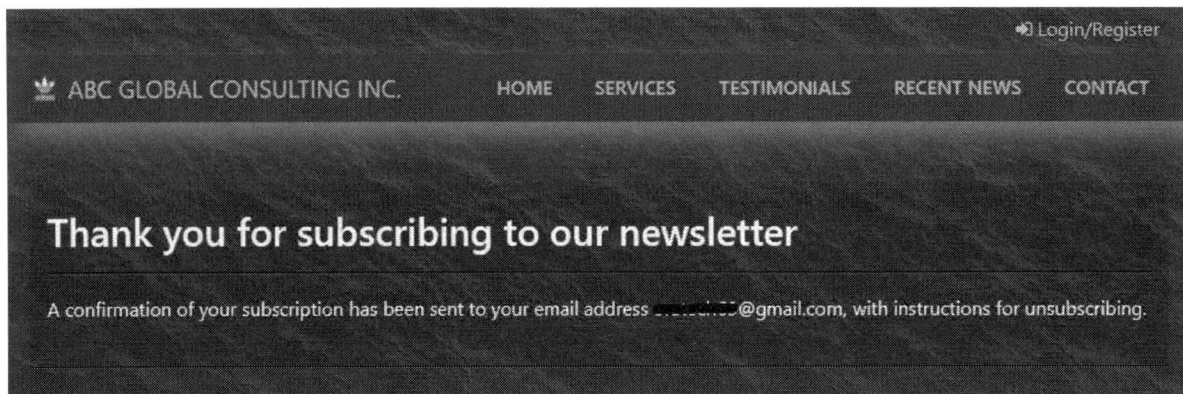

Figure 6-13

Test this module:

1. Type **http://localhost/abcglobal** in the browser and hit Enter.

2. In the main navigation menu, click **Contact** to access the page footer.

3. In the email input box, in the newsletter subscription section, enter your e-mail address and click the **Subscribe** button.

4. The next page, as illustrated in the previous screenshot, will acknowledge your subscription with the text "*Thank you for subscribing to our newsletter*". Check your e-mail account for a message similar to the one shown below.

Newsletter Subscription Confirmation

Administrator admin@abc.com via sha.com
to me

Hi. This message is sent to you from ABC Global Consulting Inc. as a confirmation to your newsletter subscription request.

Reply   Forward

Figure 6-14

Manage Website Dynamically – Admin Modules

In this part, you'll create different modules to help administrators manage the dynamic areas of the project. Starting with the login module, you will create pages that will allow site admins to manage categories, products, orders, and their own accounts. Now that you've become familiar with the page creation and calling procedures, I'm going to explain code from relevant files with the process flow of individual module.

Task 3 – Admin Login Module

1. Copy all files and folders from the source project directory to the site folder (abcglobal) - overwriting all existing files and folders in the site directory.

2. Type **http://localhost/abcglobal/admin** in your browser's address bar. If you see the following screen, click the **Advance** button, and then click the **Proceed to localhost** link (A).

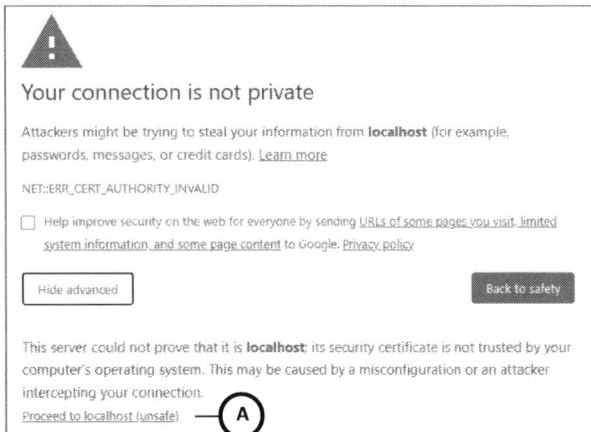

Figure 6-15

3. The admin login page, as shown in Figure 6-16, should come up.

4. Enter **admin@abc.com** in the E-mail Address box and **gemini** for the Password. Click the **Login** button. This account was created by the script file while creating the ABCGLOBAL database. However, if there are no accounts in the Admins table, the application will present a form to create the initial admin account. The next page (Figure 6-17) will show Admin menu with four links. Each link is a separate task that you'll evaluate in this part of the book. Also note that the main navigation bar is replaced by these admin task links and the Login link is changed to Logout with a welcome text displaying the name of the logged in admin user.

5. Click the **Logout** link.

This is the whole process that will be explained in the next few pages.

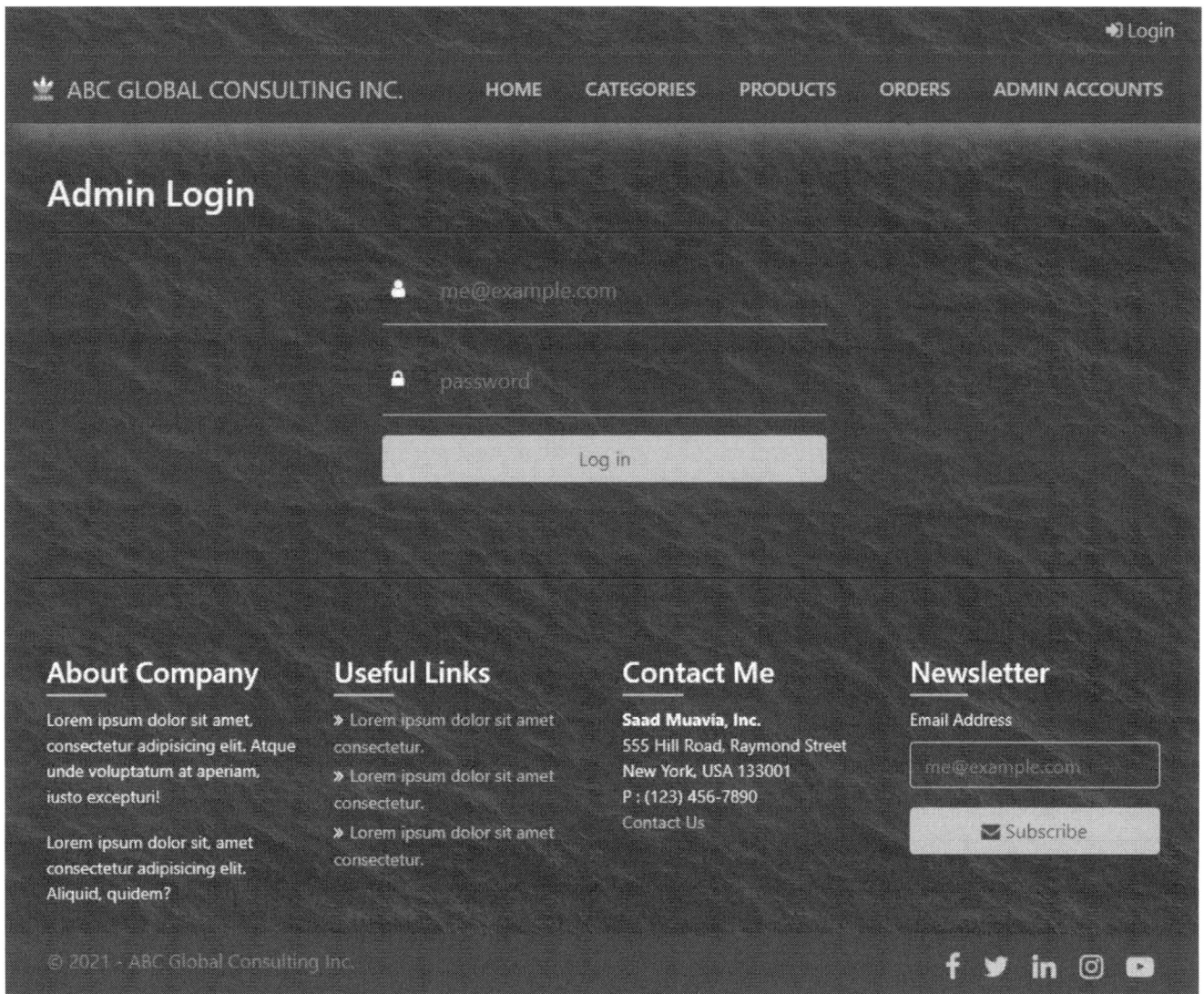

Figure 6-16

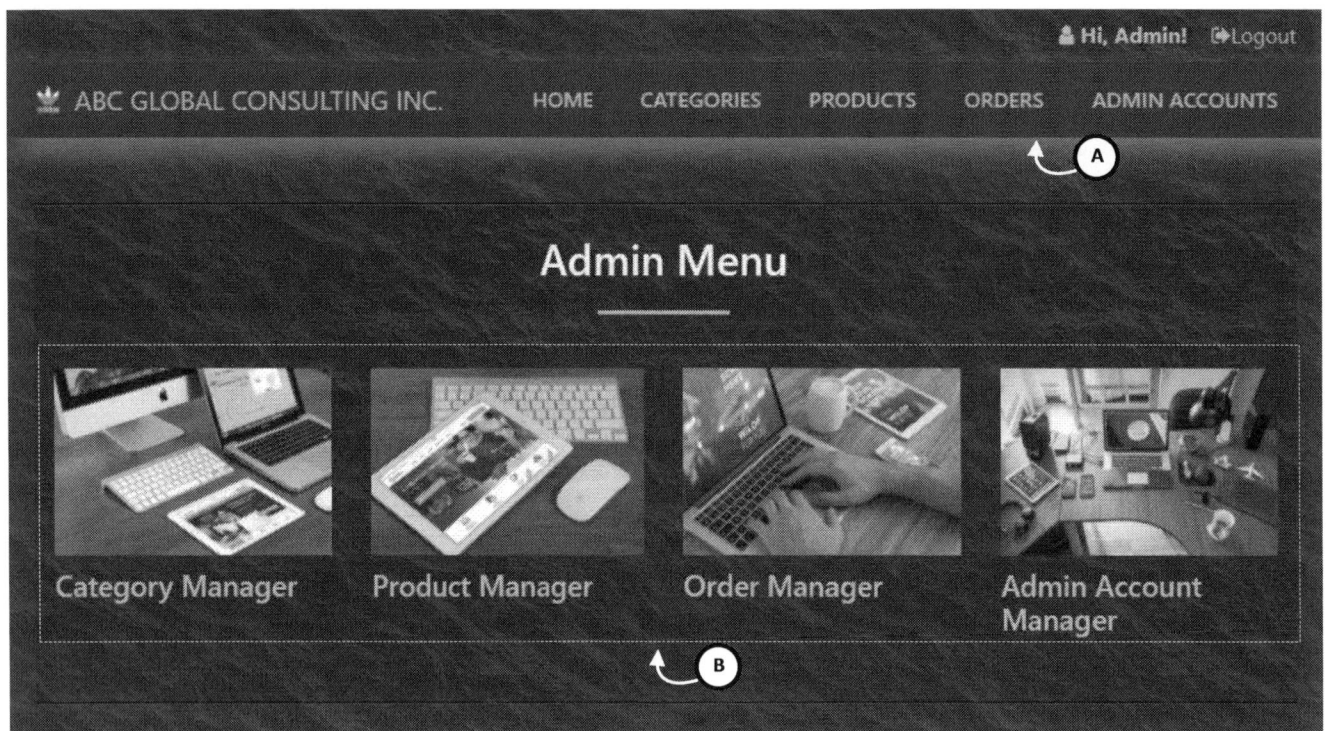

Hi, Admin! Logout

ABC GLOBAL CONSULTING INC.   HOME   CATEGORIES   PRODUCTS   ORDERS   ADMIN ACCOUNTS

Ⓐ

Admin Menu

Category Manager   Product Manager   Order Manager   Admin Account Manager

Ⓑ

Figure 6-17

Admin/Index.php

```php
<?php
    require_once('../utility/main.php');
    require_once('utility/secure.php');
    require_once('utility/check_admin.php');
?>
```

The Index.php file is also called the controller file because it controls the execution of a particular process. Each directory in this project contains a controller file, which is the default file that runs for each directory. This file in turn calls relevant functions and presentation files stored in respective directories. It comprises both PHP and HTML code to process and display web pages. Under the Admin directory, this file initiates the admin login process by calling the three files from the Utility directory. The Utility directory lies under the root (ABCGLOBAL). The files under this directory perform some basic functions and are discussed below. The *require_once* function is used to forward request to relevant files. The double dot (..) prefix used in the first *require_once* statement is pointing to the parent directory i.e. the application root directory (ABCGLOBAL in the current scenario, because the Utility is a child directory to ABCGLOBAL). A single dot (.) represents current directory.

Forward vs Redirect
*In PHP, you call one file from another either through **include** or **require** functions. This is called request forwarding. In this case, all processing takes place on the server and there is only one round trip to the server. In PHP, another term **redirect** exist which is used instead of forwarding a request. A redirect should be used if you need to transfer control to a different domain or to achieve separation of tasks. For example, database update and data display can be separated by redirect. Do the PaymentProcess and then redirect to displayPaymentInfo. If the client refreshes the browser only the displayPaymentInfo will be done again and PaymenProcess will not be repeated. But if you use forward in this scenario, both PaymentProcess and displayPaymentInfo will be re-executed sequentially, which may result in inconsistent process. For other than the above two scenarios, forwarding is efficient to use since it is faster than redirect. To redirect a request, you use the header() function. This function returns an HTTP response to the browser that contains a Location header. The header causes the browser to request the specified URL resulting in a second round trip to the server.*

```php
<?php include 'view/header_admin.php'; ?>

<div id="admin_home">
  <div class="container section page-overlay">
    <div class="row">
      <div class="col-12">
        <h2 class="section-head">Admin Menu</h2>
      </div>
      <div class="col-md-3">
        <div class="news-post">
          <img src="<?php echo $app_path ?>images/pexels-2.jpg" alt="">
          <h3><a href="category">Category Manager</a></h3>
        </div>
      </div>
      <div class="col-md-3">
        <div class="news-post">
          <img src="<?php echo $app_path ?>images/pexels-3.jpg" alt="">
          <h3><a href="product">Product Manager</a></h3>
        </div>
      </div>
      <div class="col-md-3">
        <div class="news-post">
          <img src="<?php echo $app_path ?>images/pexels-5.jpg" alt="">
          <h3><a href="orders">Order Manager</a></h3>
        </div>
      </div>
      <div class="col-md-3">
        <div class="news-post">
          <img src="<?php echo $app_path ?>images/pexels-6.jpg" alt="">
          <h3><a href="users">Admin Account Manager</a></h3>
        </div>
      </div>
    </div>
  </div>
</div>

<?php include 'view/footer.php'; ?>
```

The first line in this code calls Header_Admin.php file to display the admin menu and other header information (A). Since the admin module is different from the member module, we created a separate header file for it. The rest of the code creates the four admin tasks (B) as links that call relevant pages. We also added images to these tasks from the Images folder. Note that we used the same News-Post class that we used earlier for the Recent News section in the Home page to style these four tasks as well. The $app_path variable is created in Main.php file - discussed next. The final line in this code calls Footer.php file, which is the same file we have been using in this project.

View/Header_Admin.php

```
<head>
...
  <script
    src="<?php echo $app_path ?>jquery-3.3.1.min.js">
  </script>
  <script>
    $(document).ready(function() {
      $("#num_rows").change(function() {
          $("#pagination_form").submit();        // A form in Product_List.php
      });
    });
  </script>
  ...
</head>
...
<?php require_once('view/navbar_admin.php'); ?>
```

The Header_Admin.php file is very similar to the Header_Member.php file that we went through earlier. The only difference is the addition of two JavaScripts, as shown in the above listing. The first one uses a jQuery file from the project root folder. This file is used to handle pagination in the Product Manager module. The second script utilizes a couple of built-in functions to support the same pagination process. The num_row variable will be declared in the module. It specifies the number of product records to show on a page. When this value is changed through a select list, the CHANGE function in this script submits the page to show the desired number of records. The last line in this code displays the admin navbar.

Utility/Main.php

```
<?php
// Get the document root
$doc_root = $_SERVER['DOCUMENT_ROOT'];
```

The purpose of this file is to set some global variables, global functions, and to start or resume a user session using the session_start() built-in function. This file is included at the beginning of all controller files. This line will store the document root value (C:/Program Files/Ampps/www) in $doc_root variable. The $_SERVER is a super global array in PHP containing information such as headers, paths, and script locations. DOCUMENT_ROOT is a variable which points to the directory under which the current script is executing.

```
$uri = $_SERVER['REQUEST_URI'];
$dirs = explode('/', $uri);
$app_path = '/' . $dirs[1] . '/';        //Get only the root directory i.e. ABCGLOBAL
```

The variable $uri holds a value from REQUEST_URI. This is the value that usually appears in browser's address bar. For example, when you call the admin login form, the value of $uri would be "/abcglobal/admin/users/". The explode() function used on the second line breaks a string into an array. The value of variable $uri is broken at the symbol "/". This creates an array that is stored in the variable $dirs as follows:

```
$dirs[1] = "abcglobal"
$dirs[2] = "admin"
$dirs[3] = "users"
```

On the final line, we stored the value of the first element i.e. ABCGLOBAL (after concatenating it with a preceding and following directory separating symbol "/") in a variable $app_path. The value of $app_path becomes "/ABCGLOBAL/" and this variable is used throughout the project to denote project's root directory.

```
// Set the include path (C:/Program Files/Ampps/www/abcglobal/)
set_include_path($doc_root . $app_path);
```

The above code sets the include path. This path tells PHP where to look for the files specified in "include" and "require" functions. The resulting concatenated value is C:/Program Files/Ampps/www/abcglobal/.

```
// Get common code
require_once('utility/tags.php');
require_once('model/db.php');
```

The Tags.php file is not applicable to this module. The file (discussed later) contains some custom functions to format text and add HTML tags. The next line shifts control to DB.php in the Model directory to establish connection with the database.

```
// Function to handle database errors
function display_db_error($error_message) {
    global $app_path;
    include 'errors/db_connect_error.php';
    exit;
}
```

The above function is defined to handle database errors. Whenever a database error occurs, this function is called by passing a message to it contained in the $error_message variable. This function makes the variable $app_path global so that it is accessible to other files. Then the function calls db_connect_error.php file under the Errors directory to post the message. Exit is used to terminate the current script and prevent execution of subsequent functions in this file.

```
// Function to handle general errors (For Admins to display errors with their headers)
function display_error($error_message) {
    global $app_path;
    include 'errors/error.php';
    exit;
}

// Function to handle general errors (For Members to display errors with their headers)
function member_error($error_message) {
    global $app_path;
    include 'errors/member_error.php';
    exit;
}
```

The display_error function is called to handle general errors. For example, when invalid login credentials are entered, this function calls Error.php file to display appropriate message to the user. Note that this function is called from a file Error.php in the Errors directory and is specific to the Admin modules. For Member modules, another file Member_Error.php is created to display corresponding page headings while displaying error messages.

```
// Redirect function
function redirect($url) {
    session_write_close();
    header("Location: " . $url);
    exit;
}
// Start session to store user and cart data
session_start();
?>
```

The last redirect() function ends the current session, stores session data through session_write_close() built-in function, and redirects the user to another location passed to it using the variable $url. For example, it is called by Index.php file under Admin/Users directory to invoke Admin/Index.php file using redirect('..') statement to show the Admin menu after a successful login attempt. The two dots used in the redirect() function refers to the parent directory Admin, which is the parent directory of the Users directory. The session_start() function creates a session or resumes the current one based on a session identifier passed via a GET or POST request, or passed via a cookie. The session_start() function prompts PHP to check for a session ID in the request and to create a new session ID and session cookie if one doesn't exit.

Model/DB.php

```php
<?php
// Connect to the ABCGLOBAL database
$dsn = 'mysql:host=localhost;dbname=abcglobal';
$username = 'root';
$password = 'mysql';

$options = array(PDO::ATTR_ERRMODE => PDO::ERRMODE_EXCEPTION);
try
{
    $db = new PDO($dsn, $username, $password, $options);
}
    catch (PDOException $e)
{
$error_message = $e->getMessage();
include('errors/db_connect_error.php');
exit();
}
?>
```

This file is called to establish a connection with the ABCGLOBAL database. As we have already discussed most of the stuff presented in this file, here we will address the un-touched areas. We set error handling options for the PDO connection using the fourth argument ($options) to the PDO constructor. By default, PDO sets an error message that can be retrieved through PDO::errorInfo() and an SQLCODE that can be retrieved through PDO::errorCode() when any error occurs. To request this mode explicitly, we set PDO::ATTR_ERRMODE => PDO::ERRMODE_EXCEPTION to throw a PHP exception to handle the error that we did in the CATCH block.

PDO gives you the option of handling errors as warnings, errors, or exceptions. However, when you create a new PDO connection object, PDO always throws a PDOException object if an error occurs. If you do not catch the exception, PHP prints a backtrace of the error information which might expose your database connection credentials, including your id and password.

To catch a PDOException object and handle the associated error gracefully, we:

- Wrapped the call to the PDO constructor in a TRY block.
- Included a CATCH block that catches the PDOException object.
- Retrieved the error message associated with the error by invoking the Exception::getMessage() method on the PDOException object.
- Finally, called the .php file to display the error.

When any database error is encountered, the CATCH block activates and calls db_connect_error.php file (listed below) from the Errors directory to display the exact error message in a new page.

Errors/Db_Connect_Error.php

```php
<?php include 'view/header_admin.php'; ?>
<div class="container section page-overlay">
    <div class="row">
        <div class="col-md-12">
            <h2 class="section-head">Database Error</h2>
            <p>The following error encountered while connecting to the database.</p>
            <p>Error message: <?php echo $error_message; ?></p>
        </div>
    </div>
</div>
<?php include 'view/footer.php'; ?>
```

The connections error, which was stored in the $error_message variable in the previous script is displayed on this page using the above code.

Utility/Secure.php

```php
<?php
    // Add https prefix to make a secure connection
    if (!isset($_SERVER['HTTPS'])) {
        $url = 'https://' . $_SERVER['HTTP_HOST'] . $_SERVER['REQUEST_URI'];
        header("Location: " . $url);
        exit();
    }
?>
```

If a successful connection is made to the database via DB.php file, the flow is returned to the next line in Admin/Index.php file, which calls the following Secure.php file in the Utility folder. This file is called to add https prefix to urls to make connections secured.

The IF condition checks whether the sever is not already using a secured connection using the isset() function prefixed with the NOT (!) operator. If so, a variable ($url) is created to hold the address with the https prefix concatenated to it. The HTTP_HOST element holds the value "localhost" whereas REQUEST_URI carries the remaining requesting address, such as "abcglobal/admin/" in the current scenario. After concatenation, the url becomes "https://localhost/abcglobal/admin/". This url is then passed to the header() function on the next line. The values within the parentheses specify the header string to send. This whole action calls Index.php in the Admin folder using a secured connection.

Utility/Check_Admin.php

After executing the instructions in the Secure.php file the flow gets back to Admin/Index.php file and the Check_Admin.php file is called.

```php
<?php
    // If administrator is not logged in, call index.php to show login form
    if (!isset($_SESSION['admin'])) {
        header('Location: ' . $app_path . 'admin/users/' );
    }
?>
```

The instructions provided in this file check whether the array "admin" exist under the superglobal $_SESSION variable. This array is set in Admin/Users/Index.php file and is discussed in a subsequent section. When the user initially tries to access the application, the *admin* session is not set, so the code on line 4 executes and invokes the following Index.php file under Admin/Users directory to initiate the admin session.

Admin/Users/Index.php

In this listing only the relevant code is shown to understand the current process flow. The remaining code will be discussed as and when needed. This controller file exists in the Users child directory under Admin and evaluates which interface is to be provided based on various conditions sorted under the SWITCH statement. For example, in the current scenario a user is trying to log in to access the admin interface. Since the 'admin' session in not yet set, the first CASE in the SWITCH statement 'view_login' is evaluated and processed to show the sign in form.

```php
<?php
require_once('model/admin_lib.php');
...
else
{
  $action = 'view_login';
}
switch ($action) {
    case 'view_login':
        include 'admin_login.php';
        break;
...
?>
```

In this script another file named Admin_Lib.php is called from the Model directory. The file contains some functions to validate administrative credentials and is described in more detail ahead. Initially, when a user tries to access the admin module, the code specified in the ELSE block is executed to present the login form using Admin_Login.php file located in the same Users directory. The *break* statement is used to terminate further processing of the script.

Admin/Users/Admin_Login.php

This is the file that actually presents the admin login form. Once again, we used PHP and HTML code combination to create this page.

```php
<?php include 'view/header_admin.php'; ?>
  <form action="index.php" method="post">
    <div class="container login-form">
      <input type="hidden" name="action" value="login">
      <h3>Admin Login</h3>
      <hr class="hr">
      <div class="row">
        <div class="col-md-5 mx-auto">  <!-- The mx-auto BootStrap class horizontally centralizes the form elements -->
          <div class="form-group text-box">
            <i class="fa fa-user"></i>        <!-- User icon -->
            <input type="email" name="usremail" maxlength="35" size="35" required="vital" autofocus
                placeholder="me@example.com" class="form-control">
          </div>

          <div class="form-group text-box">
            <i class="fa fa-lock"></i>        <!-- Lock icon -->
            <input type="password" name="password" required="vital" placeholder="password"
                class="form-control">
          </div>

          <div class="form-group">
            <button class="btn btn-warning btn-block">Log in</button>
          </div>

        </div>
      </div>
    </div>
  </form>
<?php include 'view/footer.php'; ?>
```

It creates the web page by first including the Header_Admin.php file. Next, it defines the login form with the POST method and calls Index.php file from the same Users directory when the form is submitted. The form contains three HTML input elements – hidden, email, and password.

In addition to email and password visible elements, the form uses a hidden element. Hidden fields are text fields that are not displayed on the web page. This type of field allows you to add hard-coded values to a form. In addition, programmers often use hidden fields to pass data from one web page to another. It is used for the same purpose here. When the form is posted (either by pressing the Enter key or by pressing the provided Login button), the value of this element (login) is passed to the called Index.php file.

The login form is styled using the following css rules defined in style.css file. These rules will be applied to the members login form as well.

CSS Rules

```css
.login-form {
    color: white;
    margin-bottom: 50px;
    padding: 13px 0;
}

.login-form h3 {
    font-size: 30px;
    margin-top: 25px;
}
```

```css
.text-box {
    width: 100%;
    overflow: hidden;
    padding: 8px 0;
    border-bottom: 1px solid #ffc107;
}

.text-box i {
    margin-top: 12px;
    width: 26px;
    float: left;
    text-align: center;
}

.text-box input {
    background: transparent !important;
    border: none;
    background: none;
    color: white;
    font-size: 18px;
    width: 80%;
    float: left;
    margin: 0 10px;
}
```

Admin/Users/Index.php (continued)

```
...
elseif (isset($_POST['action']) == 'login')
{
  $action = 'login';
}
```

When the control is received again by Index.php file from the previous section, the ELSEIF condition is evaluated and processed because the value of 'action' is now 'login' passed on by the hidden element specified in the previous listing. This value is moved to the variable $action and is evaluated in the SWITCH statement listed below.

```
...
switch ($action) {
...
    case 'login':
      // Get username & password
      $email = $_POST['usremail'];
      $password = $_POST['password'];
      // If valid username/password, log in
      if (is_valid_admin_login($email, $password)) {
        $_SESSION['admin'] = get_admin_by_email($email);
      } else {
        display_error('Login failed. Invalid email or password.');
      }
      // Display Admin Menu page
      redirect('..');
      break;
```

E-mail and password of the administrator are retrieved from the previous Admin_Login.php script and stored in corresponding variables ($email and $password). Next, a function named is_valid_admin_login is called by passing the two variables as parameters to validate the provided information. This function exists in Admin_Lib.php file, which was included in the process via Admin/Users/Index.php file. If the provided credentials are correct, another function named get_admin_by_email from the same library file is called using the email id supplied by the administrator. This function fetches the complete record of the user. The record is then stored in an array named *admin* that is created under the $_SESSION global variable. The following behind the scene illustration presents this array and the corresponding values that it holds:

If the login information provided by the user is incorrect, the display_error function specified in the ELSE block is called (see Utility/Main.php listing) passing the message *'Login failed. Invalid email or password'*. The function displays the message in a new page and terminates the script.

If the provided information is correct, the redirect() function (also discussed in Utility/Main.php listing) is called passing parent directory argument – i.e. *Admin*. Note that the current process is executing in the *Users* child directory which is under the parent Admin directory. This action invokes Admin/Index.php file using the ('..') parameter (which represents parent directory) and displays the page (as illustrated in Figure 6-17) to perform administrative tasks.

Model/Admin_Lib.php

The file Admin_Lib.php is a library of admin related functions. The following listing provides the two functions utilized in the current admin login module.

```php
<?php
function is_valid_admin_login($email, $password) {
    global $db;
    $password = sha1($email . $password);
```

The is_valid_admin_login function validates administrators by receiving their email ids and passwords. The most common type of authentication is to store encrypted user email address and password in a database. Initially, the function uses the $db variable by making it global. Note that this variable was created in DB.php and carries a PDO object to connect to the database. On the next line, it concatenates the email address with the password and uses the sha1 function to encrypt this data. Here, the email address has been included to make the password longer and more complex which makes it more difficult to crack. The sha1 function, which uses the Secure Hash Alogrithm 1, converts the password to a 40-character hexadecimal string. This function is a hash function that accepts a variable-size string and returns a fixed-size string known as the hash value. The four types of SHA are: SHA-0, SHA-1, SHA-2, and SHA-3. Of these, SHA-1 is the most widely used.

```php
$query = '
    SELECT * FROM admins
    WHERE adminemail = :email AND adminpw = :password';
```

The code above stores a SELECT statement in the variable $query. This statement retrieves complete record of the administrator - trying to log in - from the Admins table. The WHERE clause compares the email and password stored in the database with those provided by the user. Here, adminemail is a column in the Admins table, whereas, :email is a bind variable that holds the supplied email address.

```php
$statement = $db->prepare($query);
$statement->bindValue(':email', $email);
$statement->bindValue(':password', $password);
$statement->execute();
```

These four lines prepare the SQL statement by binding the variables ($email and $password) to the place holder parameter (:email and :password) – $email is bound to :email and $password to :password. Finally, the prepared SQL statement is executed and the query is sent to the database.

```
    $valid = ($statement->rowCount() == 1);
    $statement->closeCursor();
    return $valid;
}
```

In the final code of this function we used the rowCount() built-in function that returns the number of rows affected by the last SQL statement. If the record is found in the database, i.e. rowCount() == 1, a value TRUE or 1 is stored in the variable $valid to indicate that the provided credentials are valid. If no record is found, i.e. rowCount() == 0, a value FALSE or 0 is stored in the $valid variable. The closeCursor() function frees up the connection to the server so that other SQL statements may be issued. The final line returns either TRUE or FALSE to the calling script for further processing.

```
function get_admin_by_email($email) {
    global $db;
    $query = 'SELECT * FROM admins WHERE adminemail = :email';
    $statement = $db->prepare($query);
    $statement->bindValue(':email', $email);
    $statement->execute();
    $admin = $statement->fetch();
    $statement->closeCursor();
    return $admin;
}
...
```

The second function get_admin_by_email receives $email parameter. This function is called to fetch complete record of the logged in administrator by using the email address. Note that this function is executed only when the previous one validates the administrator and returns TRUE. The process is same as mentioned before. The only difference is the fetch() built-in function, which is used to get a row from a result set associated with a PDOStatement object. It fetches the complete record in an array ($admin). The array is then returned to the calling script ($_SESSION['admin'] = get_admin_by_email($email) in Admin/Users/Index.php) that creates an admin session and displays the Admin Menu to manage categories, products, orders, and admin accounts.

Errors/Error.php

This script is called to display generic errors in a new web page. For example, it is called from Main.php to display a message to the user if the supplied login information doesn't match with those in the database.

```php
<?php include 'view/header_admin.php'; ?>
<div class="container section page-overlay">
    <div class="row">
        <div class="col-md-12">
            <h2 class="section-head">Error</h2>
            <p style="text-align:center"><?php echo $error_message; ?></p>
        </div>
    </div>
</div>
<?php include 'view/footer.php'; ?>
```

Task 4 – Manage Categories

After successfully logging into the website, the following page is displayed to perform administrative tasks. The welcome text displays the first name of the logged in administrator (A) along with the Logout link. For login credentials, see Task 3 – Admin Login Module.

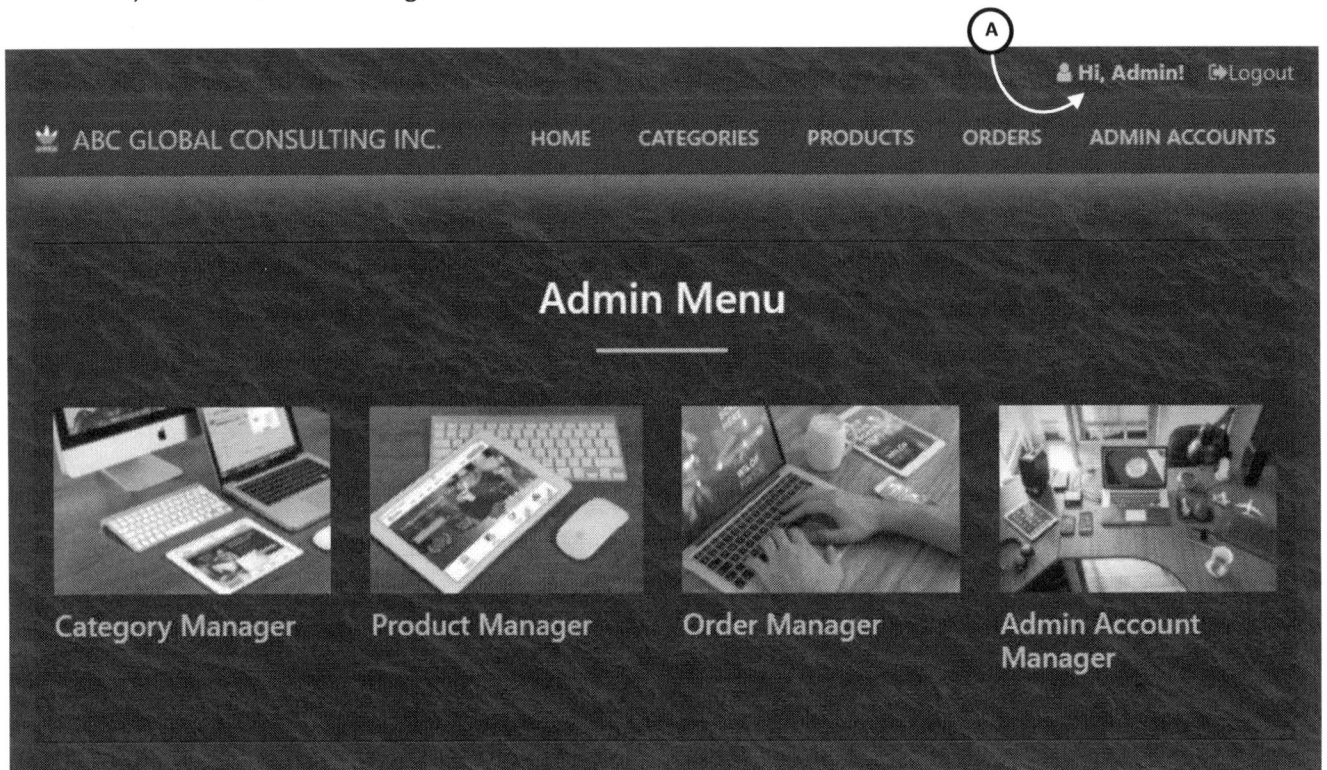

Figure 6-18

The Administrative Tasks

As you can see, the Admin Menu has four options:

Category Manager: This option lets administrators add, modify, or delete a product category. You'll complete this task in this section.

Product Manager - Task 5: This module will allow administrators to add, modify, or delete an individual product.

Order Manager - Task 6: With the help of this module, an administrator can view, process, or delete an order.

Account Manager - Task7: You can add more administrators and modify or delete existing admin accounts.

When you click the Category Manager link in the Admin Menu, the following page appears. The Category Manager section (A) lets you update or delete an existing category. The *Add Category* section (B) has a text box where you can input a new category. When you press the *Add* button (+) next to the text box, the category is added to the categories list. To modify the name of a category, change it directly in the categories list and then click the modify button (C) next to it. Similarly, use the delete button (D) to remove a category. Note that the delete button only appears when a category is not associated to a product. If a product is bind to it, the delete button won't appear on this screen – see the first three products.

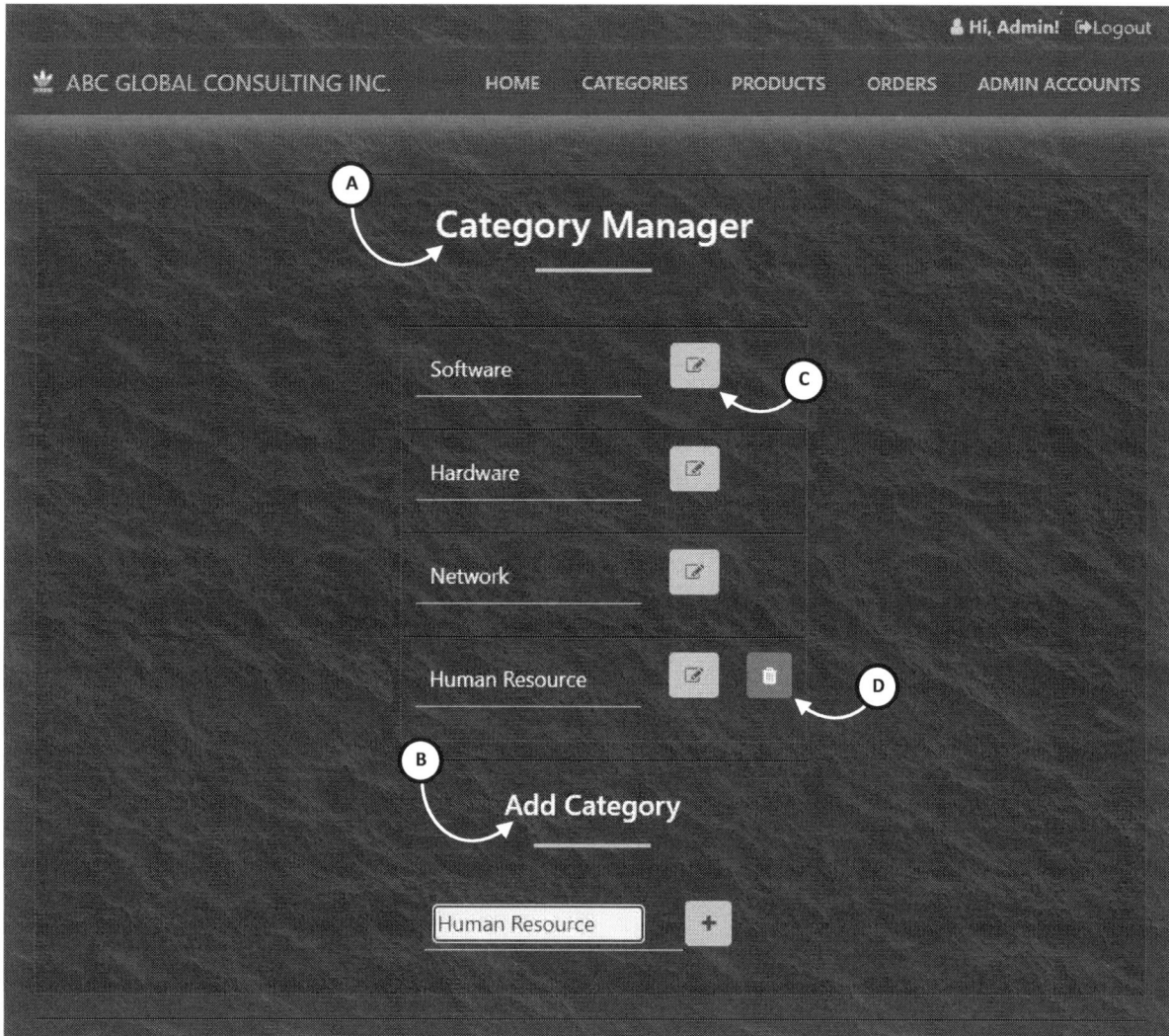

Figure 6-19

This page has four main processes:

1. View categories
2. Update category
3. Delete category
4. Add a new category

To better understand, you'll see all these processes individually. Let's begin with the first one: View categories.

Admin/Category/Index.php

```php
<?php
...
require_once('model/category_lib.php');
...
else {
   $action = 'list_categories';
}
$action = strtolower($action);
switch ($action) {
   case 'list_categories':
     $categories = get_categories();
     include('category_list.php');
     break;
}
...
```

This controller file is located under Admin/Category directory to control the category management process. The initial function of this file is to display a list of categories. On the same page, administrators have the option to add, modify, and remove categories from the Categories table in the database. The file category_lib.php is exclusive to this module. It's a library file that contains various functions related to category management. All other files specified in this controller file, such as Main.php, Secure.php etc. have already been discussed.

Initially, the code specified in the ELSE block is executed, which assigns a string value 'list_categories' to a variable named $action. The next line uses the strtolower() function, which converts a string to lowercase to match it with the static lower case values defined in the SWITCH block.

Initially, the first case condition 'list_categories' is processed and executed. On the next line, a function named get_categories() from the category_lib.php file is called to fetch all records from the categories table. The result is stored in an array named $categories. The next line calls category_list.php to display the fetched records. The break statement terminates the script and no other case statement is evaluated at this stage.

Model/Category_Lib.php

```php
<?php
function get_categories() {
    global $db;
    $query = 'SELECT *,
            (SELECT COUNT(*)
            FROM products
            WHERE products.categoryID = categories.categoryID)
            AS productCount
            FROM categories
            ORDER BY categoryID';
    try {
        $statement = $db->prepare($query);
        $statement->execute();
        $result = $statement->fetchAll();
        $statement->closeCursor();
        return $result;
    }
    catch (PDOException $e) {
        $error_message = $e->getMessage();
        display_db_error($error_message);
    }
}
...
```

The file carries five functions to handle this module. The one listed above get_categories() is the first among them. The SELECT statement retrieves all records from the Categories table. There is a sub-query defined within the main SELECT statement to evaluate how many products exist under a specific category. The result of this sub-query is stored in a column named *productCount* (A). This evaluation is done to eliminate deletion of those categories that have associated products. If the productCount column holds a value greater than zero, the Delete button hides on the web page.

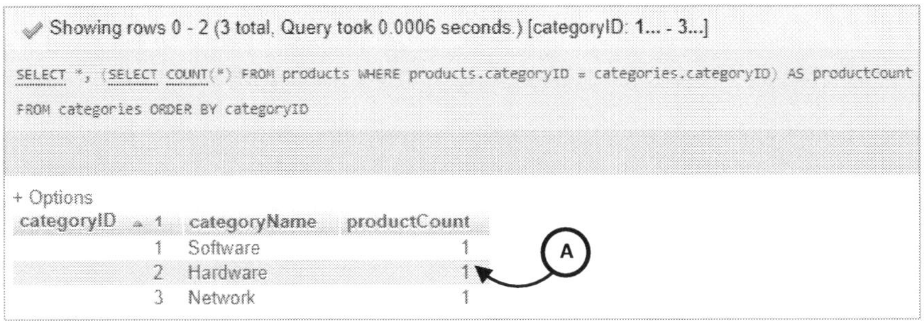

Figure 6-20

The statements in the TRY block prepare and execute the query. The fetchAll() statement returns an array containing all rows from the Categories table. This result set in then stored in the variable $result. Next, the result set is returned to the calling script through the *return* statement. The CATCH block has already been discussed in DB.php listing. It calls a function display_db_error with the argument $error_message. This function exists in Main.php, which calls db_connect_error.php in the Errors directory to display the error message. The CATCH block usually throws an error message if any database table used in the SELECT statement is missing. Also note that the CATCH block used in DB.php only handles connectivity exceptions. After connecting to the database, the block defined here handles further exceptions such as a missing table. After executing the function the flow returns to the previous list (Admin/Category/Index.php), where the file category_list.php is called before the BREAK statement.

Admin/Category/Category_List.php

```php
<?php include 'view/header_admin.php'; ?>
  <div class="container section page-overlay table-border">
   <div class="row">
    <div class="col-12">
     <h2 class="section-head">Category Manager</h2>
    </div>
    <div class="col-md-4 mx-auto">
     <table class="table table-content table-border">
      <?php foreach ($categories as $category) : ?>
```

This is the script that creates the page to manage categories. The page displays a list of categories in a table fetched through the get_categories() function specified in the previous listing. The FOREACH loop is used to iterate through all the rows of the result set, one row at a time. The $categories array stores the PDOStatement object for a multi-row result set, which was retrieved through the get_categories() function and returned to Admin/Category/Index.php file. The result set was forwarded to this script by the final two lines in Index.php file – $categories = get_categories() and include('category_list.php'). The following rules exist in Style.css file to style the table and its elements.

CSS Rules

```css
.table th,
.table td {
   border-top: none !important;
}

.table th {
   border-bottom: solid 1px #333 !important;
   box-shadow: #000 0 1px 0 !important;
}
```

```css
.table-border {
   border: solid 1px #333 !important;
   box-shadow: #000 0 -1px 0 !important;
   margin: 10px 0 20px;
}

.table-content {
   background: transparent;
   color: white !important;
}
```

```
<form action="index.php" method="post" >
 <td>
  <div class="form-group text-box">
   <input type="text" name="name" value="<?php echo $category['categoryName']; ?>">
  </div>
 </td>
 <td>
   <input type="hidden" name="action" value="update_category">
   <input type="hidden" name="category_id" value="<?php echo $category['categoryID']; ?>">
   <div class="form-group">
    <button class="btn btn-warning btn-block" value="Update">
   <span class="fa fa-edit"></span></button>
   </div>
 </td>
</form>
```

The first line here defines a form and calls the controller file of this module when the form is posted. The form contains a text element, two hidden elements, and an update button. The text input element holds the category name. You can modify the name of a category directly in this element. The first hidden element holds the value update_category. When you submit the form after modifying a category and clicking the Update button, this value is posted to the controller file. This element is created to tell the controller that an update operation is performed. The other hidden element holds value from the categoryID column. When the Update button is clicked, it carries value of the selected categoryID from the $category array to Index.php file along with the update_category action value. After receiving these values, the Index.php file executes the code under update_category case – discussed later.

```
  <td>
   <?php if ($category['productCount'] == 0) : ?>
    <form action="index.php" method="post" >
     <input type="hidden" name="action" value="delete_category">
     <input type="hidden" name="category_id" value="<?php echo $category['categoryID']; ?>">
     <div class="form-group">
      <button class="btn btn-danger btn-block" value="Delete"><span class="fa fa-trash"></button>
     </div>
    </form>
   <?php endif; ?>
  </td>
 </tr>
<?php endforeach; ?>
</table>
<hr class="hr">
```

This code is added to evaluate whether the productCount column is equal to zero. The productCount column was created in the previous script to show number of products under each category. If the condition is true and there are not products under the current category, a delete button is placed to allow the administrator to remove the category from the database. Note that this evaluation is done for each category record because we're in a FOREACH loop. If the productCount has a value greater than zero for any category, the delete button will not be displayed in front of that category. Here again, we used a couple of hidden elements to delete the exact record.

```
<h4 class="section-head">Add Category</h4>
<table>
  <tr>
    <form action="index.php" method="post">
      <input type="hidden" name="action" value="add_category">
      <td>
        <div class="form-group text-box">
          <input type="input" name="name">
        </div>
      </td>
      <td>
        <div class="form-group">
          <button class="btn btn-warning btn-block" value="Add"><span class="fa fa-plus"></button>
        </div>
      </td>
    </form>
  </tr>
</table>
        </div>
       </div>
      </div>
<?php include 'view/footer.php'; ?>
```

The above code forms a sub-section that will allow you to add a new category. When the administrator enters a new category and presses the Add button, the form is posted to Index.php file along with a hidden element value add_category. In the next listing we're going to see how these hidden values are handled by Index.php file. The final line of this code renders the page footer.

Admin/Category/Index.php (continued)

```
...
if (isset($_POST['action'])) {      // The update_category action is retrieved into $action variable and the
   $action = $_POST['action'];    // the code under the corresponding CASE is executed
...
   case 'update_category':
      $category_id = $_POST['category_id'];
      $name = $_POST['name'];
      // Validate input
      if (empty($name)) {
         display_error('You must include a name for the category. Please try again.');
      }
      else {
         update_category($category_id, $name);        // The following update_category function is executed
      }
      header("Location: .");
      break;
...
```

Model/Category_Lib.php (continued)

```
...
function update_category($category_id, $name) {
   global $db;
   $query = '
      UPDATE categories
      SET categoryName = :name
      WHERE categoryID = :category_id';
   try {
      $statement = $db->prepare($query);
      $statement->bindValue(':name', $name);
      $statement->bindValue(':category_id', $category_id);
      $statement->execute();
      $statement->closeCursor();
   }
   catch (PDOException $e) {
      $error_message = $e->getMessage();
      display_db_error($error_message);
   }
}
```

The above code snippets enables administrators to update category names in the Categories table. The web page displaying the categories list carries an update button next to each category. Administrators can just modify the category name and click this button to apply the change. The process is executed using the UPDATE SQL statement.

Admin/Category/Index.php (continued)

```
...
if (isset($_POST['action'])) {
    $action = $_POST['action'];
} else if (isset($_GET['action'])) {
    $action = $_GET['action'];
} else {
    $action = 'list_categories';
}
...
    case 'delete_category':
        $category_id = $_POST['category_id'];
        delete_category($category_id);
        header("Location: .");
        break;
...
```

Model/Category_Lib.php (continued)

```
...
function delete_category($category_id) {
    global $db;
    $query = 'DELETE FROM categories WHERE categoryID = :category_id';
    try {
        $statement = $db->prepare($query);
        $statement->bindValue(':category_id', $category_id);
        $statement->execute();
        $statement->closeCursor();
    } catch (PDOException $e) {
        $error_message = $e->getMessage();
        display_db_error($error_message);
    }
}
```

The delete operation can be performed for newly added categories and for those that have no associated product. When this criteria is met, the delete button appears next to the category. When the administrator clicks the delete button corresponding to a category, the process flows back to Index.php file, as shown in the above listing. As usual, the first IF statement (presented in bold) is executed since the delete process uses the post method. This time statements under the delete_category case are assessed and executed, because when the Delete button is clicked this value is forwarded through a hidden form element that we have already discussed in a previous listing.

Then, the received category id is stored in the $category_id variable. This variable is passed as an argument to the function delete_category(). After removing the record from the database, the page is refreshed and the controller is re-run to display a fresh list.

The delete_category function in Category_Lib.php file receives the category id and prepares a DELETE SQL statement. This statement is executed in the TRY block and thus the category record is deleted from the database.

Admin/Category/Index.php (continued)

```
...
if (isset($_POST['action'])) {
  $action = $_POST['action'];
...
  case 'add_category':
    $name = $_POST['name'];
    if (empty($name)) {
      display_error('You must include a name for the category. Please try again.');
    }
    else {
      $category_id = add_category($name);
    }
    header("Location: .");
    break;
...
```

Model/Category_Lib.php (continued)

```
...
function add_category($name) {
  global $db;
  $query = 'INSERT INTO categories (categoryName) VALUES (:name)';
  try {
    $statement = $db->prepare($query);
    $statement->bindValue(':name', $name);
    $statement->execute();
    $statement->closeCursor();
    // Get the last category ID
    $category_id = $db->lastInsertId();
    return $category_id;
  } catch (PDOException $e) {
    $error_message = $e->getMessage();
    display_db_error($error_message);
  }
}
...
```

The value add_category of the hidden input element is passed to Index.php when the Add button is clicked. Another information that this files receives through the post method is the name of the category. The categories table has two columns: categoryID and categoryName. The property of the id column is set to increment automatically, therefore, we do not need to consider a new value for it. On line 5 we put a condition to check whether the received name value is empty. If so, the function display_error is invoked from Main.php file to display the associated message. The ELSE block calls add_category function from the category library. After insertion, the header() function calls Index.php that repeats the process to display the newly added category. The add_category function defined in the Category_Lib file receives the category name and uses the INSERT SQL statement to add the new category to the database. The lastInsertID() built-in function used in this snippet is called to store id of the last saved category in the $category_id variable.

Task 5 – Manage Products

This module will allow administrators to manage individual product information. It is similar in functionality to the categories management section. However, here you'll learn some more techniques, such as how to handle images on a web page and present information in a tabular format using rows and columns.

This module has the following processes to help administrators view, modify, delete, and add products:

1. **List Products:** When the administrator selects the Product Manager link in the Admin Menu or clicks the Products link in the main navigation bar, a page appears that lists all the products under a specified category.
2. **View Product:** This page presents details of a selected product such as its image, price, description and more.
3. **Delete Product:** A Delete button will be provided on the View Product page to remove the selected product from the database.
4. **Edit Product:** Using this process, administrators will be able to modify products' information. For example, the administrator can change a product's category from one to another, put a new price, add more features in the description section, etc.
5. **Handling Products Images:** On product detail page, a sub-section will be provided to upload product images. These images will be displayed along with other details.
6. **Add Product:** As the name implies, this process allows administrators to add new products to the database through this interface.

After looking at the main processes, let's go through all of them individually.

Listing Products on a Web Page From the Database

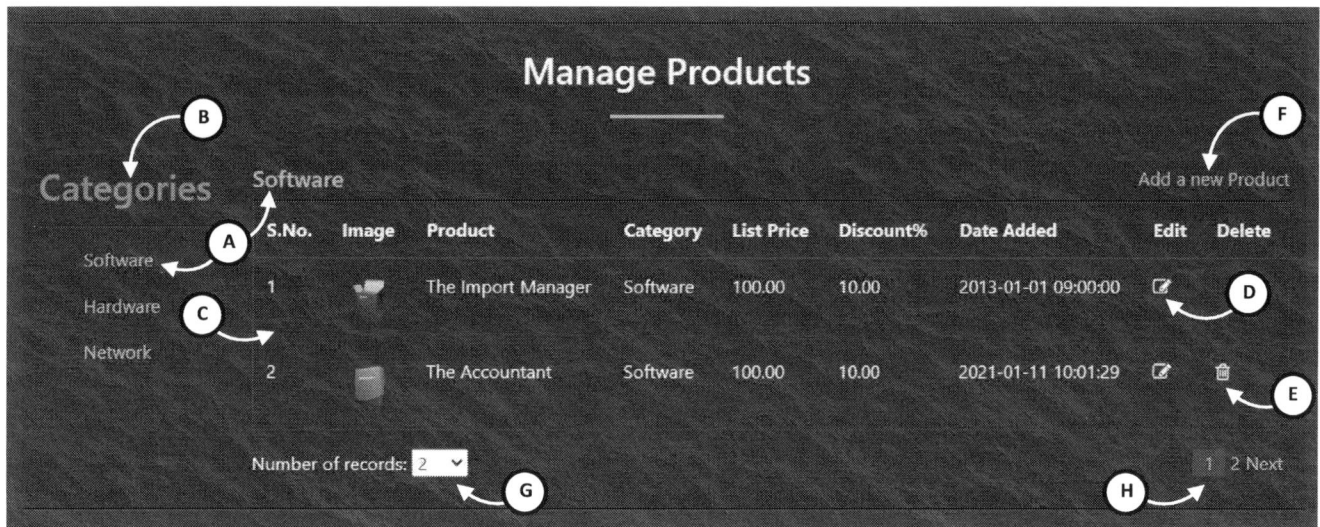

Figure 6-21

As just mentioned, the page illustrated above lists all products from the selected category (A). This page is divided into two sections.

1. The Categories section (B) displays category names on the left side, and a list of associated products (C) on the right side. Selecting a category in the Categories section refreshes this page and products related to the selected category are displayed on the right side along with the selected category name (A). For instance, the above figure displays the Software category and a list of all software products. Clicking the corresponding Edit icon (D) calls a page that reveals complete details about the selected product. The administrator can modify product's content, upload image, and can also delete it from the database on the details page. A product can also be deleted on the current page using the Delete icon (E).
2. The Add a new Product link (F) calls another page where you can add a new product to the database.

Let's go through all the php files that formulate this module, starting with the main controller file.

Admin/Product/Index.php

```
...
<?php
...
require_once('utility/images.php');
require_once('model/product_lib.php');
...
else {
  $action = 'list_products';
}
```

This file also includes six other php files (not visible in the snippet) from different folders to smoothly execute the process. Since no POST or GET actions are set so far, the ELSE block is processed, which assigns the value list_products to the variable $action. This variable is then assessed in the first CASE statement below.

```
$action = strtolower($action);
switch ($action) {
  case 'list_products':
    // get categories and products
    if (isset($_GET['category_id'])) {
      $category_id = $_GET['category_id'];
    } else {
      $category_id = 1;
    }
```

The IF/ELSE block in the above code checks whether category_id is set in the current session. If so, this value is moved to a variable $category_id to fetch products stored under this category. Usually, the IF block is not executed the first time you call this page. Instead, the ELSE block is triggered and a default value 1 is moved into the variable to get all products for the first category – i.e. Software in our instance.

```
    if(isset($_POST['num_rows'])){
      $rowperpage = $_POST['num_rows'];
    } else {
      $rowperpage = 10;
    }
    if (isset($_GET['rowperpage'])) {
      $rowperpage = $_GET['rowperpage'];
    }
```

The above code adds pagination functionality to the current page. Here too, the ELSE block in the first IF condition is processed initially to display 10 rows per page. Subsequently, when you select a value from the select list (G), the page starts to display the selected number of records. If the number of records in the Products table are more than the selected number, then pagination (H) is displayed to the right side as links that allows access to any page.

```
if(isset($_GET['page'])){
  $page = $_GET['page'];
} else {
  $page = 1;
}
$offset = ($page - 1) * $rowperpage;
```

This code will get the current page number with the help of $_GET array. Note that initially the ELSE block code is processed because the page value is not yet set. The ELSE block sets the default page number to 1. The final line of code is a formula for php pagination that calculates the offset for SQL query – discussed ahead.

```
$current_category = get_category($category_id);
$categories = get_categories();
// The get_product_count function is called to get number of products by category for pagination
$products_records = get_product_count($category_id);
$products = get_products_by_category($category_id, $offset, $rowperpage);

// display product list
include('product_list.php');
break;
...
```

This code calls the get_category() function from the Category_Lib file by passing $category_id as a parameter. The function returns id and name of the specified category which is then stored in $current_category array. The next line stores the returning result from the get_categories() function in an array $categories. We've already discussed this function in a previous section. The next line stores number of products under the selected category. This evaluation is done through the get_product_count() function that resides in Product_Lib.php file. On the next line get_products_by_category() function is called using three parameters. It fetches all products in $products array for the specified category.

Model/Product_Lib.php

```
...
function get_products_by_category($category_id, $offset, $rowperpage) {
  global $db;
  $query = "
    SELECT *
    FROM products p
      INNER JOIN categories c
      ON p.categoryID = c.categoryID
    WHERE p.categoryID = :category_id LIMIT $offset, $rowperpage";
  try {
    $statement = $db->prepare($query);
    $statement->bindValue(':category_id', $category_id);
    $statement->execute();
    $result = $statement->fetchAll();
    $statement->closeCursor();
    return $result;
  } catch (PDOException $e) {
    $error_message = $e->getMessage();
    display_db_error($error_message);
  }
}
...
```

This function returns all products for a given category. The SELECT statement uses an inner join on the categoryID column from both products and categories tables. If you use the above SELECT statement in SQL table, the output would be something like this:

productID	categoryID	productCode	productName	description	listPrice	discountPercent	dateAdded	featured	categoryID	categoryName
1	1	TIM	The Import Manager	The Import Manager is a unique imports information...	100.00	10.00	2013-01-01 09:00:00	1	1	Software
4	1	TA	The Accountant	Accounting Software	100.00	10.00	2021-01-11 10:01:29	1	1	Software
5	1	SCM	Supply Chain Management	Supply Chain Management Software	200.00	5.00	2021-01-11 10:03:17	1	1	Software

Figure 6-22

SQL joins are used to query data from two or more tables, based on a relationship between certain columns in these tables using the JOIN keyword. The INNER JOIN keyword returns rows when there is at least one match in both tables. If there are rows in "Categories" that do not have matches in "Products", those rows will NOT be listed. Note that the database script (ABCGLOBAL.TXT) has only one product for each category. I added two software products (product 4 and 5) through the Add Product interface. The first nine columns in the above figure arrived from the Products table, while the last two (categoryID and categoryName) came from the Categories table. Since you have already copied all project files from the source folder, you can add the two new software products (using the details provided in the above screenshot) through the Add a New Product link.

Returning a large number of records can impact on performance. MySQL provides a LIMIT clause that is used to specify the number of records to return. The LIMIT clause makes it easy to code multi page results or pagination with SQL, and is very useful on large tables. Suppose we want to fetch all records from 1 - 5 (inclusive) from the Products table. The SQL query would then look like this:

$query = "SELECT * FROM Products LIMIT 5";
When the SQL query above is run, it will return all records.

The following query will fetch first two records.
$query = "SELECT * FROM Products LIMIT 2";

What if we want to select records 3-5 (inclusive)? This scenario is handled by Mysql using OFFSET. The SQL query below says "return only 3 records, start on record 3 (OFFSET 2 i.e. exclude record number 1 and 2)":
$query = "SELECT * FROM Products LIMIT 3 OFFSET 2";

```
SELECT * FROM Products LIMIT 3 OFFSET 2
```

+ Options

	productID	categoryID	productCode	productName
☐ ✐ Edit ⪼ Copy ◎ Delete	3	3	CAM	Gemini IP Camera
☐ ✐ Edit ⪼ Copy ◎ Delete	4	1	TA	The Accountant
☐ ✐ Edit ⪼ Copy ◎ Delete	5	1	SCM	Supply Chain Management

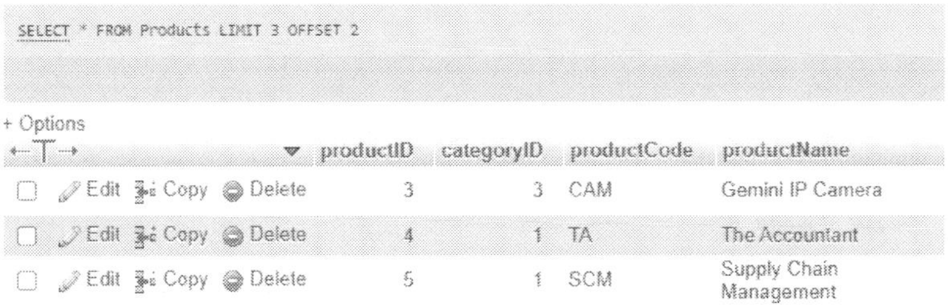

Figure 6-23

You could also use the following shorter syntax to achieve the same result. Notice that the numbers are reversed when you use a comma. You use the OFFSET value first, followed by number of records to return.
$query = "SELECT * FROM Products LIMIT 2, 3";

Admin/Product/Product_List.php

```
...
<div class="container section page-overlay">
 <div class="row">
   <div class="col-md-12">
     <h2 class="section-head">Manage Products</h2>
   </div>
   <?php include '../../view/sidebar_admin.php'; ?>
...
```

View/Sidebar_Admin.php

```
<div class="col-md-2">
   <?php if (isset($categories)) : ?>
   <h2>Categories</h2>
   <hr class="hr">
   <?php foreach ($categories as $category) : ?>
   <ol style="list-style-type:none">
     <li>
       <a href="<?php echo $app_path . 'admin/product?action=list_products' . '&amp;category_id=' .
         $category['categoryID']; ?>">
         <?php echo $category['categoryName']; ?>
       </a>
     </li>
   </ol>
   <?php endforeach; ?>
   <?php endif; ?>
</div>
```

The Product_List.php file creates the Manage Products page. It calls Sidebar_Admin.php file to display a list of all categories in a two columns sidebar using the FOREACH loop.

Admin/Product/Product_List.php (continued)

```
...
<div class="col-md-10">
<?php if (count($products) == 0) : ?>
     <p style="color:#ffc107; font-size: 1.75rem">There are no products for this category.</p>
<?php else : ?>
     <h2 style="color:#ffc107; font-size: 1.25rem; float: left">
           <?php echo $current_category['categoryName']; ?>
     </h2>
<?php endif; ?>
<a style="float: right; color: #fff" href="index.php?action=show_add_edit_form">Add a new Product</a>
```

This section displays a list of products in tabular format in the remaining ten columns. The count() function used in this code checks whether the $products array carries any record. If no record exists, the message defined on the next line informs the unavailability of products for the selected category. The ELSE block displays the name of the selected category at the top of the products table (A). The last line in this snippet adds a link that will be used to add a new product (F).

```php
<?php
 if (count($products) > 0) {
?>
 <table class="table table-content table-border">
  <thead>
    <th>S.No.</th>
    <th>Image</th>
    <th>Product</th>
    <th>Category</th>
    <th>List Price</th>
    <th>Discount%</th>
    <th>Date Added</th>
    <th>Edit</th>
    <th>Delete</th>
  </thead>
```

If some products are found for the selected category, an HTML table is created to show the products in a tabular format. The above code initiates the table creation by adding table headings.

```
<tbody>
<?php
$serial = $offset + 1;
foreach ($products as $product) : ?>
  <tr>
    <td><?php echo $serial; ?></td>
    <?php $image_filename = $product['productCode'] . '_m.png'; ?>
    <td><img src="<?php echo $app_path.'images/'.$image_filename; ?>" width="50" height="50"></td>
    <td><?php echo $product['productName']; ?></td>
    <td><?php echo $product['categoryName']; ?></td>
    <td><?php echo $product['listPrice']; ?></td>
    <td><?php echo $product['discountPercent']; ?></td>
    <td><?php echo $product['dateAdded']; ?></td>
    <td><a href="?action=view_product&amp;product_id=
    <?php echo $product['productID']; ?>"><i class='fa fa-edit'></i></a></td>
    <?php $product_order_count = get_product_order_count($product['productID']);
    if ($product_order_count == 0) : ?>    <!-- If not used in any Order -->
      <td><a href='?action=delete_product&amp;product_id=
        <?php echo $product['productID']; ?>&category_id=
        <?php echo $product['categoryID']; ?>'><i class='fa fa-trash-o'></i></a></td>
    <?php else: ?>
      <td></td>
    <?php endif; ?>
  </tr>
  <?php
  $serial++;
  endforeach; ?>
</tbody>
</table>
<?php
} else {
  echo "<h3>No Results Found.</h3>";
}
...
```

The remaining code in this block displays column values under corresponding headings in the HTML table. The first column in the table shows serial number that is calculated in conjunction with the offset value. When you create a new product, you also add an image of that product. That image is stored in the Images folder. The second column in the table displays the corresponding product image from this folder. Image handling is discussed in detail in a subsequent section.

We also added two icons (D and E) to the table to perform modification and deletion tasks. The edit icon acts as a link which, when clicked, passes a parameter named action with a value view_product and the productID to the controller (Index.php). The view_product value is assessed in a CASE statement and another file (Product_View.php - coming up next) is called to display details of the selected product. The code echo $product['productID'] is enclosed in the opening <a> tag and is associated with the = operator. If you edit the first product, the complete expression would appear in the browser like this:

http://localhost/abcglobal/admin/product/index.php?action=view_product&product_id=1

To confirm the above URL, hover your mouse over each edit icon in the list and see the complete expression in the status bar each time with the same action value but with a new product id.

The delete icon works in similar way. When this icon is clicked, the action delete_product is evaluated in a CASE statement, and the delete action is performed to remove the selected product from the Products table in the database. Note that the IF condition specified before the delete icon link checks whether the selected product is used in any customer order. This evaluation is done through the get_product_order_count() function. If the product is used in any order, the delete icon is not shown in the table for that product. The No Results Found message is displayed when no product exists for the selected category. Try this out by adding a new category using the Category Manager interface. Switch back to Manage Products page, and click the new category in the left sidebar to see this message.

```
if (count($products) > 0) { ?>
 <div>
  <form method="post" action="" id="pagination_form">
   <label for="num_rows" style="color:white">Number of records:</label>
   <select id="num_rows" name="num_rows">
    <?php
    $numrows_arr = array("1","2","3","10","25","50","100");
    foreach($numrows_arr as $nrow){
     if(isset($_POST['num_rows']) && $_POST['num_rows'] == $nrow){
      echo '<option value="'.$nrow.'" selected="selected">'.$nrow.'</option>'; // set 1 as default value
     } else {
      echo '<option value="'.$nrow.'">'.$nrow.'</option>';
     }
    }
    ?>
   </select>
```

This block of code creates pagination and is executed when some products exists under a selected category. When you apply pagination to a web page, all your fetched records are displayed in multiple pages instead of one page. Displaying all records on a single page makes that page so long and takes so much time to load. In this code, we created a form that is referenced in the JavaScript code discussed earlier in Header_Admin.php file to refresh the page when you select the number of records you want to see on this page. You choose this number from the select list defined on line 5. When you select a number, the value of the select list changes, and the JavaScript anticipates this change and submits the form (pagination_form) to display the desired number of records on the products page. Note that the id of the Select List is num_rows, and the JavaScript identifies the change using this id.

```php
<?php
 $total_pages = ceil($products_records / $rowperpage);
 echo '<ul class="pagination">';
```

This code will create the pagination (H). The value held in $products_records variable is divided by $rowperpage (value picked from the select list) on the first line in this code to evaluate total number of pages. The ceil() function rounds a number up to the nearest integer. The $products_records variable contains number of products in the selected category. A value was assigned to this variable via get_product_count() function in Admin/Product/Index.php file. The pagination is styled using a custom pagination class – listed after this code.

```php
 $first_category = first_category();
 If ($page > 1) {
   if (is_null($_GET['category_id'])){
     echo '<li><a href="index.php?page='.($page - 1).'&amp;rowperpage=' . $rowperpage .
       '&amp;category_id=' . $first_category .'">Previous</a></li>';
   } else {
     echo '<li><a href="index.php?page='.($page - 1).'&amp;rowperpage=' . $rowperpage .
       '&amp;category_id=' . $_GET['category_id'] .'">Previous</a></li>';
   }
 }
```

This code is executed when the value of $page is greater than 1 – i.e. when you are on page 2,3,… etc. If the condition is true, you will see a link labeled Previous that will allow you to move back. The initial line gets the id of the first category using the first_category() function that exists in Model/Product_Lib.php file to display products related to this category if the category_id is not set in the current session. The link is formed as follow: https://localhost/abcglobal/admin/product/index.php?page=1&rowperpage=2&category_id=1

```php
 For ($i = 1; $i <= $total_pages; $i++){
   if($i == $page){
     $active = "active";
   } else {
     $active = "";
   }
   if (is_null($_GET['category_id'])){
     echo '<li class="'.$active.'"><a href="index.php?page='.($i).'&amp;rowperpage=' . $rowperpage .
'&amp;category_id=' . $first_category .'">'.$i.'</a></li>';
   } else {
     echo '<li class="'.$active.'"><a href="index.php?page='.($i).'&amp;rowperpage=' . $rowperpage .
'&amp;category_id=' . $_GET['category_id'] .'">'.$i.'</a></li>';
   }
 }
```

The above code deals with the middle part of pagination – page numbers. The first IF condition highlights the number of the current page in the pagination list using a class named active defined in style.css file – listed below.

```
    if($total_pages > $page){
      if (is_null($_GET['category_id'])){
        echo '<li><a href="?page='.($page + 1).'index.php?&amp;rowperpage=' . $rowperpage .
          '&amp;category_id=' . $first_category . '">Next</a></li>';
      } else {
        echo '<li><a href="?page='.($page + 1).'index.php?&amp;rowperpage=' . $rowperpage .
          '&amp;category_id=' . $_GET['category_id'] . '">Next</a></li>';
      }
    }
    echo '</ul>';
  ?>
  </form>
  </div>
  <?php } ?>
...
<?php include '../../view/footer.php'; ?>
```

The final code in this file presents the Next pagination link, which is displayed unless you access the last page. The last line includes Footer.php file. The following CSS rules are applied to style the pagination.

CSS Rules

```
.pagination {
  float: right;
  display: inline-block;
  text-align: center;
  margin: 0;
}

.pagination li {
  display: inline-block;
  margin: 0 5px 0 0;
}
```

```
.pagination li a {
  border: none;
  color: #fff;
}

.pagination .active {
  padding: 0 10px;
  background: #333;
}
```

View Product Details

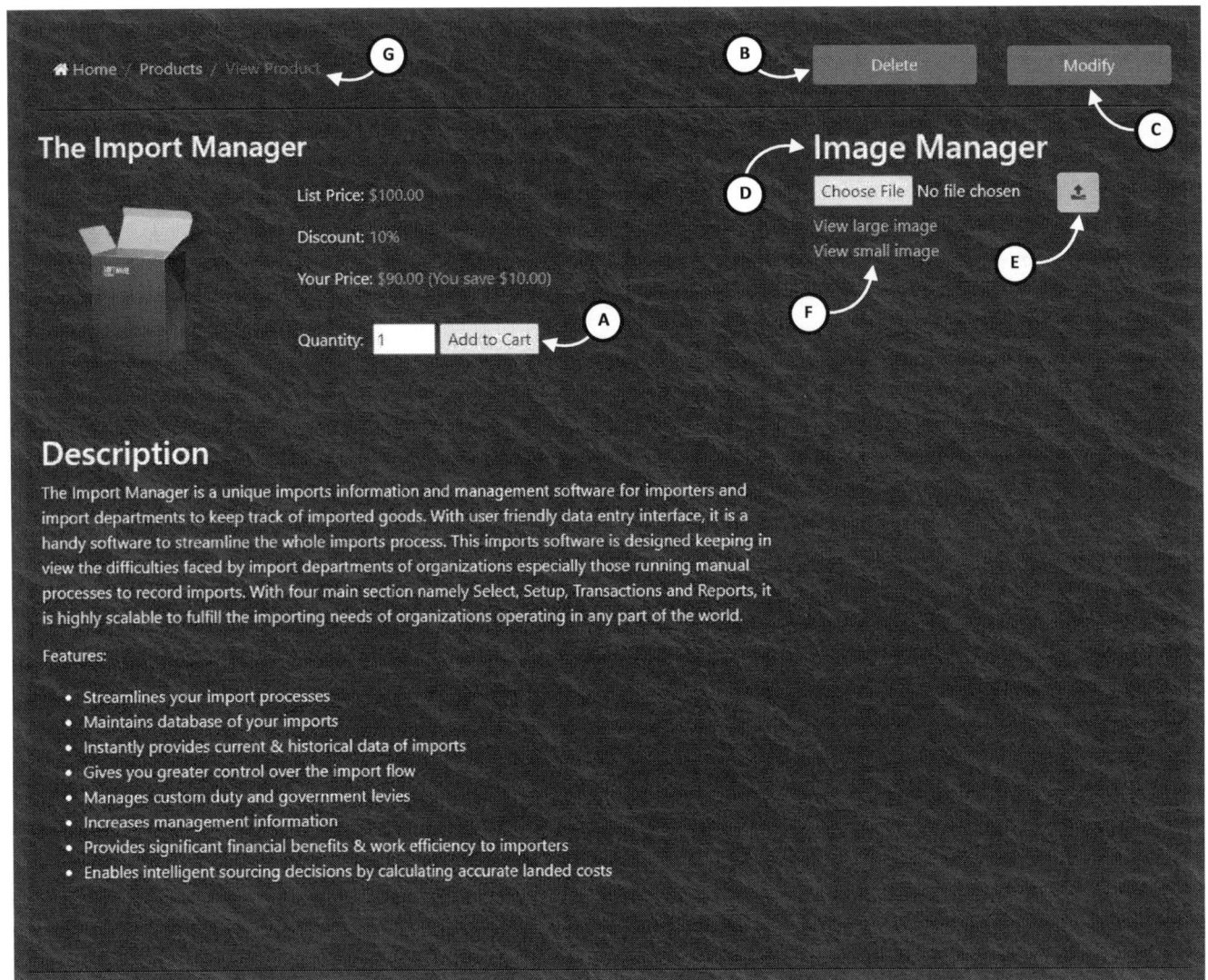

Figure 6-24

After clicking the edit link in the Manage Product page, you'll see the page illustrated above. The main Content section displays details of the selected product. It has an Add to Cart button (A) that is provided for placing order and will be discussed in the members module. The Delete button (B) removes the product from the database. Note that this button appears only if no orders are placed against a product. We will discuss it shortly. Using the Modify button (C) administrators can save modified content to the database table.

The page also contains the Image Manager sub-section (D), which is used to upload images of products. Use the Choose File button to locate the image. After selecting the image, clicking the Upload Image button (E) moves the selected image to the Images folder in the site directory. This process creates three versions of an image: actual, medium, and small. The one you see on this page is the actual one. You can see other versions using the links (F) provided under the Choose File button.

Admin/Product/Index.php

```
...
else if (isset($_GET['action'])) {
  $action = $_GET['action'];
}
...
  case 'view_product':
    $product_id = $_GET['product_id'];
    $product = get_product($product_id);
    $product_order_count = get_product_order_count($product_id);
    include('product_view.php');
    break;
...
```

When you click the edit icon on the Manage Products page, the product id parameter is passed (appended to the url) to this controller file along with the view_product action value via the GET method. This time, the ELSE IF condition is processed because the request is received appended to the URL which corresponds to the GET method. In the current scenario, the $_GET array (as shown in the figure below) is defined with two elements. The first element [action] has the value view_product while the second one is [product_id] with a value of 1. The variable $action is assigned the value view_product in the ELSE IF block and is processed in the corresponding CASE statement.

$_GET	array[2]	
[action]	string	"view_product"
[product_id]	string	"1"

Figure 6-25 - $_GET Array Structure

The code in the CASE block fetches required data through function calls. The get_product() function from the product function library is called to retrieve complete record of the selected product into the $product array. The get_product_order_count() function is called from the product function library to check whether there are any orders already placed for the selected product. This check is performed on the Orderitems table. If there are no orders, a zero value will be stored in the $product_order_count variable. This check is performed to evaluate whether to show the Delete button. If the value indicates zero, the Delete button will appear on the web page and the administrator will be able to remove the product. If in case a single order is placed for the selected product, the delete button will not appear on the page to prevent deletion of that product. The final line of this code calls Product_View.php file (discussed next) to display complete details of the selected product.

Admin/Product/Product_View.php

```
...
<?php include '../../view/header_admin.php'; ?>
    <div class="container page-overlay">
     <div class="row">
      <div class="col-md-8">
       <ol class="breadcrumb">
        <li class="breadcrumb-item"><a href="<?php echo $app_path.'admin/'; ?>">Home</a></li>
        <li class="breadcrumb-item"><a href="<?php echo $app_path.'admin/product'; ?>">Products</a></li>
        <li class="breadcrumb-item active">View Product</li>
       </ol>
      </div>
```

CSS Rules

`.breadcrumb {`
`  background: transparent !important;`
`}`
	`.breadcrumb>li:first-child:before {`
	`  content: "\f015";`
	`  font-family: FontAwesome;`
	`  padding-right: 4px;`
	`  color: rgb(255, 255, 255);`
	`}`

The above code adds a breadcrumb region (G) to display a hierarchy that contains a couple of links (Home and Products) and the label of the current page (View Product). Using the two links, you can directly access the corresponding page. For example, you can go to the Home page by clicking its link in the breadcrumb region. The region utilizes eight column from the left side. The :first-child selector adds the font awesome Home icon (\f015) before the first breadcrumb element (Home).

```
      <div class="col-md-2">
       <?php if (get_product_order_count($product_id) == 0) : ?> <!-- If not used in any Order. -->
       <form action="index.php" method="post">
        <input type="hidden" name="action" value="delete_product">
        <input type="hidden" name="product_id" value="<?php echo $product['productID']; ?>">
        <input type="hidden" name="category_id" value="<?php echo $product['categoryID']; ?>">
        <button class="btn btn-danger btn-block" style="margin: 5px 0px">Delete</button>
       </form>
       <?php endif; ?>
      </div>
      <div class="col-md-2">
       <form action="index.php" method="post">
        <input type="hidden" name="action" value="show_add_edit_form">
        <input type="hidden" name="product_id" value="<?php echo $product['productID']; ?>">
        <input type="hidden" name="category_id" value="<?php echo $product['categoryID']; ?>">
        <button class="btn btn-primary btn-block" style="margin: 5px 0px">Modify</button>
       </form>
      </div>
     </div>
```

This block of code places Delete (B) and Modify (C) buttons next to the breadcrumb region, and utilizes the remaining four columns to place these buttons side-by-side. The buttons are styled using BootStrap btn classes. The Modify button takes you to another page, where you can amend the contents of the selected product.

```
<hr class="hr" style="margin-top: 0rem">
<div class="row">
 <div class="col-md-8">
  <?php include '../../view/product.php'; ?>
 </div>
```

This code calls Product.php file (discussed next) from the View directory. The file moves information received from the database into appropriate variables and also performs some calculations. These variable values are then displayed on this page.

```
<div class="col-md-4">
 <h2>Image Manager</h2>
 <form action="index.php" method="post" enctype="multipart/form-data" id="upload_image_form">
  <input type="hidden" name="action" value="upload_image">
  <input type="hidden" name="product_id" value="<?php echo $product['productID']; ?>">
  <input type="file" name="file1">
  <button class="btn btn-warning" style="margin-left:-60px"><span class="fa fa-upload"></span></button>
 </form>
 <p style="margin-bottom:0px"><a href="../../images/<?php echo $product['productCode']; ?>.png">
View large image</a></p>
 <p style="margin-bottom:0px"><a href="../../images/<?php echo $product['productCode']; ?>_s.png">
View small image</a></p>
 </div>
 </div>
 </div>
<?php include '../../view/footer.php'; ?>
```

The above code creates the Image Manager section (D) of the page. Note that we added a new attribute enctype to the form which sends form-data encoded as multipart/form-data. The enctype attribute specifies how the form-data should be encoded when submitting it to the server. This value is required when you are using forms that have a file upload control – input type="file". The View large image and View small image links are created to display large and small versions of the uploaded product images. The whole image handling process will be discussed shortly in a subsequent section.

View/Product.php

```php
<?php
    // Parse data
    $category_id = $product['categoryID'];
    $product_code = $product['productCode'];
    $product_name = $product['productName'];
    $description = $product['description'];
    $list_price = $product['listPrice'];
    $discount_percent = $product['discountPercent'];

    // Add HMTL tags to the description
    $description = add_tags($description);

    // Calculate discounts
    $discount_amount = round($list_price * ($discount_percent / 100), 2);
    $unit_price = $list_price - $discount_amount;

    // Format discounts
    $discount_percent = number_format($discount_percent, 0);
    $discount_amount = number_format($discount_amount, 2);
    $unit_price = number_format($unit_price, 2);

    // Get image URL and alternate text
    $image_filename = $product_code . '_m.png';
    $image_path = $app_path . 'images/' . $image_filename;
    $image_alt = 'Image filename: ' . $image_filename;
?>
```

This code deals with data handling process. It fetches values from the $product array and stores them in relevant variables. For example, the database value productCode is retrieved from the array element $product['productCode'] and then stored in the variable $product_code. The next line calls a function named add_tags() from Tags.php file sited under the Utility directory. This function will be discussed later.

The next line calculates the discount value. It initially divides the value of $discount_percent by 100, then multiplies it with $list_price, and rounds the resulting value up to 2 decimal places. Suppose the values of $discount_percent and $list_price are 10 and 100 respectively. The value received after the initial division would be 0.1. Multiplied by 100 would yield 10, which is the discount value. The next line subtracts discount value from the list price to render actual unit price.

The number_format() function used in the next three lines formats a number with grouped thousands. The first one formats value in the $discount_percent variable with zero, while in the remaining variables two digits are added.

The next line concatenates the product code with _m.png string. Here the letter m represents medium sized image file. After joining, the resulting value is stored in $image_filename variable. For example, the product code retrieved from the database is TIM. After concatenation, the value TIM_m.png will be stored in the designated variable. The value of $image_path variable defined on the next line would be formed as /abcglobal/images/TIM_m.png. The final code creates an alternate text for the image. This text will be displayed when the browser fails to show the image on the web page.

```
<h3><?php echo $product_name; ?></h3>
<div class="row">
   <div class="col-md-4" style="margin-top:10px">
      <img src="<?php echo $image_path; ?>" alt="<?php echo $image_alt; ?>">
   </div>
   <div class="col-md-8" style="margin-top:12px">
      <!-- display: inline-block does not add a line-break after the element, so the element can sit next to other
      elements. Here, product price, discount percent, and unit price sit next to their respective labels -->
      <p style="display: inline-block;">List Price:</p>
      <p style="display: inline-block; color: rgb(165, 165, 165)"><?php echo '$' . $list_price; ?></p><br>
      <p style="display: inline-block;">Discount:</p>
      <p style="display: inline-block; color: rgb(165, 165, 165)"><?php echo $discount_percent . '%'; ?></p><br>
      <p style="display: inline-block;">Your Price:</p>
      <p style="display: inline-block; color: rgb(165, 165, 165)"><?php echo '$' . $unit_price; ?>
         (You save <?php echo '$' . $discount_amount; ?>)</p>
      <form action="<?php echo $app_path . 'cart' ?>" method="GET" id="add_to_cart_form">
         <input type="hidden" name="action" value="add">
         <input type="hidden" name="product_id" value="<?php echo $product_id; ?>"> Quantity: 
         <input type="text" name="quantity" value="1" size="3" maxlength="3">
         <input type="submit" value="Add to Cart">
      </form>
   </div>
</div>
<h2>Description</h2>
<?php echo $description; ?>
```

This part of the php file carries HTML elements with embedded PHP code to display product details.

A medium size image of the selected product is displayed in the first <div>. The $image_path variable holds the full path to the image including the Images directory and the image file name. The next lines display List Price, Discount percentage, and discounted price.

A form is also added to display the quantity that a member wishes to place in the cart. Note that this form uses the GET method and passes a value add in a hidden element to the Cart directory controller. The controller evaluates the value in a CASE statement for further processing and which is described in detail in the Cart module (Task 14). The text input element defined in the form receives the desired quantity from the visitor. This element has a default value of 1. The final couple of lines in this file display formatted description of the product. The next listing describes how description column content is formatted.

Utility/Tags.php

```
...
function add_tags($text) {
    $text = str_replace("\r\n", "\n", $text);  // convert Windows
    $text = str_replace("\r", "\n", $text);    // convert Mac
```

This function was called in the previous script to add HTML tags to the Description column before displaying it on the product details page. If you had a chance to look at the INSERT statement that added three products in abcglobal.txt file, you might have noticed some special tags such as \r, \n and * used in the content for the Description column. This technique is called escape sequences to include special characters in strings. The \r is used for carriage return while \n adds a new line. The last one '*' is used to represent <li> tags.

The function begins by receiving raw description in a variable $text. The next two lines use a built-in function str_replace which replaces all occurrences of the search string with the replacement string. On line # 2, the string "\r\n" is searched in the variable $text and is replaced with "\n".

```
"The Import Manager is a unique imports information and management software
...... in any part of the world.

Features:
* Streamlines your import processes
...
...
* Enables intelligent sourcing decisions by calculating accurate landed costs"
```

```
// Get an array of paragraphs
$paragraphs = explode("\n\n", $text);
```

The EXPLODE built-in function breaks (explodes) content in the $text variable and stores the result in an array $paragraphs. The string "\n\n" specifies where to break the string. The following picture depicts the values held in the $paragraphs array. The first element [0] stores the main description from "The Import Manager" to "any part of the world". The second element [1] stores the sub-heading "Features:" and the third element [2] stores the eight features, each preceded by the symbol '*'.

$paragraphs	array[3]	
[0]	string	"The Import Manager is a unique import···
[1]	string	"Features:"
[2]	string	"* Streamlines your import processes* ...
$text	string	"The Import Manager is a unique import:...

Figure 6-26

```
// Add tags to each paragraph
$text = '';
foreach($paragraphs as $p) {
    $p = ltrim($p);
    $first_char = substr($p, 0, 1);
    if ($first_char == '*') {
        // Add <ul> and <li> tags
        $p = '<ul>' . $p . '</li></ul>';
        $p = str_replace("*", '<li>', $p);
        $p = str_replace("\n", '</li>', $p);
    } else {
        // Add <p> tags
        $p = '<p>' . $p . '</p>';
    }
    $text .= $p;
}
return $text;
}
...
```

The $text='' statement empties the $text string variable to create fresh content with HTML tags using the statement $text .= $p specified at the bottom. In the FOREACH loop all special characters are replaced with relevant HTML tags. The ltrim() function is used to remove whitespaces or other predefined character from the left side of the $p variable value. The substr() function returns a part of the $p variable. It fetches one character (1) from the first position (0 is the starting point) in the $p variable. The IF condition checks whether the first character is '*'. If so, the subsequent statements add <ul> and <li> tags to the $p variable, as illustrated below.

> "<ul><li> Streamlines your import processes</li><li> Maintains database of your imports</li>
> <li> Instantly provides current & historical data of imports</li><li> Gives you greater
> Control over the import flow</li><li> Manages custom duty and government levies</li>
> <li> Increases management information</li><li> Provides significant financial benefits & work
> efficiency to importers</li><li> Enables intelligent sourcing decisions by calculating accurate
> landed costs</li></ul>"

The ELSE block adds the <p> tag to the rest of the paragraphs.

> "<p>The Import Manager is a unique imports information and management software for importers
> ...
> ...
> Operating in any part of the world.</p><p>Features:</p>"

The $text .= $p statement re-creates the $text variable content by adding text from the $p variable and returns this content (containing the HTML tags) to Product.php file.

Delete Product

The purpose of this process is to remove only those product records from the database which are not used in any order. A product can be deleted either by clicking the trash icon on the Manager Product page (E) Figure 6-13, or by clicking the Delete button on the View Product page (B) Figure 6-14. When the administrator clicks the Delete button on the product details page, a hidden element value delete_product is forwarded to the controller. The controller assesses the delete_product value in a CASE statement and then calls a function named delete_product from the functions library file, which consequently removes the specified product record from the database. After deletion, the process is switched back to the controller. Using the Header() function, controller calls itself to refresh the products page.

Admin/Product/Product_View.php

```
...
    <div class="col-md-2">
     <?php if (get_product_order_count($product_id) == 0) : ?> <!-- If not used in any Order -->
     <form action="index.php" method="post" >
      <input type="hidden" name="action" value="delete_product"/>
      <input type="hidden" name="product_id" value="<?php echo $product['productID']; ?>" />
      <input type="hidden" name="category_id" value="<?php echo $product['categoryID']; ?>" />
      <button class="btn btn-danger btn-block" style="margin: 5px 0px">Delete</button>
     </form>
     <?php endif; ?>
    </div>
...
```

This is a partial code taken from the file Product_View.php. We saw some part of it earlier. This is the point where the administrator initiates the product deletion process. Line 1 ensures whether to show the Delete button on the web page. It does so by calling the get_product_order_count() function (from model\product_lib.php) by passing the id of the selected product. If the returned value is zero (as mentioned in the IF condition), a form is created with the POST method. The form holds the Delete button and relevant hidden elements to complete the process. The first hidden element holds the value delete_product. When the button is clicked, this value is passed to the controller for further processing. The next two hidden elements are created to hold product and category id. These two values are forwarded to the controller through the POST method. Finally, the Delete button is placed in the form. When this button is clicked, the control transfers to Index.php (listed next) in the current directory.

Admin/Product/Index.php

```
...
if (isset($_POST['action'])) {
  $action = $_POST['action'];
}
...
    case 'delete_product':  // Delete product via POST method when Delete button is clicked in Product_View.php
      if (isset($_POST['action'])) {
        $category_id = $_POST['category_id'];
        $product_id = $_POST['product_id'];
        delete_product($product_id);
        // Display the Product List page for the current category
        header("Location: .?category_id=$category_id");
        break;
      } else {          // Delete product via GET method when trash icon is clicked in Product_List.php
        $category_id = $_GET['category_id'];
        $product_id = $_GET['product_id'];
        delete_product($product_id);
        header("Location: .?category_id=$category_id");
        break;
      }
...
```

When the Delete button is clicked in the product details page, the controller evaluates and processes the POST condition and moves the delete_product value into $action. The controller also receives product and category ids from the previous list through the POST method and calls the delete_product() function from the library file (model\product_lib.php). After deletion, the flow returns to the final line where the controller calls itself through the header() function (using the single dot notation) to refresh the products list page. The code in the ELSE block is triggered when the trash icon is clicked on the Manage Products page. Note that in this case the GET method is used and executed to delete the selected product.

Model/Product_Lib.php

```
...
function delete_product($product_id) {
  global $db;
  $query = 'DELETE FROM products WHERE productID = :product_id';
  try {
    $statement = $db->prepare($query);
    $statement->bindValue(':product_id', $product_id);
    $statement->execute();
    $statement->closeCursor();
  } catch (PDOException $e) {
    $error_message = $e->getMessage();
    display_db_error($error_message);
  }
}
...
```

The function receives product id on line 1 from the previous list and uses the DELETE SQL statement for record removal using the forwarded parameter.

Update Product

Figure 6-27

After adding a product, an administrator can always modify its content through the interface illustrated above. In this section you'll learn how this process works. Note that both these processes are very similar and use same set of php files to update and to add a product. The process starts when the administrator clicks the Edit icon on the Manage Products page. This action calls the View Product page that displays details of the selected product. The page carries a button labeled Modify, which is used to modify the contents of the product. When this button is clicked, the Edit Product page as illustrated in the above figure is displayed. A hidden element having value show_add_edit_form is passed to the controller. The controller calls Product_Add_Edit.php file based on the above parameter. The file Product_Add_Edit.php contains a form comprising text elements to allow modification, as shown in the above figure. After amendment, the form is submitted back to the controller through a hidden element's parameter value update_product. After receiving the parameter, the controller evaluates it through a CASE statement and calls Product_View.php file. At this point, the update process terminates and the called file Product_View.php displays the product with updated content.

Admin/Product/Product_View.php

```
...
    <div class="col-md-2">
     <form action="index.php" method="post">
      <input type="hidden" name="action" value="show_add_edit_form">
      <input type="hidden" name="product_id" value="<?php echo $product['productID']; ?>">
      <input type="hidden" name="category_id" value="<?php echo $product['categoryID']; ?>">
      <button class="btn btn-primary btn-block" style="margin: 5px 0px">Modify</button>
     </form>
    </div>
...
```

This code is similar to the delete process discussed in the previous section. The only exception is the value parameter which passes a string show_add_edit_form to the controller.

Admin/Product/Index.php

```
...
  case 'show_add_edit_form':
    if (isset($_GET['product_id'])) {
      $product_id = $_GET['product_id'];
    } else {
      $product_id = $_POST['product_id'];
    }
    $product = get_product($product_id);
    $categories = get_categories();
    include('product_add_edit.php');
    break;
...
```

After receiving the control, the Index.php file processes the ELSE condition to get product id from the POST method, executes couple of functions, and calls Product_Add_Edit.php file located in the same directory. Note that this case (show_add_edit_form) is executed for both add and edit operations. When a new product is added through the link <a href="Index.php?action=show_add_edit_form">Add a new Product</a> (listed in Product_List.php file under Admin\Product directory), this case is evaluated again and the IF condition executes the $_GET statement (line 2) because in this case the parameter (action) and the corresponding value (show_add_edit_form) are forwarded to the controller in the url. Whenever this type of call is made, php creates a $_GET array, which is accordingly evaluated in the IF condition.

Admin/Product/Product_Add_Edit.php

```
...
<?php include '../../view/header_admin.php'; ?>
  <?php
    if (isset($product_id)) {
      $heading_text = 'Edit Product';
    } else {
      $heading_text = 'Add Product';
    }
  ?>
```

As the name indicates, this file generates a page that is used to both edit and add a product. The IF condition specified above determines an appropriate page title (A) according to the selected process and stores it in the $heading_text variable, which is then used in the breadcrumb region ahead to display the title of the current page. Existence of the variable $product_id is an indication that a product is being edited.

```
<form action="index.php" method="post">
  <div class="container page-overlay">
    <ol class="breadcrumb">
      <li class="breadcrumb-item"><a href="<?php echo $app_path.'admin/'; ?>">Home</a></li>
      <li class="breadcrumb-item"><a href="<?php echo $app_path.'admin/product'; ?>">Products</a></li>
      <li class="breadcrumb-item active"><?php echo $heading_text; ?></li>
    </ol>
    <hr class="hr">
    <div class="row">
      <div class="col-md-8">
        <?php if (isset($product_id)) : ?>
          <input type="hidden" name="action" value="update_product">
          <input type="hidden" name="product_id" value="<?php echo $product_id; ?>">
        <?php else: ?>
          <input type="hidden" name="action" value="add_product">
        <?php endif; ?>
          <input type="hidden" name="category_id" value="<?php echo $product['categoryID']; ?>">
```

This form displays input elements for amendment and for addition. Once again, a condition is used based on the variable $product_id. If it exists, two hidden elements are created to inform the controller that an update_product process is to be executed for a product whose identity is held in $product_id. The code under the ELSE block is executed when a new product is added. It passes a value add_product. The last line in the above code creates another hidden element to hold category id.

```php
<div class="form-group">
  <label>Category</label>
  <select name="category_id" class="form-control">
    <?php foreach ($categories as $category) :
      if ($category['categoryID'] == $product['categoryID']) {
        $selected = 'selected';
      } else {
        $selected = '';
      }
    ?>
      <option value="<?php echo $category['categoryID']; ?>"
        <?php echo $selected ?>>
        <?php echo $category['categoryName']; ?>
      </option>
    <?php endforeach; ?>
  </select>
</div>
```

The code above displays categories (B) in a drop-down list and which is done using the <select> and <option> elements. A FOREACH loop is initiated to populate the list with all categories. The IF condition in the loop matches the value of categoryID in both $category and $product arrays. If the match is found, the category is marked as selected on the next line. This marking indicates that the category was initially selected by the administrator while creating this product record. Conversely, if no match is found, a null value is moved into the $selected variable, which generally means that a new product is being added and no value is selected yet. In case of product modification, the selected string will be echoed to display the selected category (saved previously in the database) in the select list. On the other hand, a null string will be put to mark no selection in case of a new product and the drop-down list will be filled with all categories with first category on top. This small piece of code is a good example of how to display values in a drop-down list from a database column and to restore the previous selection in the list when a record is called for editing.

```
<div class="form-group">
  <label>Code</label>
  <input type="text" maxlength="10" name="code" required="vital" class="form-control"
        value="<?php echo $product['productCode']; ?>">
</div>
<div class="form-group">
  <label>Name</label>
  <input type="text" maxlength="50" name="name" required="vital" class="form-control"
        value="<?php echo $product['productName']; ?>">
</div>
<div class="form-group">
  <label>List Price</label>
  <input type="text" maxlength="12" name="price" required="vital" class="form-control"
        value="<?php echo $product['listPrice']; ?>">
</div>
<div class="form-group">
  <label>Discount Percent</label>
  <input type="text" maxlength="12" name="discount_percent" required="vital" class="form-control"
        value="<?php echo $product['discountPercent']; ?>">
</div>
<div class="form-group">
  <label>Description</label>
  <textarea name="description" class="form-control" rows="10">
        <?php echo $product['description']; ?>
  </textarea>
</div>
```

This bunch of code simply generates input and textarea elements to display product information. The elements are presented as blank text boxes when the process is called to enter a new product.

```
<div class="form-group">
  <input type="checkbox" name="featured"
    <?php if ($product['featured']) : ?>
      checked="checked"
    <?php endif; ?>
  >
  Featured Product
</div>
<div class="form-group">
  <button class="btn btn-warning btn-block">Save</button>
</div>
```

These lines put a check box labeled Featured Products. Products marked as featured products are displayed on the main Product page of the website. If the administrator checks this box while adding or updating a product, a value of 1 is inserted in the Featured column of the Products table. The administrator can always remove a product from the featured product list by un-checking this box which moves a value of zero into the specified column. Next, we placed a Save button, which passes control to Index.php file defined in the form's action attribute.

```
<div class="col-md-4">
    <!-- Inline style applied because this section is unique and appeared only once -->
    <h2 style="margin-left:60px">How to work with the description</h2>
    <ul style="margin-left:20px">
        <li>Use two returns to start a new paragraph.</li>
        <li>Use an asterisk to mark items in a bulleted list.</li>
        <li>Use one return between items in a bulleted list.</li>
        <li>Use standard HMTL tags for bold and italics.</li>
    </ul>
</div>
    </div>
  </div>
</form>

<?php include '../../view/footer.php'; ?>
```

The rest of the code in this file provides help to administrators on how to enter data in the Description column. Note that we applied inline styles to <h2> and <ul> elements to align them with other page content. The last point in this list suggests using standard HTML tags to make text bold and italicized. Let's see how it's done. Follow the steps below to make the Features: sub-title (in the Description field) bold:

1. Login to the admin interface by typing **localhost/abcglobal/admin** in your browser.
2. Enter **admin@abc.com** in the E-mail address box and **gemini** in the password. Click the **Login** button.
3. Click the **Product Manager**.
4. Under Software, click the **edit** icon for the The Import Manager software.
5. Click the **Modify** button.
6. Scroll down in the Description area and add tags to the Features subtitle like this: **Features:**
7. Click the **Save** button and note the Features subtitle in the Description section, which should now be presented as bold-faced text.

Handling Products Images

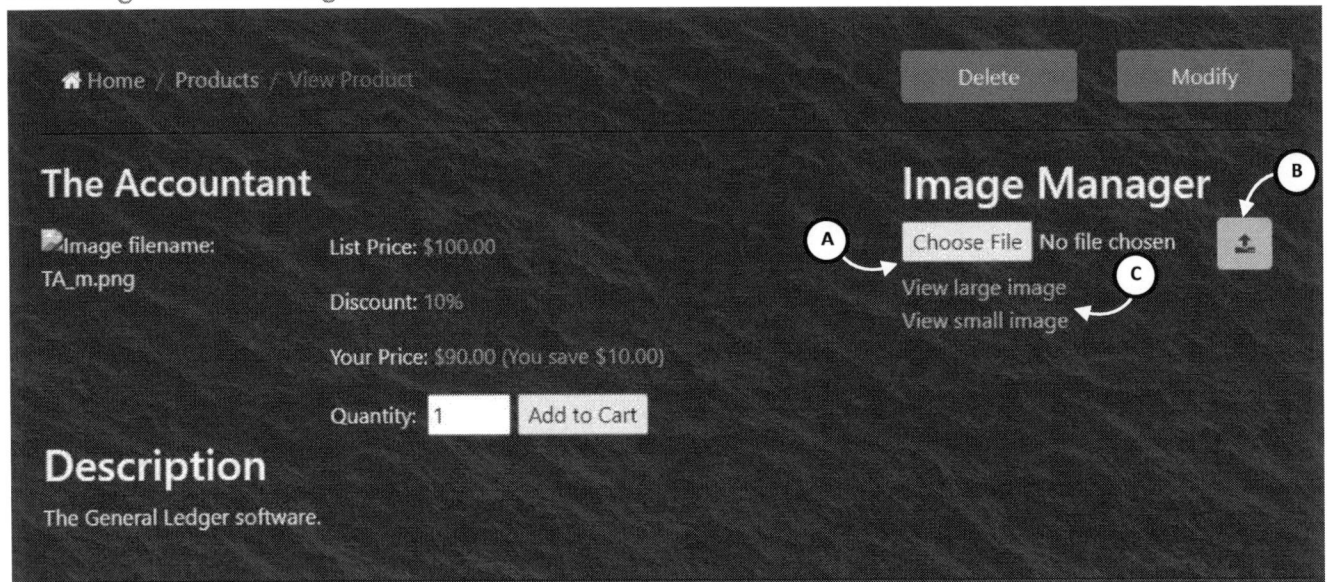

Figure 6-28

In this section you will get instructions on how to handle images of products. When an administrator adds a new product using the Add a new Product link on the Manage Products page, fills in the Add Product form, and clicks the Save button, the View Product page comes up displaying details of the new product without the image, as illustrated in the above figure. This page lets you add an image for the newly added product. The image handling process initiates when the administrator selects an image using the Choose File button (A) and clicks the upload button (B). The controller (under Admin\Product folder) comes into action to handle the process. The controller calls the get_product() function from the Product_Lib.php file. The function returns complete record of the selected product. Then, the controller calls Images.php file in the Utility directory to process the uploaded image. The function resize_image() specified in Images.php file is called twice to create medium and small versions of the uploaded image. After adding three image versions (Large - which is the actual uploaded image, Medium, and Small), the flow returns to the controller. The controller calls Product_View.php file to display the new image.

Admin/Product/Product_View.php

```
...
        <div class="col-md-4">
         <h2>Image Manager</h2>
         <form action="index.php" method="post" enctype="multipart/form-data" id="upload_image_form">
          <input type="hidden" name="action" value="upload_image">
          <input type="hidden" name="product_id" value="<?php echo $product['productID']; ?>">
          <input type="file" name="file1">
          <button class="btn btn-warning" style="margin-left:-60px"><span class="fa fa-upload"></span></button>
         </form>
         <p style="margin-bottom:0px"><a href="../../images/<?php echo $product['productCode']; ?>.png">
             View large image</a></p>
         <p style="margin-bottom:0px"><a href="../../images/<?php echo $product['productCode']; ?>_s.png">
             View small image</a></p>
        </div>
...
```

The Image Manager section utilizes last four columns on the web page. After adding an <h2> heading element, a form is created to hold image handling elements. Note that we added a new attribute enctype to the form, which sends form data encoded as multipart/form-data. The enctype attribute specifies how the form-data should be encoded when submitting it to the server. This value is required when you are using forms that have a file upload control – input type="file". It can be used only when the form method is POST. When you make a POST request, you have to encode the data that creates the body of the request in some way. HTML forms provide three methods of encoding. In the default application/x-www-form-urlencoded method all characters are encoded before they are sent (spaces are converted to "+" symbols, and special characters are converted to ASCII HEX values). The one we used here, multipart/form-data, is a more complicated encoding. In this method, no characters are encoded but it allows entire files to be included in the data. In the third method, text/plain, spaces are converted to "+" symbols, but no special characters are encoded.

Line 4 sets a value (upload_image) in a hidden element for controller. Line 5 passes the product id through a hidden element. On line 6 we used the required input type. This control permits administrators to upload a product image to the web server. Line 7 places a button to upload the image. When clicked, this button passes the values mentioned above to the controller in Admin/Product directory.

On line 9 and 10 two links are created to display large and small images of the product. When a product image is uploaded, the Image Manager process creates three versions of the image: large, medium, and small. The actual uploaded file is considered as a large image. The remaining two versions are created by the process that we'll see shortly. The medium size image is saved in the Images directory with a '_m' suffix. Similarly, '_s' is added to the small thumbnail version. For example, the code of the first software product provided in the dummy data (abcglobal.txt) is TIM. The three versions of this image file would be: TIM.png, TIM_m.png, and TIM_s.png. Note that the image files are moved to the Images folder under the site directory. The final two lines in the above code forms links (C) by providing complete path (../../images/) and file name ($product['productCode'] _s.png).

Admin/Product/Index.php

```
...
  case 'upload_image':
    $product_id = $_POST['product_id'];
    $product = get_product($product_id);
    $product_code = $product['productCode'];
    $image_filename = $product_code . '.png';
    $image_dir = $doc_root . $app_path . 'images/';
    if (isset($_FILES['file1'])) {
      $source = $_FILES['file1']['tmp_name'];
      $target = $image_dir . DIRECTORY_SEPARATOR . $image_filename;
      // save uploaded file with correct filename
      move_uploaded_file($source, $target);
      // add code that creates the medium and small versions of the image
      process_image($image_dir, $image_filename);
      // display product with new image
      include('product_view.php');
    }
    break;
...
```

The controller receives the process flow from Product_View.php file and executes code under the upload_image CASE statement. Assuming that you're uploading file for the first software product (The Import Manager), the following values will be stored in the variables defined above.

Line 2: $product_id = 1

Line 3: The $product array stores complete record of the first product fetched using the get_product() function.

Line 4: $product_code = TIM

Line 5: $image_filename = TIM.png

Line 6: $image_dir = c:\inetpub\wwwroot\abcglobal/images/

Line 7: The $_FILES array has the following values. Note that by using the global $_FILES array you can upload files from a client computer to the remote server.

$_FILES	array[1]	
[file1]	array[5]	
[name]	string	"TIM.PNG"
[type]	string	"image/png"
[tmp_name]	string	"C:\WINDOWS\Temp\phpD.tmp"
[error]	integer	0
[size]	integer	21581

Figure 6-29

Line 8: $source = C:\WINDOWS\Temp\phpD.tmp

Line 9: $target = c:\inetpub\wwwroot/abcglobal/images/\TIM.png

Line 10: The PHP built-in move_uploaded_file() function moves an uploaded file to a new location. It returns TRUE on success, or FALSE on failure. The syntax of this function is move_uploaded_file(file,newloc), where the file parameter specifies the file to be moved and the newloc parameter tells the new location for the file.

Line 11: Calls a function named process_image() from Images.php file, which is positioned under the Utility directory.

Line 12: Displays the product's page with the uploaded image.

Utility/Images.php

```
...
function process_image($dir, $filename) {
    // Set up the variables
    $i = strrpos($filename, '.');
    $image_name = substr($filename, 0, $i);
    $ext = substr($filename, $i);
    // Set up the read path
    $image_path = $dir . $filename;
    // Set up the write paths
    $image_path_m = $dir . $image_name . '_m' . $ext;
    $image_path_s = $dir . $image_name . '_s' . $ext;
    // Create an image that's a maximum of 200x200 pixels
    resize_image($image_path, $image_path_m, 200, 200);
    // Create a thumbnail image that's a maximum of 100x100 pixels
    resize_image($image_path, $image_path_s, 100, 100);
}
...
```

This function is called by Index.php to process images of products. The two parameters $dir and $filename receive values c:\inetpub\wwwroot/abcglobal/images and TIM.png respectively from the controller file. Values held in other variables are:

Line 2 $i = 3 - The strrpos() function finds the position of the last occurrence of a string (.) inside another string ($filename). This function returns 3 as the position of the sought period character, starting with 0 as the first position.

Line 3 $image_name = TIM - The substr() function returns a part of a string. Here, the function fetches 3 characters ($i) from the string ($filename) and from the starting position (0).

Line 4 $ext = .png - Stores the extension part of the file name along with period by taking all onward characters from the third position. Remember that zero possess the first place in the string.

Line 5 $image_path = c:\inetpub\wwwroot/abcglobal/images/TIM.png

Line 6 $image_path_m = c:\inetpub\wwwroot/abcglobal/images/TIM_m.png

Line 7 $image_path_s = c:\inetpub\wwwroot/abcglobal/images/TIM_s.png

Line 8 calls a function resize_image() residing in the same Images.php file to create a medium sized version of the provided product image.

Line 9 calls the function again to create a thumbnail version of the image. The resize_image function is called twice to create the two smaller versions of the image 200x200 and 100x100 pixels. Since the image we are using is smaller than the first measure, only the second image will be created in the called function.

Utility/Images.php (continued)

```
...
function resize_image($old_image_path, $new_image_path, $max_width, $max_height) {
  // Get image type
  $image_info = getimagesize($old_image_path);
  $image_type = $image_info[2];
  // Set up the function names
  switch($image_type) {
    case IMAGETYPE_JPEG:
      $image_from_file = 'imagecreatefromjpeg';
      $image_to_file = 'imagejpeg';
      break;
    case IMAGETYPE_GIF:
      $image_from_file = 'imagecreatefromgif';
      $image_to_file = 'imagegif';
      break;
    case IMAGETYPE_PNG:
      $image_from_file = 'imagecreatefrompng';
      $image_to_file = 'imagepng';
      break;
    default:
      echo 'File must be a JPEG, GIF, or PNG image.';
      exit;
  }
...
```

This function exhibits how to resize an image and is described in two parts. As mentioned earlier, the uploaded image file has three versions: Large (the original one), medium, and small. This function creates the last two after receiving all the required parameters from the previous one.

Line 2: The getimagesize() function determines the size of any given image file and returns the dimensions along with the file type and a height/width text string. The following figure presents values from the $image_info array for TIM.png that is obtained through the function getimagesize().

$image_info	array[6]	
[0]	integer	163
[1]	integer	178
[2]	integer	3
[3]	string	"width="163" height="178""
[bits]	integer	8
[mime]	string	"image/png"

Figure 6-30

Line 3-20: The value of $image_type is 3 which is obtained from index [2]. Index 2 returns a constant that identifies the type of the image. Here, the image is a PNG, so index 2 returns the IMAGETYPE_PNG constant. If the image were a JPEG or GIF, this index would return the IMAGETYPE_JPEG and IMAGETYPE_GIF constants, respectively. This constant is evaluated in the SWITCH statement to set up an appropriate function name to read and write the image to and from a file. For example, in the current scenario, the third CASE statement (line 13), for PNG image type, will be executed because we are using a .png file. PHP provides three functions: imagecreatefromjpeg, imagecreatefromgif, and imagecreatefrompng to create an image from a file. After assessing the image type, the code creates the new image using the function name stored as a string in the $image_from_file variable. The code uses the imagecreatefrompng function because we're using a PNG type image. However, if the image were of the JPEG or GIF type, this code would use the other functions mentioned in other CASE statements. If the image isn't among the listed types, the message on line 18 will be displayed. The process will upload the file to the Images folder on your PC. Once this code processes the image, it uses the function that's stored in the $image_to_file variable to write the image to the second file path. Again, since this example uses a PNG image, this code executes the same CASE block for writing a PNG image.

Utility/Images.php (continued)

```
...
// Get the old image and its height and width
$old_image = $image_from_file($old_image_path);
```

This code reads the image from the specified file. To do so, it uses the function imagecreatefrompng that's stored as a string in the $image_from_file variable (see line 14 in the previous listing), and passes the argument $old_image_path. This path is also received as an argument from the process_image() function.

```
$old_width = imagesx($old_image);
```

This code gets the width of the old image through the imagesx() function. Since the width of the image TIM.PNG is 163, the value is stored in the variable $old_width.

```
$old_height = imagesy($old_image);
```

Just like the previous code, this one uses imagesy() function to get the height of the uploaded image. The height (178) is then stored in the variable $old_height.

```
// Calculate height and width ratios
$width_ratio = $old_width / $max_width;
$height_ratio = $old_height / $max_height;
```

The first line above calculates the width ratio. The result stored in the variable $width_ratio will be 1.63 (163/100). The next line calculates the height ratio. The current height ratio is 1.78 (178/100). These ratios are calculated to keep the image within the specified limit.

```
// If image is larger than specified ratio, create the new image
if ($width_ratio > 1 || $height_ratio > 1) {
    // Calculate height and width for the new image
    $ratio = max($width_ratio, $height_ratio);
    $new_width = round($old_width / $ratio);
    $new_height = round($old_height / $ratio);
```

The IF condition checks that either the height ratio or the width ratio is greater than 1, which means that the old image is larger than maximum height or width. The code uses max() function to get the larger of the two ratios. The values stored in $ratio variable will be the $height_ratio (1.78) because it is the maximum between the two. The third line calculates the new image width. The value, after rounding, will be 92 (163/1.78). The final line determines the new height. This value will be 100 (178/1.78).

```
// Create the new image
$new_image = imagecreatetruecolor($new_width, $new_height);
```

This line uses the imagecreatetruecolor function that create a new truecolor image of 92 x 100 pixels.

```
// Set transparency according to image type
if ($image_type == IMAGETYPE_GIF) {
    $alpha = imagecolorallocatealpha($new_image, 0, 0, 0, 127);
    imagecolortransparent($new_image, $alpha);
}
if ($image_type == IMAGETYPE_PNG || $image_type == IMAGETYPE_GIF) {
    imagealphablending($new_image, false);
    imagesavealpha($new_image, true);
}
```

In this block of code transparency for GIF and PNG is handled. Note that JPEG doesn't allow parts of an image to be transparent. The first IF condition performs some processing that needs to be done only for GIF images. The first statement in this block calls the imagecolorallocatealpha function that allocates black color (RGB value 0, 0, 0) as alpha color and an alpha value of 127 to indicate that the alpha color should be completely transparent. The next statement uses the imagecolortransparent function to set the alpha color as the transparent color in the image. The next IF statement checks whether the image is a GIF image or a PNG image. The first statement in this block turns off alpha blending which is necessary to save complete alpha channel information that is done using the imagesavealpha function.

```
// Copy old image to new image - this resizes the image
$new_x = 0;
$new_y = 0;
$old_x = 0;
$old_y = 0;
imagecopyresampled($new_image, $old_image, $new_x, $new_y, $old_x, $old_y, $new_width, $new_height,
                   $old_width, $old_height);
```

This block of code creates the new image and copies the old image to the new image. To do that, this code uses a value of 0 for the x and y values of the old and new images to indicate that both images should start at the upper left corner. In addition, it specifies the correct values for the height and width of the old and new images.

The imagecopyresampled function copies a rectangular portion of the source image (old) to the destination image (new) resizing the image if necessary.

```
// Write the new image to a new file
$image_to_file($new_image, $new_image_path);
```

This code writes the new image to the specified file path.

```
// Free any memory associated with the new image
imagedestroy($new_image);
```

This line uses imagedestroy() function to free any memory used by the new image.

```
} else {
    // Write the old image to a new file
    $image_to_file($old_image, $new_image_path);
}
```

The ELSE block is executed when the old image is smaller than the maximum width and height limits. In such situation, the image is not resized and a copy of the old image is written to the new path.

```
// Free any memory associated with the old image
imagedestroy($old_image);
}
...
```

Frees any memory used by the old image.

Add New Products

The add product process is similar to the update process and uses the same PHP files that we used while editing a product. The process starts when the administrator clicks the Add a New Product link under the list of products. The controller executes the code under the case show_add_edit_form. This parameter is passed to it through the GET method when the above link is clicked. The function get_product() is called from Product_Lib.php file. Next, the get_categories() function is called from Category_Lib.php file. The Product_Add_Edit.php is inducted in the process, which presents the form to input content for the new product. It was discussed in a previous listing. The new product is added to the database through the add_product() function in the library file. The get_product() function is executed again to get details of the newly added product. Since most of the code in this process has already been discussed, we'll move on to the next task - Manage Orders.

Task 6 – Manage Orders

The administrators can view, process and delete orders placed by members of the website with the help of this module which has the following three pages:

1. **Orders List:** After clicking the initial Order Manager link in the Admin Menu, the administrator is presented with a list of Outstanding and Shipped orders. See Figure 6-31 below.

2. **Order Information:** Both these sections (Outstanding and Shipped Orders) carry links to corresponding orders which, when clicked, display details of individual orders on Order Information page. The page contains two buttons - Delete and Ship Order. An administrator can either process the order through the Ship Order button or cancel the order by using the Delete button. Note that these buttons are displayed only when an order is outstanding.

3. **Delete Order:** If an order is not shipped, the administrator can delete it. The Delete Order page confirms the process before removing the order from the database.

   Let's see how this process works beginning with the first one – Orders List.

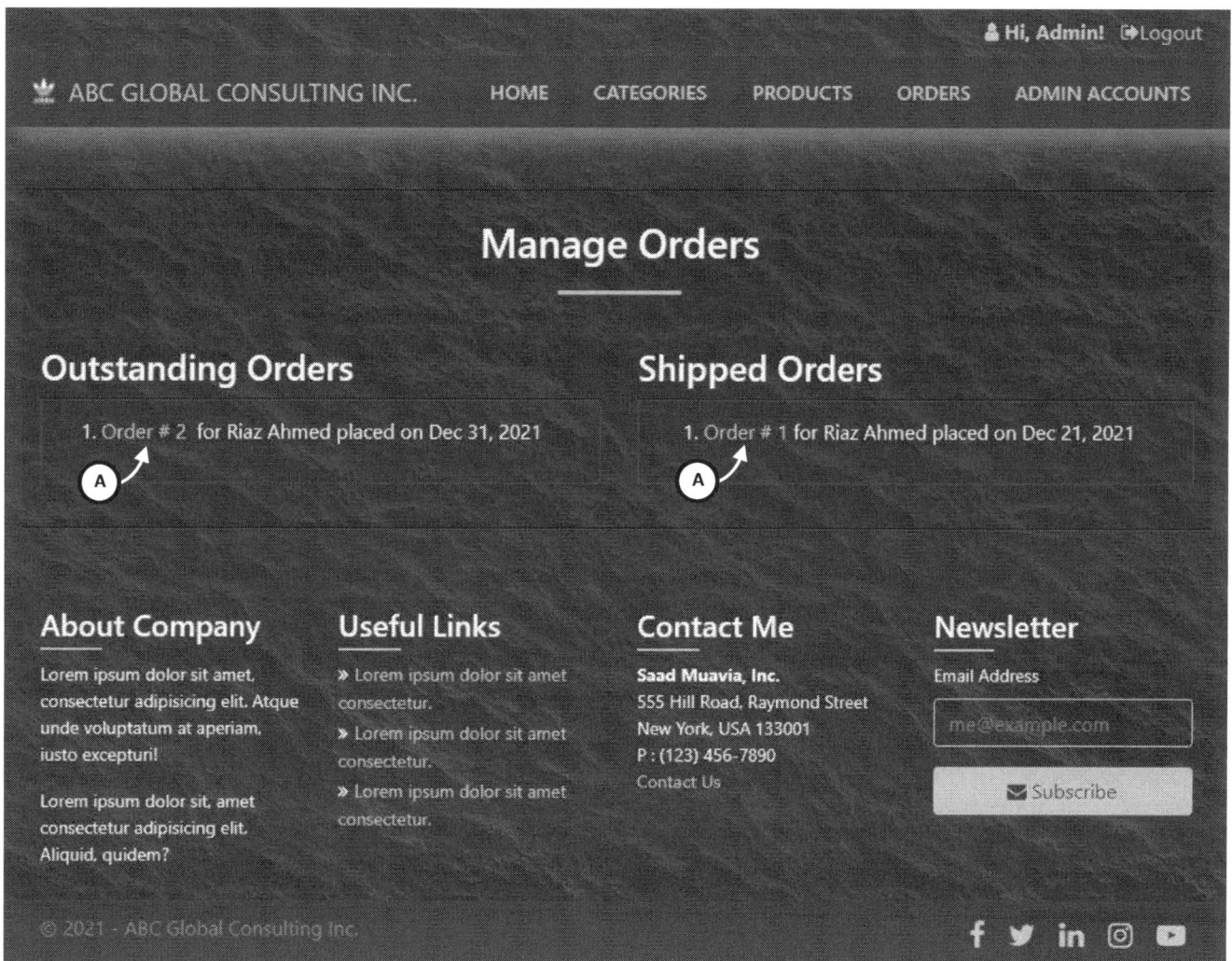

Figure 6-31

The page illustrated above lists all orders, either shipped or yet to be shipped, under two sections. Each section has links (A) to individual orders. These links call another page to display details of the selected order. Orders under the Shipped section can only be viewed, while those under the outstanding category can either by shipped or deleted through the order details page.

Orders List

The process initiates when the Order Manager link is clicked in the Admin home page, or the Orders option is clicked in the main menu. The control is transferred to Index.php in the Orders directory under the Admin folder. The controller calls some utility files to check connectivity. Here, some new files are included in the process. These files are Member_Lib, Address_Lib, and Order_Lib. All these library files contain several functions to interact with the database. Two functions, Outstanding_Orders and Shipped_Orders, are called from the Order_Lib.php library file. These functions return matching orders for display. The controller calls Order_Status.php file which displays the result on the page.

Admin/Orders/Index.php

```
...
case 'list_orders':
   $new_orders = outstanding_orders();
   $old_orders = shipped_orders();
   include 'order_status.php';
   break;
...
```

Model/Order_Lib.php

```
...
function outstanding_orders() {
   global $db;
   $query =
       'SELECT * FROM orders
       INNER JOIN members
       ON members.memberID = orders.memberID
       WHERE shipDate IS NULL ORDER BY orderDate';
   ...
}
function shipped_orders() {
   global $db;
   $query =
       'SELECT * FROM orders
       INNER JOIN members
       ON members.memberID = orders.memberID
       WHERE shipDate IS NOT NULL ORDER BY orderDate';
   ...
}
```

At this stage you must be comfortable with the process flow and can also understand what's happening. The above listings show related code from two different files. The code from Index.php file is executed when the orders' list page is initially called. Line 2 and 3 in Index.php file receive results from the two functions in $new_orders and $old_orders variables. Line 4 calls Order_Status.php from the same Admin/Orders directory to display the result.

The outstanding_orders() and shipped_orders() functions from Order_Lib.php file use SELECT SQL statements to collect order data. The first query filters data on IS NULL basis while the second one uses the reverse IS NOT NULL criterion.

The output of the two queries is show in the following figure:

Outstanding Orders Query		Shipped Orders Query	
orderID	2	orderID	1
memberID	1	memberID	1
orderDate	2021-12-31 10:35:15	orderDate	2021-12-31 10:35:15
shipAmount	200.00	shipAmount	200.00
taxAmount	64.64	taxAmount	64.64
shipDate	NULL	shipDate	2021-01-05 09:43:13
shipAddressID	1	shipAddressID	1
cardType	2	cardType	2
cardNumber	1111111111111111	cardNumber	1111111111111111
cardExpires	04/2021	cardExpires	04/2021
billingAddressID	2	billingAddressID	2
memberID	1	memberID	1
fName	Riaz	fName	Riaz
lName	Ahmed	lName	Ahmed
shipAddressID	1	shipAddressID	1
billingAddressID	2	billingAddressID	2
memberEmail	realtech@cyber.net.pk	memberEmail	realtech@cyber.net.pk
memberPW	4ee29c1079121336a....	memberPW	4ee29c1079121336a....

Figure 6-32

Admin/Orders/Order_Status.php

```
...
<div class="container section page-overlay">
  <div class="row">
    <div class="col-md-12">
    <h2 class="section-head">Manage Orders</h2>
    </div>
  </div>
  <div class="row">
    <div class="col-md-6">
      <table class="table table-content table-border">
        <h3>Outstanding Orders</h3>
        <tbody>
          <?php if (count($new_orders) > 0 ) : ?>
            <tr>
              <td>
                <ol>
                  <?php foreach($new_orders as $order) :
                    $order_id = $order['orderID'];
                    $order_date = strtotime($order['orderDate']);
                    $order_date = date('M j, Y', $order_date);
                    $url = $app_path . 'admin/orders' . '?action=view_order&order_id=' . $order_id;
                  ?>
                    <li>
                      <a href="<?php echo $url; ?>">Order #
                      <?php echo $order_id; ?></a> for
                      <?php echo $order['fName'] . ' ' . $order['lName']; ?> placed on
                      <?php echo $order_date; ?>
                    </li>
                  <?php endforeach; ?>
                </ol>
              </td>
            </tr>
          <?php else: ?>
            <p>There are no outstanding orders.</p>
          <?php endif; ?>
        </tbody>
      </table>
    </div>
  </div>
```

The above listing creates a six columns section to display outstanding orders. These orders are judged through the count of $new_orders variable. If the value of this variable is greater than zero, a list of outstanding orders is generated under <ol> element. If the value is zero, the message There are no outstanding orders is displayed. The strtotime() function used in this code parses an English textual date or time. It parses the $order['orderDate'] time string parameter. The date() function is used to present value in the $order_date variable in Mon dd, YYYY format. Here, the three letters represent:

M: For three letters month (Jan-Dec)
j: For day of month (1-31)
Y: For four digits year (2021)

When the administrator clicks an order link, the next line calls Index.php in the Admin/Orders directory. It passes two values view_order and $order_id to the controller. The former one is evaluated in a Case statement, as shown in the following code, while the later one is used to fetch details of the specified order.

```
elseif ( isset($_GET['action']) ) {
   $action = $_GET['action'];
}

case 'view_order':
   $order_id = $_GET['order_id'];
   // Get order data
   $order = get_order($order_id);
   $order_date = date('M j, Y', strtotime($order['orderDate']));
   $order_items = get_order_items($order_id);
   ...
```

The <li> element displays order links and concatenate other values such as member name and order date to it. The code produces a text like: Order # 2 for Riaz Ahmed placed on Dec 31, 2021. The text, Order # 2, is a link that calls details of the specified order when clicked.

```
<div class="col-md-6">
  <table class="table table-content table-border">
    <h3>Shipped Orders</h3>
    <tbody>
      <?php if (count($old_orders) > 0 ) : ?>
        <tr>
          <td>
            <ol>
              <?php foreach($old_orders as $order) :
                $order_id = $order['orderID'];
                $order_date = strtotime($order['orderDate']);
                $order_date = date('M j, Y', $order_date);
                $url = $app_path . 'admin/orders' . '?action=view_order&order_id=' . $order_id;
              ?>
                <li>
                  <a href="<?php echo $url; ?>">Order #
                  <?php echo $order_id; ?></a> for
                  <?php echo $order['fName'] . ' ' . $order['lName']; ?> placed on
                  <?php echo $order_date; ?>
                </li>
              <?php endforeach; ?>
            </ol>
          </td>
        </tr>
      <?php else: ?>
        <p>There are no shipped orders.</p>
      <?php endif; ?>
    </tbody>
  </table>
</div>
</div>
</div>
...
```

The above code generates a list of shipped orders. It is similar to the previous code with one distinction, and that is the $old_orders variable, which is used to check number of shipped orders to display.

Order Information, Confirmation and Deletion

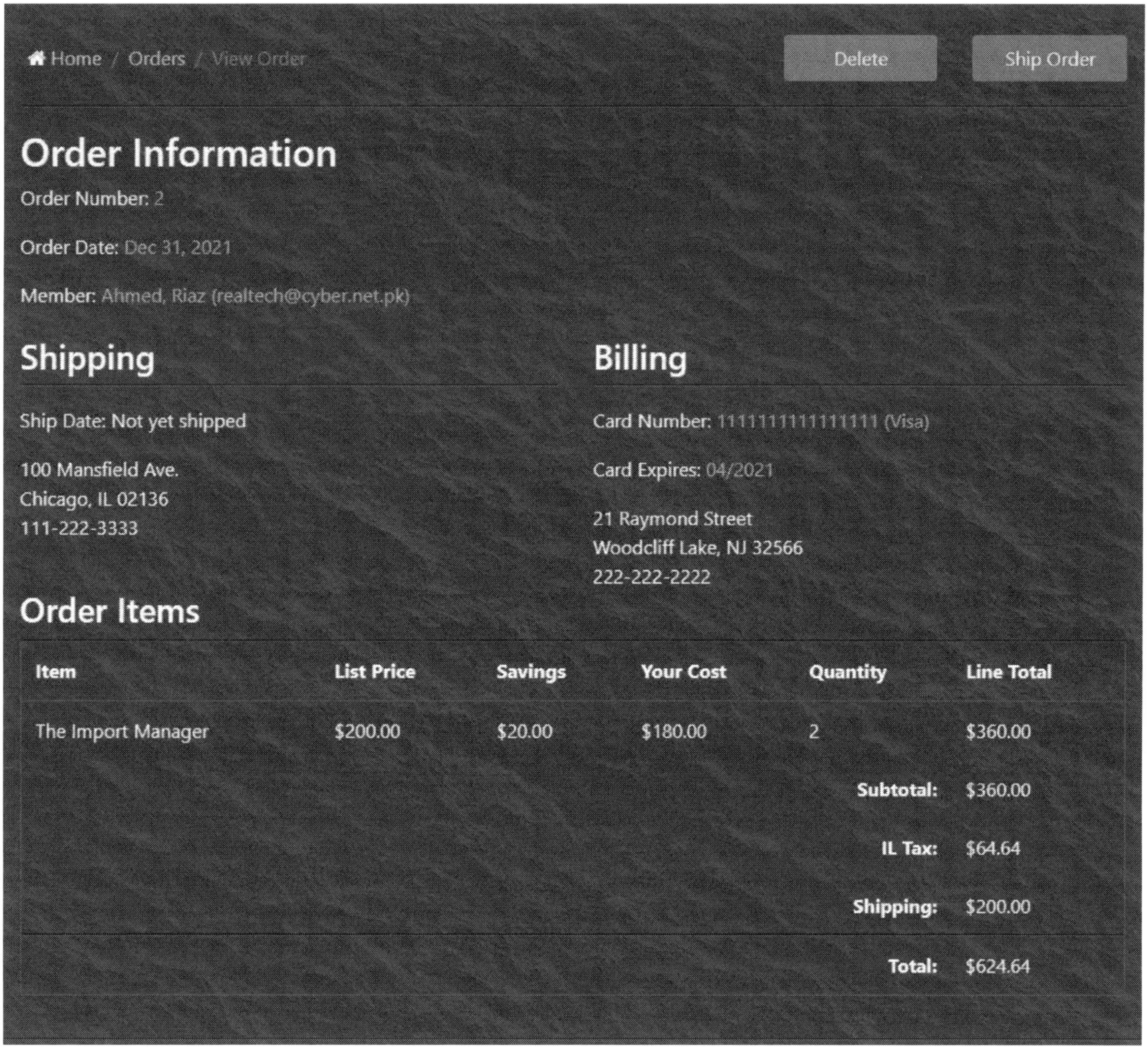

Home / Orders / View Order   Delete   Ship Order

Order Information

Order Number: 2

Order Date: Dec 31, 2021

Member: Ahmed, Riaz (realtech@cyber.net.pk)

Shipping

Ship Date: Not yet shipped

100 Mansfield Ave.
Chicago, IL 02136
111-222-3333

Billing

Card Number: 1111111111111111 (Visa)

Card Expires: 04/2021

21 Raymond Street
Woodcliff Lake, NJ 32566
222-222-2222

Order Items

Item	List Price	Savings	Your Cost	Quantity	Line Total
The Import Manager	$200.00	$20.00	$180.00	2	$360.00
				Subtotal:	$360.00
				IL Tax:	$64.64
				Shipping:	$200.00
				Total:	$624.64

Figure 6-33

The web page illustrated above presents details of a selected order. The existence of two buttons (Delete and Ship Order) is an indication that the order is yet to be shipped. An administrator can either delete or process it using these two buttons.

The process starts when an order link is clicked in either the outstanding or the shipped orders list. Two parameters, view_order and $order_id, are passed to the controller which executes the code associated with the case view_order. The three library files are called from the Model directory to fetch relevant records. The first one is called to execute get_order() and get_order_items() functions, the second one is accessed to run get_member() function, while the last one fetches shipping and billing addresses through get_address() function. After receiving the required data, the controller calls Order.php file which displays order details as illustrated in the previous figure.

Admin/Orders/Index.php

```
...
elseif ( isset($_GET['action']) ) {
    $action = $_GET['action'];
}
...
```

The controller makes all the files available to this process using the initial require_once statements. Then, it executes the above ELSEIF code, which provides couple of arguments to it. One of these arguments is view_order which, in this case, is evaluated and found true.

```
...
    case 'view_order':
        $order_id = $_GET['order_id'];
        // Get order data
        $order = get_order($order_id);
        $order_date = date('M j, Y', strtotime($order['orderDate']));
        $order_items = get_order_items($order_id);
        // Get member data
        $member = get_member($order['memberID']);
        $name = $member['lName'] . ', ' . $member['fName'];
        $email = $member['memberEmail'];
        $card_number = $order['cardNumber'];
        $card_expires = $order['cardExpires'];
        $card_name = card_name($order['cardType']);
```

The above code retrieves data from the master table (Orders) through a call to the function get_order() from Order_Lib.php file. The next line formats order date in the specified format - see previous section for details. The get_order_items() function fetches all rows from the detail table (OrderItems) for the selected order. The get_member() function retrieves complete record of the member who placed that order. After retrieving the row, information contained within columns is stored in corresponding variables using subsequent code.

```
//Get Shipping Address
$shipping_address = get_address($order['shipAddressID']);
$ship_line1 = $shipping_address['line1'];
$ship_line2 = $shipping_address['line2'];
$ship_city = $shipping_address['city'];
$ship_state = $shipping_address['state'];
$ship_zip = $shipping_address['zipCode'];
$ship_phone = $shipping_address['phone'];
//Get Billing Address
$billing_address = get_address($order['billingAddressID']);
$bill_line1 = $billing_address['line1'];
$bill_line2 = $billing_address['line2'];
$bill_city = $billing_address['city'];
$bill_state = $billing_address['state'];
$bill_zip = $billing_address['zipCode'];
$bill_phone = $billing_address['phone'];
include 'order.php';
break;
...
```

The above code stores shipping and billing address data in appropriate variables after fetching them from the database through the get_address() function. Note that this function is called twice but with different parameters to fetch the two addresses - $order['shipAddressID'] & $order['billingAddressID']. The final line in this code calls the controller file to display the gathered information on the Order Information page.

Admin/Orders/Order.php

...

```html
<!-- display buttons only for outstanding orders -->
<?php if ($order['shipDate'] === NULL) : ?>
<div class="col-md-2">
  <form action="index.php" method="post" >
    <input type="hidden" name="action" value="confirm_delete" />
    <input type="hidden" name="order_id" value="<?php echo $order_id; ?>" />
    <button class="btn btn-danger btn-block" style="margin: 5px 0px">Delete</button>
  </form>
</div>
<div class="col-md-2">
  <form action="index.php" method="post" >
    <input type="hidden" name="action" value="set_ship_date" />
    <input type="hidden" name="order_id" value="<?php echo $order_id; ?>" />
    <button class="btn btn-primary btn-block" style="margin: 5px 0px">Ship Order</button>
  </form>
</div>
<?php endif; ?>
```

...

This file is used to display both outstanding and shipped orders. Using the shipDate column value (line # 2), it distinguishes the two. If the value of shipDate is NULL, which indicates that the order is yet to be shipped, the code in the IF block is executed to display Delete and Ship Order buttons. The identical operator (===) checks that the two values are true and have the same type. After clicking any one of these buttons, the process takes hidden values (set_ship_date or confirm_delete) to Index.php file. Based on these values the controller proceeds to perform the desired action. The value set_ship_date indicates that the administrator has requested to ship the order. On the other hand, the value confirm_delete sends a request to delete the selected order. In the former case, the controller calls a function set_ship_date() from the order library file (order_lib.php) which uses the UPDATE SQL statement to put current system date in the shipdate column. A date value in this column signifies that the order has been shipped. NULL stands for outstanding orders. Once the administrator processes an order, it is listed in the shipped category and the two buttons are removed as well.

Clicking the Delete button executes the confirm_delete case in the controller file. The code under this block fetches some basic information such as order date and member details. Next, it calls order_delete.php file. This file displays a confirmation page with two buttons and the above basic information. If the administrator clicks the Cancel button, nothing happens; but, if he/she clicks the Delete button, the process flows back to Index.php file with a hidden value 'delete'. The 'delete' case in the controller file calls delete_order() function which removes the selected order from two database tables (orders and orderitems). Both these case statements use a built-in intval() function which gets the integer value of a variable. In our case, it returns the integer value of the variable order_id on success, or 0 on failure.

```html
<div class="row">
  <div class="col-md-12">
    <h2>Order Information</h2>
    <p style="display: inline-block;">Order Number:</p>
    <p style="display: inline-block; color: rgb(165, 165, 165)"><?php echo $order_id; ?></p><br>
    <p style="display: inline-block;">Order Date:</p>
    <p style="display: inline-block; color: rgb(165, 165, 165)"><?php echo $order_date; ?></p><br>
    <p style="display: inline-block;">Member:</p>
    <p style="display: inline-block; color: rgb(165, 165, 165)"><?php echo $name . ' (' . $email . ')'; ?></p>
  </div>
</div>
```

The above code display order header information, such as order number, date, and member name and email address.

```html
<div class="row">
  <div class="col-md-6">
    <h3 style="margin-top: 20px;">Shipping</h3>
    <hr class="hr" style="margin-top: 0rem">
    <?php if ($order['shipDate'] === NULL) : ?>  <!-- If the shipment date is null, display Not yet shipped message -->
      <p>Ship Date: Not yet shipped</p>
    <?php else: $ship_date = date('M j, Y', strtotime($order['shipDate'])); ?>
      <p style="display: inline-block;">Ship Date:</p>
      <p style="display: inline-block; color: rgb(165, 165, 165)"><?php echo $ship_date; ?></p>
    <?php endif; ?>
    <p><?php echo $ship_line1; ?><br />
      <?php if ( strlen($ship_line2) > 0 ) : ?>
      <?php echo $ship_line2; ?><br />
      <?php endif; ?>
      <?php echo $ship_city; ?>, <?php echo $ship_state; ?>
      <?php echo $ship_zip; ?><br />
      <?php echo $ship_phone; ?>
    </p>
  </div>
  <div class="col-md-6">
    <h3 style="margin-top: 20px;">Billing</h3>
    <hr class="hr" style="margin-top: 0rem">
    <p style="display: inline-block;">Card Number:</p>
    <p style="display: inline-block; color: rgb(165, 165, 165)"><?php echo $card_number . ' (' . $card_name . ')';
            ?></p><br>
    <p style="display: inline-block;">Card Expires:</p>
    <p style="display: inline-block; color: rgb(165, 165, 165)"><?php echo $card_expires; ?></p>
    <p><?php echo $bill_line1; ?><br />
      <?php if ( strlen($bill_line2) > 0 ) : ?>
      <?php echo $bill_line2; ?><br />
      <?php endif; ?>
      <?php echo $bill_city; ?>, <?php echo $bill_state; ?>
      <?php echo $bill_zip; ?><br />
      <?php echo $bill_phone; ?>
    </p>
  </div>
</div>
```

The above block of code shows shipping and billing addresses of the logged in member along with credit card information.

```php
<div class="row">
  <div class="col-md-12">
    <h3>Order Items</h3>
    <table class="table table-content table-border">
      <thead>
        <th>Item</th>
        <th>List Price</th>
        <th>Savings </th>
        <th>Your Cost </th>
        <th>Quantity </th>
        <th>Line Total</th>
      </thead>
      <?php
      $subtotal = 0;
      foreach ($order_items as $item) :
        $product_id = $item['productID'];
        $product = get_product($product_id);
        $item_name = $product['productName'];
        $list_price = $item['itemPrice'];
        $savings = $item['discountAmount'];
        $your_cost = $list_price - $savings;
        $quantity = $item['quantity'];
        $line_total = $your_cost * $quantity;
        $subtotal += $line_total;
      ?>
      <tr>
        <td><?php echo $item_name; ?></td>
        <td>
          <?php echo sprintf('$%.2f', $list_price); ?>
        </td>
        <td>
          <?php echo sprintf('$%.2f', $savings); ?>
        </td>
        <td>
          <?php echo sprintf('$%.2f', $your_cost); ?>
        </td>
        <td>
          <?php echo $quantity; ?>
        </td>
        <td>
          <?php echo sprintf('$%.2f', $line_total); ?>
        </td>
      </tr>
      <?php endforeach; ?>
      <tr>
        <td colspan="5"><b style="float:right">Subtotal:</b></td>
        <td>
          <?php echo sprintf('$%.2f', $subtotal); ?>
        </td>
      </tr>
      <tr>
        <td colspan="5"><b style="float:right"><?php echo $ship_state; ?> Tax:</b></td>
        <td>
          <?php echo sprintf('$%.2f', $order['taxAmount']); ?>
        </td>
```

```
        </tr>
        <tr>
          <td colspan="5"><b style="float:right">Shipping:</b></td>
          <td>
            <?php echo sprintf('$%.2f', $order['shipAmount']); ?>
          </td>
        </tr>
        <tr style="border-top: solid 1px #333; box-shadow: #000 0 -1px 0">
          <td colspan="5"><b style="float:right">Total:</b></td>
          <td>
            <?php
              $total = $subtotal + $order['taxAmount'] + $order['shipAmount'];
              echo sprintf('$%.2f', $total);
            ?>
          </td>
        </tr>
      </table>
    </div>
  </div>
</div>
...
```

A above code creates a table to display line item details from the detail table (orderitems) in the database. The sprintf() function writes a formatted string. For example, the code sprintf('$%.2f', $list_price) writes list price of items preceded with a $ sign and with two decimal places.

Task 7 – Manage Admin Accounts

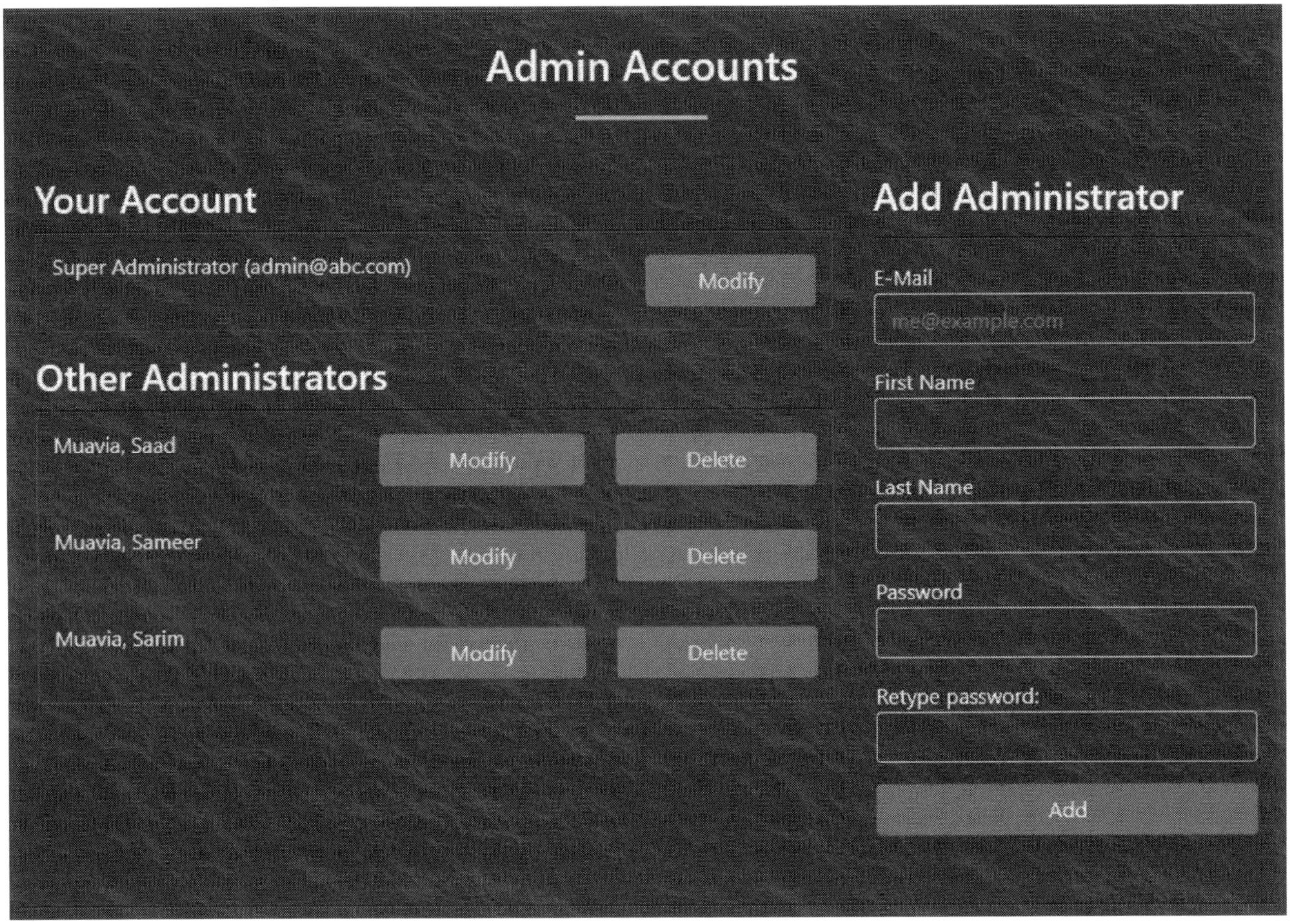

Figure 6-34

Using this module, an administrator can view, add, modify, or delete admin accounts, as illustrated in figure 6-19. The first section, allows the logged in administrator to modify his credentials. The second Other Administrators section lets him modify or delete other admin accounts. The Add Administrator section is used to add new site administrators. Let's see how this Admin Accounts page is generated.

The process starts when Admin Account Manager link is clicked on the Admin home page. As usual, the main controller passes flow to the respective controller in the Admin/Users directory which initially calls subordinate routine files under the Utility and View directories. Index.php calls Admin_Lib.php library file to collect data from Admins table. After receiving the data, the controller calls Admin_View file from the same directory to display all admin records.

Admin/Users/Index.php

```
...
if (isset($_SESSION['user'])) {
  display_error('Already logged in as a member.');
}
```

The above code checks if you're already logged in as a member. In a situation like this, you'll have to log off before performing any administrative tasks.

```
...
if ( admin_count() == 0 ) {
  if ( $_POST['action'] == 'create' ) {
    $action = 'create';
  }
  else {
    $action = 'view_account';
  }
}
...
```

The first four lines in the above code are incorporated to present the 'Add Administrator' interface when there are no admin accounts in the database. You can test it by removing the sole admin record from the Admins table. Once the record is removed, type http://localhost/abcglobal/admin in the browser and you'll be asked to create the first admin account. The admin_count function exists in the Admin_Lib.php file which counts number of admin records in the Admins table. Upon return, code in the ELSE block is executed to store a string 'view_account' in $action variable. Based on this value, code under the Case statement 'view_account' is executed.

```
...
  case 'view_account':
    // Get admin user data from session
    $name = $_SESSION['admin']['fName'] . ' ' . $_SESSION['admin']['lName'];
    $email = $_SESSION['admin']['adminemail'];
    $admin_id = $_SESSION['admin']['adminID'];
    // Get all accounts from database
    $admins = get_all_admins();
    // View admin accounts
    include 'admin_view.php';
    break;
...
```

This code fetches values from the admin session (credentials of the currently logged in administrator) into appropriate variables for display in the Your Account section. The get_all_admins() function is called to store all records from the Admins table in the $admins array. These records are displayed under the Other Administrators section. The final line includes Admin_View.php file to display the two sections along with a blank form that is used to add a new admin account, as shown in the above figure. Note that if the admin session is empty and the Admins database is also blank, only the 'Add Administrator' section will be displayed. This situation happens when the first admin account is created, as discussed above.

Admin/Users/Admin_View.php

```
...
 <div class="row">
  <div class="col-md-12">
    <h2 class="section-head">Admin Accounts</h2>
  </div>
 </div>
 <div class="row">
  <div class="col-md-8">
    <?php if (isset($_SESSION['admin'])) : ?>
    <h3>Your Account</h3>
     <form action="index.php" method="post">
      <input type="hidden" name="action" value="view_edit" />
      <table class="table table-content table-border">
       <tr>
        <td><?php echo $name . ' (' . $email . ')'; ?>
          <input type="hidden" name="admin_id" value="<?php echo $admin_id; ?>" />
        </td>
        <td><button class="btn btn-primary btn-block" style="margin: 5px 0px">Modify</button></td>
       </tr>
      </table>
     </form>
    <?php endif; ?>
...
```

The code in Admin_View.php file is explained in three parts. This one elaborates the Admin Accounts section. As discussed, the Admin Accounts page holds three sections. The above code structures the first Admin Accounts section, which displays information of the currently logged in administrator and allows him/her to modify personal credentials. It uses a table inside a form to put the information on the web page. The information it displays using the $name, $email, and $admin_id variables arrive from the previous listing. The admin id is stored in a hidden element for further referencing.

When clicked, the Modify button passes the view_edit value as a parameter to the controller which calls another interface (admin_edit.php) where administrators can change their e-mail address, first name, last name and even their passwords.

After modification, a hidden value 'update' is forwarded to the controller which executes instructions under the update case. These instructions are straight forward. First, the admin id value, received through $_POST, is converted to integer using the intval() function. This conversion is done to match the variable value with the table column value (which is an integer) in the WHERE clause of the UPDATE statement. Next, the update_admin() function is called from the functions library to put new values in the Admin table. Finally, the admin session is re-created to get updated values from the database and the page is refreshed through the redirect() function to reflect updates.

...

```php
<?php if ( count($admins) > 1 ) : ?>
  <h3>Other Administrators</h3>
  <table class="table table-content table-border">
   <?php foreach($admins as $admin):
     if ( $admin['adminID'] != $admin_id ) :
   ?>
   <tr>
    <td><?php echo $admin['lName'] . ', ' . $admin['fName']; ?></td>
    <td>
      <form action="index.php" method="post">
       <input type="hidden" name="action" value="view_edit" />
       <input type="hidden" name="admin_id" value="<?php echo $admin['adminID']; ?>" />
       <button class="btn btn-primary btn-block" style="margin: 5px 0px">Modify</button>
      </form>
    </td>
    <td>
      <form action="index.php" method="post">
       <input type="hidden" name="action" value="view_delete_confirm" />
       <input type="hidden" name="admin_id" value="<?php echo $admin['adminID']; ?>" />
       <button class="btn btn-danger btn-block" style="margin: 5px 0px">Delete</button>
      </form>
    </td>
   </tr>
   <?php endif; ?>
   <?php endforeach; ?>
  </table>
<?php endif; ?>
```

...

The above code forms the Other Administrators section. The FOREACH loop iterate through all admin records. The IF statement on the subsequent line ensures that only other admin records are displayed in this section (because detail of the logged in administrator has already been displayed in the Your Account section through the previous listing). You also have two buttons (Modify and Delete) for each admin account. These buttons are defined in separate forms and take hidden values (view_edit and view_delete_confirm respectively) to the controller when they are clicked. An administrator can use these buttons to either modify an account or delete it altogether.

```
...
    <h3>Add Administrator</h3>
    <hr class="hr">
    <form action="index.php" method="post">
      <input type="hidden" name="action" value="create">
      <table class="table table-content table-border">
        <div class="form-group">
          <label style="margin-bottom:-0.5rem !important">E-Mail</label>
          <input type="email" required="vital" class="form-control" name="email" placeholder="me@example.com"
                      value="<?php echo $_SESSION['form_data']['email']; ?>">
        </div>
        <div class="form-group">
          <label style="margin-bottom:-0.5rem !important">First Name</label>
          <input type="text" required="vital" class="form-control" name="first_name" required="vital"
                      value="<?php echo $_SESSION['form_data']['first_name']; ?>">
        </div>
        <div class="form-group">
          <label style="margin-bottom:-0.5rem !important">Last Name</label>
          <input type="text" required="vital" class="form-control" name="last_name" required="vital"
                      value="<?php echo $_SESSION['form_data']['last_name']; ?>">
        </div>
        <div class="form-group">
          <label style="margin-bottom:-0.5rem !important">Password</label>
          <input type="password" required="vital" class="form-control" name="password_1">
        </div>
        <div class="form-group">
          <label style="margin-bottom:-0.5rem !important">Retype password:</label>
          <input type="password" required="vital" class="form-control" name="password_2">
        </div>
        <div class="form-group">
          <button class="btn btn-primary btn-block" style="margin: 5px 0px">Add</button>
        </div>
      </table>
    </form>
...
<?php
if (isset($_SESSION['form_data'])) {
    unset($_SESSION['form_data']);
}
?>
...
```

The above code creates the third and final section (Add Administrator) of this web page that enables an administrator to add more admin accounts. One line # 4, the hidden element named action takes the value 'create' to the controller when the 'Add' button is clicked. The subsequent lines generate table rows to take input for the new admin account. The <label> tag defines a label for an <input> element. The $_SESSION['form_data'] is a session variable array declared under the 'create' case in Index.php file (discussed later). It sets new admin user data in session and is used to preserve form values. If not used, the user will have to re-type the data as in the two password elements. The final lines in this code release memory space by unsetting form_data session.

Admin/Users/Index.php

```
...
  case 'create':
    // Get admin user data
    $email = $_POST['email'];
    $first_name = $_POST['first_name'];
    $last_name = $_POST['last_name'];
    $password_1 = $_POST['password_1'];
    $password_2 = $_POST['password_2'];
```

This part of Index.php file is executed when the Add button is clicked to create a new admin user account. The code receives values from the $_POST superglobal variable.

```
    // Set new admin user data in session
    $_SESSION['form_data'] = array();
    $_SESSION['form_data']['email'] = $email;
    $_SESSION['form_data']['first_name'] = $first_name;
    $_SESSION['form_data']['last_name'] = $last_name;
```

We saw $_SESSION['form_data'] array in action in the last listing. It is created here to preserve admin user data in a session named form_data.

```
    // Validate admin user data
    if (!filter_var($email, FILTER_VALIDATE_EMAIL)) {
      display_error('The e-mail address ' . $email . ' is not valid.');
    } elseif (is_valid_admin_email($email)) {
      display_error('The e-mail address ' . $email . ' is already in use.');
    }
```

The filter_var() built-in function filters a variable with the specified filter. Here, it is filtering the $email variable using the filter FILTER_VALIDATE_EMAIL to validate the value in this variable as a valid e-mail address. It returns the filtered data on success or false on failure. For example, if you input someone@exa mple.com or me@example...com, the invalid e-mail address message defined on the subsequent line will be displayed. The is_valid_admin_email() function in the ELSIF block is called from Admin_Lib.php to check whether the provided e-mail address already exist in the Admins table. If found, the message defined on the next line is triggered.

```
    if (empty($first_name)) {
        display_error('First name is a required field.');
    }
    if (empty($last_name)) {
        display_error('Last name is a required field.');
    }
    if (empty($password_1) || empty($password_2)) {
        display_error('Password is a required field.');
    } elseif ($password_1 !== $password_2) {
        display_error('Passwords do not match.');
    } elseif (strlen($password_1) < 6) {
        display_error('Password must be at least six characters.');
    }
```

The above code is included to check the required fields. It checks that both passwords are not empty (the sign ||
represents the OR operator). It ensures that both passwords match. The message is displayed only when they
are not equal (!==). The strlen() function is used to see whether the minimum length of the provided password is
met.

```
    // Add admin user
    $admin_id = add_admin($email, $first_name, $last_name, $password_1, $password_2);

    // Set up session data
    unset($_SESSION['form_data']);
    if (!isset($_SESSION['admin'])) {
        $_SESSION['admin'] = get_admin($admin_id);
    }

    redirect('.');
    break;
...
```

If all the provided information is correct, then the add_admin() function is called by providing five parameters.
The function executes a routine that inserts the new account in the Admin table. The final lines in the above
code releases the form_data session array and sets the admin session if not already there. This code is also
executed when the first admin account is created. In the final line the file calls itself using the redirect function
to refresh the page with the new content.

This concludes the administration part of our website project. Try out different aspects of these modules
keeping relevant code in front to observe the process flow. The next section discusses member modules that
allow them to register and place orders online.

Purchase Products Over the Internet – Members Module

This part enables site visitors to become a member and purchase products online. Existing and new member can:

- Login to the website to place orders
- Put desired products into their carts
- Place orders by providing payment information

The following figure illustrates a general process flow for the steps mentioned above.

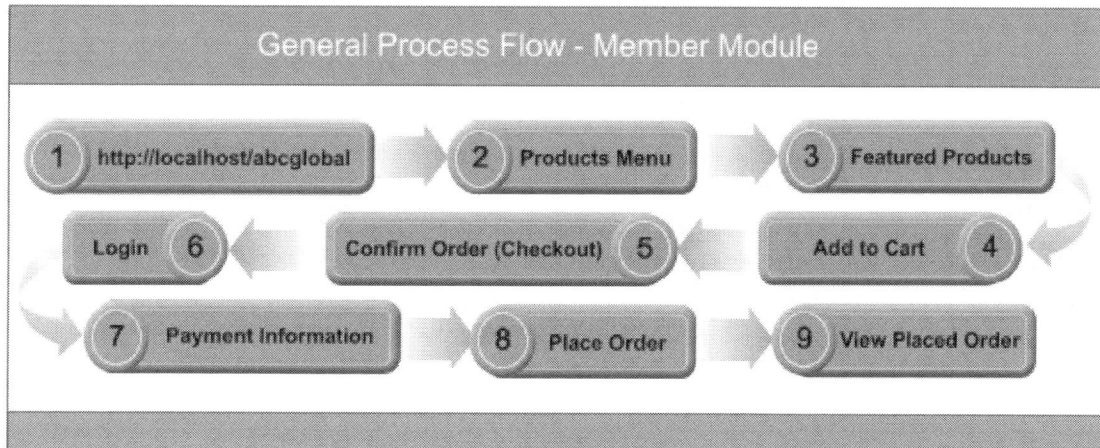

Figure 6-35

1. The process begins when a visitor enters the website by entering the specified url.
2. Clicks Product link on the main navigation bar.
3. Selects a product from the list of featured products.
4. Enters the desired quantity and places the product in his/her cart.
5. Clicks the Checkout link to confirm order.
6. At this stage, the visitor is asked to login. If the visitor doesn't have an account, he/she can register using a link provided on the login form.
7. After successful login/registration, the visitor becomes a member and is presented with a form to enter payment information.
8. On the payment form, the member clicks the Place Order button to complete the process.
9. The final step of this process displays details of the placed order to the member.

Let's continue the project and see in detail how the above mentioned steps work. Realizing that you should now be comfortable with PHP code, we'll be discussing only the unique code in the module files provided for this section.

Task 8 – Member Login Module

Considering the functionality, this module is similar to the Admin Login Module that we discussed in detail in Task 1. However, there are some additional links provided on the member login page presented in the following figure. For example, the *Register* link allows new visitors to become site members and an existing member can use the *Forgot password* link to receive a new password in his/her e-mail. Similarly the sidebar section, generated through sidebar_member.php file in the View directory, presents some navigation links relevant to site members and visitors. Also note the main navigation bar which is different from the Admin module. This page appears either when the user clicks the Checkout link to confirm order and is not logged in, or when he/she clicks the Login/Register link provided on top of all static pages. After successful log in attempt, the former case takes users to the payment information page while in the later scenario the members are landed on the Manage Your Account page where they can view and change their personal information such as e-mail, passwords and addresses.

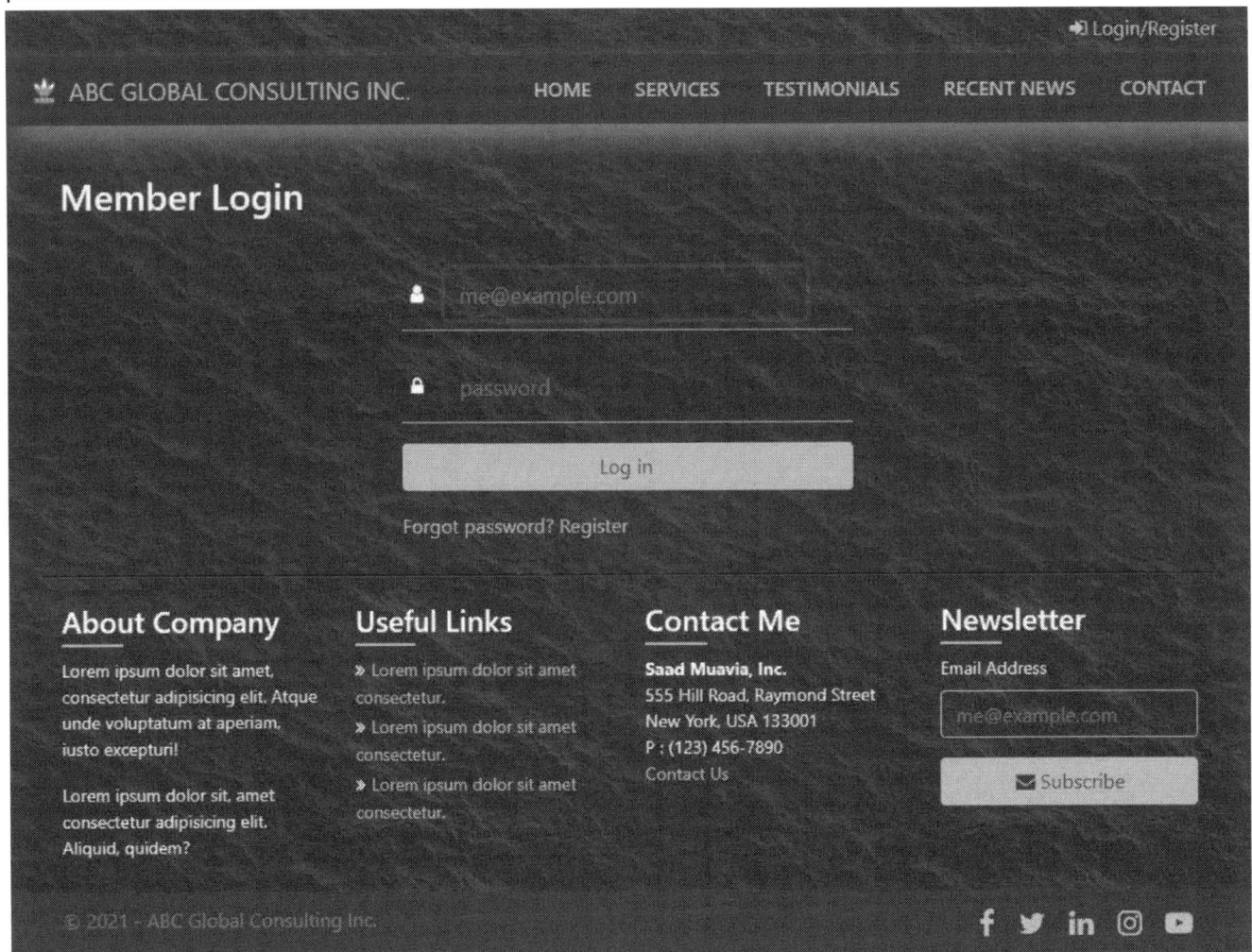

Figure 6-36

Member/Index.php

```
...
else {
    $action = 'view_login';
}
switch ($action) {
    case 'view_login':
        include 'member_login.php';
        break;
...
```

The process initiates when the site visitor clicks the Login/Register link provided on all static (.html) pages. See Header_Member.php file earlier in this chapter. After clicking the link, the process passes control to the controller Index.php file under the Member directory. Index.php executes the initial code under the default *view_login* case and calls Member_Login.php file from the same directory.

Member/Member_Login.php

```php
<?php include 'view/header_member.php'; ?>
<form action="index.php" method="post" id="login_form">
    <div class="container login-form">
        <input type="hidden" name="action" value="login" />
        <h3>Member Login</h3>
        <hr>
        <div class="row">
            <div class="col-md-5 mx-auto">
                <div class="form-group text-box">
                    <i class="fa fa-user"></i>
                    <input type="email" name="email" maxlength="35" size="35" required="vital" autofocus
                            placeholder="me@example.com" class="form-control">
                </div>
                <div class="form-group text-box">
                    <i class="fa fa-lock"></i>
                    <input type="password" name="password" required="vital" placeholder="password"
                            class="form-control">
                </div>
                <div class="form-group">
                    <button class="btn btn-warning btn-block">Log in</button>
                </div>
                <p class="register">
                <a href="member_password.php">Forgot password?</a>
                <a href="member_register.php">Register  </a>
                </p>
            </div>
        </div>
    </div>
</form>
<?php include 'view/footer.php'; ?>
```

Member_Login.php file displays the login form. Besides the e-mail and password boxes, it contains code for the two links: *Forgot password* and *Register*. It calls Member_Register.php when the Register link is clicked to display a form to the visitor to become a member. After taking user's credentials, it passes the control back to Index.php file with e-mail address, password and a hidden value: 'login'.

Member/Index.php

```
...
case 'login':
    $email = $_POST['email'];
    $password = $_POST['password'];
    if (is_valid_member_login($email, $password)) {        // If username/password are valid, then login
        $_SESSION['user'] = get_member_by_email($email);
    } else {
        member_error('Login failed. Invalid email or password.');
    }
    if (isset($_SESSION['checkout'])) {        // If necessary, redirect to the Checkout module
        unset($_SESSION['checkout']);
        redirect('../checkout');
    } else {
        redirect('.');
    }
    break;
...
```

Model/Member_Lib.php

```
...
function get_member_by_email($email) {
    global $db;
    $query = 'SELECT * FROM members WHERE memberEmail = :email';
    $statement = $db->prepare($query);
    $statement->bindValue(':email', $email);
    $statement->execute();
    $member = $statement->fetch();
    $statement->closeCursor();
    return $member;
}
function is_valid_member_login($email, $password) {
    global $db;
    $password = sha1($email . $password);
    $query = 'SELECT * FROM members WHERE memberEmail = :email AND memberPW = :password';
    $statement = $db->prepare($query);
    $statement->bindValue(':email', $email);
    $statement->bindValue(':password', $password);
    $statement->execute();
    $valid = ($statement->rowCount() == 1);
    $statement->closeCursor();
    return $valid;
}
...
```

The controller calls couple of functions - *is_valid_member_login()* and *get_member_by_email()* (located in Member_Lib.php file) to validate the provided information. If the provided information is correct, the controller sets a user session. It also checks for the existence of another session named checkout. The existence of checkout session indicates that the user has arrived here from the order confirmation page. So to keep the process in flow, the user is redirected to the checkout process. If the checkout session doesn't exist, the controller runs itself to display the Manage Your Account page through Member_View.php file (Task 11). This is a normal flow in which the user tries to login through the provided links on the static pages. For further details on login process, refer to Task1.

Task 9 – Member Registration Module

It is necessary for the site visitor to become a member before placing orders. The member login form provides a registration link that presents a form, illustrated below, to visitors. The visitor immediately becomes a member after submitting the form.

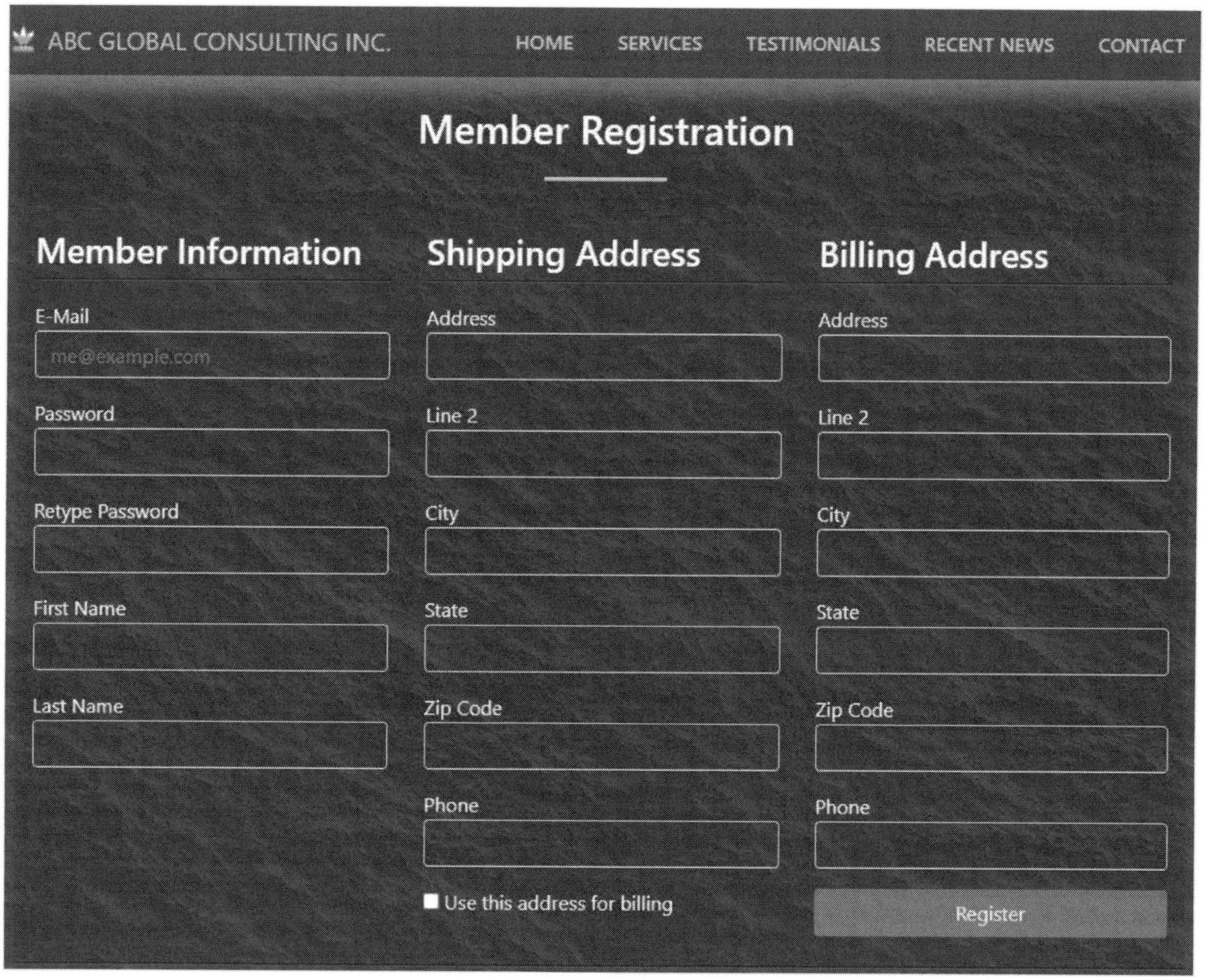

Figure 6-37

The member login form has a link named Register which initiates the registration process – see Task 8. The Register link calls Member_Register.php file. This file contains code to display the registration form as illustrated in figure 6-22. The code is similar to the one you went through in Add Admin Account. It also uses the form_data session variable to store all form information except passwords. The form has a checkbox named use_shipping. Its status is also stored in the form_data session variable. A check mark placed in this box indicates that both shipping and billing addresses are same and values entered in the Shipping Address fields are inserted automatically for Billing Address.

```
<input type="checkbox" name="use_shipping"
    <?php if ($_SESSION['form_data']['use_shipping']) : ?>
        checked="checked"
    <?php endif; ?>
> Use this address for billing
```

Member/Member_Register.php

```
...
<?php include '../utility/main.php'; ?>
<?php include '../utility/secure.php'; ?>
<?php include '../view/header_member.php'; ?>


<div class="container section page-overlay">
    <div class="row">
        <div class="col-md-12">
            <h2 class="section-head">Member Registration</h2>
        </div>
    </div>
    <form action="index.php" method="post" id="register_form">
        <input type="hidden" name="action" value="register" />
        <div class="row">
            <div class="col-md-4">
                <div><h3>Member Information</h3></div>
                <hr class="hr" style="margin-top: 0rem">
                <div class="form-group">
                    <label style="margin-bottom:-0.5rem !important">E-Mail</label>
                    <input type="email" required="vital" class="form-control" name="email"
                                    placeholder="me@example.com"
                                    value="<?php echo $_SESSION['form_data']['email']; ?>">
                </div>
                <div class="form-group">
                    <label style="margin-bottom:-0.5rem !important">Password</label>
                    <input type="password" required="vital" class="form-control"
                        name="password_1"><?php echo $password_message11111; ?>
                </div>
                <div class="form-group">
                    <label style="margin-bottom:-0.5rem !important">Retype Password</label>
                    <input type="password" required="vital" class="form-control" name="password_2">
                </div>
                <div class="form-group">
                    <label style="margin-bottom:-0.5rem !important">First Name</label>
                    <input type="text" required="vital" class="form-control" name="first_name"
                        value="<?php echo $_SESSION['form_data']['first_name']; ?>">
                </div>
                <div class="form-group">
                    <label style="margin-bottom:-0.5rem !important">Last Name</label>
                    <input type="text" required="vital" class="form-control" name="last_name"
                        value="<?php echo $_SESSION['form_data']['last_name']; ?>">
                </div>
            </div>
            <div class="col-md-4">
                <div><h3>Shipping Address</h3></div>
                <hr class="hr" style="margin-top: 0rem">
                <div class="form-group">
                    <label style="margin-bottom:-0.5rem !important">Address</label>
                    <input type="text" class="form-control" name="ship_line1"
                        value="<?php echo $_SESSION['form_data']['ship_line1']; ?>">
                </div>
                <div class="form-group">
                    <label style="margin-bottom:-0.5rem !important">Line 2</label>
                    <input type="text" class="form-control" name="ship_line2"
```

```
                    value="<?php echo $_SESSION['form_data']['ship_line2']; ?>">
        </div>
        <div class="form-group">
            <label style="margin-bottom:-0.5rem !important">City</label>
            <input type="text" class="form-control" name="ship_city"
                value="<?php echo $_SESSION['form_data']['ship_city']; ?>">
        </div>
        <div class="form-group">
            <label style="margin-bottom:-0.5rem !important">State</label>
            <input type="text" class="form-control" name="ship_state"
                value="<?php echo $_SESSION['form_data']['ship_state']; ?>">
        </div>
        <div class="form-group">
            <label style="margin-bottom:-0.5rem !important">Zip Code</label>
            <input type="text" class="form-control" name="ship_zip"
                value="<?php echo $_SESSION['form_data']['ship_zip']; ?>">
        </div>
        <div class="form-group">
            <label style="margin-bottom:-0.5rem !important">Phone</label>
            <input type="text" class="form-control" name="ship_phone"
                value="<?php echo $_SESSION['form_data']['ship_phone']; ?>">
        </div>
        <div class="form-group">
            <input type="checkbox" name="use_shipping"
                <?php if ($_SESSION['form_data']['use_shipping']) : ?>
                    checked="checked"
                <?php endif; ?>
            > Use this address for billing
        </div>
    </div>
</div>
<div class="col-md-4">
    <div><h3>Billing Address</h3></div>
    <hr class="hr" style="margin-top: 0rem">
    <div class="form-group">
        <label style="margin-bottom:-0.5rem !important">Address</label>
        <input type="text" class="form-control" name="bill_line1"
            value="<?php echo $_SESSION['form_data']['bill_line1']; ?>">
    </div>
    <div class="form-group">
        <label style="margin-bottom:-0.5rem !important">Line 2</label>
        <input type="text" class="form-control" name="bill_line2"
            value="<?php echo $_SESSION['form_data']['bill_line2']; ?>">
    </div>
    <div class="form-group">
        <label style="margin-bottom:-0.5rem !important">City</label>
        <input type="text" class="form-control" name="bill_city"
            value="<?php echo $_SESSION['form_data']['bill_city']; ?>">
    </div>
    <div class="form-group">
        <label style="margin-bottom:-0.5rem !important">State</label>
        <input type="text" class="form-control" name="bill_state"
            value="<?php echo $_SESSION['form_data']['bill_state']; ?>">
    </div>
    <div class="form-group">
        <label style="margin-bottom:-0.5rem !important">Zip Code</label>
```

315

```
                    <input type="text" class="form-control" name="bill_zip"
                        value="<?php echo $_SESSION['form_data']['bill_zip']; ?>">
                </div>
                <div class="form-group">
                    <label style="margin-bottom:-0.5rem !important">Phone</label>
                    <input type="text" class="form-control" name="bill_phone"
                        value="<?php echo $_SESSION['form_data']['bill_phone']; ?>">
                </div>
                <button class="btn btn-primary btn-block" style="margin: 5px 0px">Register</button>
            </div>
        </div>
    </form>
</div>

<?php
if (isset($_SESSION['form_data'])) {
    unset($_SESSION['form_data']);
}
?>

<?php include '../view/footer.php'; ?>
```

When the visitor clicks the Register button after completing the form, the data is submitted to the controller with a hidden value 'register'.

Member/Index.php

```
...
case 'register':
    // Store user data in local variables
    $email = $_POST['email'];
    $first_name = $_POST['first_name'];
    $last_name = $_POST['last_name'];
    $ship_line1 = $_POST['ship_line1'];
    $ship_line2 = $_POST['ship_line2'];
    $ship_city = $_POST['ship_city'];
    $ship_state = $_POST['ship_state'];
    $ship_zip = $_POST['ship_zip'];
    $ship_phone = $_POST['ship_phone'];
    $use_shipping = isset($_POST['use_shipping']);
    $bill_line1 = $_POST['bill_line1'];
    $bill_line2 = $_POST['bill_line2'];
    $bill_city = $_POST['bill_city'];
    $bill_state = $_POST['bill_state'];
    $bill_zip = $_POST['bill_zip'];
    $bill_phone = $_POST['bill_phone'];

    // Store data in the session
    $_SESSION['form_data'] = array();
    $_SESSION['form_data']['email'] = $email;
    $_SESSION['form_data']['first_name'] = $first_name;
    $_SESSION['form_data']['last_name'] = $last_name;
    $_SESSION['form_data']['ship_line1'] = $ship_line1;
    $_SESSION['form_data']['ship_line2'] = $ship_line2;
    $_SESSION['form_data']['ship_city'] = $ship_city;
```

```php
$_SESSION['form_data']['ship_state'] = $ship_state;
$_SESSION['form_data']['ship_zip'] = $ship_zip;
$_SESSION['form_data']['ship_phone'] = $ship_phone;
$_SESSION['form_data']['use_shipping'] = isset($use_shipping);
$_SESSION['form_data']['bill_line1'] = $bill_line1;
$_SESSION['form_data']['bill_line2'] = $bill_line2;
$_SESSION['form_data']['bill_city'] = $bill_city;
$_SESSION['form_data']['bill_state'] = $bill_state;
$_SESSION['form_data']['bill_zip'] = $bill_zip;
$_SESSION['form_data']['bill_phone'] = $bill_phone;

$password_1 = $_POST['password_1'];
$password_2 = $_POST['password_2'];

// Validate user data
if (!filter_var($email, FILTER_VALIDATE_EMAIL)) {
    member_error('The e-mail address ' . $email . ' is not valid.');
} elseif (is_valid_member_email($email)) {
    member_error('The e-mail address ' . $email . ' is already in use.');
}
if (empty($first_name)) {
    member_error('First name is a required field.');
}
if (empty($last_name)) {
    member_error('Last name is a required field.');
}
if (empty($password_1) || empty($password_2)) {
    member_error('Password is a required field.');
} elseif ($password_1 !== $password_2) {
    member_error('Passwords do not match.');
} elseif (strlen($password_1) < 6) {
    member_error('Password must be at least six characters long.');
}

// Validate shipping address
if (empty($ship_line1)) {
    member_error('Shipping address line 1 is required.');
}
if (empty($ship_city)) {
    member_error('Shipping city is required.');
}
if (empty($ship_state)) {
    member_error('Shipping state is required.');
}
if (strlen($ship_state) > 2 ) {
    member_error('Use two-letter code for shipping state.');
}
if (empty($ship_zip)) {
    member_error('Shipping ZIP code is required.');
}
if (empty($ship_phone)) {
    member_error('Shipping phone number is required.');
}
```

```php
// If necessary, validate billing address
if (!$use_shipping) {
  if (empty($bill_line1)) {
    member_error('Billing address line 1 is required.');
  }
  if (empty($bill_city)) {
    member_error('Billing city is required.');
  }
  if (empty($bill_state)) {
    member_error('Billing state is required.');
  }
  if (strlen($bill_state) > 2 ) {
    member_error('Use two-letter code for billing state.');
  }
  if (empty($bill_zip)) {
    member_error('Billing ZIP code is required.');
  }
  if (empty($bill_phone)) {
    member_error('Billing phone number is required.');
  }
}

// Add the member data to the database
$member_id = add_member($email, $first_name, $last_name, $password_1, $password_2);

// Add the shipping address
$shipping_id = add_address($member_id, $ship_line1, $ship_line2, $ship_city, $ship_state, $ship_zip,
                           $ship_phone);
member_change_shipping_id($member_id, $shipping_id);

// Add the billing address
if ($use_shipping) {
    $billing_id = add_address($member_id, $ship_line1, $ship_line2, $ship_city, $ship_state, $ship_zip,
                              $ship_phone);
} else {
    $billing_id = add_address($member_id, $bill_line1, $bill_line2, $bill_city, $bill_state, $bill_zip,
                              $bill_phone);
}
member_change_billing_id($member_id, $billing_id);

// Set up session data
unset($_SESSION['form_data']);
$_SESSION['user'] = get_member($member_id);

// Redirect to the Checkout application if necessary
if (isset($_SESSION['checkout'])) {
  unset($_SESSION['checkout']);
  redirect('../checkout');
} else {
  redirect('.');
}
break;
...
```

The controller executes the above code under the Register case. It creates the form_data session array to preserve form values (except the two passwords). Then it validates the e-mail address provided by the visitor through the filter_var function that we've already discussed in the Admin module. If the provided e-mail address is valid, the code checks whether the address already exist in the database using the is_valid_member_email() function. It also validates all the required fields, matches the two passwords and verifies their minimum length. The statement, *if (!$use_shipping)*, evaluates whether the user has put a check mark on the *Use Shipping Address* box. If not, the code under the statement is executed to verify the billing information.

After verification, the controller calls *add_member()* and *add_address()* functions in respective library files to insert the provided information in relevant tables. The add_member() function inserts e-mail address, names, and passwords in the Members table leaving the two address ids. The add_address() function is called twice to insert shipping and billing addresses. Each call returns a value in a variable $address_id which it gets through the built-in lastInsertID() function. The lastInsertID() function returns the ID of the last inserted row. These values are used as arguments in member_change_shipping_id() and member_change_billing_id() functions to replace shipping and billing ids in the Members table that were initially left blank.

Next, the controller sets user's session by calling *get_member()* function. This function retrieves complete record for the member who's just joined.

After successful registration, the member is redirected to the checkout page - *if (isset($_SESSION['checkout'])) ...redirect('../checkout'...* - if he came to the registration page from there, otherwise, the code calls Index.php file - *redirect('.')* - to display Manage Your Account page using Member_View.php file.

Model/Member_Lib.php

```
...
function get_member($member_id) {
   global $db;
   $query = 'SELECT * FROM members WHERE memberID = :member_id';
   $statement = $db->prepare($query);
   $statement->bindValue(':member_id', $member_id);
   $statement->execute();
   $member = $statement->fetch();
   $statement->closeCursor();
   return $member;
}

function add_member($email, $first_name, $last_name, $password_1, $password_2) {
   global $db;
   $password = sha1($email . $password_1);
   $query = '
      INSERT INTO members (fName, lName, memberEmail, memberPW)
      VALUES (:first_name, :last_name, :email, :password)';
   $statement = $db->prepare($query);
   $statement->bindValue(':first_name', $first_name);
   $statement->bindValue(':last_name', $last_name);
   $statement->bindValue(':email', $email);
   $statement->bindValue(':password', $password);
   $statement->execute();
   $member_id = $db->lastInsertId();
   $statement->closeCursor();
   return $member_id;
}
...
```

Model/Address_Lib.php

```
...
function add_address($member_id, $line1, $line2, $city, $state, $zip_code, $phone) {
   global $db;
   $query = '
   INSERT INTO addresses (memberID, line1, line2, city, state, zipCode, phone)
   VALUES (:member_id, :line1, :line2, :city, :state, :zip_code, :phone)';
   $statement = $db->prepare($query);
   $statement->bindValue(':member_id', $member_id);
   $statement->bindValue(':line1', $line1);
   $statement->bindValue(':line2', $line2);
   $statement->bindValue(':city', $city);
   $statement->bindValue(':state', $state);
   $statement->bindValue(':zip_code', $zip_code);
   $statement->bindValue(':phone', $phone);
   $statement->execute();
   $address_id = $db->lastInsertId();
   $statement->closeCursor();
   return $address_id;
 }
 ...
```

Task 10 – Password Reset Module

This module is included to help website members in recovering their lost passwords. There is a link labeled *Forgot Password* on the member login form. When clicked, this link asks the member to provide his/her e-mail address. After verification, the module creates a new random password, stores it in the database, and sends it to the member's e-mail account. After receiving the e-mail, the member can login with the new password and can change it on Manage Your Account page that we'll discuss in the next task.

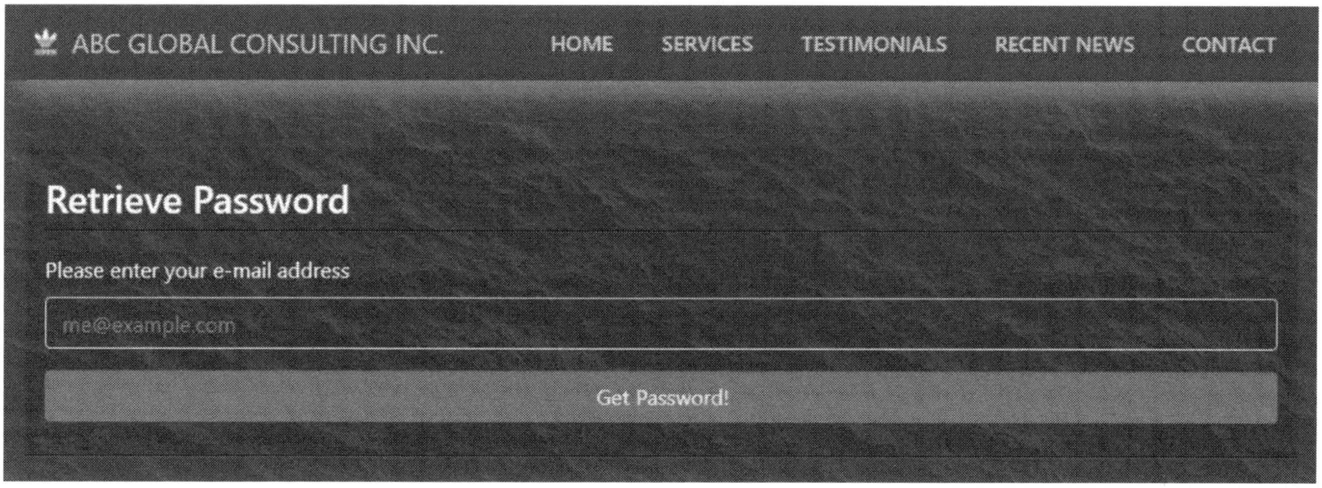

Figure 6-38

Member/Index.php

```
...
  case 'assign_password':
    $email = $_POST['email'];

    $_SESSION['password'] = get_member_by_email($email);
    $member_id = $_SESSION['password']['memberID'];

    if ($member_id <= 0) {
      member_error('E-mail address does not exist in our database.');
    }
    $new_password = update_pw($member_id, $email);

    function sanitize_email($recipient_email) {
      $recipient_email = filter_var($recipient_email, FILTER_SANITIZE_EMAIL);
      if (filter_var($recipient_email, FILTER_VALIDATE_EMAIL)) {
        return true;
      } else {
        return false;
      }
    }
    $to = $email;
    $subject = "Your New Password From ABC Global Consulting";

    $message = "<b>Hello!</b>";
    $message .= "<h1>This is ABC Global Consulting Admin</h1>";
    $message .= "\n\nYour new password on ABC Global Consulting domain is: " . $new_password;

    $header = "From:it.ho@shafi.com \r\n";
    $header .= "Cc:techies81@gmail.com \r\n";
    $header .= "MIME-Version: 1.0\r\n";
    $header .= "Content-type: text/html\r\n";

    $valid_email = sanitize_email($to);
    if ($valid_email == false) {
      echo "Invalid input - message not sent";
    } else { //send email
      mail($to, $subject, $message, $header);
      include 'member_pw_sent.php';
    }
      unset($_SESSION['password']);
    break;
...
```

The member forgets her password and clicks the *Forgot Password* link on the login form. The Retrieve Password page, as shown in figure 6-23, comes up and asks the user to provide her e-mail address. A hidden value *'assign_password'* is forwarded to the controller. Based on this value, the controller runs instructions under the corresponding case. The controller calls *get_member_by_email()* function in *Member_Lib.php* file and stores the sole returned row in a session named *password*. It takes memberID value from the session variable (password) and stores it in a variable *$member_id*. Next, it evaluates whether the *$member_id* has a value. A value of zero indicates that the database doesn't have any record for the provided e-mail address and thus an appropriate message is displayed to the user. Note that this time we called the *member_error()* function from Main.php file which consequently calls member_error.php in the Errors directory to display the message. To distinguish page headings from the Admin module, we used another file to display appropriate member module headings using Header_Member.php file. The controller then calls *update_pw()* function by passing two arguments: *$member_id* and *$email*. The returned value (a new random password) is received in *$new_password*. This function is explained ahead. The rest of the code in this case statement is already known to you. It uses the PHP Mail function to send the new password to the member using her e-mail address that exists in the database. Note that you have already configured and tested the PHP Mail function in the previous chapter and the same configuration will be used for this module. After transmitting a successful e-mail, the controller calls *member_pw_sent.php* file. This file informs the member to check her mailbox for the new password.

Errors/Member_Error.php

```php
<?php include 'view/header_member.php'; ?>
<div class="container section page-overlay">
    <div class="row">
        <div class="col-md-12">
            <h2 class="section-head">Error</h2>
            <p style="text-align:center"><?php echo $error_message; ?></p>
        </div>
    </div>
</div>
<?php include 'view/footer.php'; ?>
```

Member/Member_PW_Sent.php

```php
<?php include 'view/header_member.php'; ?>

<div class="container section page-overlay">
    <div class="row">
        <div class="col-md-12">
            <h2 class="section-head">Password Reset</h2>
            <p>A message has been sent to your email address <?php echo $to ; ?>,
    with your new password.</p>
        </div>
    </div>
</div>

<?php include 'view/footer.php'; ?>
```

Model/Member_Lib.php

```php
...
function update_pw($member_id, $email) {
  $pw_length= 8;
  $symbols = '~!@#$%^&*()-_=+[]{};:,.<>?';
  $symbol_count = strlen($symbols);
  $index = mt_rand(0, $symbol_count - 1);
  $password = substr($symbols, $index, 1);
  $password .= chr(mt_rand(48, 57));
  $password .= chr(mt_rand(65, 90));
  while (strlen($password) < $pw_length) {
    $password .= chr(mt_rand(97, 122));
  }
  $new_password = str_shuffle($password);
  if (!empty($new_password)) {
    global $db;
    $password = sha1($email . $new_password);
    $query = '
      UPDATE members
      SET memberPW = :password
      WHERE memberID = :member_id';
    $statement = $db->prepare($query);
    $statement->bindValue(':password', $password);
    $statement->bindValue(':member_id', $member_id);
    $statement->execute();
    $statement->closeCursor();
  }
  return $new_password;
}
...
```

The update_pw function is called from the controller file. It performs two tasks: generate a random password and update member's record with this new password in the database. After updating the new password in the database, it is returned to the controller which sends it through an e-mail to the requesting member.

To start, the first line of this function receives two arguments to identify the member. Line # 2 defines length for the new password. The new password consists of single uppercase letter, number, symbol, and five lowercase letters. Line # 3 defines the list of symbols to be added. Code on line 4-5 selects a random position for the symbol using strlen() and mt_rand() functions which is then added to the password using the substr() function on line # 6. Line # 7 picks a random number while line # 8 gets a random uppercase letter. In the ASCII character set, numbers 0 through 9 have the decimal values 48 to 57 while the uppercase letters fall between 65 and 90. The while loop (line 9-11) generates random lowercase letters (using the decimal values 97-122) to fill in the remaining 5 positions. The str_shuffle() function used on line # 12 randomly shuffles all the characters in the $password variable and stores it in the variable $new_password which looks something like this: a6zRa_rm.

You can also test this function independently in your browser to see how it returns different values when you refresh the browser. To do so, open a Notepad session and copy code from line 2-12. Add <?php to the beginning of this file and ?> to the end to inform the browser that it's a PHP file. Add echo $new_password; on the second last line just above the ?> symbol. Save this file as pw.php under the wwwroot folder. In your browser type http://localhost/pw.php. You'll see a random password. Press the browser's refresh button and note the symbol position along with the new password.

The IF conditional block from line 13 to 25 updates the memberPW column in the Members database table with this new password using the technique mentioned earlier. This is done to authenticate the member with the new random password created in this function when she attempts to login after receiving the password in her e-mail. Line # 26 returns the new password to the controller to transmit it to the member.

Task 11 – Manage Your Account Module

This module enables site members to:

- Change their e-mail address, names, and passwords
- Change their Shipping and Billing addresses
- View the status of their orders
- View individual order details

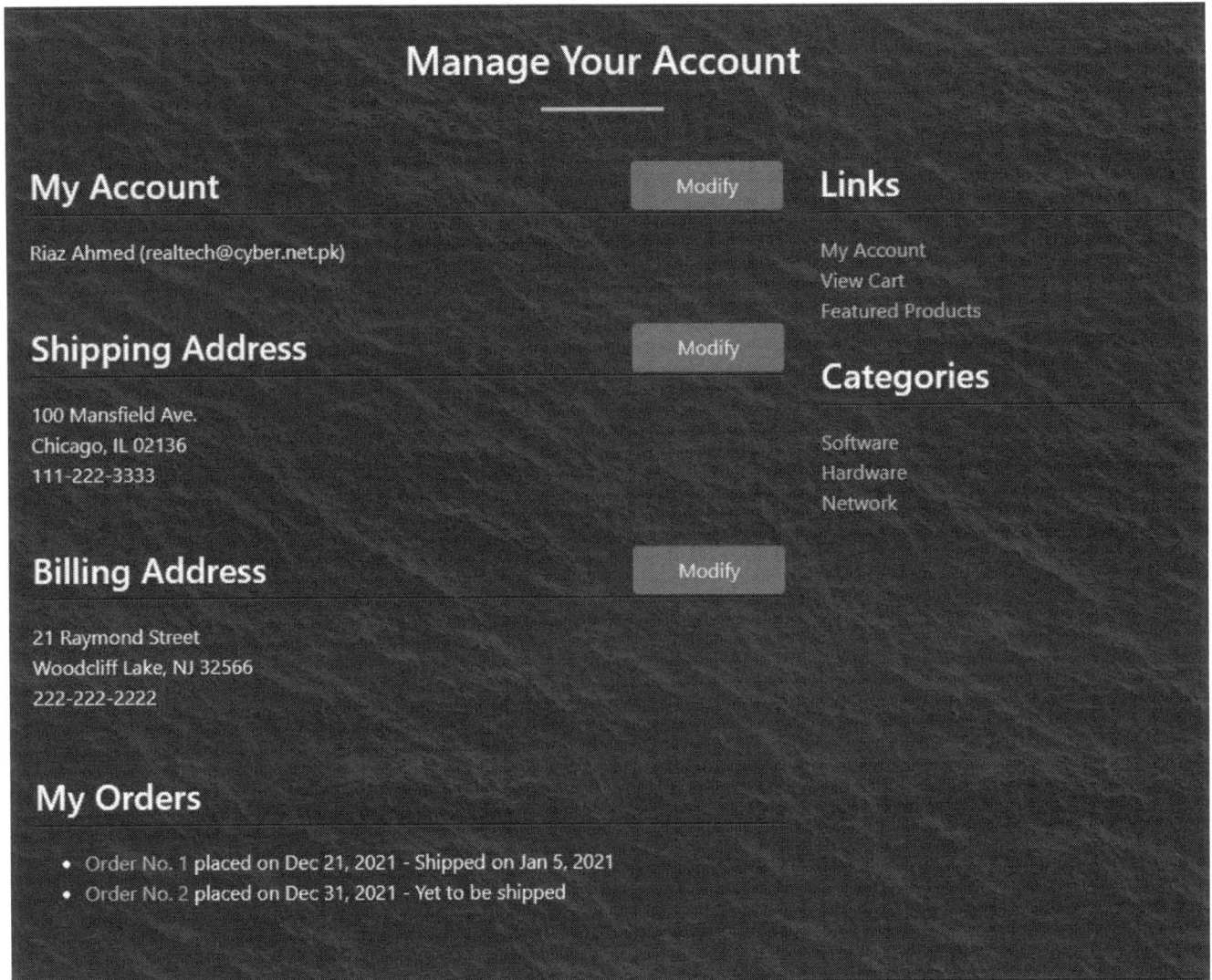

Manage Your Account

My Account   [Modify]   ### Links

Riaz Ahmed (realtech@cyber.net.pk)   My Account
                                                      View Cart
                                                      Featured Products

Shipping Address   [Modify]

100 Mansfield Ave.   ### Categories
Chicago, IL 02136
111-222-3333   Software
                                                      Hardware
                                                      Network

Billing Address   [Modify]

21 Raymond Street
Woodcliff Lake, NJ 32566
222-222-2222

My Orders

- Order No. 1 placed on Dec 21, 2021 - Shipped on Jan 5, 2021
- Order No. 2 placed on Dec 31, 2021 - Yet to be shipped

Figure 6-39

Manage Your Account is the initial page that appears when a member logs into the website and is displayed using Member_View.php file located under the Member directory. It passes a value *view_account_edit* to the controller. In reply, the controller calls Member_Edit.php file to display a page wherein members can modify their accounts. As this module is similar to Manage Admin Accounts, we will not dig deeper.

The first Edit button enables members to modify their personal profile while the next two buttons allow them to edit their shipping and billing addresses. Both shipping and billing addresses use the same Member_Address.php file under the Member directory to change existing data. Based on the member's action, the controller forwards a value either 'Update Shipping Address' or 'Update Billing Address' in a variable named $heading to the Member_Address.php file which uses it to display a suitable heading.

The final section 'Your Orders' will be displayed only when the logged in member has at least one order on record. The Member_View.php file iterates through $orders array using the FOREACH loop to display a list of all orders (either shipped or pending) placed by the current member. Each order is presented as a link, which calls the View Order page to display details of an individual order.

Member/Member_View.php

```php
...
<?php include '../view/header_member.php'; ?>
<div class="container section page-overlay">
    <div class="row">
        <div class="col-md-12">
            <h2 class="section-head">Manage Your Account</h2>
        </div>
    </div>
    <div class="row">
        <div class="col-md-8">
            <form action="index.php" method="post">
                <!-- Display h3 and button side by side using display:inline-block and float:right attributes -->
                <h3 style="display: inline-block">My Account</h3>
                <button class="btn btn-primary btn-block" style="float:right; width:20%">Modify</button>
                <hr class="hr" style="margin-top: 0rem">
                <p><?php echo $member_name . ' (' . $email . ')'; ?></p>
                <input type="hidden" name="action" value="view_account_edit" />
            </form>

            <form action="index.php" method="post">
                <h3 style="margin-top: 30px; display: inline-block">Shipping Address</h3>
                <button class="btn btn-primary btn-block" style="float:right; margin-top: 30px; width:20%">Modify
                </button>
                <hr class="hr" style="margin-top: 0rem">
                <p><?php echo $ship_line1; ?><br>
                    <?php if ( strlen($ship_line2) > 0 ) : ?>
                        <?php echo $ship_line2; ?><br>
                    <?php endif; ?>
                    <?php echo $ship_city; ?>, <?php echo $ship_state; ?>
                    <?php echo $ship_zip; ?><br />
                    <?php echo $ship_phone; ?>
                </p>
                <input type="hidden" name="action" value="view_address_edit">
                <input type="hidden" name="address_type" value="shipping">
```

```
            </form>

            <form action="index.php" method="post">
                <h3 style="margin-top: 30px; display: inline-block">Billing Address</h3>
                <button class="btn btn-primary btn-block" style="float:right; margin-top: 30px; width:20%">Modify
                </button>
                <hr class="hr" style="margin-top: 0rem">
                <p><?php echo $bill_line1; ?><br>
                    <?php if ( strlen($bill_line2) > 0 ) : ?>
                    <?php echo $bill_line2; ?><br>
                    <?php endif; ?>
                    <?php echo $bill_city; ?>, <?php echo $bill_state; ?>
                    <?php echo $bill_zip; ?><br>
                    <?php echo $bill_phone; ?>
                </p>
                <input type="hidden" name="action" value="view_address_edit">
                <input type="hidden" name="address_type" value="billing">
            </form>

            <?php if (count($orders) > 0 ) : ?>
            <br>
            <h3>My Orders</h3>
            <hr class="hr" style="margin-top: 0rem">
            <ul>
                <?php foreach($orders as $order) :
                    $order_id = $order['orderID'];
                    $order_date = strtotime($order['orderDate']);
                    $order_date = date('M j, Y', $order_date);
                    if ($order['shipDate'] != NULL){
                        $ship_date = strtotime($order['shipDate']);
                        $ship_date = date('M j, Y', $ship_date);
                    } else {
                        $ship_date='';
                    }
                    $url = $app_path . 'member' . '?action=view_order&order_id=' . $order_id;
                ?>
                <li>
                    <a href="<?php echo $url; ?>">Order No.
                        <?php echo $order_id; ?></a> placed on
                        <?php echo $order_date; ?>
                        <?php if ($ship_date != '') {
                        echo ' - Shipped on ' . $ship_date;} else {echo ' - Yet to be shipped';}?>
                </li>
                <?php endforeach; ?>
            </ul>
            <?php endif; ?><br/>
        </div>
        <div class="col-md-4">
            <?php include '../view/sidebar_member.php'; ?>
        </div>
    </div>
</div>

<?php include '../view/footer.php'; ?>
```

Member/Index.php

```php
...
  case 'view_address_edit':
    // Set up variables for address type
    $billing = $_POST['address_type'] == 'billing';
    if ($billing) {
      $address_id = $_SESSION['user']['billingAddressID'];
      $heading = 'Update Billing Address';
    } else {
      $address_id = $_SESSION['user']['shipAddressID'];
      $heading = 'Update Shipping Address';
    }

    // Get the data for the address
    $address = get_address($address_id);
    $line1 = $address['line1'];
    $line2 = $address['line2'];
    $city = $address['city'];
    $state = $address['state'];
    $zip = $address['zipCode'];
    $phone = $address['phone'];

    // Display the data on the page
    include 'member_address.php';
    break;
```

Member/Member_Address.php

```php
<?php include '../view/header_member.php'; ?>
<div class="container section page-overlay">
  <form action="index.php" method="post" id="edit_address_form">
    <div class="row">
      <div class="col-md-10">
        <ol class="breadcrumb">
          <li class="breadcrumb-item"><a href="<?php echo $app_path.'member'; ?>">Home</a></li>
          <li class="breadcrumb-item active"><?php echo $heading; ?></li>
        </ol>
      </div>
      <div class="col-md-2">
        <div class="form-group">
          <input type="hidden" name="action" value="update_address" />
          <button class="btn btn-primary btn-block" style="margin: 5px -0.5rem">Update</button>
        </div>
      </div>
    </div>
    <hr class="hr" style="margin-top: 0rem">
    <?php if ($billing) : ?>
      <input type="hidden" name="address_type" value="billing" />
    <?php else: ?>
      <input type="hidden" name="address_type" value="shipping" />
    <?php endif; ?>

    <div class="row">
      <div class="col-md-8">
        <div class="form-group">
          <label style="margin-bottom:-0.5rem !important">Address</label>
```

```html
          <input type="text" required="vital" class="form-control" name="line1" value="<?php echo $line1; ?>">
        </div>
        <div class="form-group">
          <label style="margin-bottom:-0.5rem !important">Line 2</label>
          <input type="text" class="form-control" name="line2" value="<?php echo $line2; ?>">
        </div>
        <div class="form-group">
          <label style="margin-bottom:-0.5rem !important">City</label>
          <input type="text" class="form-control" name="city" value="<?php echo $city; ?>">
        </div>
        <div class="form-group">
          <label style="margin-bottom:-0.5rem !important">State</label>
          <input type="text" class="form-control" name="state" value="<?php echo $state; ?>">
        </div>
        <div class="form-group">
          <label style="margin-bottom:-0.5rem !important">Zip Code</label>
          <input type="text" class="form-control" name="zip" value="<?php echo $zip; ?>">
        </div>
        <div class="form-group">
          <label style="margin-bottom:-0.5rem !important">Phone</label>
          <input type="text" class="form-control" name="phone" value="<?php echo $phone; ?>">
        </div>
      </div>
      <div class="col-md-4">
        <?php include '../view/sidebar_member.php'; ?>
      </div>
    </div>
  </form>
</div>
<?php include '../view/footer.php'; ?>
```

Task 12 – Display Products Catalog

The Featured Products link (A) in the side bar calls a page as illustrated in the following figure. The page grabs products (marked as featured products) from the database through an administrative task performed earlier. The site members can see all products, offered by the company, using the sidebar links (B) under the Categories section. Moreover, members can click product's title (C) to see further details of that particular product.

Figure 6-40

Abcglobal/Products.php

```php
<?php
 require_once('utility/main.php');
 require_once('model/product_lib.php');
 $products = get_featured_product();
 // Display products
 include('show_product.php');
?>
```

The page you're looking at in figure 6-40 is generated through Products.php and Show_Product.php files. Both these files are located in the site folder (root directory). The Products.php file is called when the visitor clicks the Featured Products link in the side bar. This file calls a function get_featured_product() from Product_Lib.php file under the Model directory. The function fetches all records from the Products table, marked as featured. After retrieving data, it calls the second file (Show_Product.php) to display featured products.

Abcglobal/Show_Product.php

```php
<?php include 'view/header_member.php'; ?>
<div class="container page-overlay">
  <h2>Featured products</h2>
  <hr class="hr" style="margin-top: 0rem">
  <p>We have a great collection of IT related products including software, hardware, and network that add
      value to your business.</p>

  <?php foreach ($products as $product) :
    // Get product data
    $list_price = $product['listPrice'];
    $discount_percent = $product['discountPercent'];
    $description = $product['description'];

    // Calculate unit price
    $discount_amount = round($list_price * ($discount_percent / 100.0), 2);
    $unit_price = $list_price - $discount_amount;

    // Get first paragraph of description
    $description = add_tags($description);
    $i = strpos($description, "</p>");
    $description = substr($description, 3, $i);
  ?>
  <!-- display products -->
  <div class="row">
    <div class="col-md-8">
      <table class="table table-content table-border">
        <tr style="border-top: solid 1px #333; box-shadow: #000 0 -1px 0">
          <td class="right">
            <img src="images/<?php echo $product['productCode']; ?>_s.png" alt=" ">
          </td>
          <td>
            <p>
              <b style="font-size: 25px"><a href="catalog?product_id=<?php echo
              $product['productID']; ?>" style="color: #ffc107 !important">
              <?php echo $product['productName']; ?>
              </a></b>
            </p>
```

```
      <p>
        <b>Your price:</b>
        $<?php echo number_format($unit_price, 2); ?>
      </p>
      <p>
        <?php echo $description; ?>
      </p>
    </td>
  </tr>
  <?php endforeach; ?>
</table>
</div>
<div class="col-md-4">
  <?php include 'view/sidebar_member.php'; ?>
</div>
</div>
</div>
<?php include 'view/footer.php'; ?>
```

The file Show_Product.php moves product information stored in the $product array to corresponding variables, performs calculation to show discounted price, and displays the information in a table. The function add_tags(), that we saw in a previous listing, is called to add html tags to product description. Couple of functions - strpos() and substr() - are also applied on the description data to remove features part from being displayed on the current page. If you comment out the following two lines, list of features would also appear on the web page.

```
$i = strpos($description, "</p>");
$description = substr($description, 3, $i);
```

As mentioned, the information is presented in a table comprising two columns. The first column holds product's small image that was generated through an automatic process in the Upload Image module. The second column carries title, price, and description. Each product title is presented as a link which calls its detail page to provide some additional information (product features) and Add to Cart utility.

Besides the featured products, you can also see all products under a selected category. For example, if you click the Software link under the Categories section in the sidebar, you'll see a list of all software products available in the database.

View/Sidebar_Member.php

```php
<h3>Links</h3>
<hr class="hr" style="margin-top: 0rem">
<?php
  // If user is logged in, display My Account link
  $account_url = $app_path . 'member';
  if (isset($_SESSION['user'])) :
?>
    <a href="<?php echo $account_url; ?>">My Account</a><br>
  <?php endif; ?>
<a href="<?php echo $app_path . 'cart'; ?>">View Cart</a><br>
<a href="<?php echo $app_path . 'products.php'; ?>">Featured Products</a>
<h3 style="margin-top: 22px;">Categories</h3>
<hr class="hr" style="margin-top: 0rem">
<!-- display links for all categories -->
<?php
  require_once('model/db.php');
  require_once('model/category_lib.php');

  $categories = get_categories();
  foreach($categories as $category) :
    $name = $category['categoryName'];
    $id = $category['categoryID'];
    $url = $app_path . 'catalog?category_id=' . $id;
?>
    <a href="<?php echo $url; ?>">
      <?php echo $name; ?>
    </a><br>
  <?php endforeach; ?>
```

Being part of this page, it is feasible to discuss the sidebar that displays some links specific to site members. The bunch of links in the sidebar is generated through Sidebar_Member.php file in the View directory. The first link, My Account (line 8), is displayed only when the user session is set (line 6) i.e. a member is logged in. In such case, the controller from Member directory is called to display profile of the logged in member. The second link, View Cart (line 4), calls Index.php from the Cart directory to display member's cart. You'll see member cart in an upcoming task. Code under the categories section calls get_categories() function and displays each category as a link using a FOREACH loop. When the member clicks any of these links, a variable $url forwards the selected category id to the controller under the Catalog directory. The controller executes the Category case, fetches all products for the selected category through get_product_by_category() function, and includes Category_View.php file. The file Category_View.php generates a page that displays title of the selected category followed by a list of associated products.

Catalog/Category_View.php

```php
<?php include '../view/header_member.php'; ?>
<div class="container section page-overlay">
  <div class="col-md-8">
    <ol class="breadcrumb">
      <li class="breadcrumb-item"><a href="<?php echo $app_path.'member'; ?>">Home</a></li>
      <li class="breadcrumb-item active">Products by Category</li>
    </ol>
  </div>
</div>
<hr class="hr" style="margin-top: 0rem">
```

```php
<div class="row">
    <div class="col-md-8">
        <h3 style="margin-left: 30px"><?php echo $category_name; ?></h3>
        <?php if (count($products) == 0) : ?>
            <p>There are no products in this category.</p>
        <?php else: ?>
        <table>
    <?php foreach ($products as $product) :
            // Get product data
            $list_price = $product['listPrice'];
            $discount_percent = $product['discountPercent'];
            $description = $product['description'];
            // Calculate unit price
            $discount_amount = round($list_price * ($discount_percent / 100.0), 2);
            $unit_price = $list_price - $discount_amount;
            // Get first paragraph of description
            $description = add_tags($description);
            $i = strpos($description, "</p>");
            $description = substr($description, 3, $i);
    ?>
        <tr style="border-top: solid 1px #333; box-shadow: #000 0 -1px 0">
            <td>
                <img src="../images/<?php echo $product['productCode']; ?>_s.png" alt=" "
                        style="margin-left: 30px">
            </td>
            <td>
                <p>
                <b><a href="<?php echo '?product_id=' . $product['productID']; ?>" style="margin-left: 30px;
                        font-size:25px">
                    <?php echo $product['productName']; ?></a></b>
                </p>
        <p>
         <b style="margin-left: 30px">Your price:</b>
         $<?php echo number_format($unit_price, 2); ?>
        </p>
        <p style="margin-left: 30px">
         <?php echo $description; ?>
        </p>
         </td>
        </tr>
    <?php endforeach; ?>
    </table>
  <?php endif; ?>
 </div>
 <div class="col-md-4">
    <?php include '../view/sidebar_member.php'; ?>
 </div>
 </div>
</div>
<?php include '../view/footer.php'; ?>
```

Catalog/Index.php

```
...
  case 'product':
    // Get product data
    $product_id = $_GET['product_id'];
    $product = get_product($product_id);

    // Display product
    include('./product_view.php');
    break;
...
```

Catalog/Product_View.php

```
<?php include '../view/header_member.php'; ?>
<div class="container section page-overlay">
 <div class="col-md-8">
   <ol class="breadcrumb">
    <li class="breadcrumb-item"><a href="<?php echo $app_path.'member'; ?>">Home</a></li>
    <li class="breadcrumb-item active">Product Details</li>
   </ol>
 </div>
 <hr class="hr" style="margin-top: 0rem">
 <div class="row">
          <div class="col-md-8">
   <!-- display product -->
   <?php include '../view/product.php'; ?>
   </div>
   <div class="col-md-4">
      <?php include '../view/sidebar_member.php'; ?>
   </div>
 </div>
</div>
<?php include '../view/footer.php'; ?>
```

When a member clicks a product's title from the list of featured products, the second case, product, in the controller (Catalog/Index.php) calls Product_View.php file. This file includes Product.php file from the View directory to display details of an individual product. The file, Product.php, was discussed earlier under View Product Details in the Admin section.

Task 13 – Product Details

Site members can see more details such as product features, list price, and discount offered for a particular product by clicking its title. This action takes them to the details page of the selected product where they can add the product to their cart by entering the desired quantity. If you compare this page with the View Product page in the Admin section, you'll observe similarity between the two except Image Manager and the two buttons (Delete and Edit) that were specifically added for administrative purposes. The reason for similarity is that both these module use the same Product.php file under the View directory described earlier to display product details. Please refer to *View Product Details* in the Admin section to see how this page is rendered.

Task 14 – Add Online Shopping Cart

This module shows how to add shopping cart to a website so that members could purchase products online. The page illustrated in the following figure comes up when the Add to Cart button on the product details page is clicked. This module has three basic operations: View, Add, and Update cart. The first one, as displayed in the figure hereunder, shows products added to the cart. The second one, Add, is performed when the member moves back using the two 'Return to' links and adds more products. The final Update operation is executed when the visitor increases or decreases values in the quantity box and click the *Update Cart* button. We'll see all these operations individually in this part of the book to understand how online shopping carts work.

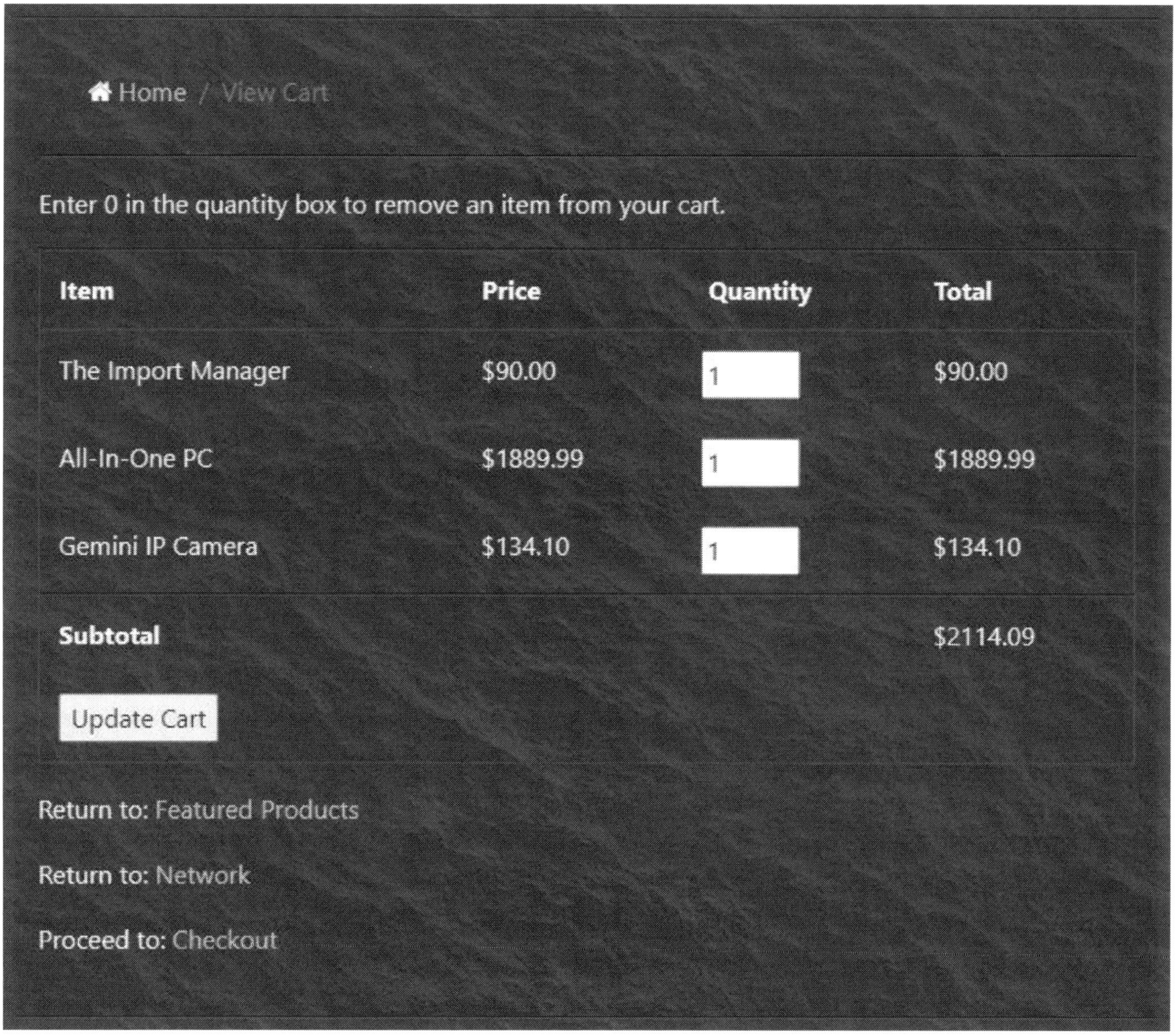

Figure 6-41

As mentioned, this process initiates when a product is added to shopping cart, which is done through Product.php file in the View directory – discussed earlier. The file, Product.php, shifts process to the controller under the Cart directory with a hidden value named add. An empty cart - $_SESSION['cart'] - is created through a call to Cart.php using the *require* statement from the controller file. In the '*add*' case the controller receives product id and quantity from Product.php file. It validates the quantity entry by calling Validation.php file in the Utility directory. The controller makes some calls to Cart.php file in the Model directory. Depending on user actions, it calls functions defined in the file to perform various operations relevant to the cart module. An internal call from these functions is made to get_product() function in the Product_Lib.php file to fetch all details of the added product and store these values in $product array. This detail is subsequently used to perform calculations and display other relevant information in the cart. Finally, the controller calls Cart_View.php to display the *View Cart* page shown in figure 6-27.

Add Products to Shopping Cart

Cart/Index.php

```php
<?php
require_once '../utility/main.php';
require_once '../utility/validation.php';
require_once '../model/cart.php';
require_once '../model/product_lib.php';

...
 elseif (isset($_GET['action'])) {
   $action = $_GET['action'];
...
switch ($action) {
...
   case 'add':
      $product_id = $_GET['product_id'];
      $quantity = $_GET['quantity'];
      // validate the quantity entry
      if (empty($quantity)) {
         member_error('You must enter a quantity.');
      } elseif (!is_valid_number($quantity, 1)) {
         member_error('Quantity must be 1 or more.');
      }
      cart_add_item($product_id, $quantity);
      $cart = cart_get_items();
      break;
...
      default:
      member_error("Unknown cart action: " . $action);
      break;
}
include './cart_view.php';
?>
```

The controller in the Cart directory requires four files to process this module. Like others, Cart.php file in the Model directory also contains various functions. Besides functions, it has the following code at the beginning of the file:

```
if (!isset($_SESSION['cart']) ) {
   $_SESSION['cart'] = array();
}
```

The above code creates an empty cart if one doesn't exist and is executed when the controller makes an initial call to the file where it resides. The Product.php file passes parameters to the controller through the GET method, so lines 6 and 7 are executed to store the hidden value 'add' in the $action variable, which is evaluated and processed from line 9-19.

Code on line 9-19 initially validates the value entered in the quantity box. It does so by calling is_valid_number() and is_present() functions in Validation.php file.

On line # 17 it calls the function cart_add_item(), again from the Model directory, to add product to the cart. The function also sets name and id of the last selected category in two separate sessions which is then displayed to the user in the 'Return to' section near the bottom of the web page illustrated above. At this point the $_SESSION array will have three arrays: [cart], [last_category_id], and [last_category_name] with the values 1, "1", and "Software" respectively assuming that the user selected the software product.

Line # 18 calls cart_get_items() function which returns an array of items shown in figure 6-42 ahead.

Finally, on line # 24 the file Cart_View.php is included to display the cart. Note that this file is included after the SWITCH statement which means that it will be called after executing every case (view, add, and update) defined under the SWITCH statement.

Model/Cart.php

```
...
function cart_get_items() {
    $items = array();
    foreach ($_SESSION['cart'] as $product_id => $quantity ) {
        // Get product data from db
        $product = get_product($product_id);
        $list_price = $product['listPrice'];
        $discount_percent = $product['discountPercent'];
        $quantity = intval($quantity);

        // Calculate discount
        $discount_amount = round($list_price * ($discount_percent / 100.0), 2);
        $unit_price = $list_price - $discount_amount;
        $line_price = round($unit_price * $quantity, 2);

        // Store data in items array
        $items[$product_id]['name'] = $product['productName'];
        $items[$product_id]['description'] = $product['description'];
        $items[$product_id]['list_price'] = $list_price;
        $items[$product_id]['discount_percent'] = $discount_percent;
        $items[$product_id]['discount_amount'] = $discount_amount;
        $items[$product_id]['unit_price'] = $unit_price;
        $items[$product_id]['quantity'] = $quantity;
        $items[$product_id]['line_price'] = $line_price;
    }
    return $items;
}
...
```

The purpose of this function is to get details of the cart products from the database. This information is stored in the array $items initialized on line # 2. Line # 3 uses the loop to iterate through all cart products. Here, we used the second form (associative array) of the FOREACH loop. Line # 4 calls get_product() function from Product_Lib.php using product id as a parameter. Complete record of each product is then stored in the $product array. From line 5-7 individual column values are retrieved from $product array and stored in corresponding variables. Lines 8-10 perform calculations to set discounts.

All the above variables are then stored in $items array (from line 11-18) and are returned to the calling script. The calling script stores this result in $cart variable which is then used in Cart_View.php (shown on the next page). The status of $items is presented in the following figure. The array [1] under $items represents product id and carries sub-arrays comprising product's details.

Name	Type	Value
⊟◇ $items	array[1]	
⊟◇ [1]	array[8]	
◇ [name]	string	"The Import Manager"
◇ [description]	string	"The Import Manager is a unique imports i...
◇ [list_price]	string	"100.00"
◇ [discount_percent]	string	"10.00"
◇ [discount_amount]	float	10
◇ [unit_price]	float	90
◇ [quantity]	integer	1
◇ [line_price]	float	90

Figure 6-42

Cart/Cart_View.php

```php
<?php include '../view/header_member.php'; ?>
<div class="container section page-overlay">
   <div class="col-md-8">
     <ol class="breadcrumb">
        <li class="breadcrumb-item"><a href="<?php echo $app_path.'member'; ?>">Home</a></li>
        <li class="breadcrumb-item active">View Cart</li>
     </ol>
   </div>
   <hr class="hr" style="margin-top: 0rem">
   <?php if (cart_product_count() == 0) : ?>
     <p>There are no products in your cart.</p>
   <?php else: ?>
     <p>Enter 0 in the quantity box to remove an item from your cart.</p>
     <form action="index.php" method="post">
        <input type="hidden" name="action" value="update">
        <table class="table table-content table-border">
        <tr class="head">
          <th class="left">Item</th>
          <th>Price </th>
          <th> Quantity</th>
          <th>Total</th>
        </tr>
        <?php foreach ($cart as $product_id => $item) : ?>
        <tr>
          <td><?php echo $item['name']; ?></td>
          <td>
            <?php echo sprintf('$%.2f', $item['unit_price']); ?>
          </td>
          <td>
            <input type="text" size="3"
                name="items[<?php echo $product_id; ?>]"
                value="<?php echo $item['quantity']; ?>" />
          </td>
          <td>
            <?php echo sprintf('$%.2f', $item['line_price']); ?>
          </td>
        </tr>
        <?php endforeach; ?>
        <tr style="border-top: solid 1px #333; box-shadow: #000 0 -1px 0;">
          <td colspan="3" ><b>Subtotal</b></td>
          <td>
            <?php echo sprintf('$%.2f', cart_subtotal()); ?>
          </td>
        </tr>
        <tr>
          <td colspan="4">
            <input type="submit" value="Update Cart" />
          </td>
        </tr>
        </table>
     </form>
   <?php endif; ?>
```

This file forms the View Cart page. On line # 10 it checks whether there are any products in the cart using cart_product_count() function. If the value is zero, an appropriate message is displayed to the user. A value greater than zero indicates that at least one product exists in the cart, so the else block is executed. This page allows members to update their cart by modifying values in the quantity box. To remove a product, they're required to simply put zero as the quantity. Upon submission, this page is posted with the update value.

The cart is displayed in a table and is styled using different classes defined in Style.css file. For example, the first row uses the 'head' class to style table headings. The FOREACH loop uses the associative approach to access each product's data individually from the cart session.

The sprintf() function writes a formatted string. For example, the code sprintf('$%.2f', $item['unit_price']) writes unit price proceeded with a $ sign and with two decimal places. The cart_subtotal() function is called from Cart.php file to calculate subtotal value.

```
<p>Return to: <a href="../products.php">Featured Products</a></p>
<!-- display most recent category -->
<?php if (isset($_SESSION['last_category_id'])) :
  $category_url = '../catalog' . '?category_id=' . $_SESSION['last_category_id'];
?>
  <p>Return to: <a href="<?php echo $category_url; ?>">
<?php echo $_SESSION['last_category_name']; ?></a></p>
<?php endif; ?>


<!-- if cart has products, display the Checkout link -->
<?php if (cart_product_count() > 0) : ?>
  <p>
    Proceed to: <a href="../checkout">Checkout</a>
  </p>
<?php endif; ?>
</div>
<?php include '../view/footer.php'; ?>
```

The bottom part of the Cart_View file provides links such as:

- Featured products
- The last category a product was selected from
- Checkout

As the name implies, the Featured Product link returns users to the main products page. Then next statement forms a url by taking category id value from the session. It then presents it as a link on the next line to return the user to the last selected category page.

The final Checkout link is displayed only when there is at least one product in the cart. An IF condition is applied to check this status. The link passes the flow to Index.php under the Checkout directory. This process will be discussed in the next task.

Update Products in Shopping Cart

Cart/Index.php

```
...
if (isset($_POST['action'])) {
   $action = $_POST['action'];
}
...
switch ($action) {
...
   case 'update':
      $items = $_POST['items'];
      foreach ( $items as $product_id => $quantity ) {
        if ($quantity == 0) {
           cart_remove_item($product_id);
        } else {
           cart_update_item($product_id, $quantity);
        }
      }
      $cart = cart_get_items();
      break;
...
include './cart_view.php';
?>
```

When the cart is updated, code defined from line 1 to 3 is executed. Since the action is update, the code retrieves the array of added products from the $_POST array on line # 6. The following snapshot illustrates values held under $_POST array. Elements [1], [2], and [3] are product ids with ordered quantity values 10, 20, & 30 respectively.

Name	Type	Value
$_POST	array[2]	
[action]	string	"update"
[items]	array[3]	
[1]	string	"10"
[2]	string	"20"
[3]	string	"30"

Figure 6-43

The FOREACH loop checks each product's quantity in the $items array. If the quantity is zero, the cart_remove_item() function is called to remove the product from the cart using the key: $product_id. The ELSE block calls cart_update_item() function to update the quantity for the product. Note that in order to pick existing products we used $items array in this loop. Line 14 calls cart_get_items() again to update $cart array.

Task 15 – Checkout Module

The checkout module asks members to confirm their orders and need their payment information to proceed. It comprises the following two pages:

- **Confirm Order:** The confirm order page (shown below) displays member's cart with tax and shipping charges. At this stage, members have the option to move back and update their carts. The Payment link at the bottom of this page advances them to the next page to complete the process.
- **Payment:** This page accepts payment information to place order and will be discussed shortly.

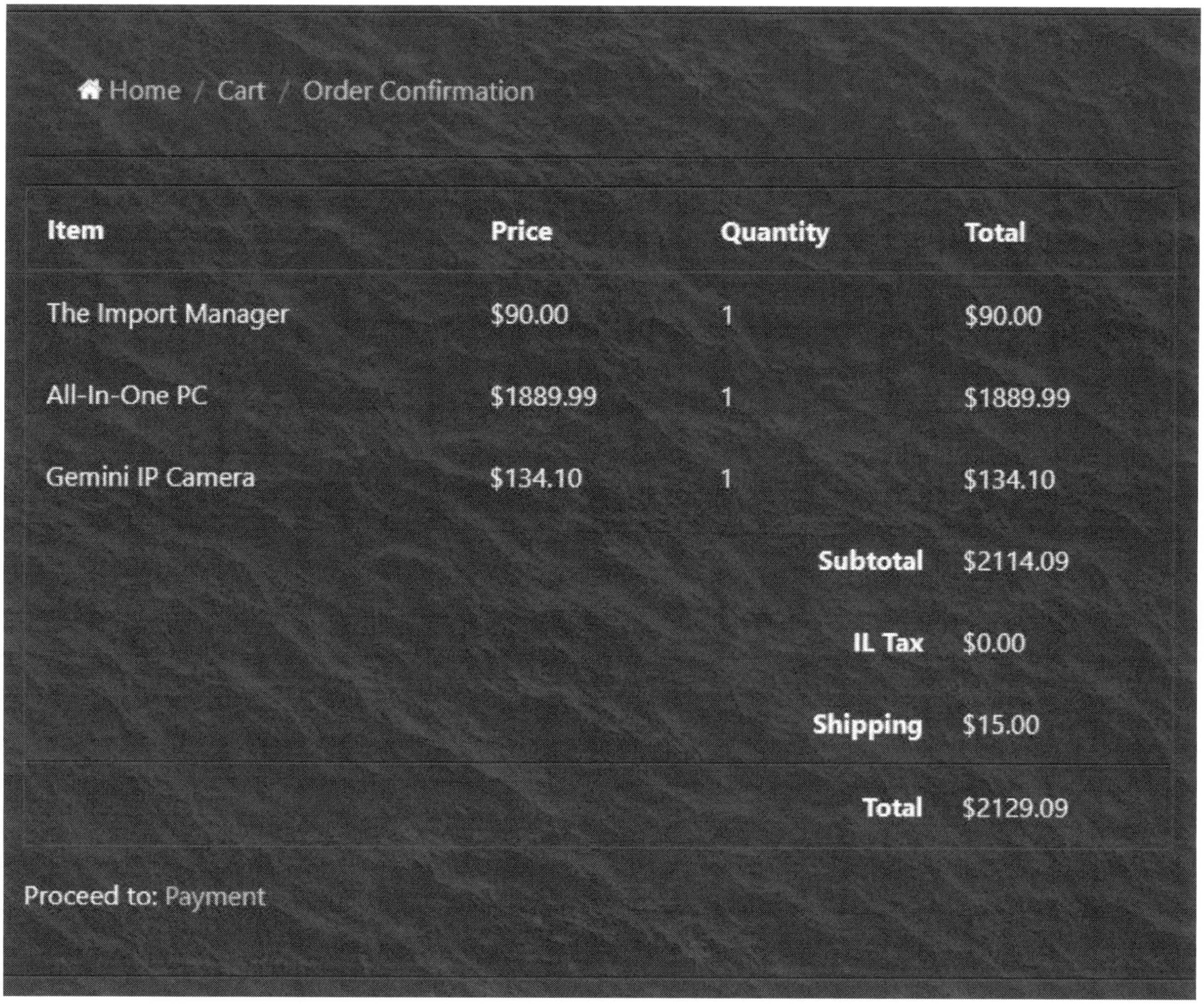

🏠 Home / Cart / Order Confirmation

Item	Price	Quantity	Total
The Import Manager	$90.00	1	$90.00
All-In-One PC	$1889.99	1	$1889.99
Gemini IP Camera	$134.10	1	$134.10
		Subtotal	$2114.09
		IL Tax	$0.00
		Shipping	$15.00
		Total	$2129.09

Proceed to: Payment

Figure 6-44

Order Confirmation

Checkout/Index.php

```php
<?php
require_once('../utility/Main.php');
require_once('../utility/secure.php');
require_once('../utility/validation.php');
require_once('../model/cart.php');
require_once('../model/product_lib.php');
require_once('../model/order_lib.php');
require_once('../model/member_lib.php');
require_once('../model/address_lib.php');
if (!isset($_SESSION['user'])) {
    $_SESSION['checkout'] = true;
    redirect('../member');
    exit();
}
...
else {
    $action = 'confirm';
}
switch ($action) {
    case 'confirm':
        $cart = cart_get_items();
        if (cart_product_count() == 0) {
            redirect('../cart');
        }
        $subtotal = cart_subtotal();  // Model/Cart
        $item_count = cart_item_count();   // Model/Cart
        $shipping_cost = shipping_cost();  // Model/Order_Lib
        $shipping_address = get_address($_SESSION['user']['shipAddressID']);
        $state = $shipping_address['state'];
        $tax = tax_amount($subtotal);   // Model/Order_Lib
        $total = $subtotal + $tax + $shipping_cost;
        include 'checkout_confirm.php';
        break;
    ...
}
?>
```

This controller receives focus from the Checkout link on the provided on the View Cart page. To complete the process, it requires various files from Utility and Model directories (line 2-9). On line # 10 it looks for the user session. The absence of this session means the user is not logged in. In such situation, the visitor is diverted to the Member directory (line # 12) where the respective controller displays the member login form. Line # 11 creates a session named checkout to remember that the user was redirected from the checkout module. For relevant information see Member Registration Module. The figure presented above fetches information from the confirm case (line 19-32). The code under this case calls cart_get_items() to retrieve complete cart information. If the cart is empty (line 21-23), the flow is redirected to cart/Index.php. From line 24 to 30 four functions (discussed next) are called to calculate subtotal, number of items in the cart, shipping cost, and tax value. All these are then presented on the order confirmation page through checkout_confirm.php file.

Model/Cart.php (Functions)

```php
function cart_subtotal() {
    $subtotal = 0;
    $cart = cart_get_items();
    foreach ($cart as $item) {
        $subtotal += $item['unit_price'] * $item['quantity'];
    }
    return $subtotal;
}


function cart_item_count() {
    $count = 0;
    $cart = cart_get_items();
    foreach ($cart as $item) {
        $count += $item['quantity'];
    }
    return $count;
}
```

Model/Order_Lib.php (Functions)

```php
function shipping_cost() {
    $item_count = cart_item_count();
    $item_shipping = 5;   // $5 per item
    if ($item_count > 5) {
        $shipping_cost = $item_shipping * 5;
    } else {
        $shipping_cost = $item_shipping * $item_count;
    }
    return $shipping_cost;
}


function tax_amount($subtotal) {
    $shipping_address = get_address($_SESSION['user']['shipAddressID']);
    $state = $shipping_address['state'];
    $state = strtoupper($state);
    switch ($state) {
        case 'CA': $tax_rate = 0.09; break;
        default: $tax_rate = 0; break;
    }
    return round($subtotal * $tax_rate, 2);
}
```

These are the four functions used in the previous listing. The cart_subtotal() function calculates and returns cart's subtotal. If fetches complete cart information from current session, uses a loop to multiply unit price with each product's quantity, stores the cumulative result in a variable ($subtotal), and returns it to line # 24 in the previous listing. The second function, cart_item_count(), adds up values in the quantity field and returns it to $item_count on line # 25 in the previous listing. The shipping_cost() function calculates a shipping charge of $5 per item for the first five items. The returned value is stored in $shipping_cost variable on line # 26 in the previous listing. The final tax_amount() function receives $subtotal parameter and calculates sales tax on this value only for orders originating from California (CA) state. This value is returned to line # 29.

Checkout/Checkout_Confirm.php

```php
<?php include '../view/header_member.php'; ?>
<div class="container section page-overlay">
   <div class="col-md-8">
     <ol class="breadcrumb">
        <li class="breadcrumb-item"><a href="<?php echo $app_path.'member'; ?>">Home</a></li>
        <li class="breadcrumb-item"><a href="<?php echo $app_path.'cart'; ?>">Cart</a></li>
        <li class="breadcrumb-item active" style="color: #ffc107">Order Confirmation</li>
     </ol>
   </div>
   <hr class="hr" style="margin-top: 0rem">
   <table class="table table-content table-border">
     <tr class="head">
        <th class="left" >Item</th>
        <th>Price </th>
        <th>Quantity </th>
        <th>Total </th>
     </tr>
     <?php foreach ($cart as $product_id => $item) : ?>
        <tr>
           <td><?php echo $item['name']; ?></td>
           <td>
             <?php echo sprintf('$%.2f', $item['unit_price']); ?>
           </td>
           <td>
             <?php echo $item['quantity']; ?>
           </td>
           <td>
             <?php echo sprintf('$%.2f', $item['line_price']); ?>
           </td>
        </tr>
     <?php endforeach; ?>
     <tr>
        <td colspan="3"><b style="float:right">Subtotal</b></td>
        <td>
          <?php echo sprintf('$%.2f', $subtotal); ?>
        </td>
     </tr>
     <tr>
        <td colspan="3"><b style="float:right"><?php echo $state; ?> Tax</b></td>
        <td>
          <?php echo sprintf('$%.2f', $tax); ?>
        </td>
     </tr>
     <tr>
        <td colspan="3"><b style="float:right">Shipping</b></td>
        <td>
          <?php echo sprintf('$%.2f', $shipping_cost); ?>
        </td>
     </tr>
        <tr style="border-top: solid 1px #333; box-shadow: #000 0 -1px 0;">
        <td colspan="3"><b style="float:right">Total</b></td>
        <td>
          <?php echo sprintf('$%.2f', $total); ?>
        </td>
```

```
        </tr>
      </table>
      <p>
        Proceed to: <a href="<?php echo '?action=payment'; ?>">Payment</a>
      </p>
    </div>
<?php include '../view/footer.php'; ?>
```

The code presented in this listing draws the order confirmation page. A table is created to hold headings and data. After creating row for table headings, the FOREACH loop is added to display individual product from the $cart array with price, quantity, and total. The next table row displays cart subtotal. Then, the next row shows tax figures along with member's state. The second last row displays shipping cost while the last row displays grand total for the order. The final lines in this code creates a link named Payment that takes member to the next page where she provides her credit card information.

Payment Information

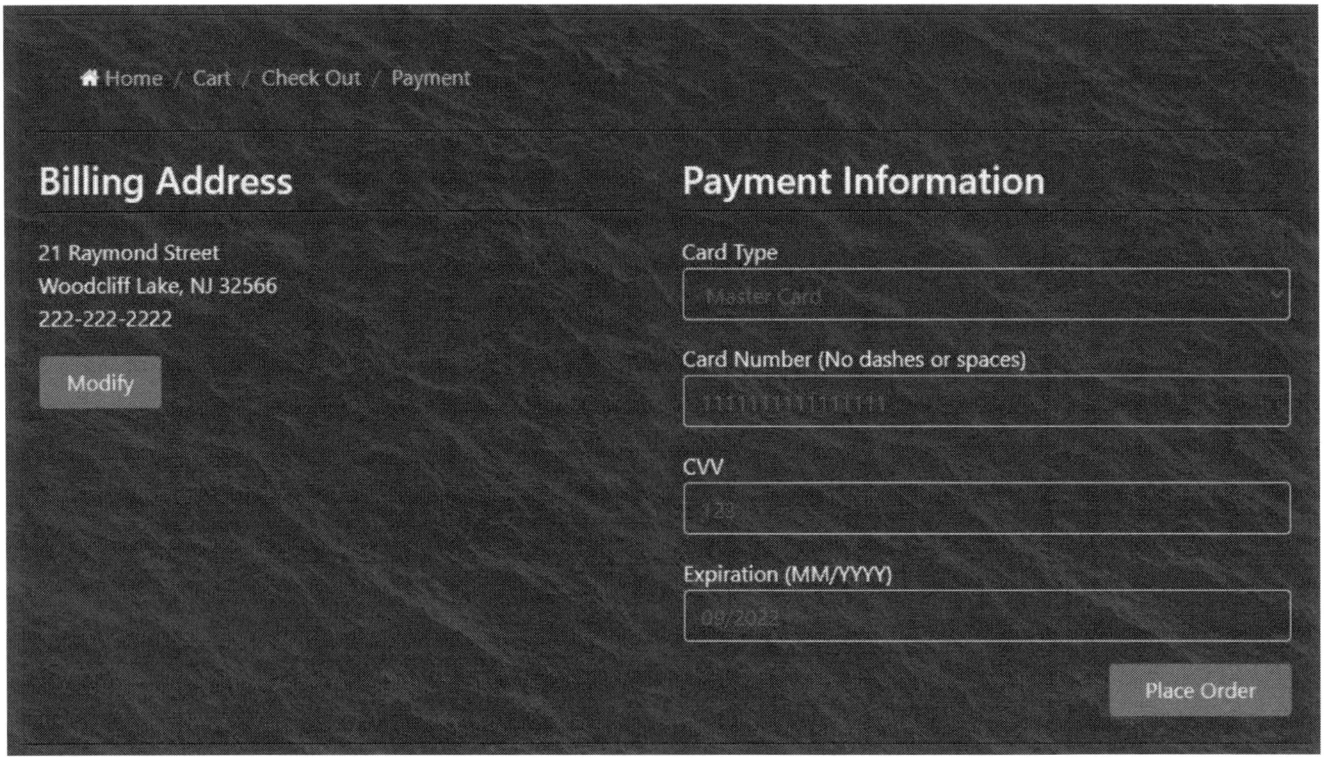

Figure 6-45

This page has two sections: Billing Address and Payment Information. The former one displays member's billing address from the database and presents a Modify button to alter this information. The latter one has a form which takes credit card information from the member. Card Type is a drop down list from which the member can select his card. It carries: Master Card, Visa, Discover, and American Express. The Card Number field accepts 15 digits for American Express and 16 for others. Similarly the CVV box takes 4 digits for American Express and 3 digits for the rest. The card expiration should be entered in MM/YYYY format. For example, 09/2022 represents September, 2022. After filling in this form, the member clicks the Place Order button to confirm his order.

Checkout/Index.php

```
...
elseif (isset($_GET['action'])) {
    $action = $_GET['action'];
}
switch ($action) {
    case 'payment':
        if (cart_product_count() == 0) {
            redirect($app_path . 'cart');
        }
        $billing_address = get_address($_SESSION['user']['billingAddressID']);   //Model/Address_Lib.php
        $bill_line1 = $billing_address['line1'];
        $bill_line2 = $billing_address['line2'];
        $bill_city = $billing_address['city'];
        $bill_state = $billing_address['state'];
        $bill_zip = $billing_address['zipCode'];
        $bill_phone = $billing_address['phone'];
        include 'checkout_payment.php';
        break;
...
}
?>
```

The code listed here initiates the payment process. In the previous list, an action named payment was forwarded on line # 38. The controller GETS and stores this value in $action (lines 1-3) and executes the 'payment' case (line # 5).

After checking the shopping cart status (lines 6-8), it calls get_address() function by passing billing address id from the user session as a parameter and stores data in individual variables (lines 10-15). This data is displayed on the payment page with an Edit button so that members could change their billing information.

Finally, on line # 16 the file checkout_payment.php is included to display the payment page.

Checkout/Checkout_Payment.php

```
...
  <div class="row">
    <div class="col-md-6">
      <h3>Billing Address</h3>
      <hr class="hr" style="margin-top: 0rem">
      <p><?php echo $bill_line1; ?><br />
        <?php if ( strlen($bill_line2) > 0 ) : ?>
        <?php echo $bill_line2; ?><br />
        <?php endif; ?>
        <?php echo $bill_city; ?>, <?php echo $bill_state; ?>
        <?php echo $bill_zip; ?><br />
        <?php echo $bill_phone; ?>
      </p>
      <form action="../member/index.php" method="post">
        <input type="hidden" name="action" value="view_address_edit" />
        <input type="hidden" name="address_type" value="billing" />
        <button class="btn btn-primary btn-block" style="width:20%">Modify</button>
      </form>
    </div>
    <div class="col-md-6">
      <h3>Payment Information</h3>
      <hr class="hr" style="margin-top: 0rem">
      <form action="index.php" method="post" id="payment_form">
        <input type="hidden" name="action" value="process" />
        <div class="form-group">
          <label style="margin-bottom:-0.5rem !important">Card Type</label>
          <select name="card_type" class="form-control">
            <option selected="selected" value="1">Master Card</option>
            <option value="2">Visa</option>
            <option value="3">Discover</option>
            <option value="4">American Express</option>
          </select>
        </div>
        <div class="form-group">
          <label style="margin-bottom:-0.5rem !important">Card Number (No dashes or spaces)</label>
          <input type="text" name="card_number" required="vital" class="form-control">
        </div>
        <div class="form-group">
          <label style="margin-bottom:-0.5rem !important">CVV</label>
          <input type="text" name="card_cvv" required="vital" class="form-control">
        </div>
        <div class="form-group">
          <label style="margin-bottom:-0.5rem !important">Expiration (MM/YYYY)</label>
          <input type="text" name="card_expires" required="vital" class="form-control">
        </div>
        <button class="btn btn-primary btn-block" style="float:right; width:30%">Place Order</button>
      </form>
    </div>
  </div>
...
```

This file displays the payment information page. The initial code in this file generates the Billing Address section. Line # 7 displays second address only when it exist, which is evaluated on line # 6 using strlen() built-in function. Lines 13-17 create a form with two hidden elements along with a Modify button. When this button is clicked, the POST method takes the two hidden values to the controller under the Member directory to present Update Billing Address page.

The second section of this page is created to receive payment information. It has a form comprising some input elements and a button labeled Place Order. The Place Order button posts this form to the controller with a hidden value 'process'. The four card types are defined in a <select> element whereas the other card information is received in three separate text elements.

Checkout/Index.php

```
...
if (isset($_POST['action'])) {
   $action = $_POST['action'];
}
...
switch ($action) {
...
   case 'process':
      if (cart_product_count() == 0) {
         redirect('Location: ' . $app_path . 'cart');
      }
      $cart = cart_get_items();
      $card_type = intval($_POST['card_type']);
      $card_number = $_POST['card_number'];
      $card_cvv = $_POST['card_cvv'];
      $card_expires = $_POST['card_expires'];
      if (!is_present($card_type)) {
         member_error('Card type is required.');
      } elseif (!is_valid_card_type($card_type)) {
         member_error('Card type ' . $card_type . ' is invalid.');
      }
      if (!is_present($card_number)) {
         member_error('Card number is required.');
      } elseif (!is_valid_card_number($card_number, $card_type)) {
         member_error('Card number ending in ' . substr($card_number, -4) . ' is invalid.');
      }
      if (!is_present($card_cvv)) {
         member_error('Card CVV is required.');
      } elseif (!is_valid_card_cvv($card_cvv, $card_type)) {
         member_error('Card CVV is invalid.');
      }
      if (!is_present($card_expires)) {
         member_error('Card expiration date is required.');
      }
      elseif (!is_valid_card_expires($card_expires)) {
         member_error('Card is either expired or the date entered is invalid.');
      }
      $order_id = add_order($card_type, $card_number, $card_cvv, $card_expires);
      foreach($cart as $product_id => $item) {
         $item_price = $item['list_price'];
         $discount = $item['discount_amount'];
         $quantity = $item['quantity'];
         add_order_item($order_id, $product_id, $item_price, $discount, $quantity);
      }
      clear_cart();
      redirect('../member?action=view_order&order_id=' . $order_id);
      break;
...
```

The previous listing posts the form with a hidden value 'process' that is evaluated from line 1 to 3 here. After receiving control, the controller executes the 'process' case (line # 5). Once again, the cart is checked for product existence. If there are no products, flow is redirected to cart directory, else, code from line # 9-13 is executed to store credit card information in different variables.

Code from line # 14 to 34 validates credit card data. All functions used here exist in Validation.php file.

The first IF block (line 14-18) checks whether the member has selected a value from the provided four card types. It calls couple of functions to validate user input. The remaining IF block validates credit card number, CVV number, and date of expiration. All these functions used for validation are discussed next.

After data validation, the controller calls add_order() function to insert provided information in master database table - Orders (line # 35). Here, the available four parameters (card type, number, cvv, and expiry) are passed to the function. The remaining information, customer id and addresses required in the Orders table, is fetched from the user session.

Line # 36 to 41 uses a loop to insert line items in the OrderItems table from the cart session. The code calls add_order_item() function to perform the insert operation.

Line # 42 calls clear_cart() function from Cart.php to clear the cart.

After successfully completing the whole process, the controller redirects flow (line # 43) to Member directory by passing an action 'view_order' together with current order id. In return, the controller in the Member directory displays a page that shows the last placed order.

Utility/Validation.php

```
function is_present($value) {
   if (isset($value) && strlen($value) > 0) {
      return true;
   } else {
      return false;
   }
}
```

This function checks the existence and length of the received argument ($value). Previously, this function was called in Add Product to Shopping Cart. This time it is called multiple times to validate credit card information. For example, the initial call (line # 14) in the previous list passes $card_type parameter to this function. Using isset($value), the IF statement checks whether the provided parameter exist and its length is greater than zero. The strlen() function returns length of the given string on success, and 0 if the string is empty. In the current scenario, for instance, if the member selects Visa as card type, a string value '2' is passed in $value. Since it's a single character, the value returned by strlen() would be 1 which is greater than zero. If both conditions are found true, the is_present() function returns true; otherwise false is returned to the calling script.

```
function is_valid_card_type($card_type) {
   if (!is_int($card_type)) return false;
   if ( $card_type < 1 || $card_type > 4 ) return false;
   return true;
}
```

This function checks whether the member selected a card type from the provided list. Recall that this list was created in Checkout_Payment.php and each card option was assigned a value. That value is received here as an argument. The first condition in this function returns false if the provided value is not an integer. The second statement also returns false if the value is either less than 1 or is greater than 4. In contrast, if the provided value is an integer and also falls within the range (1-4), the value true is returned to the calling script, validating the card type.

```php
function is_valid_card_number($card_number, $card_type) {
  switch ($card_type) {
    case 4:
      $pattern = '/^\d{15}$/';
      break;
    default:
      $pattern = '/^\d{16}$/';
      break;
  }
  return preg_match($pattern, $card_number);
}
```

As shown, two parameters are received by this function to validate credit card number. The first parameter, $card_number, holds the card number whereas the second one, $card_type, holds a value ranging from 1 to 4 to represent each card type. As mentioned earlier, the American Express card (given the value 4) accepts 15 digits as card number while the other three types take 16 digits. To receive valid input, we used the SWITCH statement and evaluated card type value on line # 3. If the value is 4, the selected card is American Express. Next, on line # 4 we defined a pattern to validate the input. Pattern strings are defined inside a pair of forward slashes. The '^' pattern marks the beginning of the string while the '$' pattern signifies the end. The '\d' pattern represents any digit. The {n} pattern must repeat exactly n times. Thus the expression, '/^\d{15}$/', checks for 15 digits for American Express card and 16 digits for others (line # 7).

The Preg_Match() PHP function on line # 10 is used to search a string, and return a 1 or 0. If the search was successful a 1 will be returned, and if it was not found a 0 will be returned. In this code, it searches the specified pattern in the card number string.

```php
function is_valid_card_cvv($card_cvv, $card_type) {
  switch ($card_type) {
    case 4:      // American Express
      $pattern = '/^\d{4}$/';
      break;
    default:
      $pattern = '/^\d{3}$/';
      break;
  }
  return preg_match($pattern, $card_cvv);
}
```

This function is similar to the previous one and validates card CVV number according to the selected option.

```
function is_valid_card_expires($card_expires) {
    $pattern = '/^\d{1,2}\/\d{4}$/';
    if (!preg_match($pattern, $card_expires)) return false;
    $date_parts = explode('/', $card_expires);
    if (intval($date_parts[0]) <= 0 || intval($date_parts[0]) > 12) return false;
    $now = new DateTime();
    $expires = new DateTime();
    $expires->setDate($date_parts[1], $date_parts[0], 1);
    $expires->add(new DateInterval("P1M"));   // $expires->modify('+1 month');
    $expires->sub(new DateInterval("P1D"));   // $expires->modify('-1 day');
    $expires->setTime(23,59,59);
    return ($now < $expires);
}
```

Let's go through each line of code individually to understand what is happening here. Assume that the member enter 02/2016 (February, 2016) as card expiration date which is received by this function through the variable $card_expires on line # 1.

Line # 2 generates a pattern for validation. The pattern incorporates month and year values in digits separated by a forward slash. Members can either enter 1 or 01 for January.

Line # 3 returns false if the card expiry value doesn't match the defined pattern expression.

Line # 4 stores values from $card_expires something like this:

Name	Type	Value
⊟◇ $date_parts	array[2]	
◇ [0]	string	"02"
◇ [1]	string	"2016"

Figure 6-46

The explode() function breaks a string into an array. Here, the value of variable $card_expires is broken at the symbol "/".

Line # 5 returns false if the month value ($date_parts[0]) is not between 1 and 12.

Line # 6 stores current system date in a date object $now. For example, January 10, 2023 will be stored as: "2023-01-10 10:25:29". The second part of this string '10:25:29' represents current system time.

Line # 7 repeats the same process and stores current system date in another date object: $expires.

Line # 8 uses the setDate() function which resets the current date of the DateTime object to a different date. This code uses the two values from $date_parts array. Where the first value, [1], holds 2016 and the second one, [0], carries 02. The third argument (1) is passed for day one. This combination sets $expires to "2016-02-01 10:25:29".

Line # 9 uses a DateInterval object that represents a span of time, or a period of time specified under the parentheses - ("P1M"). The letter P begins the interval code. nM specifies the number of months. The add() method adds the amount of time specified by the DateInterval object. Note that this code requires PHP version 5.3.0 or higher. If the version is lower, use the alternate code provided next to it as a comment. After adding the duration of one month, the value of $expires becomes: "2016-03-01 10:25:29".

Line # 10 uses the same technique to subtract 1 day ("P1D") from $expires. This time the sub() method is used to subtract the specified amount of time. After subtraction, the value of $expires becomes: "2016-02-29 10:25:29".

Line # 11 sets the time portion in $expires using 24 hours format. It makes the timestamp in $expires to: "2016-02-29 23:59:59" and this is the value that we wished to obtain through this function. It is the last day and time when the card expires.

Line # 12 compares current date with the expiry date and returns the result. If current date is less than expiry, the card is accepted.

After providing all valid information, the member clicks the Place Order button. This action records order details in relevant master and detail tables (Orders and OrderItems) and calls the Order Information page that displays the last placed order. This is the same page you saw in the Admin module.

With the completion of this task, the development phase of our website project concludes. After completion, the site is ready for deployment on a hosting server and that is what the next task deals with.

Task 16 – Website Deployment

After completing the website and giving it a thorough test run, you're ready to deploy it on a hosting server from where the world could access it. The following steps need to be completed in order to accomplish this task.

1. Host the website
2. Install FileZilla FTP Client and upload files
3. Access control panel
4. Create a blank database and a database user. Grant database access privileges to the new user.
5. Call phpMyAdmin tool to create database tables using the Import option.

Step-1 Hosting the Website

To make your website visible to the world, it has to be hosted on a web server. Every website on the Internet needs to be stored somewhere, and that's what referred to as "web hosting". A website host is just a computer that is on all the time and connected to the Internet. When you visit a website, you download some files from the machine that stores that particular website. Any computer can be used to host a website, even the one you are using now – but the computers used by professional hosting companies are incredibly powerful with lots of hard disks and memory, highly optimized to deliver the website files to thousands of readers simultaneously.

The two basic ways of hosting a website are: self and commercial.

Self-Hosting

If you want to go the DIY free route, then it is in fact entirely possible to host your own website at home, on your own Internet connection. With advances that allowed Internet access to move away from dial-up services and into a realm of faster and more robust use of Internet resources, the possibility of self-hosting became more viable. As is true with many forms of electronic equipment, the hardware necessary to create and manage a hosting network became more affordable. At the same time, software packages that could help configure and operate the networks also became more cost-effective. Coupled with the fact that more people began to make use of the Internet for both personal and commercial purposes, and also became more familiar with how to design sites and understand bandwidth, the idea of self-hosting is now well worth consideration.

While self-hosting is certainly more viable than in years past, the process still requires securing the right equipment, using software to manage the resources, and protect the host from all the threats that could filter into the hosting process via the Internet connection. This means that users who are not comfortable with these types of management processes are likely to find that working with a hosting company rather than trying to handle the processes alone may still be the best bet. For others who feel competent to engage in self-hosting, the strategy can mean greater ease in managing resources and even allowing the entire project to be much more cost effective.

There are a lot of security issues that can come up when self-hosting. Configuration issues can take a bit of doing to get the right software installed, and set up to behave correctly. Also, a commercial host will usually have some monitoring set up, so they know if the site goes down. They'll also normally have redundancy set up, so that even if a hard drive or one of their internet connections goes down, your site doesn't lose connectivity or otherwise stop working.

Unless you are an extremely tech savvy individual and have some strong need to run everything from your home, hosting your own website is not going to be a good option for most people.

Just to give you an idea, here are some of the things you'd need to host your own site:

- A computer that is powerful enough to keep up with the server requests when your site receives traffic
- A copy of the Linux operating system
- Make sure your ISP will even allow this. Some may, but will charge you an additional fee
- Cable and DSL are not good enough. You should probably have a dedicated T1 line

It's also important to remember that the computer you use must be dedicated for this task. It is not recommended you use your personal computer to double as a web host because it could interrupt your website's performance levels. So as you can see the costs for hosting your own site will start piling up. First you'll need a second computer, then you'll have to pay your ISP additional money so they will allow you to even host your site. Plus you'll have to buy an additional T1 line and that may cost you several hundred dollars per month. Not to mention you'll spend a lot of time setting this up unless you know a great deal about computers, servers, etc.

Commercial Hosting

Here you have three flavors: shared, virtual private server and dedicated server.

Shared Hosting: So called because you share a hosting server with other websites that are also stored on the same computer. Shared hosting is the budget option where prices and packages vary. Shared hosting is a very cost effective solution to host your website. With shared hosting, your web site gets its own domain name, and is hosted on a powerful server along with other websites. Shared solutions often offer multiple software solutions like e-mail, database, and different editing options with good technical support.

VPS and Dedicated Servers: These are the top 2 levels of website hosting, and mean you get the whole server to yourself. The difference between Virtual Private Server (VPS) and Dedicated Server is that a Dedicated Server is a single, physical system which you essentially "rent" inside of a data center. A virtual private server (VPS) is a virtual machine provided by an Internet hosting service. Although a VPS runs in software on the same physical computer as other customers' virtual machines, it is in many respects functionally equivalent to a separate physical computer. A VPS is dedicated to the individual customer's needs, has the privacy of a separate physical computer, and can be configured to run server software.

Initially I'd suggest heading straight to a shared hosting plan. Besides cost effectiveness, it saves you so many headaches down the line. When the time comes to upgrade, you can easily migrate to a more professional solution.

| Step-2 | Install FileZilla FTP Client and Upload Files |

After purchasing a hosting plan, the next step is to upload your website files to the hosting server using some FTP client software.

FileZilla client is a cross-platform graphical FTP, FTPS and SFTP software with lot of features, supporting Windows, Linux, Mac OS X and more. It is used to transfer files between computers. It is open source software distributed free of charge under the terms of the GNU General Public License and can be downloaded from http://filezilla-project.org/. In order to use FileZilla client on your client PC, you must disable FTP Access Filter if you're behind a firewall, such as Microsoft ISA Server.

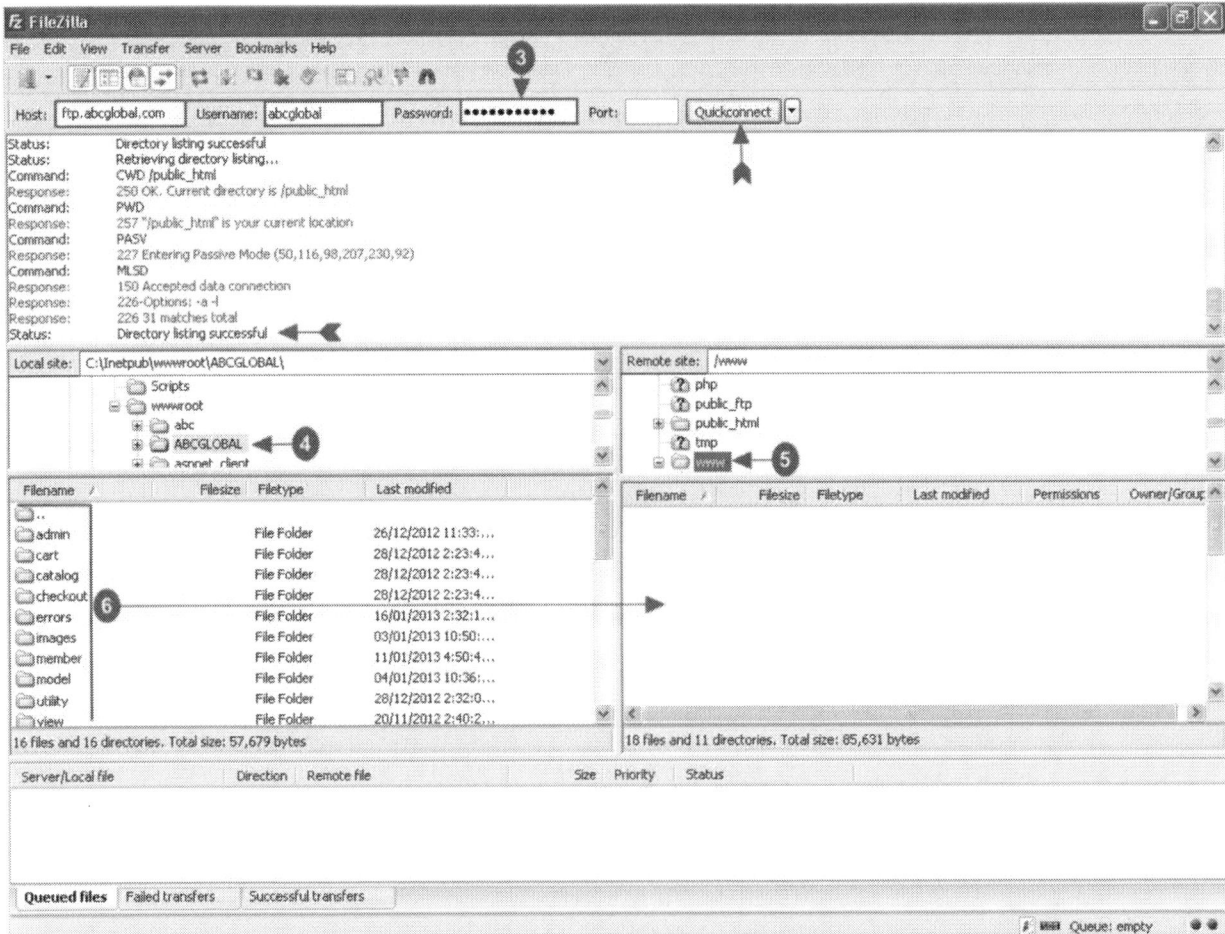

Figure 6-47

1. Launch the downloaded FileZilla_x.x.x.x_win32-setup.exe file on your PC and follow the wizard to complete the setup.
2. Run FileZilla client either from your desktop or from the program group
3. Enter the information (Host, Username, and Password) provided by your hosting company and click the Quickconnect button. After a while you will see a message *'Directory listing Successful'* in the upper pane which indicates that you're ready to upload your website files to the hosting server. Prior to uploading the files, make sure you've made necessary changes (especially to modules developed to send e-mails) described earlier.

4. From the Local site pane to the left, expand wwwroot directory and select ABCGLOBAL folder from your PC. This would list all the files being held in this directory as shown above.

5. Similarly, select www folder from the Remote site to your right which is the target directory on the hosting server where you'd transfer your website files.

6. From the lower Local site pane, select all files and drag them to the lower pane under the Remote site. This will start file transfer process which you can observe in the bottom pane.

After completion, a message *File transfer successful* will appear indicating that the hosting server is now ready to deliver your website. Your work is not over yet. Besides static pages that the world can access at this stage, you also have dynamic content that resides in your database and this is what you are going to configure next. But first, you'll have to access the control panel to create your database on the hosting server.

Step-3   Access Web Hosting Control Panel

In web hosting, a control panel is a web-based graphical interface provided by the hosting company that allows customers to manage their various hosted services in a single place.

Some of the commonly available modules in most control panels are:

- Web-based file manager
- Configure and manage e-mail accounts
- Manage database
- Access to server logs
- Web log analysis software to provide traffic statistics
- Details of available and used web space and bandwidth
- Maintaining FTP users' accounts

It allows you to control all aspects of your site. You can upload files, create sub domains for your blogs like yourblog.yoursite.com, setup disk partition and bandwidth partition if you are hosting multiple sites, limit the use of MySQL database, install PayPal for your e-commerce site, and much more.

There are many kinds of control panels out in the web hosting market but the following three control panels are recommended and are widely used by many hosting companies.

C panel: http://cpanel.net - If you are new to web hosting control panel, c panel would be your best choice because it provides video tutorials which are very informative for new webmasters.

Plesk control panel: https://www.plesk.com - Plesk panel is best suited with MS based applications which make it unique. Plesk is very tough for both crackers and hackers to perform any malicious task on the server.

H-Sphere: https://www.psoft.net - H-sphere is known for its compatibility with windows, UNIX and Linux and offers a special support ticketing system to keep you in touch with your hosting providers.

A Web hosting control panel plays a vital role when selecting a web host for your website. With many kinds of control panels and many web hosting companies out there - each with their own standard and resources - you need to understand your own specific web hosting requirements like which control panel you actually require and then only you can make a mature decision to go after a particular web hosting company.

In this exercise, you will use cpanel interface to create your database and install couple of PHP packages.

1. In your browser type the url provided by your hosting company to access the control panel such as http://cpanel2.hostingserver.net:1234/.
2. Enter the username and password, also provided with the above information. After providing valid credentials, the following page appears. Note the four marked utilities under three different sections. In the upcoming exercises you'll be asked to select these utilities to perform some specific tasks according to the number displayed on top of them.

Figure 6-48

Check uploaded files from control panel

1. In the Files section click File Manager (marked as 1 in figure 6-31).
2. In Directory Selection, select *Document Root for* (fourth option), select *abcglobal.com* from the provided list and click *Go*. The File Manager page comes up with a list of files you uploaded in step 2. Some common functions that you can perform on this page are: Upload/Download files, rename a file or folder, and modify your code using the Edit button.

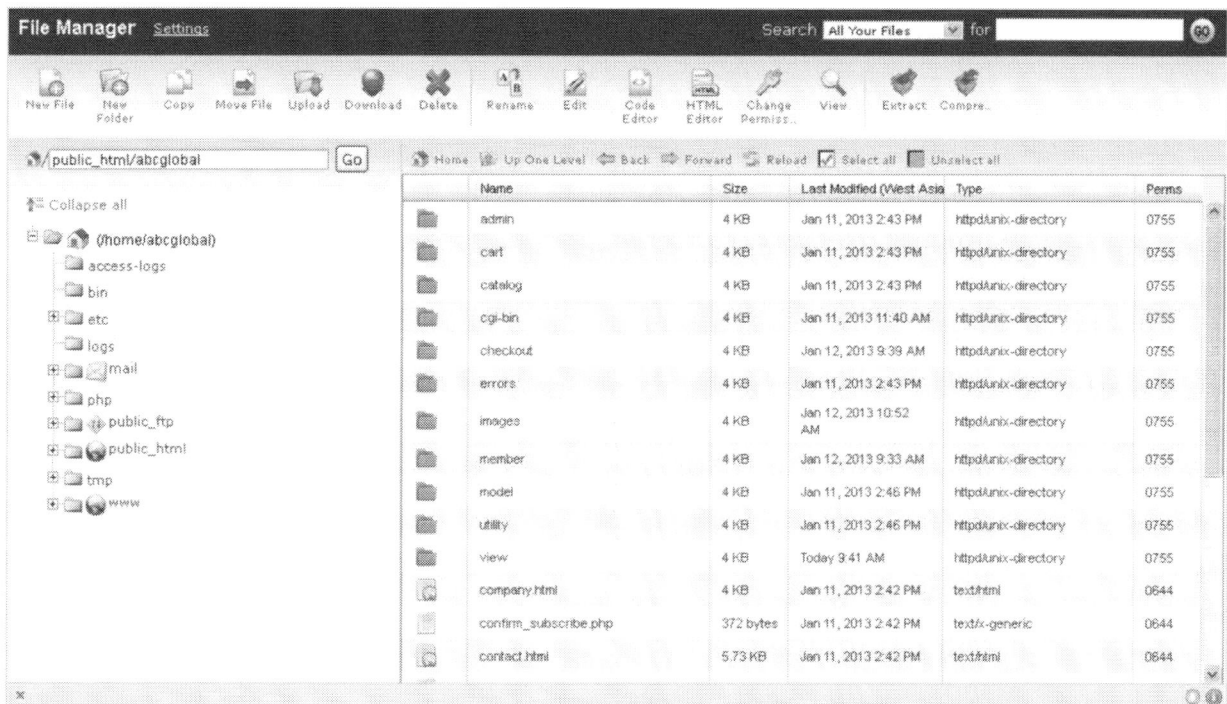

Figure 6-49

Step-4 Create Database and Users

In this step you'll create a blank database and an internal database user who will be authorized to access and manipulate the database. Database access and manipulation consists of four actions: Select, Insert, Update, and Delete. These privileges will also be granted to the database user in this exercise.

1. On the cpanel home page click *MySQL Databases* utility (marked as 2). This will bring up the MySQL Database page.
2. In the New Database box type *db* and click the *Create Database* button. A confirmation page with the message *Added the Database abcglobal_db* appears.
3. Click the *Go Back* link.

Figure 6-50

Many web hosting environments, including cPanel, use a database prefix (DB Prefixing) to designate which database resources belong to which account. cPanel uses the account name followed by an underscore. For example, if an account named 'myacct' were to create a database with the name 'somedb', the resulting database would actually be 'myacct_somedb.' Database users created and administered by the account would also have the prefix.

Add a new database user from the Add New Users section as illustrated below

1. In the Username box, type *admin*. Note that just like the database name; the user is also prefixed with the domain name.

2. To create a strong password for this user, click the *Password Generator* button which will return a password. Note down this password and keep it in a secure place.

3. Click the *Create User* button which will add a new user.

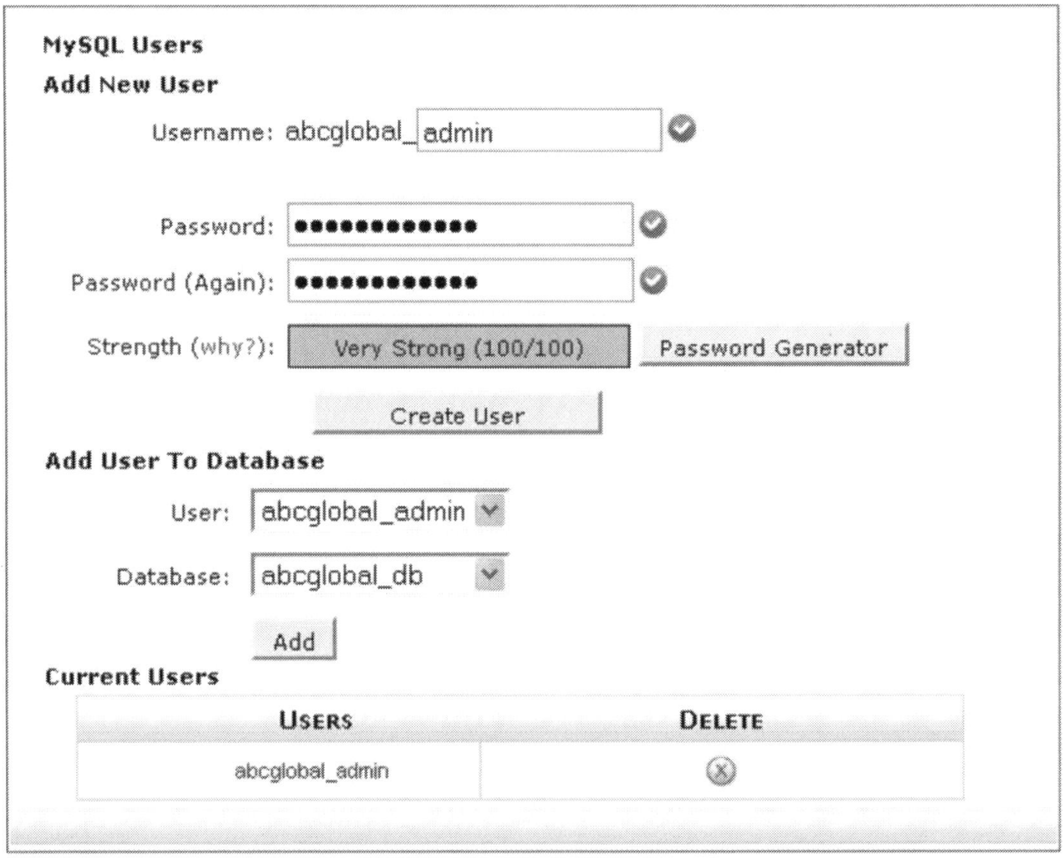

Figure 6-51

Note that while developing the website on your PC, you used the combination of root and mysql in your php files (such as db.php under the Model directory) to connect to the local database. To connect successfully in the hosting environment, that information needs to be updated with the current database name (abcglobal_db), username (abcglobal_admin), and password (provided by the Password Generator).

Grant database access privileges to the new user

1. Click the *Add* button under Add User To Database section in the above screen shot. MySQL Account Maintenance page comes up.
2. Click the *ALL PRIVILEGES* check box to grant all the listed rights to the new user and click the *Make Changes* button. A confirmation message *User "abcglobal_admin" was added to the database "abcglobal_db"* should appear. Click the *Go* Back link.

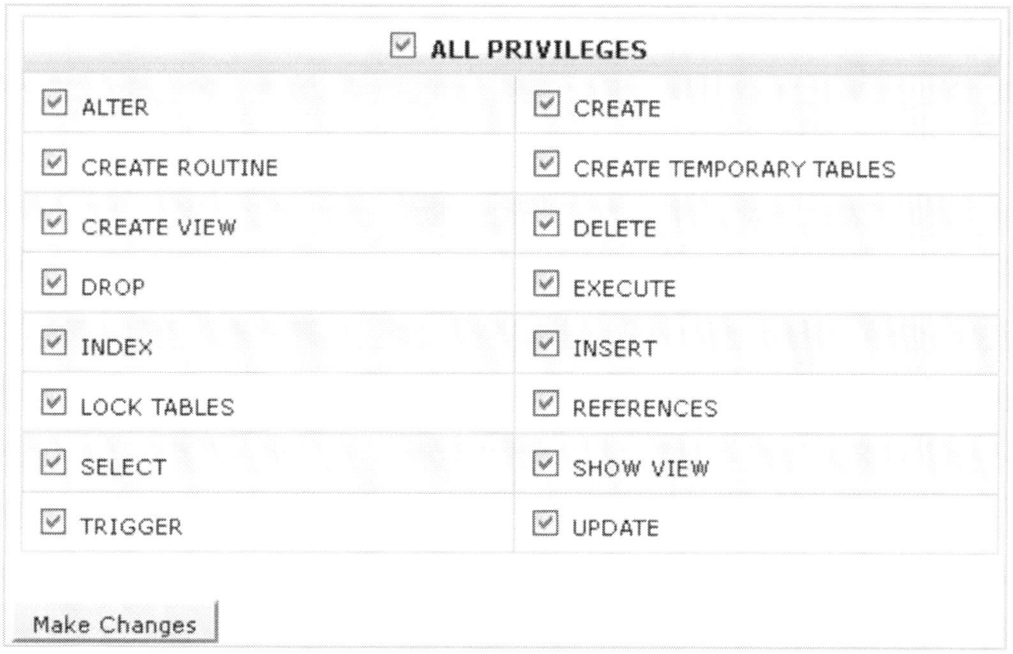
ALL PRIVILEGES
ALTER
CREATE
CREATE ROUTINE
CREATE TEMPORARY TABLES
CREATE VIEW
DELETE
DROP
EXECUTE
INDEX
INSERT
LOCK TABLES
REFERENCES
SELECT
SHOW VIEW
TRIGGER
UPDATE
Make Changes

Figure 6-52

The above two steps would allow the new user to perform all operations on the abcglobal_db database tables that you are going to create next. The file db.php under the Model directory and subscribe.php file under the root folder provide authentication data (dbname, username, and password) to connect to the database. You need to alter those credentials with the information you defined here. For example, you need to replace dbname "abcglobal" with abcglobal_db, username "root" with abcglobal_admin, and password "mysql" with the newly generated password. Note that the user, you just created, would act as a super administrator of the site with all privileges. In the real world scenario, however, you have to create separate users with different rights. For example, a site member should not be allowed either to ALTER or DROP a database table, so these two privileges should be revoked from him.

Step-5 | Create Database Tables

In step 4 you created a blank database with the name abcglobal_db. In this step you'll populate it with some tables along with dummy data through a script - abcglobal.txt. The file abcglobal.txt, provided with this book code, generates all the nine tables that you've been working with throughout this book. For further details, see Database Structure discussed earlier in this chapter.

1. Click *phpMyAdmin* (point 3) on cpanel home page. This will call phpMyAdmin page.
2. Click the _db link being displayed in the left pane.
3. Click the Import tab - 📥 **Import**. Before clicking this tab, make sure the drop down list to your left is showing _db which is the database the script will run in. The next page will also confirm this with the text: Importing into the database "abcglobal_db".
4. Click the *Browse* button, select the file *abcglobal.txt* from the source folder on your PC , and click the *Go* button appearing at the bottom of the page. A message "Import has been successfully finished, 16 queries executed. (abcglobal.txt)" will be displayed with all nine files appearing in the left pane.

■ Conclusion

After fitting in all the blocks at their proper locations, you should run this project on your hosting server to see how it works on the web. Refer to all the stuff provided in this book as you review this website project and explore new ways to improve it.

You have been introduced to the huge website development topic and taken to a position from where you can learn more about it on your own. This book served as a crucial starting point. The concepts covered herein provided invaluable information for your future projects. Specifically you learned about the various components that make up what we know as a tiered architecture model in that you have a client, the Web server, and a data store. You learned about the role client-side technologies such as HTML, CSS, and JavaScript play in the architecture model. You also saw how server-side technologies such as PHP and MySQL database fit into the model.

Aside from the theoretical material provided in this book, you also learned how to install and configure all the required software such as Microsoft's Web server IIS, PHP with its packages and MySQL database.

You also went through how to build static and dynamic web pages. Created a prototype on your development machine and were guided on how to deploy a website on a hosting server with all necessary base information.

While this book introduced what seems like a ton of concepts, terminology, and so on, it's merely a stepping stone to move you forward to explore the enormous world of web development.

ABOUT THE AUTHOR

Riaz Ahmed is an IT professional with over twenty five years of hard-earned experience. He started his career as a programmer in early 90's and is currently working as the head of IT for a reputed group of companies. His areas of interest are web-based development technologies and he has written eighteen books so far on different technologies. You can reach him via his email address oratech@cyber.net.pk

INDEX

Printed in Great Britain
by Amazon